The Heart of Dublin

PETER PEARSON, artist and writer, has been passionately interested in his native city, Dublin, for most of his life. He devoted many years, particularly during the 1980s, to working in a voluntary capacity to save historic buildings and districts. In 1985 he, along with a small group of architects and historians, campaigned the government to retain and revive the Temple Bar area.

As an artist he is widely known for his city paintings, which, at different times, have symbolised the decay, the change and the vigour of Dublin and show a love for its character and colour, its history and people. As a conservationist and art historian he has been a leading figure in developing public interest in the protection of the visual and built heritage of Ireland. Much of his research is based on his own records of vanished houses, factories, shops and churches, which are included in this book, and his collection of salvaged artefacts ranging from shopfronts and plasterwork to coal-hole covers and fanlights.

Peter has been involved in numerous publications: *Dunlaoghaire/Kingstown, Between the Mountains and the Sea, Dublin's Victorian Houses, The Forty-Foot – a monument to sea bathing* and *The Royal St George Yacht Club*.

Published in association with James Adam & Sons, Auctioneers

the *Heart* of *Dublin*

RESURGENCE OF AN HISTORIC CITY

PETER PEARSON

Peter Pearson

THE O'BRIEN PRESS
DUBLIN

First published 2000 by The O'Brien Press Ltd.,
20 Victoria Road, Dublin 6, Ireland.
Tel. +353 1 4923333; Fax. +353 1 4922777
E-mail books@obrien.ie
Website www.obrien.ie

ISBN: 0-86278-668-1

British Library Cataloguing-in-Publication Data
A catalogue record for this title is available from the British Library

1 2 3 4 5 6 7 8 9 10
00 01 02 03 04 05 06 07

The O'Brien Press receives
assistance from

The Arts Council
An Chomhairle Ealaíon

Editing, typesetting, layout and design: The O'Brien Press Ltd.
New photographs: Robert Vance
Index: Gráinne Farren
Colour separations: C&A Print Services Ltd.
Printing: MPG Books Ltd.

Contents

For Adam and Jerome

Introduction

There are many different Dublins. Dublin is a city firmly defined to the south by the Dublin–Wicklow Mountains, and fringed to the east with the sandy shores of Dollymount and Sandymount. It is a city of north and south, with a division created by the River Liffey. Today's Dublin is also a busy European capital, an administrative city with spreading suburbs, new housing schemes, schools and shopping centres that stretch west beyond Leixlip, Clonsilla and Clondalkin, north beyond Swords and Malahide, and south beyond Bray and Greystones. Large tracts of County Dublin's former countryside have disappeared completely.

This book examines the centre of the historical city of Dublin, its streets and buildings, assembling a rich collection of sources, early photographs and prints. It attempts to create a bridge between modern Dublin and the historic city, much of which has so recently almost completely vanished.

Street directories and word-of-mouth records are often invaluable sources of information, as are the decorative trade cards and bills of old-time businesses. These sometimes depict business premises or stock, and they often represent the only souvenir of a vanished industry. Even throw-away paper bags, old bottles and tins help to paint a fuller picture. Links with the past can be found in many places – a much-altered building can

Above: Almost a symbol of Georgian Dublin, this type of door knocker is still very popular.

Left: A view the Liffey and Temple Bar area, c.1980s, before the rejuvenation of this part of the city.

A PROSPECT of the CITY of DUBLIN from the NORTH

A MAP of the CITY and Suburbs of DUBLIN. And also the ARCH-BISHOP & EARL of MEATHS Liberties with the Bounds o

Above: A panoramic view of the city of Dublin made in 1728 for Charles Brooking's map of the city.

Below: The Millennium Bridge has provided Dublin with a new pedestrian link between the north and south sides of the river.

tell its own story. Records are few concerning the craftsmen who, with their families, lived and worked in Dublin all their lives. However, there are a small number of businesses still operating from the same premises after several generations or even centuries.

Dublin's past was a lively, colourful one, with its fine buildings and interesting old streets, esteemed noblemen and nameless paupers, heroic deeds and acts of treachery. The tenements, the taverns, the brothels ... it was all there. Some might say that it is already too late to write this book, that already too much has disappeared, sacrificed to the relentless march of progress. For example, most of the Liberties, with their old industries – the leather tanneries, the breweries, the warehouses and the red-brick, Dutch-gabled houses of the eighteenth century – have vanished.

There are those who see the conservation of a city's old buildings as a cause that can be taken too far. However, the protection of our heritage is not some kind of zealous religious adherence to a rigid set of rules which dictate that everything old must be retained. It is simply about keeping the best of our past so we can make the best of the present. It is about

preserving our identity and maintaining a link with our roots. It is about knowing who we are and where we have come from. At this time, with our successful economy, we are, in a very real sense, in danger of losing our identity – and not just in terms of our old buildings, but in our use of language and in social, familial and cultural relationships. This can be seen in the bland sameness of the new apartment blocks and shopping centres in the city and suburbs of Dublin. The hackneyed argument that 'you can't preserve everything', becomes the justification for clearing sites and eradicating all evidence of past lives.

Time and time again, the city has been faced with choices. For example, we could have completely erased all traces of two of Dublin's most important industries – the world-famous distilleries Power's and Jameson's. But by preserving and adapting even part of them, an important link has been maintained with two hundred years of history and an important part of Dublin's identity.

In a sense, Dublin's recent renewal has meant that the city is now more complete than it has been for nearly fifty years, especially south of the Liffey. The very intactness of certain older streets, such as South William Street, Capel Street, Camden Street and Thomas Street, shows just how much has been lost elsewhere. Who can begin to imagine what Bride Street or Jervis Street were like before they were largely cleared away in the 1950s and 1960s? Who can remember Eccles Street with its Georgian houses – before one whole side of the street was demolished in the 1980s to make way for the Mater Hospital car park?

Above: An elegant Georgian hallway, Merrion Square.

Above top: Plasterwork fragments from Leeson Street.

Below: Dublin's Georgian doors are renowned for their classical proportions and beautiful fanlights.

The expansion and redevelopment we are now experiencing is not the first time radical change has swept through the city. From the 1760s, over a period of about 100 years, the work of the Wide Streets Commissioners created Georgian Dublin with its streets of uniform character – necessarily destroying much of the fascinating, more ancient city in the process. The Commissioners created Parliament Street, widened Dame Street and opened Westmoreland and D'Olier Streets to join the new Sackville (now O'Connell) Street. The general appearance of Baggot Street, for instance, undoubtedly owes much to their work as well. They were instrumental in shaping the brick-built streetscapes that were – and are – so characteristic of Dublin. But were they vandals or improvers? How many timber-framed buildings or Dutch-gabled houses did they demolish during their work? How much did they value the past, and what can we learn from their activities? The contribution of the Wide Streets Commissioners is well documented in the Dublin City Archives through maps and records, and while much has been written about their involvement with the better-known thoroughfares of Dublin, such as Dame Street, less has been said about their contribution in areas like George's Street and the environs of

the two cathedrals, St Patrick's and Christ Church. These areas are examined here and highlight an important episode in the city's growth.

Robert Ballagh's photographic memoir, *Dublin*, depicts the city at a particular moment in time in the early 1980s. This was Dublin at one of its lowest points, with many landmarks either derelict or abandoned. The city is seen as an artistically fascinating, but stagnant, still life of truncated buildings and abused doorways. The grim reality of Dublin during the 1980s was also catalogued by Frank McDonald in a long series of articles published in the *Irish Times*. He described a whole city of derelict properties, usually owned by individuals or companies with no sense of civic pride or duty, who saw the old buildings as liabilities and their sites as potential gold mines. Much of this property was owned by public bodies who should have known better. The list included almost all semi-state organisations, religious, financial and healthcare institutions, along with the Office of Public Works and Dublin Corporation itself.

Dublin encompasses many contradictions: It is busily modern, yet it is filled with the narrow laneways and solid buildings of earlier centuries; it is European, yet it has a distinct and proud sense of its own identity; it is a capital city, yet it is of a size to encourage a sense of familiarity and friendliness. The subject of this book is Dublin's city centre – its heart – which was founded in the Viking era and grew through medieval times to burst out of its city walls and spread eastwards in the eighteenth century. The city is explored, street by street, area by area. It is examined through the tangible remains of old houses and other structures, often using maps and prints to piece together the story, drawing threads from medieval times, through the eighteenth and nineteenth centuries, and right up to the present day. The last thirty years, in particular, represent a period of unprecedented change; whole streets of buildings have disappeared. During this time, the recording of such streets, their buildings and the lives that were lived there has been at best haphazard; often no descriptions or photographic records survive.

It is a particular intention of this book to look at the streetscape of Dublin, to examine the fabric of the city, including the individual houses, shops and other buildings that give the city its personality. It is these buildings that define the character of a city, perhaps more than the great public buildings, however majestic or important they may be.

Below: The dismantling, in the 1980s, of a fine ceiling in a house on Dawson Street.
Below bottom: A monthly horse fair still takes place, now against the backdrop of the radically modernised Smithfield area.

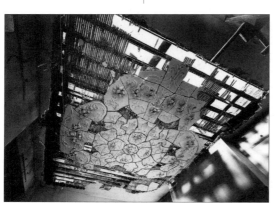

In earlier times, as now, Dublin Corporation played an important role in the planning and development of the city. In the seventeenth century, for example, it granted leases of lands within its jurisdiction to entrepreneurs like Sir John Rogerson, who then divided them up for the development of houses and businesses. The Corporation was, in essence, the head landlord of all the land outside the old medieval walls of the city, excepting certain religious properties and the Liberties. By agreement with the City Surveyor, tracts of land were parcelled out for development. In this way, the Corporation has behaved as a sort of planning authority since the late seventeenth century.

It is hard to understand how, after centuries of great civic pride and intense loyalty to the heritage of Dublin, Dublin Corporation sometimes played such a destructive role in the second half of the twentieth century. It became a bureaucratic body, often incapable of imaginative decision-making. The squalor of Dublin's tenements in the nineteenth and early twentieth century had bred an intense distaste and distrust of the past, and many old areas, such as Pimlico and Bridgefoot Street, were wiped out and blocks of flats akin to those found in East London or Birmingham were erected, without regard to the streetscape or a sense of community.

Above: In a most dramatic turn-around of the dockland area, Dublin's tallest apartment block, was recently completed on the Grand Canal Dock.

It is unfortunate that, during that period, so many of the Corporation's decisions seemed to facilitate the relentless development of roads and new buildings at the expense of people and their collective past. These policies resulted in much of the city becoming depopulated, with the closure of many businesses. The quays of Dublin were badly hit, with most of the western section being demolished. The area around St Patrick's Cathedral, including Bride Street, Cuffe Street and Kevin Street, became a wasteland. Much of Queen Street, North King Street and Parnell Street suffered the same fate. Institutions, for example many of Dublin's noted schools, closed in the 1970s, and, in the following decade, hospitals, churches, libraries and swimming pools followed suit. Well-known firms, many of which were based in the city for more than a century, either disappeared or moved to the suburbs. Prospects looked bleak for State-owned property, such as military barracks, and even for Dublin Castle itself.

The clearance of such areas as High Street for road-widening resulted in the complete eradication of all of the old houses and buildings that once

created the streetline. Ironically, it also created the opportunity for archaelogical excavation of the medieval city. There was, perhaps, a feeling that an undesirable period of history was being removed and being replaced with a more satisfying or comfortable 'early' (ie. Viking or medieval) history, while at the same time the sites were being cleared for future developments.

By the mid-1980s Dublin was a much neglected city – battered and exhausted by traffic, many of its old buildings abused or torn down. The very spirit of the city seemed in danger of being extinguished forever. Having been left derelict by their owners, many historic buildings were destroyed by fires – some set deliberately. In this way, many fine buildings were lost, particularly on the quays, in the Liberties and in the Smithfield area. Recent examples of historic buildings that were burnt down are: St Luke's Church in the Coombe, number 12 Fumbally Lane, houses on Bachelor's Walk and Ormond Quay, and Bow Street Distillery. Unfortunately, a full list would run to many pages.

But things have been changing. In the late 1980s, tax-designated areas were introduced by the government, slowly at first, to generate interest in redeveloping some of the most neglected parts of the city. A number of symbolic improvements at last began to take place. These included the creation of a new paved mall in O'Connell Street, the pedestrianisation and paving of Grafton Street

and the beginning of stone paving in the Temple Bar area. Although some regarded these works as merely cosmetic or as a last-ditch attempt to paper over the cracks in the façade of a once great city, they were, in fact, the seeds of a new civic pride, fostering a change in attitudes towards the city. Some owners renovated their shopfronts, removed unsightly advertisements and repainted their premises more regularly. The celebration of Dublin's millennium in 1988 and the choice of Dublin as European City of Culture in 1991 both helped to regenerate pride in the city. These events were not responsible in themselves for any great move to restore or rebuild the city, but they gave the capital a much-needed boost as a venue for tourists and they revived Dubliners' sense of pride in their city. Happily, Dublin Corporation have, in recent years, taken the lead in many projects both in sensitive development and in conservation.

All of this coincided with the conversion of the Royal Hospital in Kilmainham into the Irish Museum of Modern Art (IMMA), the restoration of the Custom House, and the revamping of Dublin Castle. Government Buildings in Merrion Street were also completely remodelled in a grandiose manner. Furthermore, by this time An Taisce, the voluntary heritage protection organisation, had successfully persuaded the government not to demolish the Temple Bar area for the purposes of building a central bus station, while groups of artists and architects went on to propose an alternative, multicultural use for the area. Temple Bar Properties was established by the State to oversee the area's conservation and renewal.

In the voluntary area, many groups were making a useful contribution. A group, assembled under the banner of the Dublin Crisis Conference and the Students Against the Destruction of Dublin (SADD), campaigned successfully for the abolition of many of the very destructive road plans for Dublin. The Dublin City Centre Business Association fought for the regeneration and protection of the main shopping districts. The Dublin Civic Trust successfully restored a number of derelict historic properties during the 1990s. For example, in cooperation with Dublin Corporation, the Trust prevented the demolition of a seventeenth-century house in Aungier Street and went on to establish an organisation to make an inventory of historic buildings in the city centre. Drimnagh Castle was being restored, An Taisce had moved into Tailors' Hall, private owners were restoring houses in North Great George's Street and plans were afoot to save a house for the James Joyce Cultural Centre. Dublin Tourism also took the initiative to restore two houses in Parnell Square, now the Irish Writers' Museum and the Irish Writers' Centre. On the commercial front, Bewley's was rescued from near extinction by Campbell Catering, who proceeded to refurbish the Grafton Street building. The General Post Office in O'Connell Street was also restored by the Office of Public Works (OPW) for An Post.

Above: Cast-iron fragment from a Georgian balcony.

Below: Carved wooden details from demolished Georgian houses.

Opposite top: A symbol of the new Dublin, the Civic Offices on Wood Quay.

Opposite bottom: Today's Dublin port is now busier than at any time in the past.

All of these events helped to bring about a mood of change, a new approach and a new pride in Dublin. This was complemented by an ever-improving standard of new urban architecture and by the many high-quality residential schemes established by the Corporation. New street paving and street furniture were introduced in many parts of the city, and helped to establish a new image.

Most of the derelict sites of 1980s Dublin have now been redeveloped, at least in the

heart of the city. In addition, the last twenty years have seen a remarkable number of fine restorations of public buildings and some private houses and shops. Many of the buildings and places photographed by Ballagh have been restored and cleaned. Pearse Street Garda Station, Sunlight Chambers, the once-forlorn Sick and Indigent Room Keepers' Society building and the grimy Fruit and Vegetable Markets have all been brought back to life. The Memorial Gardens in Islandbridge, Sir John Rogerson's Quay and the South Wall have also been repaired, and are now more accessible to the public.

Since 1993 remarkable changes have taken place in Dublin. The transformation of Dublin Castle from being a home for government departments in the 1980s into a major visitor attraction, comprising archaeological excavations, restored gardens and coach house, a restaurant, and the new Chester Beatty Library, is symbolic of the change that has occurred in the city in general. The opening of new pedestrian routes to districts like Temple Bar and Smithfield and the building of a new pedestrian bridge over the River Liffey

Below: Traffic control and parking are major issues confronting Dublin in the twenty-first century.

demonstrate the Corporation's current commitment to the pedestrian and to the human scale of the city.

In the coming years, great improvements are expected in the Smithfield area, where many residential developments have already been completed. It is hoped that historic buildings with a local community use, such as the Father Matthew Hall, will be retained and will again become part of the identity of the established population and new communities.

The greatest change is the extraordinary number of new apartment blocks that have been built, mostly due to the special tax designations that were introduced. Much of central Dublin has changed from being dead at night and empty at the weekend to being a place of twenty-four-hour vibrant activity. In less than ten years, Dublin has become a major tourist destination, with a full calendar of cultural events, bustling shops and an ever-increasing choice of restaurants and cafés. In 1984 over twenty of Dublin's traditional family-run hotels had closed; a decade and a half later, Dublin is building hotels as fast as it can and there is still a shortage of rooms. Dublin is famed for its small, intimate public houses, but the 1990s saw the arrival of the mega-pub, able to cater for large numbers but sometimes lacking in character.

Despite an increasingly sensitive approach to Dublin's architectural heritage, there are still glaring omissions in the cultural repertoire. For example, there is a lack of properly organised public markets in the city. A weekly flower market and a good second-hand or antiques market would prove very popular. Perhaps more seriously, Dublin has no major museum dedicated to the city itself. The existing museums are excellent, from the

National Gallery to Collins Barracks, and from the Royal Hospital in Kil-mainham to the Municipal Gallery in Parnell Square and the superbly laid-out new Chester Beatty Library galleries in Dublin Castle. (Unlike any other capital city in Europe or the USA, all of the national museums in Ireland's capital are free of charge.) The Dublin Civic Museum has oper-ated for many years on a semi-voluntary basis with an inadequate budget and no plans for the future.

Dublin needs a full-scale City of Dublin museum. It needs an appropriate home for all those artefacts that are, at present, either in storage or scattered about the city. Gathered together, these artefacts would make a collection worthy of a capital with a long and noble history. Such precious items would tell the story of the city: the guilds – the strongbox of the Linen Hall Guild is still in existence; shop signs and shopfronts, some of which are in the Civic Museum; the Molyneux coat of arms from the magnificent Molyneux House near Bride Street; the statues and coat of arms from the original Tholsel, which stood in Skinner's Row; the statue of St Andrew that lies forgotten in a car park but once graced the eighteenth-century Church of St Andrew; frag-ments of plasterwork decoration from the city's great houses; pieces of wallpaper and glass from Dublin Castle; tools from a Dublin tannery; printed ephemera from shops; bills, documents and letters; shoemakers' lasts; dance cards from Dublin Castle; swords and scissors made in Dublin in the eight-eenth century; book bindings; glass; theatre programmes. The expansion and development of the city; the politics of Dublin, its Parliament House; its educational establishments; its archaeological past; the history of shipping, the early Custom House, the port; the street sellers; the nobles; the lives of the poor and the work of Dublin's many charities – all of these stories, along with the great events of history, need to be recorded and fully presented in a City of Dublin museum.

The story of Dublin is a story of contrasts. Right beside the elegant Georgian city epitomised by Merrion Square, there is the city of grubby streets lined with beggars and homeless people sleeping rough. Beside the Dublin of great architecture – the magnificently restored City Hall, the Custom House and Trinity College – there is a city of mediocre buildings, many of which were built in tax-designated areas over the last twenty-five years. Alongside the sparkling new city – the Custom House Docks with its shiny, glazed office blocks reflected in the water – there is the age-old Dublin of historic monuments, cathedrals and ancient city walls. There is Smithfield with its chimney converted to a viewing tower and its striking row of giant steel masts, whose lamps illuminate the square. There is Temple Bar, crammed with a choice of restaurants and pubs, new photo-graphic galleries, street markets and visitors from across the globe. And there is that other Dublin, whose doorways are used as urinals and where the pavements, from the Liberties to Temple Bar, and from Sheriff Street to Smithfield, are often scattered with broken glass and anti-social behav-iour of all kinds seems to be tolerated.

Above: Two stunning details from the recently restored ceiling at 20 Lower Dominick Street.

In Dublin, the venerable public profiles of the Church of Ireland in the eighteenth century, and the Roman Catholic Church in the twentieth century, have largely passed. Many of the churches belonging to the Church of Ireland, Methodist, Presbyterian and Quaker denominations have closed, as well as some Roman Catholic churches, such as St Paul's on Arran Quay and SS Michael and John's. But the magnificent bells of Christ Church Cathedral continue to toll as they have done for centuries.

In the year 2000 Dublin is a more European city than any of its British counterparts. While London may be cosmopolitan and hectic, Dublin has a special charisma, sometimes more akin to a continental city, with its young population and vibrant street life. City living has become more and more popular, with a massive number of new apartments, and restaurants and cafés in the city centre that open late into the evening and all through the weekend. The perception of the city has changed, for tourists and residents alike. Dublin is continuously evolving, and now, perhaps more than ever, it is building a new identity. The new heart of Dublin still beats with the pulse of its fascinating history – it is that rhythm that draws people to it and it is that rhythm that this book seeks to record.

Above: Many of Dublin's old-style streets, with their family houses, have vanished.

Below: Map of the heart of Dublin, showing the principal streets which are discussed in this book.

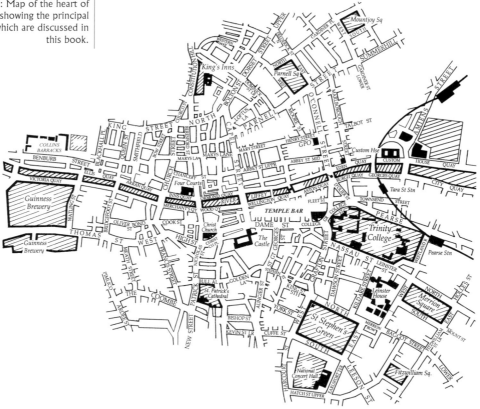

CHAPTER ONE

The Liffey and its Bridges

*T*he Liffey is for many people the spiritual heart of Dublin, and the crossing of the river at the Ha'penny Bridge is a ritual for visitors and Dubliners alike. Besides being the reason for the city's location and very existence, the Liffey is a welcome natural feature in today's city, which has become a dense creation of man-made structures with continuous traffic and bustle. There are occasions, especially in winter, when the smell of the sea steals its way up the river on a full tide, accompanied by seagulls and even the occasional heron. At other times in winter it carries branches, leaves and all the usual human debris of plastic bags and bottles downstream. In the evening the light plays on the surface of the water and reflects the quayside buildings and bridges. The river is as fascinating by day as it is by night, when the many lights of the city are reflected in it.

Left: The uncluttered quays of the 1950s showing Ha'penny Bridge, Bachelor's Walk and the Liffey.

Many artists are drawn to rivers, especially when fine buildings and bridges complement nature's work. Architecture and water make a fine marriage and the old houses of Dublin's riverside are no exception. During the late Georgian period various noted painters, such as James Malton and Samuel Brocas, depicted the Liffey with the Four Courts and the quays. What is remarkable about their paintings is that very little seems to have changed over the last 200 years. For example, monuments such as the Four Courts and the Custom House remain dominant and the modest width of the quays and the scale of the houses are still the same. The three- and four-storey rows of buildings that once lined the river were a varied but harmonious collection of historic structures, but only a small number of the original eighteenth-century houses still stand today.

Above: The lower reaches of the Liffey, such as Sir John Rogerson's Quay, were once part of the commercial port and are now in the process of being pedestrianised and converted to recreational use.

Below: The river unchannelled, with its quays still largely unbuilt, is depicted in Speed's map of Dublin (1610).

At low tide the Liffey is a shallow river, one which it is not difficult to imagine in its natural state, making its way towards the sea with a wide and unchannelled flow. John Speed's map of Dublin, dated 1610, shows the river east of the medieval city flowing where it liked, spreading over sandbanks and through channels out towards the sea. It was during the eighteenth century that most of the new quays were built and large tracts of land were reclaimed from the sea. One of the most noted reclaimers was Sir John Rogerson, whose quay dates from 1728. Rogerson, who reclaimed almost 150 acres of land east of Trinity College, was Lord Mayor of Dublin in 1693 and had also been an MP for the city. In 1713 Rogerson acquired a lease of all the tidal lands stretching as far as the Donnebrook (Dodder) River. At about the same time an area north of the Liffey, known as North Lotts, was also reclaimed. The semi-tidal wasteland was divided into allotments, which were then sold by public subscription.

There are at present sixteen bridges over the Liffey, if we include all those from Islandbridge to the East Link and the new footbridge known as 'Millennium Bridge'. Two more are planned, in the docklands area and near Watling Street. The enclosure and bridging of the Liffey, achieved for the most part during the last three centuries, has been well documented by many authors. The history of Dublin city is itself inextricably bound up with the life of the river. Most schoolchildren know that the name Baile

Above top: The scale of the quays and their adjoining buildings remains much the same today as in the 1790s.

Above: These ferries, depicted on John Rocque's map (1756), were once the principal means of crossing the Liffey.

Left: Queen Street Bridge is one of the few bridges that kept its curved gradient, rather than being rebuilt as a flat bridge to accommodate traffic.

Átha Cliath refers to a time long ago when Dublin had no bridges and that a ford made of woven branches or hurdles was the only crossing in the river. There is some debate as to the exact location of this ancient ford, but it is thought to have been somewhere near the Four Courts.

Upstream from the Ha'penny Bridge

A plan of the city of Dublin in 1661 shows just one bridge, which gave access from the north, from the present Church Street, over the river and through an arched gate into the medieval walled city of Dublin. If you needed to cross anywhere downstream, there were a number of ferries to transport you across. Records exist of the many ferries that plied the Liffey since medieval times and continued to do so right up until 1984, when the last crossing was made by the Ringsend boat.

Several new bridges were erected towards the end of the seventeenth century – one at Watling Street, near Collins's Barracks, one at Queen Street, one at Winetavern Street, near the Four Courts, and another at Capel Street, which was named Essex Bridge and is now called Grattan Bridge. All of these were rebuilt or modified during the Georgian period and were renamed at various times. One of the most attractive of these early bridges is that at Queen Street, now officially called Liam Mellowes Bridge. This elegantly curved, three-arched bridge was erected during the 1760s and has a distinguished appearance with its granite stonework, niches and balustraded parapet. Such bridges, with their high central arch, not only allowed large boats to pass beneath, but also created a more satisfactory visual effect.

A remarkable addition was made to Watling Street Bridge, now called Rory O'Moore Bridge, in 1812, in the form of a mock-medieval gateway that straddled the southern quay. A very substantial limestone structure, it was later dismantled and moved as it proved an obstruction to traffic. It

Above: The latest addition to Dublin's bridges is the Millennium Bridge, completed in 1999, which has provided a useful link between the Jervis Street area and Temple Bar.

Below: The newly pedestrian-ised Sir John Rogerson's Quay.

now forms one of the entrances to the Royal Hospital, Kilmainham. The Ha'penny Bridge, erected shortly after 1816, is certainly one of the most striking early nineteenth-century cast-iron structures in Ireland. Equally attractive and certainly more ornate is King's Bridge, erected in 1821 to commemorate the visit of King George IV to Ireland. The bridge has recently been thoroughly restored and repainted by Dublin Corporation, who have lately cleaned, painted and lit all of the city centre bridges. A pair of cast-iron crowns and cushions were discovered in the water underneath King's Bridge, where they had been discarded around 1952!

A new footbridge was first proposed at Ormond Quay / Wellington Quay in the late 1980s as part of the overall plan for the Temple Bar area, but the scheme was not approved. The design, with its canopy and undulating profile, was perceived by many as being too radical or avant garde. In 1998 a competition was held to design a pedestrian bridge for the same site, and the architectural team of James Howley and Sean Harrington, along with their engineers, won the contract. The Millennium Bridge, as it is now called, provides access from the Abbey Street area on the northside to the Temple Bar district on the southside. The new bridge is restrained in design and does not compete with its older sister the Ha'penny Bridge, or with the wide and solid Grattan Bridge upstream. Through its elegant simplicity it respects the historic nature of its surroundings, the quay walls and the old quayside houses. An historic event was witnessed by many

Below: The graceful curve of the Ha'penny Bridge has become a popular symbol of Dublin. The ha'penny toll was once collected at either end of the bridge.

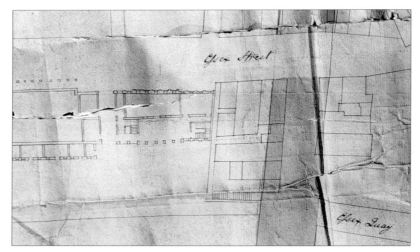

Above: A plan from the 1750s showing the proposed line of Parliament Street (the dark strip) and the open-arcaded front of the old Custom House.

Below: A map, made prior to 1815, showing the layout of Wellington Quay, the octagonal cockpit on the right, and part of the old Custom House Quay.

passers-by when, one Sunday, early in November 1999, the bridge was lifted into place. The operation took little more than half an hour, as the largest telescopic crane in Ireland swung it over the river.

The Ha'penny Bridge, which is 140 feet long, springs from two rusticated masonry bases which project a little from each of the quay walls. The bridge replaced a ferry which had operated at this point on the river. The ferry service was privatised in the early 1800s by Alderman Beresford and William Walsh and it was they who erected the bridge at their own expense. It was said to have cost £3,000 and was described in 1821 as, 'a great ornament and convenience to the city'.

The Ha'penny Bridge, so called because of the toll which was once charged at each end of the bridge, conveniently connects the passage at Merchants' Arch with the pedestrian route through Liffey Street and on to Mary Street. The railings that form the sides of the bridge are joined in three places by delicate archways in cast iron, surmounted by lamps. The Regency bridge, which is close to 200 years old, will soon be fully restored.

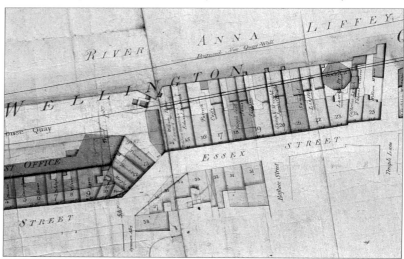

Merchants' Arch is so named because it was built by the Merchant Tailors' Guild of Dublin. The building was erected in 1821 when the Guild left their original premises in Tailors' Hall, in Back Lane near Christ Church. The striking, late Georgian-style Merchants' Arch with its stone front was designed by Frederick Darley, an architect who came from a distinguished family of stone-cutters. One of the most surprising features of the building is an attractive, oval, granite staircase, which leads to the first floor where there is a large meeting room, almost forty feet square. The first floor has an exceptionally high ceiling that allowed for the later addition of a gallery. The building was used by a shirt manufacturer in recent times and has lately become a wine bar and night club.

One of Dublin's most important quayside buildings, the old Custom House at Wellington Quay, was demolished in the 1790s when the present Custom House was opened. It is hard for us to imagine the presence which this wonderful building must have had and to picture the daily life around

Above: An engraving by Wirsing, a German artist of the mid-eighteenth century, is one of the best impressions we have of the old Custom House, showing a number of sailing ships and smaller barges full of barrels, probably waiting to sail upstream into the old medieval city.

Below: The design for the new Essex Bridge, made by the architect George Semple in the mid-eighteenth century, which replaced an earlier structure.

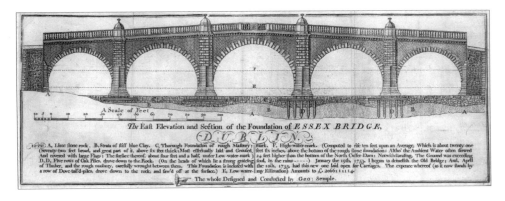

Right: A late nineteenth-century impression of Dollard's Printing House on Wellington Quay, showing the mansard windows, which resemble those in the original Custom House. Grattan Bridge and Parliament Street are in the foreground, and the corner building, which is also still standing, was owned by Goodbody's, the snuff manufacturers.

it. However, some early prints and maps give us an insight into the appearance of this building, which was rebuilt in 1707 and lay at the heart of the city, close to Dublin Castle. The old Custom House, which replaced a smaller and plainer building, stood almost exactly on the site of Dollard's Printing House and the Clarence Hotel. It was a large building in the Queen Anne style, fifteen windows wide with a striking roof carrying a row of mansard windows. The ground floor consisted of an open arcade where business could be done and shelter could be found in bad weather, and above it were three storeys of offices and rooms. The quay in front of the Custom House was broad, and here ships lay waiting to load or unload. Just upstream stood the elegant five-arched Essex Bridge. Grattan Bridge now stands in its place. It is worth noting that the line of today's Essex Street, with its bend at the Photographic Centre and Design Yard, is a direct result of the presence of the Custom House, with its broad quayside space in front of it. The street known as Temple Bar, which becomes Essex Street, had to make a detour around the back of the Custom House.

A mid-eighteenth-century painting of Essex Bridge viewed from upriver shows the old Custom House with a public clock in the pediment and a small cupola above. A large four-storey building and a flight of steps stood directly adjacent to the bridge. The bridge itself had a pair of niches on either side, a place perhaps for a watchman to guard the bridge by day or night. A large equestrian statue of King George I stood on a pedestal built on a projection upriver of Essex Bridge. The statue, erected in 1722, was removed to the garden of the Mansion House in Dawson Street in 1753. Early maps show that the Custom House Quay was approached from Essex Street through two passageways beside the Custom House. There was also a narrow passage leading from the Custom House onto Essex Bridge. On a busy day, prior to 1790, the small stretch of river between Ormond Quay and today's Wellington Quay must have presented a very picturesque sight, crammed with small sailing vessels, barges and ferries.

In 1757 it was proposed to connect Capel Street and the fine new Essex Bridge with Dublin Castle, by means of a grand thoroughfare that would later be called Parliament Street. At that time the route to the castle from the Custom House or Essex Bridge involved taking the twisting passage through Blind Quay and Cork Hill. There were also narrow passageways such as Crane Lane and Sycamore Alley, which led onto Dame Street and through Castle Lane (now Palace Street) into the Lower Castle Yard. It was also at this time proposed to create a grand square or piazza in front of the castle on the site of what would later become City Hall. It was intended that the equestrian statue of George I would be moved from its original position at Essex Bridge and erected in the middle of this square.

Ormond Quay, which joins Bachelor's Walk on the north side of the river, dates from the late seventeenth century and some of its houses survive. It is named in honour of James Butler, the First Duke of Ormond, who, as Lord Lieutenant, was effectively the ruler of Ireland in the 1680s. His brother, Charles, Earl of Arran, gave his name to Arran Quay, which is of a similar vintage.

Wood Quay is one of the best-known of the Liffey's quays, due to the great controversy over the archaeological excavations of Dublin's Viking past and the subsequent erection in 1982 of the first of the Civic Offices, some of Dublin's least-loved buildings. The name Wood Quay is thought by some to have

Above: Ornamental lamps, on Grattan Bridge, which replaced Essex Bridge in 1875.

Below: Plan for creating Wellington Quay, showing the properties which had been 'valued by jury' for the Wide Streets Commissioners.

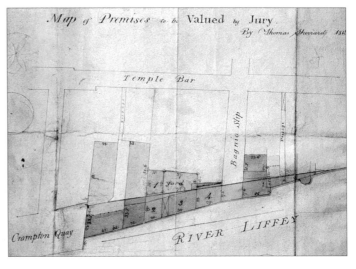

Above: This photograph, taken in the 1940s, records the annual Liffey swim. Note the almost intact line of houses along Essex Quay, all of which have since been demolished.

Below: In the eighteenth century the river was crowded with ships, shown here on Rocque's map (1756).

come about because the quay itself was made of wood, and archaeological findings have revealed that there was such a quay here as far back as Viking times. In the eighteenth century it was known as the Coal Quay, as the city coal yard was situated nearby.

Wellington Quay, below Grattan Bridge, is in fact one of the last quays to have been built on the Liffey. As already mentioned, there was a wharf or quay at the original Custom House throughout the eighteenth century, located on the site of the present Clarence Hotel and Dollard's Printing House, but Wellington Quay as we know it today was not built until about 1817, and was named after the Duke of Wellington, who had made his name by defeating Napoleon at the Battle of Waterloo in 1815.

On the south bank of the Liffey, towards the west, we have Usher's Island, which was literally an island between the River Camac (now largely culverted) and the River Liffey. The name Usher's Island comes from John Usher's house, which was located here in the late sixteenth century. His house is said to have stood not far from the back of the present Brazen Head Hotel and public house.

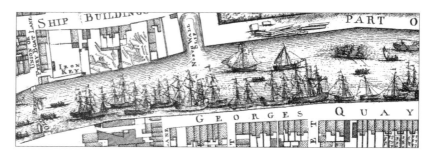

Richmond Bridge, standing just down-stream of the Four Courts, and Whitworth Bridge, standing just upstream of the Four Courts, are both elegant structures. Both carry a classical balustrade with a granite coping, which is continued along the quay in front of the Four Courts and is a very elegant feature of the Liffey at this point. There are also many mature trees along this stretch, which lend a sense of grace to the river. Richmond Bridge, erected in the early nineteenth century, replaced an older structure known as Ormond Bridge. It is said that a gentleman from Chapelizod was riding over Ormond Bridge in about 1802, at the time of a great flood, and as he approached the arch of the bridge, it sud-denly collapsed before him. His horse, with one spring, cleared the great gulf beneath him and carried him on to the other side of the river in safety. Richmond Bridge, named after the Duchess of Richmond, was begun in 1813. It was opened on St Patrick's Day 1816 and is built of Portland stone. The arches of the bridge are elabo-rately ornamented with keystones which carry the heads of *Plenty*, the *Liffey* and *Industry* on one side and *Commerce, Hibernia* and *Peace* on the other.

Above: The balustraded Liffey-side walk in front of the Four Courts is one of the most pleasant aspects of the river.

Downstream from the Ha'penny Bridge

Since the late seventeenth century when the city started to expand, there has been a steady movement eastwards. As each new bridge was con-structed further seaward, the port of Dublin continued to move east. Since the eighteenth century ships have evolved into larger and larger vessels, requiring ever deeper berths. A glance at any of the paintings or prints of Dublin port in the 1790s, for example, shows that most of the vessels at that time were no bigger than one of today's large trawlers. The fact that the Liffey and the port of Dublin were one and the same place accounts for the continued involvement of the Dublin Port and Docks Board in the con-struction and maintenance of the quay walls and the bridges in the city. The finance to do much of this work came from a levy on shipping. Follow-ing the building of Carlisle (now O'Connell) Bridge in 1790, the quays lying to the west were no longer accessible by ships and the responsibility for them and various older bridges was largely taken over by Dublin Corpo-ration. Ships continued to berth at Eden Quay and Burgh Quay until the latter half of the nineteenth century, as many contemporary photographs reveal. Clusters of vessels with their tall masts and rigging could be seen lying close to what is now O'Connell Bridge. The building of Butt Bridge, with its opening section, in 1879 still allowed vessels through to reach these quays.

Above: The Guinness barges were used to transport barrels of beer from the brewery downstream to their larger ships.

Below: The challenge of the quays is to remove heavy traffic and large trucks, which still pose a threat to the safety of pedestrians.

Some of the last traces of this maritime commerce only disappeared within the last year or two, with the loss of a building carrying the inscription of the Dublin Sack Company on George's Quay, and the closure of McCann Verdon's Ships' Chandlers on Burgh Quay. This part of our history has slipped away as the city has progressed into a new era. The year 1888 saw the last sailing ships pass upstream of Butt Bridge, for in that year what many would consider to be the Liffey's ugliest structure was erected: the Loopline Bridge. However, this important new railway bridge linked, for the first time, the railways of the south and north of the country, but sadly it created a crude separation of one of Dublin's loveliest public buildings from the rest of the city. The Custom House was blocked from view and cut off from the city centre. The opening of the Matt Talbot Bridge in 1978 once again pushed shipping further downstream. Regrettably, from both a historical and a visual point of view, this took away the possibility of ships ever mooring in front of the Custom House again. The now vanished blue-and-cream-painted Guinness ships that berthed here until the mid-1970s were a familiar and much-loved sight. So too were the Guinness barges, which twenty years earlier could be regularly seen transporting barrels of beer up and down the Liffey between the brewery and the ships.

Few residents of the once-isolated fishing and boat-building village of Ringsend could ever have imagined 100 years ago that there would be a road bridge across the Liffey at this point. (There had, of course, been a Liffey ferry, which was used by dock workers and the local inhabitants.) The East Link Toll Bridge, a low structure capable of opening up to allow shipping through, was opened to traffic in 1984 and further emphasised the position of Dublin port as being to the east. The quays beyond it are now rarely used by shipping. For some years the East Link took the pressure of traffic off the city centre at Butt Bridge and its success prompted the development of the West Link Toll Bridge, carrying traffic from Blanchardstown across to Palmerstown, some years later. But the increasing problem of traffic congestion has led to suggestions that a tunnel running under the Liffey from east to west might be the only way to completely solve the problem, by taking traffic off the quays, and returning the centre of Dublin to pedestrians. At present, the pedestrian has little more than eight seconds to cross the road at the Ha'penny Bridge, while great juggernauts pound past, coming to and from the port.

Further downriver, Burgh Quay is said to date from 1808. The name derives from Elizabeth Burgh, the wife of Anthony Foster, whose eldest son, the Right Honourable John Foster, was the last Speaker of the Irish

Left: The view from Bachelor's Walk, looking east across the foot of O'Connell Street, c.1860. Note the Georgian buildings erected by the Wide Streets Commissioners all along Eden Quay.

House of Commons. In the early nineteenth century, Burgh Quay was very much a busy part of Dublin port and it was here that the Corn Exchange was built in 1816. The Corn Exchange, built by the grain merchants of Dublin for the purpose of selling and dealing in grain, is a handsome two-storey arcaded building that fronts on to Burgh Quay. For many years the Corn Exchange lay abandoned, with only its façade standing on the quays. Originally it contained a large hall, 130 feet long, which extended right back to Poolbeg Street. GN Wright, in his book *An Historical Guide to the City of Dublin*, tells us that the interior of the Corn Exchange was quite elaborately decorated with plasterwork, and that a clock was ornamented with plasterwork featuring sheaves of corn and implements of farming.

Carlisle Bridge, now known as O'Connell Bridge, was originally built in 1794, three years after the opening of the new Custom House, and named after a Lord Lieutenant of Ireland, the Earl of Carlisle. Ships could now no longer proceed upriver past this point. The building of Carlisle Bridge commenced in 1791 and took about three years. The original bridge was only forty feet wide and was considered too narrow, and so was rebuilt in 1880 in its present form. At 151 feet wide, it has the distinction of being at least as wide as it is long. The Carlisle Building, a four-storey commercial building dating from around 1800 and matching the Ballast Office at the corner of Westmoreland Street, originally overlooked the bridge. The

Right: The view across O'Connell Bridge to the Carlisle Building during a royal visit in the early 1900s. The Carlisle Building was demolished to make way for O'Connell Bridge House.

building was sold to a Mr Kinahan for £4,000 in the early nineteenth century. It was then leased to the Commissioners of Irish Lights in 1897. The Carlisle Building was replaced in the 1960s with O'Connell Bridge House. The new and rather ungainly office building was the first large-scale intrusion into the quays.

Eden Quay was constructed in 1796. The name Eden is derived from the Right Honourable William Eden, who was Chief Secretary in Dublin Castle in about 1780. It is interesting to see how Eden's name became applied to the quay. He wrote to the Right Honourable John Beresford in 1782:

> If our great plans should ever go into execution for the improvement of Dublin, I beg that you will contrive to edge my name into some street or into some square, opening to a bridge, the bank or the Four Courts.

Bachelor's Walk was first developed in the 1720s and a few houses from this period still survive. It is thought that the name Bachelor's Walk comes from an early owner of property here, and not from the quay, which some believe might have been a promenade for bachelors!

Heading eastwards, both Crampton Quay and Aston Quay are of early eighteenth-century date. Crampton Quay is said to have been named after Philip Crampton, a prosperous bookseller, who also developed Crampton Court adjoining the Olympia Theatre. Aston Quay was developed on the property of Henry Aston, a merchant who was active in Dublin in the eighteenth century and was a friend of Dr Richard Steevens, the founder of Steevens's Hospital.

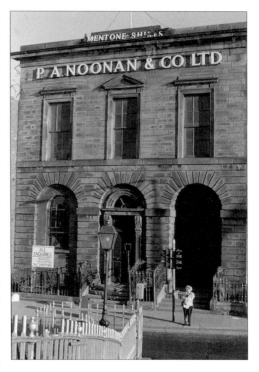

Above: Merchants' Arch, constructed in 1821, cleverly accommodates a pedestrian route from Dame Street through Crown Alley to the Ha'penny Bridge.

In 1960 an extraordinary proposal was put forward to solve the city's car parking problem, which at that time must have been a relatively minor one. Dublin Corporation rejected the plan, which involved covering the River Liffey to create two massive car parks, from O'Connell Bridge to Butt Bridge on one side, and to the Ha'penny Bridge on the other.

As recently as the early 1980s there were plans to widen the road on both sides of the quays. The creation of such a traffic route on either side of the Liffey would have required the demolition of every single quayside house. The only listed buildings which stood in the way were St Paul's Church on Arran Quay, the wonderful Sunlight Chambers building on the corner of Parliament Street and Essex Quay, which has recently been refurbished and cleaned, and the stone structure of Merchants' Arch beside the Ha'penny Bridge. Virtually all of the western quays on both sides – the area of the Guinness's Brewery and Collins's Barracks – were wiped out during the 1980s and, after many years of vacant and derelict sites, nondescript apartment blocks were eventually erected in their place. Many of these quayside houses were the homes and businesses of merchants and traders in the eighteenth century, whose ships would have tied up in places like Bachelor's Walk and Ormond Quay. The houses had modest but interesting features, such as cut-stone doorcases, decorative fanlights, wrought-iron railings and good internal details. Some of them were panelled inside.

The appearance of these new apartments in the late 1980s was, however, part of the new vote of confidence in the city centre, which for so long had been ignored in favour of the suburbs. There can also be little doubt that the historically dubious celebration of Dublin's Millennium in 1988, and the designation of Dublin as European City of Culture in 1991, did much to focus attention on the city and to raise its profile generally. These events mark the turning of the tide in Dublin's fortunes, and help to explain the recent phenomenal resurgence of the social, economic and architectural life of the city.

Dublin now, at the turn of the century, is a very different place to the Dublin of even ten or twenty years ago. Several entirely new streets of apartments have been created in the city, most of the derelict sites have gone and the propped-up and vandalised Georgian houses have mostly been replaced.

CHAPTER TWO

Temple Bar

*T*emple Bar derives its name from the Temple family, who had a large house and gardens in this area since the seventeenth century. Sir John Temple, who became Master of the Rolls in Ireland, published a history of the Rebellion of 1641. His son, Sir William Temple, was also involved with public life and became a Member of the Irish Parliament. It would appear that the development of the Temples' property took place in the late seventeenth and early eighteenth centuries. Similar parcels of land adjoined the Temple property, such as that held by Sir William Fownes, which

Below: Meeting House Square is a new urban space created out of a derelict area during the 1990s. On the left is the Gaiety School of Acting and on the right is the Photographic Centre.

Above: A pair of carved nineteenth-century shopfront brackets in Anglesea Street. Unfortunately, many decorative features of this type have disappeared in Temple Bar.

Right: The weekly Temple Bar food market in Meeting House Square, which has become very popular.

eventually became Fownes Street. Another important property holding was that of Henry Aston, whose land includes the site of the present telephone exchange in Crown Alley. Alderman Crampton also held a substantial plot of land leased from the City of Dublin. His name is recorded in Crampton Quay and Crampton Court. All of the land in this area was owned originally by the City of Dublin and was leased to these various property owners who in turn sublet their holdings. For instance, in the eighteenth century, Sir John Temple leased his holding from the City at £40 per annum. John Temple's lease of this area was renewed in 1735 and includes the site of the present Temple Bar Square. The Earl of Anglesey held a substantial parcel of land, now occupied by Anglesea Street, which in the eighteenth century included a coal yard for the poor.

Much of the character of this area has miraculously survived over a 250-year period, with the ancient street pattern and names remaining almost unchanged. Twenty years ago few could have predicted that this part of Dublin would become the focal point of tourism in the city itself and that the name would be a byword for all that is trendy and up-to-date. Nobody could have foreseen then that this area would be packed with restaurants and pubs, crowded even on a winter Sunday afternoon. The result, though not to everybody's liking, is a vibrant tourist attraction, an area that manages to blend a sense of the old city with an image that is also very contemporary. This was achieved by various architectural interventions, by giving generous tax incentives to developers and by inventing a variety of cultural focal points or centres in the area. The introduction of these cultural facilities in this one relatively small area, including the Irish Film Centre and Film Archive, the Photographic Centre and Photographic Archive, Design Yard, the Music Centre, Art House and the refurbished Projects Arts Centre, is an interesting experiment whose ultimate success will have to be evaluated in the years to come.

The property holdings of CIÉ (the state transport company) originally included a block of property between Eustace Street and Fownes Street, Dame Street and Wellington Quay on the River Liffey. This block, it was proposed, would be demolished and a large bus station built there with a six- or seven-storey shopping and office facility above it.

At the same time, north of the river, a development of similar scale, which would accommodate the buses of the north city, was planned for a site between Ormond Quay and Abbey Street, Jervis Street and Liffey Street. It was also suggested that this transportation centre would, at some point, be linked to an underground railway, which might extend as far as Tallaght. By the mid-1980s there appeared to be very little likelihood that the government would proceed with either the rail link to Tallaght or the grandiose transportation centre. Furthermore, many of the older areas in the city centre, including the quays and Temple Bar, were in an extremely rundown state and the property market was at an all-time low. There was simply no demand for such buildings, and neither was there any great demand for new offices.

Above top: In the 1980s buses rumbled through Temple Bar, shaking the foundations of the old buildings.

Above: The street called Temple Bar, which gave its name to the whole area, is now one of the busiest pedestrian streets in Ireland.

Above: Through the common practice of retaining a façade while destroying everything else, many interesting internal features have been lost, as in the case of this building in Eustace Street.

Below: The 1970s plan for a CIÉ transportation centre, which would have extended north and south of the Liffey, was not scrapped until the late 1980s.

The result was that Temple Bar had become completely stagnant, with little if any commercial activity being carried on there. There were a few sleepy pubs in the area, such as Flannery's, the Foggy Dew and the Norseman. The Clarence Hotel struggled on, while its rivals, the Dolphin and the Exchange, had closed their doors during the 1970s. The Olympia Theatre was finding it difficult to attract audiences and the collapse of the proscenium arch in the magnificent Victorian theatre was a major setback. There were a number of small trading companies, stationery businesses and a few clothing manufacturers who occupied the various warehouses of the district. A quiet area by day, it was completely deserted at night and at weekends.

In 1986, An Taisce called on the government to reassess the plan for CIÉ to locate its transportation centre in Temple Bar. An Taisce had prepared a thorough survey of the area between Parliament Street and Anglesea Street, and pointed out that this part of Dublin, though much neglected, had a unique architectural character and important streetscape, which would be destroyed if the CIÉ scheme were allowed to go ahead. An Taisce was not opposed to the transportation centre in its own right, but suggested that it should be located elsewhere in the city, perhaps on the vacant site at George's Quay, beside the existing Dart line. The importance of this area, which was in 1986, for convenience, described as the Temple Bar area, was the very fact that so much historical detail remained intact, and An Taisce pointed to the possibility of the area becoming a type of Parisian Left Bank.

Some have maintained that it is not possible to integrate cultural activity by means of new buildings and facilities. It could be argued that culture and inspiration must come from the individual and cannot be planted there by a state body and operated by administrators. Others see the projects in the Temple Bar area as a great act of public funding for the arts – an action never instigated on such a scale before and unlikely to be repeated in the same way. It is interesting to note that, before Temple Bar Properties undertook its mission to create a cultural quarter in this area, there were many artists of all sorts active in the various old buildings there. Now, apart from two designated buildings, there are no artists active in the area – they have moved to other parts of the city where rents are cheaper and facilities come without strings attached.

The buildings of Temple Bar Properties were seen as flagship projects, where the architects involved expressed their vision in a striking contemporary style. Some of the new buildings succeed admirably and are undoubtedly monuments of their time, while others seem to hit a discordant note in the overall pattern of Dublin's streetscape, with too much steel, too many hard angles, too much Germanic geometry for the largely vertical houses and buildings of Dublin's old city. The achievements of Temple Bar in terms of building conservation and historical authenticity have been disappointing and fall far short of the expectations of An Taisce, who first proposed the protection of the area. No inventory of the architectural heritage of the district was carried out until most of the demolition work had been completed. Some thirty-two buildings within the area were either gutted, leaving only façades standing, or were fully demolished. This was bitterly disappointing to An Taisce, who had opposed the CIÉ plan for the area on the basis that it would have wiped out the old buildings there and destroyed the area's authenticity. Now An Taisce were witnessing the erosion of the heritage of the area by stealth and with the assistance of a semi-state body and tax incentives.

Above: Fownes Street, which included early eighteenth-century panelled houses, narrowly escaped demolition at the hands of CIÉ when they were drawing up plans for a new transportation centre.

From an historical perspective this was the part of Dublin that once boasted the most famous printers, bookbinders, booksellers and engravers, and some of the most famous craftsmen – carvers and gilders, makers of mirrors, clocks, bookbindings and jewellery – that Ireland ever produced. This district contained three of Dublin's most famous theatres in the eighteenth century – Smock Alley Theatre, Crow Street Theatre, also known as the Theatre Royal, and the Musick Hall in Fishamble Street. It was a cultural quarter in the truest sense. Here

Above: A typical Gibbs-style stone doorcase in Fownes Street.

Left: Most of the small artisans, such as Byrne's the clockmakers in Fownes Street, have now disappeared from the area.

Above: The Temple Bar area in 1985 with Essex Street in the foreground. The parking lot on the right is now the site of new apartments and a pedestrianised street.

locksmiths, silversmiths, tailors and craftsmen of every sort worked side by side with merchants and entrepreneurs. Seen in this context, it is particularly unfortunate that so many craftsmen and artisans have left the area. Sadly, throughout the wave of development that has taken place during the last ten years, much of the rich detail has disappeared, including stone doorcases, shopfronts, interior fittings, carved brackets and indeed whole buildings. However, in fairness to Temple Bar Properties and Dublin Corporation, the planning authority, they have insisted on the correct pointing of brick façades and the reinstatement of traditional Georgian windows and many other original details.

The Central Bank, constructed amid considerable controversy in the early 1970s, was at that point the only major new building to have been erected in this part of the old city. The construction of the Central Bank had necessitated the demolition of several old houses on Fownes Street, and a number of historic buildings on Dame Street. The massive eight-storey structure, which overhangs the surrounding streets and dominates the entire area, was at the time seen by many to be 'the way forward' for the city. Many people, especially developers, envisaged a city where all old buildings, houses and streets would be erased and bold new emblems of the twentieth century, in the form of office blocks of glittering glass and white concrete, would take their place. It was Frank MacDonald, in a series of articles in the *Irish Times*, who wrote about the disgraceful dereliction in this part of town, where surface car parks covered much of the streetscape. MacDonald also highlighted the many heavy-handed road-widening plans of the Dublin Corporation Roads Department. These plans involved the demolition of all of Wellington Quay, most of Essex Street East and Temple Bar, much of Eustace Street and Fownes Street and indeed part of Dame Street. All things considered, the prospects for the Temple Bar area in 1985 were grim.

Following An Taisce's campaign to save the area, which involved much political lobbying by them and other groups, an announcement was eventually made by the government in 1987 that the Temple Bar area would be spared. The provision of studio space for musicians and artists at very low rents had allowed the area to evolve as a district for artistic pursuits and alternative lifestyles. Premises had been rented by such groups as the Gay and Lesbian Federation, the Green Party, the Resource Centre and the Project Arts Centre. Small businesses selling second-hand furniture and clothes and enterprises such as the Square Wheel Cycle Works had been established in the buildings rented out by CIÉ. Many tenants now feared that the likely gentrification of the district would mean a rise in rents that would force their ultimate departure. Dublin Corporation demonstrated their commitment to conserving this area by immediately embarking on a plan to resurface every street in the district with stone setts. The result was spectacular and instantly changed the whole character of the district. Suddenly people began to look on this shabby area in a new light. Simultaneously, a group of young architects called the Temple Bar Study Group prepared plans and designs for new buildings to be built on the various derelict sites in the area.

Below: This nineteenth-century Temple Lane warehouse, of which only the unusual façade and circular windows remain, is representative of the early manufacturing and commercial nature of the Temple Bar district.

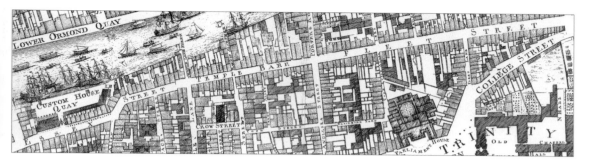

In 1991 Temple Bar Properties was established by government act and its brief was to develop a cultural quarter in the city alongside a residential and small business area. The area was now defined as extending from Westmoreland Street in the east all the way to the Civic Offices in the west. In the same year a competition was held which would develop an architectural framework for the renewal of the entire area. Several new open spaces for public squares were proposed and various pedestrian routes planned, which would create an east–west movement in the district. The competition was won by a consortium of architects called Group '91. All of the former CIÉ property was handed over to Temple Bar Properties for redevelopment. Traffic was largely eliminated from the area and most of the district is now fully pedestrianised. This is an extremely pleasant aspect of Temple Bar.

The success of the area has brought its own problems. Pubs and restaurants have proliferated to an extraordinary extent and pavements are frequently blocked by large wheelie bins and even stacked barrels of beer.

Opposite: Curved Street, constructed in the 1990s, is one of the most adventurous architectural innovations in Temple Bar.

Above: Rocque's map (1756) shows how the street pattern of the Temple Bar area has remained virtually unchanged. The density of housing indicates how populous and busy the area was in the mid-eighteenth century.

Below: This painting, attributed to Phillip Hussey, is a rare representation of a typical mid-eighteenth house. The family are shown in their first-floor drawing room.

Above: A panelled staircase from number 17 Eustace Street before restoration.

Below: An early nineteenth-century map of Eustace Street, showing its extension to Wellington Quay and the Presbyterian Meeting House.

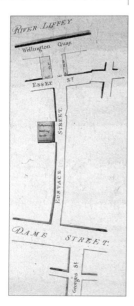

Right: A rare surviving example of a panelled staircase at number 25 Eustace Street, carefully restored by the Irish Landmark Trust.

The area has developed a European reputation as a lively night spot, and the results are unfortunately often to be seen the following morning on the streets: broken glass, vomit and urine in doorways and alleyways. But perhaps no one should be surprised – some of the city's inhabitants had exactly the same reputation in the eighteenth century!

The presence of the Civic Offices, occupying the entire Wood Quay site along with Christ Church Cathedral, the major network of roads there and Dublin Castle created a barrier between Temple Bar and the medieval city of High Street, Thomas Street and the Liberties. This break in the fabric of the old city in terms of streets and buildings will be difficult, if not impossible, to make good.

Among the first buildings in Temple Bar to be refurbished was 18 Eustace Street, the head office of Temple Bar Properties. This handsome early nineteenth-century house, which was one of the largest in the street, has been carefully restored. In 1993 a former warehouse in Essex Street was refurbished for Design Yard as a high-quality jewellery gallery and display area for Irish crafts and furniture. The contemporary interior has worked well and Design Yard has been very successful. The Children's Cultural Centre, located in Eustace Street, incorporates a purpose-built theatre behind the façade of the oldest Presbyterian meeting house in Ireland. The centre, now known as the Ark, is extremely popular with school groups and children of all ages. Almost directly opposite the Ark, the presence of a vacant site presented an opportunity to create a new street, which has been named Curved Street. Two new buildings fronted Curved Street, Arthouse on the south and the Temple Bar Music Centre on the north. Arthouse, a temple to the contemporary world of multimedia arts, with its

curved façade and somewhat nautical lines, is perhaps one of the most successful modern buildings in Temple Bar. A steel girder that projects from the façade is reminiscent of the timber cranes which were once commonplace in the many warehouses of the district.

The Photographic Centre, in a new building at the corner of Meeting House Square and East Essex Street, houses the nation's Photographic Archive and is funded by the National Library. This provided an ideal opportunity for the National Library to relocate all its photographic holdings to one building and to establish a permanent exhibition space for its photographic collections.

Several smaller infill developments, most of which were residential, are also worthy of note. An unusual residential complex at 25 Essex Street includes a raised interior courtyard. Another interesting building occupies the corner of Fownes Street and Cecilia Street and was built on the partly excavated Augustinian Monastery. Now occupied by Malone's restaurant, this building features a façade of coursed limestone and is rendered on the upper floors. A semicircular glass-brick staircase is an unusual feature.

The Green Building is an experimental structure erected between Temple Lane and Crow Street. The façade of the building adds interest to the streetscape of Crow Street, with its semicircular projecting bow and double balconies. The main entrance of the Green Building is ornamented with a sculpture created from recycled copper pipes, incorporated into a beaten-copper entrance door.

Above: A general view of Eustace Street. Unlike the neighbouring lanes, Eustace Street was fashionable and mostly residential. It was described as a 'new street' in 1709.

Temple Bar in the Eighteenth Century

When John Rocque produced his map of Dublin in 1756, he depicted a sophisticated city that had already spread rapidly in an easterly direction towards Dublin Bay. His map, entitled 'An exact survey of the city and suburbs of Dublin in which is expressed the ground plot of all public buildings, dwelling houses, warehouses, stables, courts, yards, etc', is a fascinating portrait of an eighteenth-century European city with a thriving port. True to his word, Rocque did indeed describe every courtyard, every alleyway and every house with as much accuracy as was possible at that time. The district of Temple Bar was then traversed by one main thoroughfare, that of Essex Street, Temple Bar and Fleet Street, while it was bounded on the

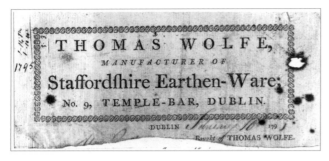

THOMAS WOLFE,

MANUFACTURER OF

Staffordshire Earthen-Ware;

No. 9, TEMPLE-BAR, DUBLIN.

DUBLIN *Janu* 10 1795

Bought of THOMAS WOLFE.

Above: The Temple Bar area was a focus of commercial activity in eighteenth-century Dublin.

Below: An eighteenth-century map showing both the Presbyterian and Quaker Meeting Houses, and Meeting House Yard.

south by Dame Street and College Green. On the river frontage we have already described the presence of the old Custom House beside Essex Bridge, but there was no Wellington Quay adjoining it until 1815. A spacious Aston Quay ran eastwards as far as Hawkins Street and many ships moored there. The quay became redundant following the building of Carlisle (now O'Connell) Bridge in the 1790s.

Rocque's map depicts the attractive but somewhat disorderly nature of the development of much of central Dublin. In general, houses were considerably smaller and the plots were narrower than they were to become in the late eighteenth century when the streets were realigned by the Wide Streets Commissioners.

Eighteenth-century Temple Bar was bordered on the east by the Parliament House (now the Bank of Ireland) and by Trinity College, and on the west by the Custom House and Dublin Castle. There were few other important buildings in the district apart from the meeting houses of the Quakers and the Presbyterians in Eustace Street. There were also a number of theatres, such as the Crow Street Theatre, the Smock Alley Theatre, which was situated on Blind Quay, otherwise known as Exchange Street, and the Musick Hall in Fishamble Street.

Charles Brooking's map, with its border of engravings of Dublin, was

made in 1728, some thirty years prior to Rocque's map. It helps to give a more three-dimensional impression of what the city was like. Most of these small houses in Temple Bar were two or three storeys high and gable-fronted. They were built of brick and had slated cruciform roofs. They had timber sash windows with small panes of glass. The interiors would have been plain, but in a more expensive house the staircase and principal rooms might have been timber-panelled. The skyline was filled with a multiplicity of brick chimney stacks. Most houses had a closet to the rear, a small room measuring seven or eight feet square, which served as a dressing room. The larger properties had a backhouse, which was a small two-storey structure situated to the back of the main house in which either work was carried out or a member of the household dwelt. Only a few of these early houses survive today in the Temple Bar area, for example 25 Eustace Street.

Eustace Street was developed on the site of a seventeenth-century house and gardens belonging to Sir Maurice Eustace, a descendant of a

Norman family who settled in County Kildare, from whom it derives its name. It would appear that much of Eustace Street was built in the early 1700s, and it is fortunate that the front of the Presbyterian Meeting House, built in 1728, survives, along with at least four houses of the same vintage. The symmetrical façade and elaborate cut-stone window and door surrounds are all that remain of the meeting house, which was rebuilt as a warehouse in the nineteenth century. Its most famous pastor, or minister, was Dr John Leland, who published many acclaimed theological and philosophical works in the mid-eighteenth century. The prosperous congregation supported an almshouse and male and female schools.

Eustace Street was certainly one of the better residential streets of Temple Bar, containing a number of good private houses, the Dissenters' (Presbyterian) Meeting House and the Quaker Meeting House, with its adjoining yard. Meeting House Yard was apparently famous for its hatters and cap-makers – thought to have been of Huguenot stock – until the middle of the nineteenth century. The presence of the Presbyterians and the Quakers in this quarter since the early eighteenth century suggests that they were only just tolerated by the Anglican authorities, provided they were housed in an unfashionable part of the city, hidden from the public eye. Dissenting Protestants as well as Catholics were discriminated against by the Irish Parliament throughout the eighteenth century.

Above: The principal meeting room in the Quaker Meeting House, which was converted in the mid-1980s into cinema one of the Irish Film Centre.

Above: One of the largest warehouses in Temple Lane, which has now been converted into apartments. The sizeable doors easily accommodated bales of material for the mainly textile-related industries.

The first meeting house of the Religious Society of Friends, or Quakers, was built in Sycamore Alley in 1692. During the eighteenth century they acquired further properties, including a passageway from Eustace Street to Meeting House Yard – now the central foyer of the Irish Film Centre. Several Quaker families owned houses in the immediate vicinity, including Joshua Bewley, whose tea and coffee importing business began there in about 1840. Numbers 4 and 5 Eustace Street were acquired by the Friends in 1815, and by 1859 the principal entrance to the meeting house was by means of Eustace Street. Extensive alterations were made to the street frontage, including the entrance to the meeting house, in the late nineteenth century, and the old yard was roofed to create a covered vestibule. The principal meeting room, clearly shown on Rocque's map of 1756, is a plain rectangular space dating from the early eighteenth century. Now somewhat modified, it houses cinema one in the Irish Film Centre. During extensive Victorian reconstruction, a gallery, dated 1877 and supported by cast-iron columns, replaced an earlier three-sided timber one, and the meeting house was furnished with plain, well-made benches. In keeping with Quaker practice, there was no altar, only a raised seating area for the Society's elders. In 1975 the Friends sought planning permission to erect a nine-storey office block, to include a conference hall, new meeting rooms, a library, bookshop, offices and bedsits, on their site at Eustace Street, but were refused permission by the Corporation. A reading room and historical library were maintained by the Quakers in Eustace Street, and when most of the meeting house was sold in 1985 it was re-established in Swanbrook House in Donnybrook. The conversion of these buildings into the IFC was the first 'cultural project' to be completed in the Temple Bar area.

Amid the undoubtedly respectable and possibly austere congregations of Quakers and Presbyterians in Eustace Street, there were also several taverns, the most notable of which was the Eagle. It was here in 1782 that the Irish Volunteers held their meetings and dinners under the auspices of the Duke of Leinster and in the presence of the Lord Mayor, Lord Charlemont, Henry Grattan and other supporters.

A fascinating parchment deed of 1709 has recently come to light which concerns the lease of property in Essex Street to William Quayle, an apothecary, and mentions that it is bounded on the east by a new street 'intended to be called Eustace Street'. It was joined on the north by Thomas Pooley's timber yard, part of which had been acquired to form the continuation of Essex Street. To the south lay 'wast' or waste ground owned by Pooley, and to the west 'Sykamore' Alley. The same holding, which must have been situated on part of what is now Meeting House Square, was let again in 1716 to a brewer named John Shelley, who was to create a passageway to Essex Street, in line with a house known as 'The Sign of the Golden Bible'.

The tall houses on the east side of Eustace Street backed onto warehouses in Temple Lane. It would appear that many of these warehouses belonged to the residences of Eustace Street. One of them, with its wide granite openings and small timber crane jutting out from the top of the building, was unfortunately demolished in the early 1980s before the development of Temple Bar began.

In 1987 yet another demolition occurred of a key building, at the corner of Eustace Street and Dame Street. Though the Victorian red-brick building with its ornate stucco shopfront was of no major architectural significance in its own right, its demolition created

Above: Clearly visible in this Temple Lane warehouse (now demolished) is the crane jutting out at roof level.

Above: An elaborate stucco capital of a demolished Victorian commercial premises at the top of Eustace Street.

Left: The restored panelled drawing room of number 25 Eustace Street, with its original corner fireplace.

Above: Temple Bar Square with its book market. The lively atmosphere of the recently regenerated Temple Bar area attracts visitors in large numbers from home and abroad.

Below: A medieval tile from the Augustinian Friary in Fownes Street.

Opposite top: An eighteenth-century map of Crown Alley.

Opposite bottom: Merchants' Arch, as it appeared prior to the building of the Central Bank, shown in a 1960s newspaper cutting.

another serious gap in the city's streetscape, which many feared would never be filled. It was a respectable late-nineteenth-century office building, with prominent gables. The structural failure of a large timber bessamer beam over the shopfront had caused concern for the safety of the façade. There is little doubt that the defect could have been remedied and demolition avoided. Fortunately a new building, now operating as a hostel, was erected there without undue delay.

Number 25 Eustace Street, dating from the 1720s, has been expertly and beautifully restored by the Irish Landmark Trust with the assistance of the Department of the Environment and Temple Bar Properties. This once gable-fronted house is one of the oldest in the area and is panelled throughout. The restored building is available for short-term rent or weekends.

An interesting feature of the staircases in these early houses are the ramp-type bannisters and handrails. The hand-turned balusters or poles are positioned on a continuous ramp, instead of on each step, which was the fashion from about 1740 onwards. Number 17, a similar house, was also very carefully restored, though more of it had to be replaced.

The great number of shop signs hanging from various shops, houses and taverns must have added to the colour of Dublin's eighteenth-century streets, but they also served an essential purpose of providing an address by means of an identifiable symbol for the many illiterate citizens. For this reason, pubs were given names such as the Punch Bowl or the Dog and Duck. The Turk's Head Chop House was a tavern in Temple Bar, and the name has been revived recently on Parliament Street. Various publishers in Dame Street could be found at the sign of Swift's Head, Cicero's Head or Virgil's Head, while Shakespeare's Head stood at the corner of Castle Lane (now Palace Street) in 1726. The term 'where do you hang out?' may derive from describing the whereabouts of your abode by the sign hanging over the door.

It is interesting to note from mid-eighteenth-century maps that Eustace Street did not run all the way to the river as it does today. Temple Lane, however, which no longer runs down to the river, did so at that time, ending in a boat slip and ferry point. Neighbouring Fownes Street ended in the well-known Bagnio Slip. Bagnio is the Italian for bath and suggests that this may at one time have been a favourite bathing or watering place. An octagonal cockpit also stood at the bottom of Temple Lane, right beside the river, on the present line of Wellington Quay. It was used for cock fighting, which was very popular in the eighteenth century. Fownes Street was the site of an Augustinian monastery, which was thought to have been founded in the thirteenth century by the Talbot family. A beautiful medieval tile showing a rampant griffin was found here during excavations, and a substantial arched stone wall was also uncovered.

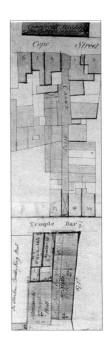

In the eighteenth century, Crown Alley was a narrow, twisty passageway running from Temple Bar up to Dame Street. The width of the alley as it is seen today at the back of Merchants' Arch would be a good guide to the width of the whole of Crown Alley at that time. The properties that fronted onto the alley were built in a random fashion, jutting in and out and leaving a passageway of irregular width. In the 1820s, when the present Ha'penny Bridge was newly completed and a proposal was put forward to build Merchants' Hall facing it, the Wide Streets Commissioners took the opportunity to widen and straighten Crown Alley. Their work was made considerably easier where it passed through the site of the present Central Bank, as this entire area was cleared in the 1790s when a new building line was established on Dame Street.

The bottom of Fownes Street approaching the Bagnio Slip was known at the end of the eighteenth century as Dirty Lane, and as already noted this part of town seemed to have quite a reputation for squalor. A report on the district that appeared in the *Irish Builder* in 1879 commented:

> Alas, there is nothing sweet or pleasant in the Temple Bar of our day! There are plenty of foul-smelling drains, dilapidated dwellings, back yards seething in filth, and poverty and rags from basements to attics and out and about.

The writer continued:

> There is still some life and huckstering trade in Temple Bar but its wealthy merchants and big and little prosperous shopkeepers of forty or fifty years are all dead and gone, or if

any of them still live, they know the place no longer. Poor Temple Bar! Ruin – black, ghastly and deadly has rained upon you in torrents!

He went on to suggest that, 'Perhaps the modern "monster" drapery shops have absorbed the hats as well as the bonnets', and that the hatters of Temple Bar had no successors. The author was surely referring to the Victorian development of large department stores such as Pim's and Brown Thomas's. He continues to describe the vanished clothing industry of the area: 'The cap makers of Meeting House Yard were once a busy and numerous race of female artisan, but they too have totally disappeared.'

The Guild of Merchants' Hall was first proposed in 1820 and included 'a passage from the Metal Bridge' leading to Crown Alley. Maps dated 1826 show that the passageway from Merchants' Arch was covered at the Temple Bar end. The bottom of Crown Alley was also covered by an archway in the same way. At the time, many passageways and alleys were built over in this manner in order to maximise space. The bottom of Temple Lane was described in a survey of 1781 as a watering slip, presumably a place where horses could be washed down and ships could take on water. A passage to the ferry with steps was also marked. Several of the houses which backed directly onto the Liffey had small square privies, or toilets, but these buildings were swept away during the construction of Wellington Quay in about 1815.

A plan for the rebuilding of the block between Fownes Street and Anglesea Street on Dame Street was proposed by the Wide Streets Commissioners in 1792. Maps prepared for the acquisition of property in this area show the jumble of small properties which surrounded the twisty Crown Alley, and the location of the old Post Office Yard. Thirteen new houses were at first proposed for the new street line, before it was decided to erect the much larger commercial buildings. It is almost certain that the Wide Streets Commissioners were behind the construction of the Ha'penny Bridge and the development of a passageway through Merchants' Arch, linking Crown Alley with Liffey Street and the north city centre. At this time, about 1820, the southern quays were being completed by joining Crampton Quay with Essex Quay through the building of Wellington Quay. The cockpit, which must have stood close to the site of the present Eliza Lodge Hotel, was probably demolished during the construction of Wellington Quay.

A map of the area dating from the late eighteenth century shows Meeting House Yard situated on what is now the foyer of the Irish Film Centre. A building called the Stamp Office stood between the Quaker Meeting House and Eustace Street, while Vallance's Auction Room occupied part of the site of the present Meeting House Square. A small passageway called Coghill's Court, which is still open, joined Meeting House Yard with Dame

Street. This passage was previously named Cockle's Court and may be a reminder of the fondness of Dubliners for shellfish over the centuries. Much of the area behind the Quaker Meeting House and Sycamore Alley was taken up with warehouses and stables in 1789. Some of these were leased to small businesses by the Huguenot families of Cope and D'Olier. The building in Sycamore Alley currently occupied by Belgo, the Belgian restaurant, incorporated an earlier warehouse building. Numbers 12 and 13 were the stores and stables of Joshua Bewley in the 1840s. These warehouses were substantially rebuilt in the nineteenth century, but the façade of one small early nineteenth-century premises remains. Its handsome granite front and archway have been incorporated into a new development.

Essex Street was divided in two by the construction of Parliament Street in the 1760s. The occupations of the inhabitants of this street did not change greatly over the next century and in 1835 we still find tallow chandlers, hat manufacturers, a printing office and an earthenware manufacturer. At 32 Essex Street East, on the corner with Eustace Street, we find the Eustace Street Male School. Part of the arched façade of the school, with its massive stucco doorcase, was incorporated into a new building here, which was raised by an extra storey.

At number 50, Mary Smith was the proprietor of the Dolphin Hotel and Tavern in 1835, while Patrick Coyne was the owner of the Castle Hotel at number 16. The Dolphin Hotel was eventually taken over and rebuilt by the Nugent family in the late nineteenth century. Now the home of the District Court, it is a very handsome red-brick building with limestone dressings and an elaborate corner entrance featuring a golden dolphin. The metal flags on the dormer windows in the roof are pierced with the initial DH. The Castle Hotel stood almost exactly on the site of the present Fitzsimons Hotel and was in existence by about 1800.

In the nineteenth century, Henry Rathborne, merchant, had premises at number 49 Essex Street, possibly backing on to Crampton Court. Rathborne's were one of Dublin's oldest and most noted candlemakers and are still in business today.

In 1905 John G Rathborne's, wax and spermaceti (from whale oil) candle manufacturers, oil refiners and general oil merchants, were again located in Crampton Court. This small court, which lies beside the Olympia Theatre, just off Dame Street,

can be approached either by a passage from Essex Street or from a narrow lane under a building in Dame Street. In the late eighteenth century, maps prepared for the Wide Streets Commissioners show that there were five houses and three small stores surrounding Crampton Court. There was a particularly large building on the site of the Olympia Theatre, which is marked on a late-eighteenth-century map as a bakehouse. By the 1830s we find twenty-one businesses located there, including boot and shoe-makers, stationers, gunmakers, watch-glass manufacturers, engravers, a grocery and provision stores and a tavern-keeper. The last remaining occupant of Crampton Court was Jordan's, the shoemakers, whose single-storey shed remained in use until 1995. Their premises were, in fact, all that remained of a three- or four-storey Georgian house that was once entered by a fine stone doorcase. All of the granite footpaths and paving of the passageways still remain intact. This area, which had been derelict for almost thirty years, has been rebuilt and will hopefully regain something of the spirit of the eighteenth-century courtyard, with small shops and residences above.

References have been found to a Crampton Court Theatre dating to the early eighteenth century, and a Widow Quinlan is mentioned as the proprie-tor. In 1879, Dan Lowry operated a music hall here. It later became the Empire Palace Theatre and finally, in the twentieth century, the Olympia Theatre. Crampton Court is dominated by the Olympia's massive Victorian façade. This was at one time the principal entrance to the theatre and the two arched doorways are still to be seen. It was only when the theatre acquired a house on Dame Street in the 1890s that a new and elaborate entrance was created with the present wonderful cast-iron canopy, added

Right: The richly decorated interior of the Olympia Theatre. There are three levels on each side to accommodate ornate private boxes, of which only the bottom two are used.

in 1897, which is filled with coloured glass. The new entrance on Dame Street means that patrons first have to descend to basement level, and then pass almost under the stage and up into the back of the theatre. The Olympia Theatre, which is partially built over the River Poddle, is famous for its elaborate Victorian interior, which includes twelve richly decorated boxes, an ornamented proscenium arch and a decorated ceiling. It is the finest Victorian theatre remaining in Dublin.

One of Dublin's most famous theatres, the Crow Street Theatre, opened in 1758 and ran until 1820. The theatre in fact stood in what is today called Cecilia Street, on the site of the present Cooke's building. It is said that at the last performance in the theatre most of the fittings, including scenery, benches and decorations, were ripped out and taken away by the audience!

Above: The coloured-glass canopy of the Olympia, once known as the Empire Palace, was added in the 1890s and projects out over the pavement of Dame Street.

An illustration from *Walker's Hibernian Magazine* of 1795 shows the theatre to have been quite substantial, with four tiers of galleries divided into boxes. The print shows a pony race in full swing with most of the audience standing in a kind of pit in the centre of the floor. A map of properties produced for the Wide Streets Commissioners in about 1815 marks it as 'Theatre Royal'. The theatre had been built at a cost of £3,000 and on its closure was converted into a hat factory. Part of it was acquired in 1836 by the Apothecaries Hall, who erected the present building which was equipped with lecture rooms and a laboratory. In 1852 it became the Cecilia School of Medicine, which in turn became the School of Medicine of the Catholic University and was, in a sense, the forerunner of University College, Dublin (UCD).

Adjoining Cecilia House are three small warehouses dating from the middle of the nineteenth century. Many of these premises were used as stores by woollen merchants and wine merchants and by manufacturers of various kinds. One of the most impressive warehouses stood at the corner of Temple Lane and Cecilia Street. Only the façade of this impressive five-storey building remains today as the structure was greatly modified to create apartments within. The opening from the timber loft doors was retained and a small iron crane also remains.

In 1835 Crow Street boasted no less than seventeen tailors and dressmakers, and was also home to John Kirkwood, engraver, copper-plate printer and globe manufacturer to His Majesty. A bill, dated 1842, from Margaret Aston's Tailoring Establishment to Thomas Brabazon of Tara Hall, shows that he paid £3 18/– for a black dress coat and £1 12/– for black doe trousers. Clothes for his servants, including livery frock coats and green livery vests, came to a further five guineas.

Number 7 Crow Street is one of the last surviving early- or mid-eighteenth-century houses in this district. Its Gibbs-style stone doorcase is typical of the period and it once had a plain Gothic-style fanlight. Similar houses survive in Fownes Street and these have been carefully restored. These double-fronted houses contained small, panelled rooms on both ground and first floor. All of this panelling, including the original timber cornices and plain corner fireplaces, has now been restored. The houses, which were on the brink of collapse and threatened with demolition, were rescued in about 1993. The mid-nineteenth-century occupants of Fownes Street included a jeweller and gold beater, tailors, printers, a picture cleaner, two bakeries and a wine store.

The Wide Streets Commissioners

The operation of the Wide Streets Commissioners is itself interesting. Established by an act of parliament, their first meeting was held in 1758 in the old Custom House beside Essex Bridge. The next meeting was held in the same year in Dublin Castle, and three years later we find them in the Tholsel at Skinner Row, near Christ Church Cathedral. The Commissioners' method of property acquisition was not unlike the system of Compulsory Purchase Order that is employed today by local government. Once they had decided on the new street or proposed line of widening, they would commission a careful survey of all the properties involved. Maps were prepared detailing the names of owners and tenants, and submissions were heard on behalf of the various parties. Each owner submitted a figure that they considered a reasonable compensation for giving up their property and moving their business, and the sums ranged from quite modest figures, such as £15, up to several thousand pounds in the case of major landowners. The premises of printer George Faulkner, for example, stood in the way of the proposed new Parliament Street, and he sought a sum of £5,000 in compensation. He eventually received about £2,000. Various witnesses were called to back up the alleged value of various people's holdings and businesses. John Nott, who was described as a grocer and 'sells wines, has tolerable business', valued his interest in numbers 14 and 16 Crane Lane at £500. In the event he received £250, although fellow vintner Charles Wynn, the owner of the Bear Tavern, swore evidence to the effect that 'if Mr Nott was obliged to remove, it would hurt him greatly'. (Nott was later the successful bidder for the plot at number 2 Palace Street and built himself a new house on that site, later to become the Sick and Indigent Roomkeepers' Society's building.) The final valuations on the various properties were made by a jury, which consisted of various worthy merchants and gentlemen of the city. In 1779, ten out of the full complement of twenty-two merchants and gentlemen who were supposed to attend the jury, including Arthur Guinness, were each fined £10 for not turning up – a heavy fine in eighteenth-century terms.

Following the acquisition of the various properties, a map was drawn up showing the proposed new street and indicating the various lots for sale.

Above: An eighteenth-century sword made by Read's the Cutlers of Parliament Street.

Opposite: The granite-paved passageway leading to Crampton Court from Essex Street.

These plans were 'fixed in several coffee houses' and indeed some of the surviving maps, which are kept in the Dublin City Archives, show clear signs of having been displayed on a notice board with tacks. When 4 Essex Street was sold to the Wide Streets Commissioners, it was specified that all materials were included with the property 'except the grates, locks and marble chimney pieces', and the Commissioners stipulated that the 'houses to be thrown down and passage cleared by the 29th September 1761'. The Wide Streets Commissioners spent what was then a very large sum, over £32,000, in acquiring the property between Essex Street and Dame Street.

Above: A decorative watch paper, often to be found inside fob watches. In the eighteenth century, Temple Bar was noted for the number and skill of its craftspeople.

Left: This impressive corner building, number 15 Parliament Street, was planned by the Wide Streets Commissioners in the late eighteenth century. The Italianate façade was added later. By 1850 it was the premises of Robert Cordner, a wealthy coach-lace manufacturer.

Opposite: The streets paved with stone setts are a vital element in the definition of Temple Bar as a place set apart from the rest of the city. In the background is the National Photographic Archive.

Above: One of a pair of elaborately carved brackets, eight feet in length, from Abrahams' Victorian shopfront in Parliament Street.

Above right: In this photograph, c.1980, Parliament Street had fallen into a state of total stagnation and was frequented only by passing traffic.

The names of some of the artisans and merchants who were displaced and compensated are recorded in the minutes of the Commissioners' meetings, and give us a flavour of the commercial life of this part of Dublin in the middle of the eighteenth century. Mr Francis Booker, who was one of the most important makers of looking glasses, or mirrors, in Dublin, was awarded £850 for his interest in a property in Essex Street and for the inconvenience of relocating his business. Fellow glass grinder and cabinet-maker William Bibby gave evidence to the effect that Mr Booker had 'twice his business, if not more'. Booker was able to acquire a site and build a new house on the west side of Parliament Street, almost directly adjacent to the present Sunlight Chambers. This and an adjoining house survived up until the 1990s, by which time, having been allowed to deteriorate, they were demolished except for the façades. Unfortunately, a rare example of a rococo plasterwork ceiling had to be dismantled from the principal first-floor room of one of these houses. The pieces of the ceiling were stored in tea chests by Temple Bar Properties and to this date have not been reinstated.

Francis Booker specialised in elaborate carved and gilded mirrors, which today bring very large sums of money in auction rooms. One of his neighbours was Isaac D'Olier, a goldsmith, whose family name is recorded in the present D'Olier Street. Other trades represented in Essex Street and Crane Lane, which were affected by the making of the new road, were sword cutlers, a seal cutter, shoemakers and a mantua-maker (a mantua was a type of cloak or mantle).

As Dublin's prime business district in the eighteenth century, this was also the location of two of the most important printers in Ireland of the day. Boulter Grierson, printer, was the son of George Grierson, whose lease of a property in Essex Street dated back to 1699. The family of Grierson had been appointed to the role of King's Printer. Several generations of Griersons continued the business at their premises in Essex Street, known as 'the King's Arms and the Sign of the Two Bibles'. The Grierson family became extremely wealthy and at the close of the eighteenth century owned various Georgian mansions in the Rathfarnham area, including at one time Rathfarnham House, now part of Loreto Convent, and Woodtown House. As King's Printer, the Griersons were responsible for printing and publishing the House of Commons Journal, Statute Books and other official publications and bills. Aside from this business, the Griersons were printers of bibles and prayer books. Following the Act of Union, George Grierson claimed compensation for his loss of business and his investment in other printing work. Grierson's patent was renewed in 1811, when he was appointed King's Printer for another forty-year term. During the acquisition by the Wide Streets Commissioners, a witness for Boulter Grierson claimed that he would lose up to £200 in moving from his premises. His printing office was later located on Cork Hill, where he also produced the *Dublin Gazette*. These offices eventually became the premises of the *Evening Mail* and occupied a building on the corner of Parliament Street.

Above: Part of a now-vanished rococo ceiling from 22 Parliament Street. Decorative plasterwork is rarely found in Temple Bar, indicating the largely commercial nature of the district.

Below: Parliament Street today.

Perhaps the best-known printer in this area was George Faulkner, whose shop and printing office in Essex Street had been leased since 1751. We learn from the minutes of the Wide Street Commissioners that Francis Booker paid him a rent of £50 per annum for the use of a crane at 25 Essex Street, and that Faulkner 'uses a vast deal of paper for his journal and much room for all his books'. Faulkner was also the owner of 26 Essex Street, which had been leased to Edward Fitzsimons since 1723 as the Merchants' Coffee House.

Samuel Goodbody, a tobacconist, was the occupant of 30–31 Essex Street, which he had leased since 1749 from Lord and Lady Molesworth. This property was described as 'very well built', with an ample warehouse attached. The Molesworths received the astonishing sum of almost £5,000 from the Wide Streets Commissioners for their interest in properties in this area. Goodbody's tobacco and snuff manufacturers remained on the corner of Wellington Quay and Parliament Street until the middle of the twentieth century and the building, with its Victorian shopfront, survives today.

Another unique survivor of this period, said to be the oldest shop in Dublin, is the premises of Thomas Read, cutler,

Above: Ancient bellows from an artisan's workshop, found in Parliament Street. They might have been used to fan a small furnace in a metalworker's shop.

Below: The impressive trade card of Francis Booker, who specialised in making carved and gilded mirrors.

located at 4 Parliament Street. Read's premises had originally fronted onto Crane Lane and he was able to relocate with a more prominent shopfront onto Parliament Street when the street was created. While Read's dates from 1670, the present shop, which was built in the 1760s, is an outstanding example of an eighteenth-century shop interior, with its mahogany display cases and delicately glazed cabinets. All of the original Chippendale-style glass-fronted cabinets with their small drawers are intact, as are all of the old counters and cash office desks. Among the fascinating collection of items in Read's shop are the world's smallest pair of working scissors, which it is said could cut a housefly's whiskers! The world's largest penknife – with 576 blades – is also in the collection, as well as other instruments. The shop boasts a fascinating collection of ancient knives, scissors and swords, and many kinds of surgeons' scalpels and needles. In 1821 the business obtained a royal charter to make needles for the British military forces. During the eighteenth century Read's produced magnificently crafted steel swords, which were supplied to the nobility and gentry as well as to the army. Such swords were usually inscribed with the maker's name and sometimes with the owner's name as well. The announcement of the closure of Read's the Cutlers caused dismay among the general public. Apart from being one of the city's finest specialist shops, it was well-known as the oldest surviving shop in Dublin. The last owner, John Read Cowle, decided to keep the business going until he could find somebody who would take it on as a going concern. The shop was eventually purchased by Hugh O'Regan, who established the Thomas Read pub on the corner with Dame Street. John Read Cowle handed over the keys of his shop to the new owners in 1989, thus ending a family association of over 300 years.

Other businesses in Crane Lane at this time included Peter McDermott, wig-maker; Zachariah Browne, stay-maker; Christopher Clarke, watchmaker; John Stewart, paper-maker; Ignatius McQuire's Bordeaux warehouse; and the Bear Tavern.

One of the first arrivals in the newly built Parliament Street was Mr Lundy Foot, who opened a tobacco shop in 1758 at the corner of Parliament Street and Exchange Street. The shop, which bore the sign of the Virginia planter, boasted a stock of tobacco including Bristol Roll, Common Roll, Pigtail, High and Low Scotch Snuff, Irish Rapees and Supefying Pigtail for ladies! Lundy Foot became famous for his snuff, and it is said that a particular batch of snuff got burnt by accident and became extremely popular with his clients, who became regular buyers of it. The business was still going strong in the nineteenth century and the name of Lundy Foot was known far and wide.

Foot became very wealthy and built himself a fine country house in Rathfarnham, which is now the Warden's Residence at St Columba's College. A ceramic coat of arms, which was once displayed over Lundy Foot's shop, was presented to the Dublin Civic Museum in 1973. The shopfront bearing his name survived here until 1998, when the letters, formed in cement, were thrown into a rubbish skip. One letter, the 'Y', was salvaged by this writer at that time. Fortunately, the building itself is still standing and has been converted into solicitors' offices.

In 1985, number 15 Parliament Street, the magnificent corner premises of Hackett's Seeds, was demolished, along with the adjoining house. The ground floor had a remarkable stone façade in the style of an Italian palazzo, dating from the middle of the nineteenth century. Dublin Corporation had ordered the demolition of the building because of some internal settlement of the walls and slight sloping of the floors. Following protests from An Taisce, it was agreed that the principal features of the building, such as its fine arched and rusticated ground floor, would be reinstated, but when it and the adjoining house were demolished a bland, new red-brick building was eventually erected in their place.

The year 1985 marked a low point in the history of Parliament Street, as first Abrahams' Tailors and next Read's the Cutlers announced that they would be closing down. The magnificent timber-carved shopfront of Abrahams' was rescued from a rubbish skip during alterations to the premises and the gigantic carved and gilded brackets are now in the Pearson collection.

Above: Read's the Cutler's on Parliament Street, is the earliest and most intact Georgian shop interior in Dublin – and possibly in Ireland. It has been closed since 1998.

Below: Some of the built-in drawers from the untouched interior of Read's shop.

Throughout the nineteenth century, Parliament Street earned a reputation as the centre of business for printing and publishing. More than thirty music sellers and publishers were located there in the early 1800s, while nearby Essex Quay was home to two noted violin makers, William Wilkinson and John Mackintosh. After a period of stagnation in the 1980s, a new paving scheme and the planting of trees helped attract some new business back into the street. Though it is greatly improved, Parliament Street still does not have the level of trade that its position deserves.

Essex Quay

A survey of the Essex Quay area of the City Estate, the property holdings of Dublin Corporation, was carried out in 1812 by AR Neville. This fascinating map clearly marks the position of Izod's Tower, a circular fortification that was part of the city wall. Today known as Isolde's Tower, it runs along the northeast side of Exchange Street and across towards Parliament Street. The position of Fyan's Tower was also clearly marked on the survey and the contemporary tenants of the buildings on that site identified. Fyan's Castle and the City Crane stood as part of a group of buildings between Essex Quay and Blind Quay, now known as Exchange Street. The City Crane, a substantial structure for lifting and weighing, stood opposite a Gothic schoolhouse that is now part of the Viking Adventure Centre, standing beside the Church of SS Michael and John. Izod's Tower was demolished in 1675.

An earlier map of the same area, made in 1781, shows the playhouse occupying the site of the Church of SS Michael and John. This, of course, was the famous Smock Alley Theatre. The site of Isolde's Tower was shown as the property of Augustus Thwaite, leased to him since 1733, and a further twenty-two houses and buildings stood between Blind Quay and the Liffey. A small covered passageway called Chester Alley gave access to Essex Quay from Blind Quay. Amid a storm of protest, the last remaining group of these houses was demolished in 1993 by Temple Bar Properties. The demolition of the five quayside buildings enraged many people, not least because the buildings had never even been recorded or examined structurally. It had been the intention of Dublin Corporation's Planning Department to list the buildings, but an early-morning demolition crew reduced the five properties to a heap of rubble, and nothing was

Above: The eighteenth-century warehouses of Lundy Foot in Essex Street.

Opposite top: A late eighteenth-century map of Essex Quay and Exchange Street, showing the property of the Foot family (bottom left). In the centre of the map is a circular structure representing the site of Izod's Tower, which was one of the defensive towers of the medieval city walls.

Opposite bottom: The premises of Lundy Foot & Co., at 26 Parliament Street, from a photograph taken in 1998.

Right: An eighteenth-century handturned baluster pole from Parliament Street.

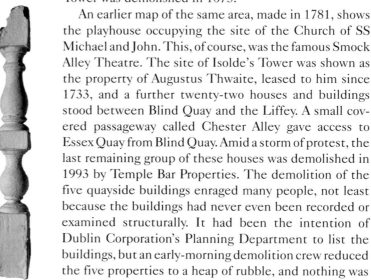

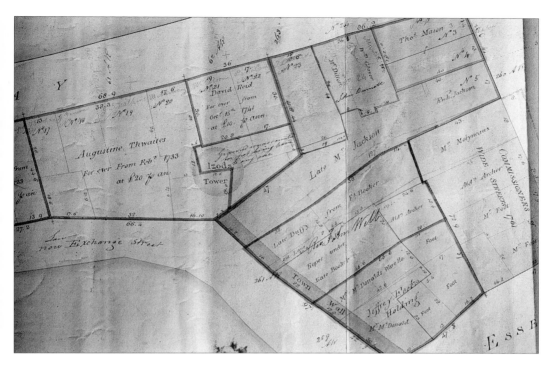

salvaged from them. Some very early timbers, probably of seventeenth-century date, were later found in the rubble. The site of these houses, which partially covered Izod's Tower, was excavated, revealing the base of the tower – it may now be seen beneath the new apartment block that has replaced the houses. It is a sad fact that there have been several instances in Dublin in the past where the perceived bene-fit of an archaeological dig has been used to justify the demolition of historic buildings that stand above ground, thus facilitating the developer, whose main objective is to build on a cleared site. A further section of the Essex Quay site was rebuilt in 1998 by another apartment building, with a distinctive bookend façade that is finished in stone.

The present Sunlight Chambers building, at the corner of Essex Quay and Parliament Street, occupies the site of houses that were erected by the Wide Streets Commis-sioners in the 1760s. One of the most noted occupants of this corner premises was Thomas Mason, an optician. Mason's business, with an address at 11 Essex Bridge, was described as 'Optician, Mathematical and Philosophical Instrument Maker'. He supplied spectacles in many varie-ties – gold, silver, tortoiseshell and horn frames – as well as telescopes and microscopes. In 1848 he also sold magic lanterns and slides with *camera obscuras*, spirit levels,

Above and above right: One of the unusual terracotta friezes, depicting the process of washing clothes, of the Sunlight Chambers.

Below: The five eighteenth-century houses of Essex Quay, adjoining the Sunlight Chambers.

theodilites, surveying chains, mariners' compasses, sundials, boxwood, ivory and brass rulers, brewers' gauges, barometers, electrifying machines and goggles for dusty weather! Mason's became the leading photographic firm in Dublin in the nineteenth century, and the business remained in the district and survived in its new premises on the corner of Dame Street and Palace Street up until the 1970s. As we have already seen, Mason's neighbours included Francis Booker, the mirror maker, whose property extended back to Exchange Street or Blind Quay, where he had extensive workshop space and showrooms. By the late eighteenth century, Lundy Foot's premises on Parliament Street also incorporated warehouses and stables to the rear in Exchange Street.

Sunlight Chambers was completed in 1901 as the Irish headquarters of Lever Brothers, manufacturers of soap. The building, which was

scheduled for demolition for road widening in the 1970s, has recently been restored and cleaned, revealing two richly ornamented terracotta friezes depicting the manufacture of soap and the process of washing. Its ornate Italianate façade is much admired and disguises a very plain interior – when it was built the *Irish Builder* commented that the ugliest building in Dublin was not a hundred miles from Grattan Bridge!

Smock Alley Theatre was built on Blind Quay by John Ogleby in about 1662. By permission of a patent from the 'Master of Revels in Ireland', he spent about £2,000 erecting a fine theatre. The theatre lived and flourished through many ups and downs until its closure in 1788. It attracted the nobility and gentry, who availed of the boxes, but also to the pit came many intoxicated audiences, who were out to cause trouble. In about 1780, Smock Alley Theatre was described as being one of the finest theatres of its type, and had a most unusual painted drop – instead of a curtain – which depicted the House of Parliament and the front of Trinity College. The theatre boasted many well-known actors of the day such as Mrs Siddons, Peg Woffington, David Garrick and Brinsley Sheridan.

By 1790 the premises had been converted and was being used as a whiskey store. In 1811 the site was taken over for the building of a church by the Catholic congregation of Rosemary Lane, which opened in 1815. It was constructed, it is said, mainly by volunteer labour, by the tradesmen of this part of Dublin.

Below: The early morning demolition in 1993 of the Essex Quay houses.

Below bottom: One of the two new apartment blocks that have been constructed on the Essex Quay site.

Before its demise in 1995, the Church of SS Michael and John was one of the earliest and finest Catholic churches in the city of Dublin.

The name of the church was derived from two defunct medieval churches in the district – St John's, formerly of Fishamble Street, and St Michael's of St Michael's Hill. The new rectangular Church of SS Michael and John was built with two façades designed in the restrained Gothic manner. The interior was ornamented with elaborate Gothic plasterwork, a large gallery and a fine altar. The great expanse of the Gothic ceiling, with its tracer-ied plasterwork, pendants and cherubs' heads, was under threat of removal and demolition until the intervention of conser-vation organisations. Though the rest of the church was indeed gutted in 1995, the ceiling was strengthened and repaired and survives. Unfortunately the galleries, including a very fine organ loft supported by four delicate wrought-iron brackets, which were orna-mented with delicate Gothic panelling, were entirely removed, along with an impressive marble altarpiece.

Above: An angel from the elaborate Gothic ceiling and wall of the Church of SS Michael and John.

The Church of SS Michael and John had closed in 1988 and lay mainly unused for a number of years. A joint project between Temple Bar Properties and Dublin Tourism planned to spend about £5.7 million to convert the church into an interactive Viking Museum. At face value, the plan appeared to be a good one, which would give the redundant church a new lease of life, but the proposal to remove every trace of the church's magnificent interior was at odds with all good conservation policy. It seemed bizarre to destroy the heritage of one period – the early nineteenth century – in order to create a museum of the heritage of an earlier period. The project also involved con-verting two former schoolhouse buildings and an impressive Georgian-style presbytery to new uses. Planning permission for the project was first sought in 1992. To quote the English *Independent* of 18 January 1995, 'this curious project, designed by Gilroy, McMahon Architects, involves the destruction of authentic history to make way for a world of conjecture and make believe'.

The church of SS Michael and John was an important example of the Regency Gothic style in a church context. The three large pendants that hung down from the centre of the ceiling were particularly striking. While the Chapel Royal in Dublin Castle had some similarities in style, and was of the same period, the only other Roman Catholic church in Dublin of similar type was St Michan's in Halston Street. The Exchange Street Chapel, as it was called by GN Wright in 1821, was one of the first Catholic chapels to be built on a large scale in Dublin prior to Catholic Emancipation. It is quite

astonishing that a building of this quality, which had been so often described in books about Dublin as having a richly ornamented interior, should have been allowed to be virtually destroyed as recently as 1995.

By the end of the 1990s most of the projects of Temple Bar Properties had been completed and only one major derelict site between Fishamble Street and Exchange Street Upper remained to be developed. This area incorporated the former music hall on Fishamble Street and adjoined Copper Alley. In recent memory it was used by the libraries service of Dublin Corporation for parking vehicles. A major series of developments has now been completed here, including the creation of a new pedestrian street from Lord Edward Street to Essex Street.

CHAPTER THREE

Dame Street

A map of Dublin was made in the year 1610 by John Speed. This unusual map, which has the qualities of a bird's eye view, shows that Dublin was still essentially a medieval city, located mostly within the city walls, although it had begun to spread, north across the river to St Michan's and St Mary's Abbey, up Thomas Street to the west, to St Patrick's Cathedral and Stephen Street in the south and down Dame Street towards Trinity College in the east.

Just outside Dame's Gate lay Dame Street and St Andrew's Church, which is depicted by Speed as having a semicircular graveyard. The church is believed to have stood on the site of the present Allied Irish Bank on Dame Street and its graveyard would have extended towards Dublin Castle. During the seventeenth century the church was used as a stables by the military in Dublin Castle and it was demolished some time after 1682. The graveyard was completely obliterated by the building of a marketplace in the early eighteenth century, called Castle Market, which was partly built on the site of St Andrew's Church and churchyard.

In the 1770s, on the same site, there was an inn called the Black Lyon. Castle Market is indicated on John Rocque's map of Dublin made in 1756, just outside the walls of Dublin Castle. Rocque shows a market surrounded by small houses and consisting of eight small buildings with room for covered stalls around them. The marketplace was connected to George's Street by a narrow laneway. It could also be entered from the Palace Street side by another short alleyway, today known as Dame Lane.

Much information can be gleaned from the minute books of the Wide Streets Commissioners, who, in 1779, were in the process of buying out the holdings in the area so that Dame Street could be widened. In Castle Market, there were thirty-four stalls leased to several butchers and poulterers, various hucksters (small traders and stall owners), and a cheese man. The market sold herbs and we

Opposite: Today's busy Dame Street is one of the main thoroughfares of Dublin, always crowded with people and traffic. It links the old medieval city with Trinity College and the eastern half of Georgian Dublin.

Below: Dame Lane occupies the site of an old route through the eighteenth-century Castle Market.

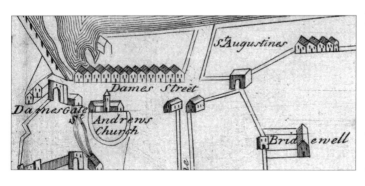

read that Messrs Cope and Meredith received a rent of three shillings and three pence a week for three stalls around the 'dirt hole in the herb market'. The market property was held on a lease from the church wardens of St Andrew's parish. Elsewhere the minutes inform us that a Mrs Elizabeth McKeon lived in the root market in Castle Market in one of the narrow houses that must have adjoined the site of the present Dame Lane. On the corner of Dame Street and George's Street was another property where we read that, 'Michael Molloy is a huckster and lives in a street cellar of Richardson House for which he pays ten guineas a year'. A stiff rent for a cellar in 1779!

Of particular interest is the mention of a long-vanished but large house known as Kildare House, the lease of which dated from 1682. The property belonged to Walter Harris and William Ellis and incorporated a number of inns on Dame Street, including the Sign of the Trumpet and the Nagg's Head. Harris's and Ellis's property, which in 1682 covered numbers 18–21 Dame Street, was bounded by St Andrew's churchyard to the west, the yard and stables of Dublin Castle to the south and Kildare House to the east, while 'abutting onto the King's pavement in Dammas Street'.

As early as 1772 the Wide Streets Commissioners were making plans for the improvement of Dame Street. The street then was not unlike a funnel, beginning with a wide space at College Green and ending with a narrow passage at Cork Hill, in front of what is now City Hall. But having successfully laid out Parliament Street, the Commissioners declared that, 'Dame Street, which is the only passage from His Majesty's said castle to the Parliament House, is a most narrow and inconvenient street and as it is a street of the greatest trade and the

greatest thoroughfare of the said city ...' they recommended that it should be widened and improved. They went on to explain that 'the vast number of different carriages and the great crowds continually passing through it' posed great dangers to 'limb and lives', especially during the sitting of parliament! It took another six years for the Commissioners to organise a survey of both sides of Dame Street, stretching from Crampton Court to the Parliament House and from Palace Street as far as Trinity Lane (now Trinity Street). In addition, the purchase of property was a slow business in the eighteenth century, just as it is today. It was not until 1784 that designs were finalised for the new elevations of the houses that would be built between Palace Street and George's Street; the drawings were prepared by Samuel Sproule.

Dame Street was once lined on both sides by a large number of eighteenth-century houses but it is almost certain that none of these survives today. It is possible that a few refronted houses near the present Olympia Theatre escaped the Wide Streets Commissioners' activities. Otherwise the entirety of Dame Street and College Green was reconstructed and a figure of almost £120,000 was spent in acquiring properties. The new buildings on both sides of the street were set back to a new line, leaving Dame Street at a new width of eighty-eight feet when finished. This meant that the old street was almost trebled in width.

Though much of Dame Street was remodelled during the nineteenth century and many premises were altered or rebuilt, there are still some

Above: Dame Street's interesting mix of house dates and types. During the eighteenth century this part of Dame Street was only twenty-five feet wide.

Opposite top: Part of Malton's view of City Hall, showing the completed work of the Wide Streets Commissioners in the block of houses to the right. These were demolished in the 1970s.

Opposite bottom: Speed's map (1610) shows the relationship of Dame Street to Dame's Gate and the original St Andrew's Church, which stood on the site of the AIB building.

Above: A decorative stucco panel, showing a vase of fruit, from Lipton's grocery establishment at the corner of Eustace Street.

Below: A 1920s photograph of Dame Street, showing the widened thoroughfare with its important business premises, such as those of Lipton's the grocer's, recognisable by the large awnings.

buildings that remain exactly as the Wide Streets Commissioners left them in the 1780s and 1790s. The best example is the block of five-storey houses between Temple Lane and Crow Street on the north side of the street. The corner premises incorporates the well-known Italian restaurant Nico's, and has a fine brick façade with granite coigns. The appearance of these buildings was dictated by the commissioners. The cost of construction was borne by the owner, but where cut-stone embellishments such as coigns, parapets or architraves were added, the cost was borne by the Wide Streets Commissioners. Though there have been many changes in Dame Street over the last 200 years, the proportion and scale of the buildings remain consistent with those that were laid down in the 1780s. Even when the various banks and insurance companies rebuilt premises in the late nineteenth century, they maintained the same building heights.

The proposed demolition and rebuilding of such an important street undoubtedly caused a great deal of upheaval for the many residents and occupants of the buildings. It was a busy commercial street, densely populated with traders of all kinds. For instance, in 1778 on the south side of Dame Street, between Palace Street and George's Street, we find three booksellers, two publicans, one embroiderer, two mercers, one glass seller, three watchmakers, two printers, three grocers, two shoemakers, one glover and a tobacconist. In number 17, for example, between Trinity Lane

and George's Street, we find no less than six different tenants, including Eleanor Cahill, a washer woman who holds the back garret; John Ryan, a servant who lives there with his huckster wife in the backhouse; Mary Hamilton, a mantua-maker, who occupies one room; a ribbon weaver, in two rooms; Brigid Bushell, a plain worker, who holds the street garret; and Lawrence Mackie, a stone cutter, who has a shed in the back yard. William Ashford, the noted painter, leased part of his premises at number 14 Dame Street to a gold beater in 1776. John T Gilbert, author of *History of the City of Dublin*, published between 1854 and 1859, mentions that among the most famous residents of Dame Street were Bartholomew Mosse, the founder of the Rotunda Lying-in Hospital, John Rocque, the map maker and James Petrie, the artist and father of the noted antiquarian George Petrie.

Above: A vignette from the stationery of a nineteenth-century business at number 54 Dame Street, on the corner of Temple Lane.

Below: An eighteenth-century map, showing the line where the Wide Streets Commissioners proposed to cut back old properties to make room for the widening of Dame Street.

The south side of Dame Street, near Dame Court, was occupied by many different tradesmen, including jewellers, opticians, paper stainers, a perfumer, a breeches-maker, a laceman, printers, stationers, booksellers, watchmakers, apothecaries and gunmakers. It is interesting to note that there was a tennis court and a puppet show house situated in Dame Court in 1781. At this time, Dame Court was formed around a square and was not simply a street as it is today. One of the largest businesses to be displaced by the Commission's plans was the sugar house and sugar bakery of Patrick Sweetman, whose premises adjoined George's Lane, now Great George's Street South. Sweetman, who was also a brewer of porter, received £4,055 in compensation and the description of his equipment is worth recording: 'a fine cistern and a scum cistern, molds and pots, syrop boxes of lead and lead on the panes'. He also had large copper pans, coolers and other utensils, and in 1775 an iron founder named J Heavisid gave evidence that he had sold Sweetman two 'cockles' in 1775. This equipment must have been extremely valuable as some years later Sweetman accepted £1,500 less in compensation in return for being allowed to keep his equipment.

It is easy to see that many people were uprooted by the proposed improvements and that those who did best in terms of compensation were the landlords or owners of properties. The representatives of the Foster Estate on the south side of Dame Street received over £3,000 in compensation. Arthur Cope and Joshua Meredith received over £5,429 for their holding in Dame Street.

Following the acquisition of the property, the various new building lots were advertised 'according to the plans, as fixed in several coffee houses'. The purchasers of the new plots, as laid down by the Wide Streets Commissioners, did not get their property cheap. For instance, the site of number 1 Dame Street was purchased by auction by James Potts for over £1,200. The plot purchased by Potts was the important corner site, now occupied by the Allied Irish Bank in Dame Street. (Potts was the printer of *Saunders News-Letter* and was also paid for doing printing for the Wide Streets Commissioners.) Other bidders on the new plots included Lundy

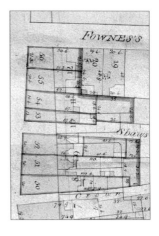

Foot, William Cope, Arthur Guinness, David La Touche and Thomas
Cooley, the successful architect of the Royal Exchange. Cope was the successful bidder for 3 Dame Street, while Cooley purchased the site of
number 4. At the east end of Dame Street, adjoining Trinity Lane, now
Trinity Street, we find number 18 owned by Mr William Sweetman, brewer, and leased to Thomas Kiernan, an ale seller or ale
draper.

Early maps give us a good picture of life in Dame Street in the
1770s. The site of the Olympia Theatre was occupied by a large
building, then shown as a bakehouse, which was entered from
Sycamore Alley. Number 78 Dame Street, which backed onto
what is now the Irish Film Centre, had a small distillery behind it
and there were slaughterhouses situated off George's Street near
the Castle Market. The site of the present Central Bank was also
very different in the eighteenth century and included Shaw's
Court, Crown Alley and the old post office yard. The old post
office yard was entered through a passage from Dame Street and
contained stables, presumably for the horses which delivered post
around the city and county.

It was not until 1792 that plans were prepared by the Wide Streets
Commissioners for the erection of twelve new houses running between
Fownes Street and Anglesea Street. These plans necessitated the

demolition of a network of old buildings, including the old post office yard, and the realignment of Crown Alley. Jury's Hotel, which occupied three of these houses, was remodelled in the 1860s with an elaborate entrance and a unifying scheme of stucco embellishment. The hotel's famous Antique Bar, as it was known, was sold to a bank in Switzerland, who erected it in their premises in Zurich. The hotel was demolished in 1980.

The Central Bank now stands on the site of Shaw's Court, another courtyard approached by a narrow passage from Dame Street. The court was occupied by a firm of wholesale silk merchants owned by William Cope. Previously it had been the home of the Shaw's Court Theatre and more significantly the first home of the Dublin Society, later known as the Royal Dublin Society (RDS). The society moved from Shaw's Court to Grafton Street in 1767. Gilbert notes that Shaw's Court was originally the site of an early eighteenth-century house, which had a large warehouse, stables and a garden.

Gilbert tells us that the General Post Office for Dublin was situated, in 1755, in Bardon's chocolate house in Shaw's Court, and that the old post office yard adjoined it. Chocolate houses were a favourite haunt in the late eighteenth century, equivalent to present-day cafés. The General Post Office moved from Dame Street to College Green in 1783, and this site was developed some ten years later by a group of Dublin merchants who erected Commercial Buildings. The new Commercial Buildings, which included a coffeehouse, were arranged around an open courtyard which backed onto Cope Street. A passageway led through this courtyard from Dame Street, connecting it with Crown Alley. Commercial Buildings, with its fine cut-stone façade, was designed by Edward Parke and was opened in 1798.

The Commercial Buildings were demolished in 1970, along with several other, mainly Victorian, office buildings. These demolitions, which were being carried out to clear the site for the new Central Bank, also included one of the last remaining Wide Streets Commissioners' houses on this block. It was a five-storey-over-basement house with an arcaded, granite-built ground floor which was originally intended as a shop. A replica of the cut-stone façade of Commercial Buildings was re-erected beside the Central Bank, while the original stones lay mouldering on bank property in Sandyford. The Royal Insurance office, a Victorian structure, was built in the Italianate style in 1869 and the ceilings of the interior were said to have been richly decorated with plasterwork. Sandwiched between the partly reconstructed commercial buildings and the ugly office block that replaced Jury's Hotel is another handsome Victorian office building with a sandstone

Above: Another building that stood in the way of the Central Bank was the Royal Insurance Office, which was located on the corner of Fownes Street and Dame Street.

Below: This block of tall Georgian houses is one of the few intact examples of the Wide Streets Commissioners' work.

façade. A stone-carved plaque bearing the symbol of the Ouzel Galley, a commercial body founded in the early eighteenth century to arbitrate on trade disputes, was re-erected on Dame Street on a clumsy brick infill beside this building.

It is not surprising that as the buildings of Dame Street merged into those of College Green they became grander and more imposing, because of their proximity to the Parliament House. Daly's Clubhouse was one of the grandest street front-ages yet to be proposed by the Wide Streets Commissioners. The architect, Richard Johnston, was asked to prepare a design for a unified façade stretching from Anglesea Street to Foster Place, incorporating the Clubhouse at its centre. In 1791 the club vacated its original premises in a chocolate house at 2–3 Dame Street and took over their new, fashionable headquarters. The club, which had been founded in a tavern by Patrick Daly, became the centre of attraction for young bucks and fashionable gentlemen. It was described as being lavishly furnished with 'grand lustres, inlaid tables, marble chimney pieces, white and gold chairs and sofas covered with the richest aurora silk'. There was a special door leading from Foster Place across a footpath to the Parliament House for the convenience of members. The Clubhouse was said to be the scene of much gambling and dissipation enacted by members of the 'hellfire club' and similar societies who used to assemble within the building. The magnificence of Daly's Clubhouse excited the surprise and admiration of travellers, who concurred in declaring it to be 'the grandest edifice of its kind in Europe'.

Above: The Commercial Buildings erected by Dublin merchants in 1798 included a courtyard through which pedestrians could gain access to Crown Alley.

Below: Daly's Clubhouse, which formed the architectural centrepiece of a block of eighteenth-century properties, was 'the chief resort of the aristocracy and Members of Parliament'.

Though the granite façade of Daly's Club-house remains more or less intact, the original flanking buildings have long since vanished. Even their Victorian replacements have also disappeared in favour of more banal office blocks. Foster Place, that wonderful leafy cul-de-sac, was originally connected with Fleet Street by means of a narrow street, once called Parliament Row and later Turnstile Alley. The houses of the west side of Foster Place were originally conceived as a single terrace by the Wide Streets Commissioners. Two of these original eighteenth-century houses survive intact at the corner of the street. They are restrained in style and have a semi-arcaded, stone-built ground floor. These two houses, along with all the other buildings on this side of the street, have been purchased by Trinity College within recent years.

The Allied Irish Bank (AIB) entrance on Foster Place incorporates part of one of the

original eighteenth-century houses. Sir Thomas Lighton's bank and account office was located here as early as 1797. Lighton's bank merged with Shaw's bank and later became the Royal Bank, at which point, in 1859, the interior was rebuilt and the present portico added. The vaulted cash office and interior of the building is supported by ornamental cast-iron columns and is one of the finest Victorian banking halls in Dublin. It was designed by the architect Charles Geoghegan.

One of the most impressive office buildings on Dame Street is the Crown Life building at the corner of Fownes Street. It was designed in 1868 in the Venetian palace style by Thomas Newenham Deane. If the original plan to build a bus station in Temple Bar had proceeded, then this building would certainly have disappeared. A stone building, it exhibits much elaborate carved detail, including Italianate balconies, an elaborate cornice, windows, chimney stack and mansard windows. An especially attractive feature is the staircase, whose arched windows may be seen on

Above: The Crown Life Insurance Building at the corner of Fownes Street is one of Dublin's most striking Victorian buildings.

the Fownes Street elevation. This fine building is now part of the Trinity Arch Hotel.

Many of the new five-storey buildings in the block facing the Central Bank, dating from the 1780s and 1790s, were revamped in the Victorian period, a good example being those at numbers 68–70, where elaborate stucco ornamentation was added to disguise the original brick façade. The ground-floor shopfront, which now incorporates the Mermaid Restaurant, bears some of the finest carved ornamental brackets, decorated with lion masks and clusters of roses.

There is a slight hill rising from the hollow of the River Poddle estuary, now that part of Dame Street in front of the Olympia Theatre, and the street rises slowly towards the junction with South Great George's Street. Standing at this junction and looking eastwards towards Trinity College, a large section of Georgian Dame Street remains intact. The five-storey

Below: A view westwards down College Green, showing the impressive streetscape.

Left: The billhead of Kavanagh the gunmaker, one of a wide variety of trades that were located in Dame Street.

Below: A carved timber bracket from Gregory Kane's, portmanteau and camp-furniture maker, at 68-70 Dame Street.

street line is broken by Victorian office buildings, such as the Pen Corner with its stone cupola. Looking back towards City Hall, the Georgian streetscape has been largely remodelled, first with the building of the Munster and Leinster Bank (now AIB) at the corner of Palace Street, then by the construction of the neo-Gothic premises of Callaghan's at 12–16 Dame Street, and finally by the 1930s corner building of Burton's the tailors.

Across the street on the corner of Eustace Street, another pair of houses was converted in the 1890s into Lipton's grocery establishment. One of the entrances to Lipton's may still be seen in Eustace Street, where baskets of fruit are represented in stucco panels beside the entrance to Shamrock Chambers. The brand name of Shamrock Foods survives since the days of the grocery business of Sir Thomas Lipton, who as a keen yachtsman owned some of the largest private yachts in the world.

A photograph of Dame Street taken by William Lawrence in about 1890 shows the premises with large lettering reading 'Liptons, the largest tea and provision dealers in the World'. As was the fashion of the day, canvas awnings projected out over the street and protected the produce in the shop window from the sunlight. At that time, Dame Street was paved with stone setts and laid out with tracks for the horse-drawn trams.

Bottom: Hely's 'Acme Works' (or factory) in Dame Court and Dame Lane. Also shown is the Stag's Head, one of the most intact Victorian pubs in Dublin.

The magnificent Allied Irish Banks premises at the corner of Dame Street and Palace Street was designed by TN Deane in 1872 and is very similar in style to his museum building in Trinity College built some twenty years earlier. The bank is modelled on the architecture of the Venetian palaces and exhibits some of the best Victorian stone carving to be found anywhere in the city. The grand corner entrance gives access to a full-height, two-storey banking chamber, the inside of which is elaborately ornamented in plasterwork and has a fine coved ceiling featuring

Right: Deane and Woodward's Venetian-style bank, which is now owned by the Allied Irish Bank, was originally located at numbers 7–9 Dame Street. This photograph shows the original part of the building. The bank was doubled in size in 1956 but this work was carried out so well that it is almost impossible to distinguish between old and new.

the coats of arms of the major towns and cities of Munster. At floor level the walls are lined to shoulder height with richly coloured marbles from Connemara and Italy, inlaid with geometric designs. A boardroom is cleverly fitted into the Palace Street frontage at first-floor level. The grey limestone masonry with the white Portland-stone decorative features are a tribute to the Irish stonemasons who crafted the building.

The adjoining premises of Callaghan's, the military and civil tailors and outfitters, were rebuilt in 1879 to the designs of JJ O'Callaghan. Callaghan's premises, which occupied the site of four of the old houses, were well known as the leading supplier of horse-riding equipment, the firm having been established in 1869. High up in the gabled roof line of this building is an old clock that was originally manufactured by Chancellor of Dublin and has recently been reactivated as a working and chiming clock. The ground floor premises are now occupied by a café, two restaurants and a chemist.

Burton's, which was the Dublin branch of the famous London tailoring establishment, was built in 1929 in a pseudo-Egyptian style, featuring a striking sandstone-coloured ceramic façade with an unusual blue-tiled roof. Unfortunately, the ground floor now incorporates several somewhat unsatisfactory shopfronts and an oriental carpet shop. William Kavanagh, gun and rifle manufacturers, was established at 12 Dame Street in 1796 and continued in business throughout the nineteenth century. Their business occupied one of the Wide Streets Commissioners' houses with its typical arched ground-floor shopfront built of granite. Kavanagh's boasted a 120-foot-long shooting gallery for customers to carry out a trial of any of their products. Adam's Trinity Hotel, established within the last five years, occupies the site of one of Dublin's best-known stationery and toy shops, Hely's. Hely's, who were also printers, had a red-brick printing works at the back of their premises in Dame Court.

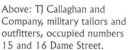

Next to the Mercantile Bar, a narrow passage leading from Dame Street brings the pedestrian out in front of the Stag's Head. A fine mosaic that advertises the Stag's Head is embedded in the pavement in front of Dame Court. The pub was built in 1895 and is elaborately decorated both inside and out. The interior is richly embellished with carved woodwork and a panelled timber ceiling. The careful retention of all of the original details, including the stained glass, creates a very opulent effect.

Number 38 Dame Street is the only building to have retained its arcaded shopfront intact from the late eighteenth-century street widening. The neighbouring Lucky Coady displays an excellent example of a fine Victorian shopfront. It is embellished with Ionic columns, masks, carved brackets and even the cornice of the building is ornamented with lion masks.

By the late nineteenth century the occupants of this part of Dame Street had largely changed from small manufacturers and merchants to solicitors, stockbrokers and insurance companies. The building on the corner of Dame Street and Trinity Street is a fine sandstone structure, built in the Italianate manner in the mid-nineteenth century. This building has been in use as an office since the nineteenth century, housing accountants, solicitors and, at one time, the Trinity Bank.

One of the most striking offices, which forms the junction between Dame Street and College Green, is the Pen Corner. This elaborately detailed office building was constructed in 1901 and has a remarkable curved elevation that terminates in a stone-built turret and clock. The upper floors are punctuated by massive Portland-stone columns, while at street level the Pen Corner shop with its 1930s vitrolite frontage is a

Above: TJ Callaghan and Company, military tailors and outfitters, occupied numbers 15 and 16 Dame Street.

Below: A Georgian door knocker from the side entrance of one of the houses built by the Wide Streets Commissioners.

distinctive feature of the area. Its neighbour, 17 College Green, has been the premises of Guinness Mahon Bank since the 1880s at least.

College Green, beginning at Trinity Street, gradually widens into the great open space that is fronted on the one hand by the Bank of Ireland and on the other by Trinity College. This part of Dublin is considered by many to be the real centre of the city. Throughout the nineteenth century, many changes were to occur in the buildings of this street as prosperous banks vied with each other to create suitable monuments to their wealth and position.

The English architectural historian Mark Girouard once suggested that if you were to flood Dame Street and College Green, the many Italianate buildings would create a Venetian Gothic vista. The love of Victorian banks for classical or Italianate architecture is very evident in Dublin, and has left us a great legacy of mercantile public buildings. The old Hibernian Bank with its French Renaissance detailing has been beautifully restored by the National Irish Bank. The coffered ceiling of the vaulted banking hall, which was designed by Thomas Drew in 1873, is a most beautiful space. The present National Irish Bank, on the corner of Church Lane, began as a relatively small building in 1867, but was enlarged in 1873 to its present size. Next door, in the 1890s, the Royal Bank built a striking premises in

Below: A view of College Green, showing Foster Place and an equestrian statue of King William III. The statue was a source of ongoing controversy until its eventual destruction in 1929.

contrasting Scottish red sandstone. Its circular tower and copper conical roof is a memorable landmark in the College Green streetscape.

The granite façade of the present Bank of Ireland at 34 College Green was originally built as the National Bank, founded by Daniel O'Connell in the mid-nineteenth century. The emblem of the bank is represented in an interesting sculpture, executed by the firm of Pearse and Sharpe, on the roof line, which bears the inscription 'Éireann go Bráth' and features a round tower, wolfhound and Irish harp beside a statue of *Hibernia*. The interior features a forest of columns surrounding a Victorian circular banking hall with various modern alterations and additions.

Above: One of the two large fragments from the destroyed marble plinth of the statue of King William III, currently in storage in the Dublin Civic Museum.

The Ulster Bank made their contribution to the Victorian architecture of College Green by building a grandiose Italian Renaissance-style façade in 1891. The ironwork lamp standards bear the hand of Ulster and the wrought-iron gates at the entrance are a remarkable piece of craftsmanship. Jeremy Williams, in his book *A Companion Guide to Victorian Architecture in Ireland 1837–1921* (1994), states that: 'Its finest feature, the banqueting hall with its richly stuccoed vault, was inexcusably destroyed in 1976 "to improve the working conditions of the staff".' The Ulster Bank went on to destroy a group of impressive buildings that adjoined Church Lane, only to replace them with a new structure of extraordinary banality.

Although College Green and Dame Street constitute one of the busiest thoroughfares in the city, the general sense of architectural grandeur has not been lost. College Green has played host to a wide variety of events, including the many visits of British royalty to Ireland during the nineteenth century, the occasion of the Eucharistic Congress in 1932, when a full-sized replica of an Irish round tower was erected in the street, and most recently the visit of US President Bill Clinton.

For over 200 years the centre of College Green, opposite Foster Place, was dominated by an equestrian statue of King William III. The statue, mounted on a high pedestal, was erected in 1701. Created by the noted English sculptor Grinling Gibbons, it was never very popular with Dublin's citizens, although it was a very striking monument in its own right. On various occasions the statue was defaced and daubed with paint and tar, and in 1836 it was successfully blown up. The lead statue was, however, repaired and remained in College Green for almost another century. Supporters of King William, who in the early 1700s included various city dignitaries, the lord mayor and the military, paraded around the statue and progressed to Dublin Castle on the anniversary of the king's birth. The statue was finally removed

Below: The west front of Trinity College dominates College Green and has often been the scene of great public gatherings.

Left: The richly ornamented Georgian interior of the Provost's House is a good example of the large and varied architectural heritage of Trinity College.

in 1929 following another explosion. It is not difficult to imagine the various eighteenth-century civic and military parades that must have passed up and down the narrow Dame Street between Dublin Castle and the Parliament House. A famous gathering of the Irish Volunteers in College Green is depicted in the well-known 1779 painting by Francis Wheatley.

College Green was originally known as Hoggen Green, due to the proximity of the Nunnery of St Mary de Hogges, dating from 1156. It was the site of the Priory of All Hallows, founded in 1162, and during the Reformation this religious establishment was granted to the citizens of Dublin by Henry VIII. During the reign of Queen Elizabeth I, the citizens transferred the ownership to the Archbishop of Dublin for the purpose of establishing a university, and so Trinity College (and College Green) was born. In 1550 the nunnery, or priory, lay in a completely derelict state and was described as 'now ruinous, and nothing remaining but the walles'. It was proposed at that time to repair some of the buildings and establish six looms where weavers and spinners would be employed to make woollen and linen cloth. The name Trinity Street or Trinity Lane derives from the existence here of Trinity Hall, a building that once accommodated students and physicians. The physicians attended to members of the college who might be ill and it was here, in association with Trinity College, that the College of Physicians in Ireland was established. Trinity Hall was demolished in the early eighteenth century and part of the site was occupied by St Andrew's parish almshouse.

In 1783 the Irish parliament passed an act to establish 'one general letter office and post office in some convenient place within the city of Dublin' and a new post office building was erected in College Green, facing the Parliament House, on the site of what was later to become the National Bank. The services of the post office were greatly improved at this time which, as we have already seen, had moved from the old post office yard near Fownes Street. The receipts of the post office increased from over

Above: The Victorian campanile in Trinity College.

AN EXTENSIVE AND WELL-SELECTED ASSORTMENT OF
Grand, Semi-Grand, Cabinet, Cottage, Grand-Square, Circular & Square
PIANO-FORTES,
Of the latest and most approved construction, by
BROADWOOD, COLLARD & COLLARD, & TOMKISON,
Constantly for Sale, at the lowest London Prices.

DOUBLE AND SINGLE ACTION HARPS, BY ERARD & OTHERS.
SPANISH GUITARS BY THE MOST EMINENT MAKERS:
Piano-Fortes, Harps, and Guitars lent on Hire.
Old Piano-Fortes taken in Exchange, and the highest value allowed.
Accordions, Flutes, Flageolets, Violins, Violoncellos, Tambourines, Music Paper, Portfolios, Blank Books,
Music Slates, Wire, superior Harp, Guitar, and Violin Strings, and every other article appertaining to Music.
The newest London and Foreign Publications.
PIANO-FORTES AND HARPS TUNED AND REPAIRED, &c.

£40,000 in 1786 to over £77,000 in 1799. In 1818, on the completion of the General Post Office (GPO) in Sackville Street, the post office moved yet again to its current home.

The creation of Westmoreland Street in the 1790s, linking College Green to Sackville Street by means of Carlisle Bridge, was to have a profound effect on the future of Dublin. Several different configurations of streets had been looked at, but in 1793 the Wide Streets Commissioners examined and approved the triangular block which today forms Westmoreland Street, D'Olier Street and College Street. Lord Mountjoy (Luke Gardiner Junior) and John Beresford, two of the eleven commissioners who approved the plan, must have been delighted to see another step made towards connecting their substantial property interests north of the Liffey with the rest of the city.

The new streets required the clearance of many old houses and businesses around Fleet Street, including an old watch house that stood at the angle of College Street and Fleet Street, a rope walk (or rope factory) that adjoined property belonging to Beresford and a sugar house (or factory) belonging to a Mr Crosthwaite. The new bridge (now O'Connell Bridge) made the so-called Lower, or Old, Ferry on the Liffey at Hawkins Street

Opposite: In this advertisement an original Wide Streets Commissioners' shopfront can be seen.

Below: An early nineteenth-century engraving of the newly created Westmoreland and D'Olier Streets. These new streets formed a link from Trinity College to O'Connell Bridge.

Right: The grand banking hall of the former Provincial Bank in College Street, designed in 1863, now owned by the AIB.

Below: The former Rooney's in College Street, with its attractive lettering, is a rare example of a Victorian shopfront.

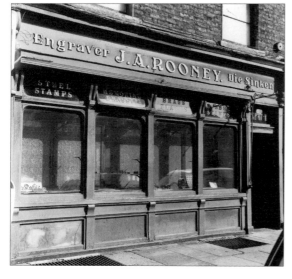

redundant. Two narrow passages named Fleet Lane and Fleet Alley suggested the line for the new Westmoreland Street.

Many of the original late Georgian buildings planned by the Wide Streets Commissioners still remain, although there were various changes made by the addition of Victorian insurance and bank buildings, and some late twentieth-century office blocks. The uniform streetscape of Westmoreland Street and D'Olier Street consisted of five-storey buildings with stone-fronted shops at ground-floor level. The restored shopfront of the *Irish Times* office in D'Olier Street is a good example. By the middle of the nineteenth century, many prestigious businesses had shops in Westmoreland Street, including Schreiber's watchmakers, Hodges ironmongers and Moses's pianoforte and harp warehouse.

The spacious, uncluttered and dignified thoroughfare was one of Dublin's most fashionable streets.

By the 1870s the street had become an extremely

popular address for insurance companies, solicitors and a new group of professionals – photographers.

Construction work is now almost complete on the large hotel that has involved the clearance and façade retention of many buildings on the College Street, Westmoreland Street and Fleet Street block. Since the early 1990s, the plans for this important site have generated much controversy, not least because of its proximity to what are two of the most important architectural monuments in Ireland – the Bank of Ireland and Trinity College.

Apart from the demolition of so many listed buildings on the site, fears about the intrusive nature of the bulky new roof structure were well founded, and the design was modified. The roof, incorporating hotel bedrooms, does not enhance the fine Victorian bank, dating from 1863, on College Street, or the attractive houses nearby, which incorporate two of Dublin's best shopfronts – the Dublin Yeast Company and the former Rooney's – and Doyle's corner pub; all built to the designs of the Wide Streets Commissioners.

The AIB building, with its richly detailed façade of Portland stone,

Above: One of the exceptionally ornate brackets from the shopfront of the Dublin Yeast Company on College Street.

Left: This red-brick building, once occupied by an Edwardian vegetarian restaurant, was demolished to make way for a new hotel.

Above: An engraving of Westmoreland Street and D'Olier
Street by Samuel Brocas,
c. 1820.
Below: College Street in a
photograph from the late
1970s, showing the AIB bank.

replaced an earlier structure of the Provincial Bank. A plain building with two cut-stone entrances stood to the east, and was originally a police office. It was more recently the offices of the Workers' Union of Ireland, until its demolition in the early 1980s.

Many bookshelves could be filled with the excellent publications which exist about the Bank of Ireland and Trinity College, and here we will confine ourselves to noting the great architectural importance of these structures, and the fact that all of the buildings in question have been expertly restored over the last twenty years. In Trinity College there are perhaps two exceptions – the extraordinary Museum Building has not been cleaned and the ancient residential block known as the the Rubrics awaits a sensitive refurbishment of its seventeenth-century features. Other major structures, including the eighteenth-century West Front, the Exam Hall, the Chapel and the Printing House have all been cleaned and repaired. The Dining Hall was fully restored following a disastrous fire in 1986.

The college boasts several interesting new buildings, including the neat timber-clad Samuel Beckett Theatre and the new Dental School building at the Lincoln Gate.

CHAPTER FOUR

Dublin Castle

*T*he history of Dublin Castle is a long and complicated one. Today it does not have the appearance of a stronghold or fortress. On approaching it many visitors are mystified, because what greets them does not resemble a conventional castle but rather a fine collection of eighteenth-century administrative buildings.

In terms of Irish history, Dublin Castle is perhaps the most politically symbolic structure or building in the State. The Upper Yard is a large and dignified space, dominated by the Genealogical Office or Bedford Tower, with its clock and copper cupola. The Bedford Tower, with its symmetrical composition and rustic gates, is really the chief decorative feature of an otherwise rather sombre collection of buildings in the Upper Yard. The enclosed rectangular space is today paved with stone setts and the front of the State Apartments is graced by sixteen flag poles, on which fly the flags of the various European States.

Left: An aerial view, c.1940s, showing the Upper and Lower Yards of Dublin Castle.

Above: Dignitaries arriving at the State Apartments during an EU summit meeting in 1990, amid tight security and the glare of cameras.

Below: The culvert of the River Poddle, which was accidentally uncovered during the 1990s. This photo reveals the substantial brick-built arched structure, which contains the surprisingly clean stream.

Dublin Castle is, of course, a Norman construction and was built on the highest ground in the city. The land slopes away to the north towards the Liffey, and to the south and east it slopes downwards and would once have been bordered by the open, flowing River Poddle, which formed the castle's moat. Much has been written about the history of Dublin Castle and the social and political events that have occured there. Today, Dublin Castle is the focus of many State occasions and government functions, but it is also a major tourist attraction. The State Apartments are open to visitors and the archaeological excavations of the Powder Tower are also on view. The castle is host to many small, semi-state bodies with an artistic or cultural brief, such as the Heritage Council, the Arts Review and Poetry Ireland. Above all, the castle is the symbolic home of the Revenue Commissioners, a role that it has fulfilled since medieval times. It also houses the traffic division of the Garda Síochána and is used extensively for important conferences.

In the late 1980s, a major conference facility was built around the Upper Yard of Dublin Castle, primarily to host the summit meeting of the European Community in 1990. Other conferences and promotional activities take place in the various apartments and in the recently refurbished coach house, which lies across the garden at the rear of Dublin Castle. Nearby stands the former Accountant General's house, which is now the new home of the Chester Beatty Library. The Chapel Royal is open to the public daily, and the Record Tower has been converted into a museum of the Garda Síochána.

Today, Dublin Castle boasts five separate venues for conferences and meetings. The crypt of the old Chapel Royal is currently used as a theatre and the Assay Office continues to perform its function by stamping and authenticating pieces of silver artwork in its small building near the Ship Street Gate. The State Apartments are used for official functions by the Government. These rooms include St Patrick's Hall, the Picture Gallery, the Throne Room and the Drawing Room. There is also a restaurant and gift shop located under the Treasury block near the Palace Street entrance.

The late twentieth-century portrait of Dublin Castle is therefore one of rich, varied and intensive activity. Three different, dignified and somewhat austere stone entrance gates provide access to the confines of the castle. The Triumphal Arch at Ship Street is now the main traffic entrance to the castle, while the pedimented and arched gate at Palace Street is the chief pedestrian entrance. The Cork Hill entrance beside City Hall is used for formal State occasions, as it leads through an impressive rusticated archway into the Upper Yard of the castle.

Above: The impressive Ship Street Gate to Dublin Castle, which is still the main entrance used by vehicles.

Below: James Malton's famous print of Dublin Castle shows the genealogical office, which is the architectural centrepiece of the Upper Yard.

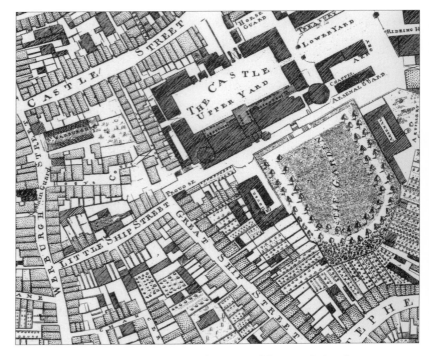

Right: Rocque's map of 1756, showing the castle – itself in many ways unchanged – set in the context of a crowded residential city.

Below: Excavations in the 1980s revealed this medieval staircase at the base of the Powder Tower in Dublin Castle.

It is difficult to imagine Dublin Castle as a Norman defensive structure, akin to the many Welsh castles with their strong circular towers and flanking walls. However, Dublin Castle was once just such a place, with four corner towers and a double-towered entrance gate that stood approximately on the site of the present Bedford Tower. The corner towers are known as: the Bermingham Tower, which still stands near the Ship Street Gate; the Record Tower, standing near the Chapel; the Storehouse Tower, whose base now remains underground near the Vaults Restaurant; and the Cork Tower, part of which may be seen in the basement area of the conference centre. The Storehouse Tower was also known as the Powder Tower, the Record Tower as the 'Gunners' or Wardrobe Tower, and the Bermingham Tower as the Kitchen Tower.

The Bermingham Tower, located at the southwestern corner of the castle, was the highest and strongest of all the towers. It was used in earlier times as a prison, but nineteenth-century maps show that the State kitchen was located on the ground floor and that surrounding it were a number of larders and special kitchens. These were, of course, adjacent to St Patrick's Hall, where many important functions were catered for. In fact, the massive meathooks still survive in what was once called the cold meat larder. The castle was very well equipped with servants' quarters, sculleries, bedrooms for staff, a fish kitchen, a pastry pantry, a pastry larder, meat larders and a still room, used for distilling liquor. Other rooms situated beneath the State Apartments, adjoining the tower, included a plate butler's office and a plate pantry, where silver was kept, a brushing room, a lamp room and a glass pantry. There was also a servants' hall. The Bermingham Tower was largely dismantled in 1775 and rebuilt in its present form. This followed structural damage caused by an accidental fire which had taken place nearby. A magnificent Gothic-style state supper room was created in the new Bermingham Tower and this dates from the 1770s. The room is lit by three elegant Georgian, Gothic-style windows, and the circular ceiling is decorated with delicate Gothic-style tracery. At present this room is no longer furnished as it

Above: The base of the circular Cork Tower revealed through excavations in the 1980s. The foundations of the eighteenth-century administrative buildings are visible above the tower.

should be, nor used as an elegant dining room, as it is required for use as a servery when dinners are held in St Patrick's Hall. This circular chamber, with the addition of suitable Regency furniture and the removal of the radiators in the windows, the net curtains and linoleum floor covering, could be transformed into one of Dublin Castle's prettiest rooms. John Cornforth suggests that this room may have been designed by James Wyatt, who carried out other similar works in Ireland, particularly at Dunsany Castle in County Meath. In 1829 the pastry pantry was described as a 'French kitchen'; and at about this time, French cuisine was becoming fashionable in Britain and Ireland. There was also plenty of space for storing wine underneath the State Apartments and the wine butler had a room of his own. The room where the kitchens once operated is now an office. Other rooms were set aside for the Battleaxe Guard, and the small octagonal room that gives on to the low bridge, providing access to the garden, was originally a library. The castle was provided with its own supply of ice and the ice house was located in a single-storey structure standing to the north of the Record Tower.

A plan of Dublin Castle made in 1673 shows many of these features very clearly and also shows a large hall, the Old Parliament House, occupying the centre of the Upper Yard. Some ten years later a fire destroyed most of the medieval castle.

The Record Tower, previously known as the Wardrobe Tower, is by far the most solidly built tower, and one of the most impressive 'medieval' features, to survive in Dublin Castle. Its walls are some twelve to fifteen feet thick at the base. A spiral staircase rises within the thickness of the walls. It was here that royal robes and other important costumes were kept for State occasions. The Record Tower was completely remodelled in 1813 to the

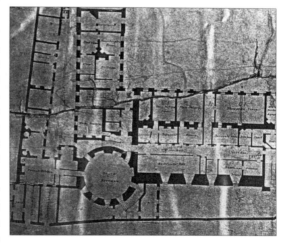

Above: A nineteenth-century plan of Dublin Castle showing the substantial walls of St Patrick's Hall and the Bermingham Tower. This basement plan also shows the State Kitchen and various stewards' rooms.

Above: Two of the many
sculpted heads ornamenting
the Chapel Royal, which dates
from 1815. These are from
the entrance to the crypt.

designs of Francis Johnson as a new and fireproof archive to store State
papers. It continued to do so until the 1980s when the papers were
removed to the Public Record Office in nearby Bishop Street. The upper
section of the Record Tower was rebuilt in the early 1800s to the design of
Francis Johnson. Johnson rearranged the spaces to house the many records
and books and he added a spectacular battlement, not unlike those at
Windsor Castle in England.

The cross block that separates the Upper Castle Yard from the Lower
Castle Yard once housed the War Office, while directly behind the Royal
Exchange, or City Hall, stood the Chief Secretary's apartments and other
offices, including a small library. These elegant rooms had fallen into disre-
pair by the 1980s and were completely demolished at that time, leaving
only the façades that faced into the Upper Castle Yard. The Lower Castle
Yard is fronted on the north side by the Treasury Building and on the south
by the Chapel. The Treasury Building, which dates from the early eighteenth century, was also the office of the Auditor General, and, in a
remarkable example of continuity, the present-day office of the Comptroller and Auditor General still use this building. A terrace fronts the treasury
block, allowing access to the building and compensating for the slope of
the Lower Castle Yard.

During the eighteenth century the moat of Dublin Castle became
redundant and much of it was filled in with rubbish and debris from the
neighbouring houses outside the castle. Excavations carried out in 1986
uncovered great quantities of mainly domestic artefacts. These included
wine and brandy bottles, quite a lot of glass, pieces of leather, settling pans
for milk, an Elizabethan penny and ha'penny and also great numbers of clay

pipes dating back to the seventeenth century. The excavations were carried out between Castle Street and the castle, behind the Genealogical Office, on the site of the present conference centre. They showed the existence of the medieval moat which in some places was over sixty feet in width. As we have seen, Dublin Castle was gradually being rebuilt. The process began in the late seventeenth century and continued through the Georgian period. The work was concluded in the early nineteenth century with the rebuilding of the Chapel Royal.

The foundation stone of the Chapel Royal, perhaps one of the most attractive buildings in Dublin Castle, was laid in 1807 by the Duke of Bedford, the then Viceroy or Lord Lieutenant of Ireland. It replaced an earlier chapel that was demolished in the same year, and was completed in 1814 at a cost of £42,000. The chapel has a simple plan and consists of a single nave or choir, with galleries on either side, and is raised above a crypt, which compensates for the sloping site. Much of the seating is laid out along each side, facing towards the central aisle. The delicate detailing of the interior, with its stucco ornamentation, clustered Gothic pillars and groin-vaulted ceiling, creates the effect of a miniature English cathedral. It is said that many of the ornamental details were copied from York Minster. It is a small church, only seventy-eight feet in length, but highly ornamented. The gallery of the chapel is carved with the royal arms and the arms and names of the Viceroys of Ireland. The dates carved into these coats of arms record the history of Norman, and later British, rule in Ireland. After 1864, when all of the

Above: The Palace Street Gate, one of the three mid-eighteenth-century classical entrances to Dublin Castle.

Below left: A painting by the author, showing the Chapel Royal and the Record Tower.

Above: A mid-nineteenth-century painting of a St Patrick's Day ball in St Patrick's Hall. The costumes are accurate representations of the various regimental uniforms, and the swirls that can be seen on the floor indicate the use of chalk dust to make the floor slippery for dancing.

Below: All the castle offices were once coded by painted numerals such as this.

gallery space was used up, the armorial inscriptions were continued in the windows. The Chapel Royal is built of a grey limestone and is highly ornamented, with carved heads, pinnacles and traceried windows. Many of the exquisitely carved stone heads which adorn the outside of the chapel were carved by Edward and John Smyth, who are best-known for their work on the Custom House. The railing in front of the Chapel Royal is carried down the slope in steps and terminates in a scroll of ironwork mounted on a stone plinth. Oil lamp brackets are situated at regular intervals along the railing. The Gothic-panelled doors and all of the joinery in the crypt and the chapel above are of the finest quality.

The Lower Castle Yard was also the site of the extensive stables of the castle and a riding house or riding school. The riding school was certainly in existence in the eighteenth century, but later maps show a series of stables allocated to the aides-de-camp, the Chief Secretary, the Under Secretary and other departments. Inside the Palace Street Gate was the aide-de-camp's house and the house of Major Henry Sirr, the town major and head of a brutal secret police service. There was also a forge and stables for the cavalry. The castle arsenal was situated in the Lower Castle Yard near the Chapel Royal, later to become the present Garda offices. The Piquet Yard, just inside the Palace Street Gate, housed the cavalry and their stables. The stables and the octagonal guard house were eventually demolished and replaced by the present office block of the Revenue Commissioners.

Early nineteenth-century prints of the Upper Yard show the spire and tower of St Werburgh's Church, which was one of the tallest in Dublin. A little later, a print depicts the same tower with the uppermost section removed. The tower was completely removed in the early nineteenth century, apparently at the request of the Lord Lieutenant, who considered its presence to be a security risk as it might provide a vantage point to a sniper.

During the nineteenth century an extra storey was added to the Genealogical Office, situated facing the State Apartments in the Upper Yard, spoiling the elegant proportions of the building. Fortunately, this addition was removed in the 1980s during the restoration of the building.

St Patrick's Hall, the largest public space in the castle, stands on the site of a much earlier hall, certainly dating from the seventeenth century and probably much earlier. The present hall, with its fluted and gilded Corinthian pillars, was originally a ballroom and the ballroom floor remains intact beneath the carpet. The present hall has a coved ceiling, highly ornamented with gilded plasterwork and three massive paintings, and would appear to date from the 1780s, around the time that the Order of St Patrick was established. Their formal ceremonies were held here, including the investiture of new knights. The paintings were the work of Vincenzo Valdre, an Italian artist, and depict 'The Munificent Government of George III', 'The Conversion of the Irish by St Patrick' and 'Henry II Receiving the Submission of the Irish Chieftains'. The symbolism of these paintings is interesting, given the significance of Dublin Castle as the centre of English rule in Ireland over a seven-hundred-year period. However, it is worth noting that many interesting relics of the British era have

THRONE, ST. PATRICK'S HALL, DUBLIN CASTLE.

Above top: The Changing of the Guard at the main Cork Hill entrance to Dublin Castle.

Above: Deep bayonet cuts made on the Guardhouse wall by bored guards in the nineteenth century.

Left: A pre-1920s cigarette card, showing the throne and elaborate regalia in St Patrick's Hall.

Above top: An ancient water-pipe, made from a quartered elm tree trunk, discovered in the old Armoury buildings.

Above: An ornamental toilet, bearing the Prince of Wales feathers, which was probably installed for a royal visit.

survived intact in the castle, such as the gilt throne in the Throne Room and the gilded, crown-shaped mirrors. Furthermore, most of the viceroys' portraits still hang in the Picture Gallery and in other rooms in the castle. Other royal emblems survive, for instance on the carved organ case in the Chapel Royal. Now elegantly redecorated in dark blue silk, St Patrick's Hall is hung with the banners of the Knights of St Patrick. These banners originally hung in the chancel of St Patrick's Cathedral. The honour of Knighthood was conferred in St Patrick's Hall by the Lord Lieutenant at a very formal ceremony.

The entrance to the State Apartments today is by means of a projecting porch or canopy above which lies the Throne Room. This leads through a hall of Doric columns into the main staircase. The double staircase gives access to the landing or hall which used to be called the Battleaxe Hall. The Battleaxe Hall was so named after the special bodyguard of the Lord Lieutenant.

The Throne Room, or Presence Chamber as it was previously known, is one of the most intact eighteenth-century rooms in the castle. The throne, which still survives (although its legs have been cut short), dates from the early nineteenth century, and may have been produced for the visit of George IV. The walls of the Throne Room are ornamented with circular paintings or medallions, which are the work of Italian artist Gaetano Gandolfi. It was in this room that a Lord Lieutenant was sworn in on arrival in Ireland and was also sworn out on his departure. Here many elaborate Throne Room dances were held, following large, lavish dinners in the castle. In the eighteenth and early nineteenth centuries, the official castle season would last for five or six weeks and over 15,000 guests might be entertained in the castle.

This lavish hospitality involved an enormous undertaking in terms of catering. The many kitchens, which have already been described, would have been full of giant fireplaces, consuming tons of coal and timber. Marble slabs were spread with delicately decorated entrées and other elaborate dishes, and tiny white statuettes moulded in suet would form the centrepieces of the supper tables. French cuisine came into fashion in about 1830 and French chefs would have been on hand throughout the nineteenth century to cook these lavish feasts, on occasion for large numbers of people. A contemporary visitor to the kitchen described seeing 800 cutlets egged and breadcrumbed ready for frying, and some 150 cold fowls, while in the fish and vegetable kitchen there was a 39lb salmon.

The Lord Lieutenant would arrive to a dinner with a great entourage, including 'his aide-de-camp, Steward and Comptroller, his Gentleman Usher, the Gentlemen of the Bed Chamber and all the gentlemen at large and pages'. At dinner many toasts were drunk! First, the Lord Lieutenant would drink to the health of the King, followed by the Prince of Wales, the Dukes and all the royal family. Following that a toast would be drunk to the glorious memory of King William and then to his victory at the Battle of the Boyne on 1 July 1690. The next toast would be to the prosperity of the city of Dublin and after that to the linen manufactory of Ireland, also to the prosperity of Ireland and her trade thereof.

In the early eighteenth century a viceregal *levee*, a formal reception held just after a grandee, or monarch, had risen from bed, usually in the early afternoon, was held on a Sunday. The castle season commenced early in February, after the arrival of the Lord Lieutenant. It consisted of an endless round of entertainments including a *levee*, a drawing room, which meant a drawing room party for ladies that usually involved playing cards, and a series of banquets and state balls. These entertainments continued until St Patrick's Day, and the season concluded with a St Patrick's Ball. Most of the *levees* and drawing rooms were held in the Throne Room. For a state ball the ladies would be dressed in the most lavish dresses with extravagant jewels, the men and officers in richly ornamented uniforms and all the staff of the castle would wear the state livery of the Viceroy or Lord Lieutenant. The castle itself was profusely decorated with palms and floral decorations, while military bands played in the dancing and supper rooms.

During the seventeenth century the old medieval castle of Dublin was in a considerable state of decay. Many Lord Lieutenants complained about the condition of the castle and described it as a miserable place. John Cornforth, in a comprehensive article on the architecture of Dublin Castle published in *Country Life* in 1970, points out that the British administration never rebuilt Dublin Castle as a single, grand piece of architecture, rather they patched here, rebuilt there, mended the castle in different areas and made do with what was there. This policy, or non-policy,

Above: A fragment of Regency wallpaper discovered behind the bookcases in the Record Tower.

Below: Demolition work in progress during the 1980s, showing the dismantling of blocks 8, 9 and 10 in the Upper Yard.

led to the development of the castle as it is today – a series of administrative buildings, with the State Apartments planted on top of a partially demolished medieval structure. Whether or not this was a deliberate plan on the part of the British, the result was the creation of a complex that does not have one particular architectural distinction, suggesting that the administration did not feel it worthwhile to spend money on a castle in such a troubled province. As we have already seen, the castle was part palace, part administration centre and part military barracks.

Though the viceroys of the sixteenth and seventeenth centuries had to make do with somewhat uncomfortable apartments, it would appear that they were well fed. An account of one week's expenses in September 1585 shows that the Viceroy's household consumed:

ten bullocks, forty sheep, sixteen hogsheads [large casks holding fifty-two gallons] of beer, one hogshead of Gascoigne wine, four gallons of sack [dry white wine, from the French *sec*],

as well as:

bread, manchets or fine white rolls, pastry, ling, stock fish, salted salmon ... bacon, fowl both wild and tame, fish, butter sweet and salted, eggs, oatmeal, salt, sauce, herbs, spices and fruits of all sorts.

Other items of expenditure included wax lights, staff torches, white lights, coal and wood. The clothing for various retainers and staff included linens, cloaks and frieze jerkins. Also required were ruches (pleats or frills of fabric), perfumes, flowers, strewing herbs and the maintenance of ninety horses and hackneys, the wages for forty-five horse boys, linens for them and loose gowns of cloth.

The twelfth and thirteenth centuries were turbulent times in the history of Dublin and the Leinster area as a whole. At that point there was no castle in Dublin and the Normans, who controlled the city, reported to King John that there was no safe place for the custody of his royal treasure. The King's response, in 1205, was to order the building of a castle in Dublin in a suitable place. The King's representative or Justiciary was Hugh de Lacy, later Archbishop Henri de Loundres, and he is credited with having built Dublin Castle, which was completed in the year 1213.

The remarkable mystery of the theft of the crown jewels from Dublin Castle in 1907 has never been solved. The jewels, which consisted of the insignia of the Order of St Patrick and other precious stones, were kept in a safe in the Library on the ground floor of the Bedford Tower by Sir Arthur Vicars, the Ulster King of Arms. The jewels disappeared just before the state visit of King Edward VII to Ireland.

In the mid-1980s the Office of Public Works came in for much criticism for what appeared to be its total neglect of Dublin Castle and its many historic buildings. Several important buildings were propped up, others were lying in a semi-derelict condition with weeds growing out of the gutters, more were completely disused and there was talk of wholesale demolition. The Upper Yard was surfaced in tarmac and was used as a car park. In a trenchant article written in 1983, the *Irish Times* declared that the care and maintenance of Dublin Castle had fallen to an all-time low. There was much evidence of badly eroded stonework, derelict buildings and a general lack of maintenance. The Genealogical Office had moved out of the Bedford Tower because it was declared unsafe. The Metropolitan Children's Court, which had also been located here, had moved too, and the Revenue Commissioners and Customs and Excise had abandoned other buildings. Professor Kevin B Nowlan, Chairman of the Dublin Civic Group said that:

> There was something quite bizarre about the way in which important State occasions are held in the sumptuous State Apartments amongst surroundings of galloping decay, buttressed buildings, virtual ruins.

It was, he said, one of the most shameful aspects of the management of historic properties by successive governments that had allowed Dublin Castle to deteriorate visibly over the years.

Although a great deal of demolition took place behind the façades of the Upper Yard in Dublin Castle, fortunately all remaining structures and buildings in the castle complex have been saved and given a new lease of life. During the 1990s the Office of Public Works carried out a programme of restoration and refurbishment of the various buildings at the rear of Dublin Castle. These included the old Ship Street Barracks, the Coach House at the back of the garden, and the various old buildings used by the Revenue Commissioners, the Garda Drug Squad and the Garda Traffic Unit. It is possible now to say, at the start of the twenty-first century, that all of the historic buildings in Dublin Castle have either been converted, restored or renovated and that the castle is in full daily use.

Plans were first mooted for the Chester Beatty Library to move to Dublin Castle from its location in Ballsbridge in the early 1990s. A new, purpose-built museum has been constructed and fitted out, and the old Accountant General's house and Ordnance Building has been restored and converted as the new library and administration building. The Chester Beatty Library contains some of the most important works of oriental art in the world. The library is surmounted by a clock turret and cupola which has an elegant peacock weather vane.

As we have seen, Francis Johnson was responsible for a number of improvements to Dublin Castle in the early nineteenth century. On the south side of the castle, Johnson created a unified Gothic design that incorporated a terrace below the State Apartments, a new battlemented entrance to the Record Tower and entrances to the crypt beneath the Chapel Royal. The wall supporting the terrace is built of ashlar limestone. It is perforated by Gothic gun loops and capped by a battlemented parapet. Similarly, the Coach House behind the Castle Garden, also designed by Johnson, is essentially a Gothic-style screen wall in front of a series of sheds. The Coach House, now a public venue, has an impressive Gothic battlemented entrance and two flanking towers.

The Castle Garden, which in the early 1990s was completely replanned and planted in a circular layout, is linked to the State Apartments by means of a shallow granite bridge. The bridge leads into an octagonal pavilion or tower, which was at one time used as a library.

The external appearance of St Patrick's Hall

Below: The army standing to attention during a State occasion in the Upper Yard of Dublin Castle in the 1950s.

Left: The converted Accountant General's house and new galleries, which provide a magnificent setting for the Chester Beatty Library's collection.

is extremely plain and recent attempts to enliven this part of the castle by painting it with bright primary colours attracted a good deal of public comment.

The arched Ship Street Gate, with its walkway and parapet above, is connected to the Guard Room and was originally part of the castle's defences.

Dublin Castle has frequently been used as a location for film-making over the last ten years. Included among these productions are *Michael Collins*, *Oliver*, *Moll Flanders* and many other period pieces that required authentic settings. During these film-making episodes it was thrilling to hear the castle resounding to the noise of horses' hooves and carriages. The Upper Yard was once laid out as an eighteenth-century marketplace.

Dublin Castle today receives over 180,000 visitors annually, making it one of the most popular monuments or public buildings in Ireland. The

Above: The reappearance of horse-drawn carriages on the streets of Dublin has given rise to an annual inspection of the roadworthiness of each vehicle. At the same time there is a veterinary check of the horses.

castle has the potential to reach back through Ireland's history with its very complex and contrasting symbols. A balanced selection of images from these different periods could be presented here to help explain its complex history: a sixteenth-century scene in the Record Tower, perhaps the escape of Red Hugh O'Donnell; a typical eighteenth-century ball in the castle with all the fine costumes, carriages arriving, the role of the Lord Lieutenant, the Throne Room and its paintings; a tableau concerning the theft of the crown jewels, including pictures or replicas of the jewels and the remarkable story; a display of some of the fabulous printed ephemera which came from the castle – invitation cards, dance programmes, etc.; the planned attack on the castle by Robert Emmet; the nineteenth-century military history – a billet or guard room scene, uniforms, swords, the cavalry and their stables; the castle and the story of 1916; 1921 and the new Irish State; the Dublin Castle of the 1990s; the history of the Customs and Excise in Dublin Castle; the history of the Revenue Commissioners in Dublin Castle; the specific role of the Police in Dublin Castle – all of these subjects could be treated and made interesting for the visitor.

CHAPTER FIVE

City Hall

*M*ost Dubliners remember City Hall as the location of the Dublin Rates Office, the Dublin City Archives and the City Manager's Department. In 2000 City Hall was reopened to the public following its full restoration. It is now one of the most majestic public buildings in Dublin.

This elegant classical building may be viewed from several different prospects. From across the River Liffey coming up Capel Street it can be seen in the distance at the end of Parliament Street. It can also be viewed from the east, approaching from Dame Street, and another attractive prospect is looking down from Castle Street to the west side of the building. Like most of Dublin's public buildings it is built of stone. Classical in concept, it has a simple plan: a large, domed space sits within a square. The exterior is ornamented with giant Corinthian columns carved from Portland stone.

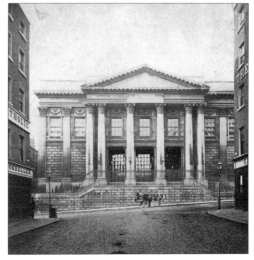

The Royal Exchange, as it was originally called, was built as a meeting place for trading and for storing goods. It was erected by the merchants of Dublin, who required a proper space in which to do business in the late eighteenth century. Located directly outside the gates of Dublin Castle, this district was the hub of commercial activity in the eighteenth century, as the River Liffey with its Custom House was only a few yards away. In 1769 a competition was held and Mr Thomas Cooley, an English architect, won the prize of 100 guineas and the job of designing the Royal Exchange. The erection of this large structure required the demolition of many older and smaller buildings, including a house which had belonged to Lord Cork, whose name was given to Cork Hill. Lucas's Coffee House was also situated in this immediate area. The building of such an elaborate and magnificent structure took ten years; the first stone was laid in 1769.

Above: An early photograph, *c*.1850s, of City Hall, showing the original entrance to the building above street level.

Above and below: The quality of the exquisite stone carving, supervised by sculptor Simon Vierpyl, is evident both outside on the cornice (top) and the capitals (middle), and inside on the carved frieze (bottom).

Opposite top: The City Hall was one of the first public buildings to make use of the giant order of classical columns, as can be seen in this pre-Restoration photograph of the Cork Hill façade.

Opposite bottom: Part of a circular window from the dome, showing eighteenth-century graffiti.

Some years ago the roof of City Hall was completely renovated and repaired, and in 2000 major work was completed on the rest of the building. These renovations involved the removal of all nineteenth-century and subsequent additions in order to restore City Hall to its original, eighteenth-century appearance. When the Royal Exchange was taken over in 1852 by Dublin Corporation as its headquarters and meeting place, walls and screens were constructed, separating the central domed area from the surrounding ambulatory spaces. These walls allowed for the creation of offices and meeting rooms within the building. A new staircase was also created at the back and a new mosaic floor and a series of murals were added underneath the dome. All of the structural features have now been removed and the inside of City Hall has been opened up, revealing an astonishingly grand interior. The Victorian conversion was well conceived and the work, including handsome joinery, doors and plasterwork, was carried out to a very high standard, but it had completely changed the character of the interior, which had once allowed for free circulation around the domed area.

The sense of grandeur, which is so striking both inside and outside City Hall, is created by the use of the giant order of composite columns. This was the second major public building in Dublin, following the Parliament House in College Green, to utilise classical architecture in this way, and was a public statement by the prosperous merchants of Dublin that they were a powerful and successful group. It may also have been their way of resisting the proposed move of the Custom House and city towards the east.

Prior to the building of the Royal Exchange, merchants had used the Tholsel, which was situated close to Christ Church Cathedral. The Tholsel was demolished in the early 1800s, and is the only major building represented in James Malton's prints of Dublin that has vanished. As early as 1765 the Wide Streets Commissioners, whose job was to create straight and noble streets in Dublin and clear away many of the small, twisty thoroughfares, had earmarked this location for a public square, standing as it did just beside Dublin Castle.

The monumental scale and elegance of the interior of City Hall is greatly enhanced by the enormous coffered dome, now completely regilded. The dome is lit by a series of circular windows, quite a number of which display interesting examples of eighteenth-century graffiti. One window bears the signatures of a glazier and a carpenter and the slogan, 'Damn the cargo'. This slogan may have been written by carriers who were asked to go and unload a ship that was waiting down at the Custom House Quay, perhaps late on a Saturday afternoon. It is a very human reminder of the original function of the Royal Exchange.

Like City Hall's exterior, the interior is also ornamented by a series of giant composite capitals, with a stone cornice above. The carving of these capitals and of the cornice is of outstanding quality, especially when viewed at close quarters. The stonework, particularly on the exterior, has been restored and cleaned.

The basement of City Hall, most of which is vaulted and domed, was designed as a storage space, and in its early years was let to the customs authorities. Parts of the basement were originally cobbled, and during removal of partitions and walls in 1999 some of these cobblestones were uncovered. In the centre of the building, beneath the domed space, a central pillar supports the floor. This area has a remarkable sculptured quality.

The Royal Exchange, as has already been mentioned, was designed as a meeting place for merchants and traders, and so an elaborate coffee room was built over the main entrance, facing today's Parliament Street. This room, a large rectangular space with a coved ceiling, is now used as the Dublin Corporation City Council chamber. These upper rooms are approached by two magnificent oval staircases, both of which are ornamented in the refined, classical Adam style. The plasterwork was carried out by Charles Thorpe, who was himself a member of Dublin Corporation in the eighteenth century, and the designs were directly copied from recent discoveries of ornamentation found

in Herculaneum, near Pompeii, in Italy. The decoration of the new Royal Exchange in 1770 shows just how up-to-date Dublin was with European trends in architecture and decoration. The Corporation took possession of the Royal Exchange in 1851, having paid the sum of £1,721, fourteen shillings and ten pence.

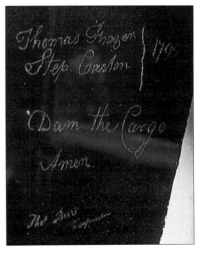

In the central domed space is a series of frescoes, carried out for the Corporation between 1914 and 1919 by James Ward. These paintings depict scenes from the history of Dublin city, such as the Battle of Clontarf. The space is also home to four very different and very interesting statues, which include Daniel O'Connell, Dr Charles Lucas, Thomas Drummond and Thomas Davis. There was originally also a statue in bronze of King George III, dressed in a Roman military outfit, but this has long since vanished. In 1797, when trade in the Royal Exchange was at its height, there was a need for more office space for the various merchants. This was answered by the

construction of Commercial Buildings in College Green, which was demolished in 1980, the site being occupied by the Central Bank. The great statue of Daniel O'Connell, now in City Hall, originally stood on a pedestal beside the front steps. In 1867 it was proposed to move the statue indoors as it was felt that the marble was being eroded and damaged by the weather. The oldest statue in City Hall, that of Dr Charles Lucas, was carved in 1772. Dr Lucas was a member of the Dublin City Assembly, the forerunner of the Corporation. The statue was the work of Edward Smyth, who is best known for his riverine heads on the Custom House.

The statues of Daniel O'Connell, Thomas Davis and Thomas Drummond are all the work of John Hogan. Daniel O'Connell, 'The Liberator', was Lord Mayor of Dublin in 1841, which accounts for the presence of this sculpture in City Hall. Thomas Drummond, who was Undersecretary for Ireland in the early nineteenth century, originally came from Scotland. He was well respected and loved by many Irish people and he adopted Ireland as his home; he is buried in Mount Jerome cemetery. The reform of the police is attributed to Drummond. He also spearheaded the building of railways in Ireland

and helped to abolish the system of tithes. Drummond's famous words are carved on his statue's plinth: 'Property has its duties as well as its rights'. Drummond is also credited with having invented an incandescent lamp that was used in lighthouses and enabled ships to navigate better in foggy conditions.

Thomas Davis, the Irish poet and patriot, founded the *Nation* newspaper. His statue was originally erected over his grave in Mount Jerome cemetery in 1852, but was brought into City Hall in 1944.

An engraving by James Malton shows that the original pedestrian approach to the front

Above top: One of the two oval staircases in City Hall, showing the delicate plasterwork by the stuccadore Charles Thorpe.

Above: A stonemason at work on an enormous, richly carved capital at City Hall.

of City Hall from Castle Street and Cork Hill was by means of a terrace or ramp, and a flight of steps descended into Dame Street at the other end. A new set of entrance steps and a balustrade were added later. One of the functions of Dublin Corporation was to control and supervise weights and measures. The Corporation held a set of correct measures and bushels and also a correct brass yardstick. These brass measuring lengths were fixed to the front wall of City Hall and, though very worn, may still be seen there today. The Dublin city coat of arms may be seen on the pedestals which form part of the nineteenth-century balustrade. Carved in Portland stone, some of these have weathered very badly while others have been replaced. The city arms depict three castles burning, a symbol of the zeal of the citizens of Dublin to defend their city. In 1814 the stone balustrade, part of the original terrace in front of City Hall, collapsed. A great crowd had

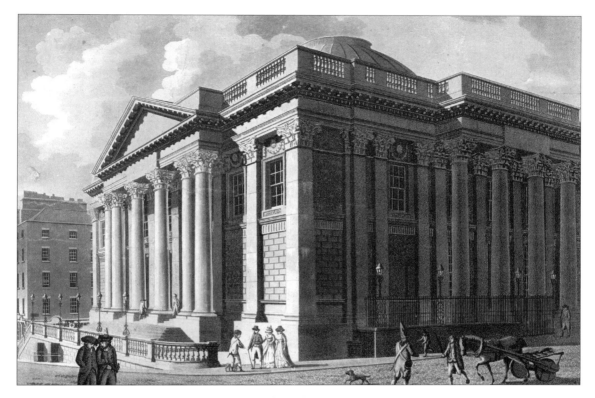

gathered to watch a public whipping in front of City Hall and the stone balustrade fell on the spectators below in the street, killing nine people.

The engravings of Samuel Brocas and James Malton of the Royal
Exchange are taken from a vantage point near Cork Hill, looking east down
Dame Street towards Trinity College. They show the street, between City
Hall and the Olympia, narrowed to a width of fifty-one
feet, a design laid down by the Wide Streets Commissioners as the new streetline in 1766. Early maps show that
prior to this Dame Street had been scarcely more than
twenty-five feet wide. The buildings which once occupied the site of the present Millennium Garden projected
out towards the Olympia Theatre. During the 1970s
Dublin Corporation road engineers planned to widen
Dame Street and this set in motion a sequence of events
that was to lead to the demolition of all the buildings in
that block except number 2 Palace Street, the former Sick
and Indigent Roomkeepers' Society building.

The street, now known as Palace Street, which inci-
dentally is one of the shortest streets in Dublin, was known as Castle Lane
in the mid-eighteenth century. Castle Lane led from Dame Street into the
Lower Castle Yard, which is the part of Dublin Castle closest to the original
moat and the River Poddle.

Above: James Malton's late
eighteenth-century view of
the new Royal Exchange.

Above: The full coat of arms of
Dublin Corporation.

2 Palace Street

Palace Street, which acquired its name after the rebuilding of the street, was so called because it led to the Palace of the Lord Lieutenant, an alternative name for Dublin Castle. The street consisted of four tall, narrow houses, each to have a frontage of eighteen feet nine inches. Of those only one original house survives, which is number 2. In 1766 four or five new houses were proposed for Palace Street/Castle Lane, which would be widened to thirty-five feet. A new arched and pedimented gate to Dublin Castle, with two pedestrian entrances, was erected on Palace Street leading into the Lower Castle Yard. This gate is still in use today as the principal pedestrian entrance to the castle. It would appear that numbers 2 and 3 were originally built together as a pair because both houses are of the same plan, having a large central chimney stack and an L-shaped projecting return. Number 2 Palace Street was modified around 1800, with a pair of bow-shaped rooms being created at the rear of the house on the ground and first floor.

During the 1970s proposals to demolish the entire street were proceeding apace and, only for the determination of the Sick and Indigent Roomkeepers' charity to stay in their original home, the building would undoubtedly have been lost forever. Due to the efforts of various councillors, including Carmencita Hederman and Alderman Alexis FitzGerald, 2 Palace Street was

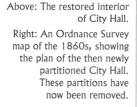

Above: The restored interior of City Hall.

Right: An Ordnance Survey map of the 1860s, showing the plan of the then newly partitioned City Hall. These partitions have now been removed.

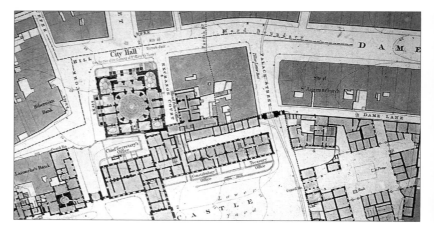

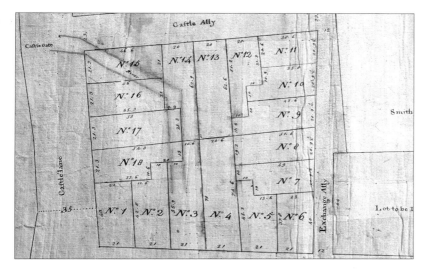

Left: One of the earliest plans of the Wide Streets Commissioners, showing the proposed layout of the Palace Street block. The diagonal line left of centre shows the course of part of the River Poddle. Castle Lane was renamed Palace Street at this time.

Below: A variation of one of the City of Dublin's coats of arms, as used on nineteenth-century stationery.

eventually designated as a listed building. In 1992 the charity decided that they could no longer look after this old and large house, which was now in need of considerable repair, and they accordingly sold it by public auction. The house was subsequently restored and refurbished as one of the few private family residences in this part of the city centre. The restoration of the house involved repairing and replacing the original inscription in plaster on the front of the building, the repair and careful retention of all the Georgian and Victorian windows and the strengthening of the building from within using steel ties.

A unique feature of this house is the presence of an old safe in the wall of what was originally a chimney. The key to the safe had been mislaid and it had not been opened for thirty years! The lock was picked open by a local locksmith in 1990, and an extraordinary collection of papers and other odds and ends, including a box of washing powder, some soap, a variety of shirts and five-and-a-half old pence, came to light. There were also some documents relating to the takeover of the building by the British military in 1921 because of its proximity to the Castle. The society claimed compensation from the British government for the takeover of their building between some time in 1921 and May 1922. Other finds in the safe included publicity posters for a sermon, 'In aid of the Society of Indigent Roomkeepers', to be preached in St Werburgh's Church in February 1796 by the Reverend Richard Graves, one of the founders of the society.

The Sick and Indigent Roomkeepers' Society is said to be one of the oldest charities in Dublin, and indeed in Ireland. Before their purchase of the house in Palace Street in 1855 the charity met at inns and other premises around the city and they dispensed aid to those who had either fallen ill or could not afford to pay their rent. An unexpected donation from Benjamin Lee Guinness in 1855 assisted the charity in their purchase of 2 Palace Street. They carried out a major renovation of the house, which included some Victorian alterations to the ground and first floors.

Above: Originally a drawing room, this room was used as the office of the Sick and Indigent Roomkeepers' Society for almost 150 years.

Above: A marble plaque, which was fixed to the wall of the building of the Sick and Indigent Roomkeepers' Society, is now in storage at the Dublin Civic Museum. It lists the founders of what is considered to be the oldest charity in Dublin.

The Sick and Indigent Roomkeepers' Society was established in 1790 and helped, in general, a class of people who were self-supporting but had been reduced to poverty. The charity would not help anyone who had begged for help, but they would give funds to help people pay their rent or, in some instances, to buy materials or equipment to assist them in earning a living. It had been a non-denominational charity since its foundation in 1790, and showed no religious or political bias to the room keepers who needed its assistance. A room keeper was simply somebody who rented rooms, and the money they received from the Society enabled them to keep on their rented accommodation and live with dignity, rather than perhaps ending up in the workhouse. One of the original founders of the charity was Samuel Roseburgh, a linen draper, whose portrait hangs in the present headquarters of the charity on Leeson Street. Many people continue to receive help from the Sick and Indigent Roomkeepers' Society today.

By 1984 the Sick and Indigent Roomkeepers' building looked decidedly shaky. It stood forlorn amid the ruins of Palace Street – the Corporation had demolished everything on one side and the Office of Public Works had demolished number 1 Palace Street (the former 'Aliens Office') on the other. A great deal of controversy surrounded the compulsory purchase of number 2 Palace Street around 1980, and the Dublin Civic Group fought the Corporation's Planning Department, which was intent on demolishing this last remaining house on the site between Dublin Castle and City Hall. The Dublin Planning

Left: An invitation to a ball in the 'Rotundo' in 1851 – one of the means by which the charity raised funds for its support of the sick and destitute.

Below: A view of the somewhat lonely looking number 2 Palace Street prior to its restoration. Neighbouring houses were demolished in the 1970s.

Officer, Charles Aliaga Kelly, described the house and district as an obsolete area that was in need of rehabilitation. The house has been and remains a landmark in the city and is the subject of a great deal of interest for Dubliners and tourists alike. Two marble plaques, one of which recorded the foundation of the charity and the names of its founders, were removed from the wall of the house in 1992 and are to be erected in the Dublin Civic Museum on South William Street.

Frank McDonald, the Environment Correspondent of the *Irish Times*, who did much to highlight the wastage and dereliction of central Dublin in the 1980s, wrote an article about the City Hall/Palace Street area in 1981. He pointed out that, contrary to the generally held belief that most derelict sites were owned by rapacious property speculators, many of the derelict sites in the city were owned by Dublin Corporation itself, and that many of them had been acquired for road widening. He went on to point out the sad irony that this area was right on the tourist trail to Dublin Castle and the city's celebrated cathedrals, yet it was one of the ugliest eyesores in the city. Number 1 Palace Street, the 'Aliens Office', which has already been mentioned, was demolished in 1979 by the then Board of Works (now the Office of Public Works). In 1994 this site, along with the former Clune Clancy buildings beside Exchange Court, was sold by the OPW and a series of new apartment buildings was erected here. Unfortunately, numbers 5 and 6 Palace Street, which had stood at the corner of Dame Street (and had been the premises of the well-known firm Thomas H Mason & Sons, opticians and photographers), were destroyed during a fire in 1967. The proposed reconstruction of Masons following the fire was refused by

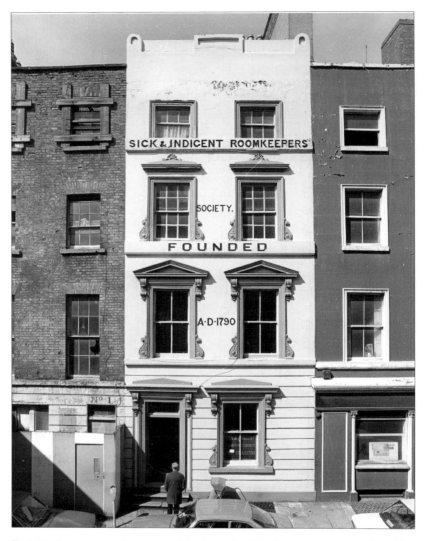

Right: Number 2 Palace Street originally dates from 1766, but was refronted by the Sick and Indigent Roomkeepers' Society in the 1850s.

Dublin Corporation because of their road-widening plans, so that by 1980 the Sick and Indigent Roomkeepers' building stood 'like a lighthouse amidst a sea of dereliction', as its secretary Mr GC Weekes remarked. Mr Weekes added that the Society had had the patronage of many lord mayors of Dublin since its foundation and he further commented that as the charity had been there for over 140 years, he saw no reason why they should move somewhere else.

I first visited the Sick and Indigent Roomkeepers' building in 1984, with a view to photographing the house, recording it and seeing what kind of condition it was in. The Dublin City Association of An Taisce, with whom I was involved for many years, were anxious to see the building preserved and to help in any way we could towards this end. I little thought then that eight years later I would be working on the house, and then living in it during the 1990s. It has been a great privilege to live in a house as old and with such a history as this one has. From it, since 1992, I have watched the centre of Dublin being transformed from a state of quiet decay into the thriving tourist centre that it is today.

Among the very old parchment deeds that we acquired on the purchase of the building was one dated 1795, naming Robert Emmet as a purchaser of a half share in the premises. The Emmet family owned considerable property around Dublin city and this may simply have been another investment for them. However, the planned attack and takeover by Robert Emmet of Dublin Castle may have had a bearing on their interest in this house, which was so strategically located. From the windows of the house much of the military comings and goings in the castle could be observed. Indeed, Major Sirr's home was in the Lower Castle Yard.

Another document mentions the presence of a family named Barrett Wadden, who lived here in 1810. They were silk merchants and ran a silk manufacturing business here. During our work in restoring the building we found some old silk bobbins and evidence of sewing machines having been fixed to the floors, along with scorch marks on the floorboards that had been made by the long, thin iron of a tailor's 'goose'. There has been a long tradition of tailoring not only in this house but in the general area around Dublin Castle. As new and more fashionable residential areas were built in the late eighteenth century, many of the older houses of the city were rented by textile workers and tailors, who both lived and worked in them. Numerous tailors and outfitters made military and naval uniforms for the incumbent soldiers of the castle. It is often forgotten that Dublin Castle was, above all, a military barracks and that great numbers of soldiers and officers were stationed there.

An earlier occupant of number 2 Palace Street, during the 1780s, was a widow named Catherine Alley, a haberdasher. In about 1830

Above: One of a pair of pewter inkwells, which were used by the Sick and Indigent Room-keepers' Society.

the building was part-leased to a tailor named Holbrooke Davis. A number of interesting artefacts came to light during work on the building, including two large pewter inkwells. These rather large inkwells, which resemble Puritan hats in shape, contained holders for quills and are probably of late eighteenth-century date. Among the many handmade bricks that were used in the construction of the building one was found bearing the thumb mark of the man who must have modelled the brick when the clay was wet. Elsewhere in the city, bricks have been found with the imprint of a cat's paw! Also used in the construction were many handmade clout nails. Such nails were about three inches long and hand-forged by a blacksmith. The basement remains in its original form, with two very old kitchens and fireplaces intact. The flagged stone floor also remains *in situ*.

The area around Palace Street and in front of the Olympia Theatre is a low-lying one. Starting at this point there is a noticeable hill as Dame Street runs east towards Trinity College. It was here that the River Poddle originally joined the Liffey, and prior to the sixteenth century this was almost certainly a tidal area. The River Poddle is today carried in a brick culvert that runs around Dublin Castle and cuts straight down the middle of Palace Street, having passed under the central arch of the gateway into Dublin Castle. It then bends under the Olympia Theatre and makes its way towards the quays to issue into the Liffey at Wellington Quay. This was not always so. Prior to 1766 the Poddle appears to have run in an open stream behind the houses of Castle Lane/ Palace Street. Another branch of the River Poddle, which was originally a mill race, shoots off just inside the Palace Street Gate into Dublin Castle and turns to run under the back of the Sick and Indigent Roomkeepers' building and across the road towards Crane Lane, where up until the eighteenth century a mill once stood. The mill, known as Dam's Mill, was powered by this branch of the Poddle. The Church of St Marie Le Dam (also referred to as Del Dam or Le Dame), which stood close to here, was so named because of this mill race and dam. The church is said to have been built in about 1179 and is famous because of the coronation of Lambert Simnel, a ten-year-old boy who was crowned King Edward VI, ostensibly as the genuine heir to the throne, in 1487. The crown used during the course of this coronation – which was later invalidated – was taken from the statue of St Mary in this church.

Above: A quadrant, or curved, sash window, which was added to the back of number 2 Palace Street in about 1800.

CHAPTER SIX

Castle Street
to Bride Street

Castle Street

Today's quiet Castle Street, which contains a number of modern apartment buildings and the old City Rates Office, gives little sense of the status it enjoyed in the medieval walled city of Dublin. Castle Street, Skinner Row and High Street then formed the main east–west thoroughfare of the city, as well as linking Dublin Castle to Christ Church Cathedral. Even after the city spread eastwards, beyond the confines of the medieval walls, into Temple Bar and towards Trinity College, Castle Street maintained its prime position. But it became a backwater in the 1880s, following the construction of Lord Edward Street.

It is hard now to imagine that this street once rattled with the sound of coaches and was filled with the noises of soldiers and horses coming to and from Dublin Castle. It is difficult to picture all the merchants and traders, the coffee houses and the shoemakers which once thronged it. *Walker's Hibernian* magazine of February 1789 provides us with a glimpse of life on this busy street:

> Last Monday night, about the hour of twelve, a buck who lodges at a house in Castle Street, having paid his devotions rather too liberally to Bacchus that evening, amused himself with tearing the firebricks from a grate, and flinging them into the street, to the terror of passengers, and though frequently admonished to forego his mischieviousness, sport could not be stopped until the neighbours, assisted by a party of the police, interfered. During this frantic diversion, the Lord Lieutenant's coach man, who had been driving his

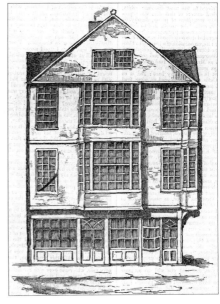

Below: The last timber-framed house in Dublin stood at the corner of Castle Street and Werburgh Street.

master to Kilmainham, narrowly escaped losing his life by one of the bricks, which struck the coach box and rebounded against the front of the carriage.

Brooking's map of 1728 illustrates the original defensive towers and the drawbridge of Dublin Castle, which faced on to the south side of castle Street. These medieval gate towers were dismantled in about 1750. Though named after its proximity to the castle, the street was never directly overlooked by it, as a row of houses came between it and the castle; the houses' yards occupied the site of the castle moat. Even the present Castle Steps did not exist – this stretch was lined on both sides by small houses and was known as Cole's Alley. These old houses, which are shown on Rocque's map of 1756, were cleared away towards the end of the eighteenth century, leaving only the La Touche Bank. The corner of Cork Hill and Castle Street just in front of the Rates Office is a perfect example of a fan of granite pavement, now quite rare in the city.

Various maps in the City Archives show that the Ware family had property interests on the south side of Castle Street, and Gilbert tells us that James Ware, who was Viceroy Fitzwilliam's secretary in 1588, lived in Castle Street. The Wares were a scholarly family – several family members from consecutive generations produced books of a historical nature about Ireland. Charles II offered James Ware a title, but he declined to accept it. James was also granted a house that had been forfeited during the 1641 Rebellion, but he presented it back to the widow of the original owner. He published several books on the antiquities of Ireland, and he maintained his position as Auditor General both before and after the political upheavals of 1649.

James Ware's house is thought to have stood on the site of Hoey's Court – a long-vanished residential enclave, under the shadow of the graveyard of St Werburgh's Church and close to the ancient city wall. Hoey's Court, surrounded in the eighteenth century and before by small houses, was approached by small passageways from Werburgh Street to the west, and from Cole Alley, later the Castle Steps, to the east. Jonathan Swift was born in 1667 at 9 Hoey's Court. This was a brick house consisting of four storeys over a basement. At first- and second-floor level it was four windows wide, narrowing to two windows on the top floor and flanked by a typical Dutch-style gable.

Gilbert lists ten booksellers and printers as resident in Castle Street during the latter half of the seventeenth century; it is reasonable to assume that many of them occupied houses of timber-frame construction. The last known timber-frame, or cagework, house in Dublin stood on the corner of

Above: Rocque's map shows the important position of Castle Street as a residential and commercial street.

Below: The gabled house at number 9 Hoey's Court was the birthplace of Dean Swift. It was located just west of the Castle Steps.

Castle Street and Werburgh Street. It was dismantled in 1813. An engraving of it, illustrated in the *Dublin Penny Journal*, is often reproduced. The house consisted of three floors, with additional rooms in the gabled attic. The engraving shows a picturesque old house with a shop on the ground floor and the upper floors projecting out over it into the street – a typical feature of sixteenth-century cagework houses. A few timber beams of an adjoining house still exist, embedded in the wall of 4 Castle Street, now the headquarters of the Dublin Civic Trust.

It is extraordinary that not one cagework house survives in Dublin, or indeed in Ireland, when we consider the large numbers which remain in England, France and elsewhere in Europe. The fear of fire in cagework houses was very real, because the chimneys were constructed of timber, lath and plaster – this was one of the main reasons why so many of them were demolished. The windows of cagework houses consisted of wooden frames with many small panes of hand-blown glass; even the simple sketch in the *Dublin Penny Journal* shows the shadows and wavy light from these irregular panes of glass.

On the streets of the seventeenth and eighteenth centuries, shops and taverns were identified by their hanging signs. Castle Street was no exception, boasting the Castle Tavern in 1680, the Garter Tavern in 1696, the Thatched House Tavern in 1728, the Drapier's Head in 1735, the Plume of Feathers Tavern in 1753 and the Carteret's Head in 1750. In the eighteenth century the Rose Tavern stood on the north side of Castle Street, almost opposite what is now called the Castle Steps. The Carteret's Head lay behind houses on the north side of Castle Street and, like the Brazen Head, was approached by a covered passage.

A survey of the Dublin street directory for 1778 reveals three shoemakers in Castle Street along with a variety of lacemakers, glovers, milliners and haberdashers, hosiers and peruke-makers. Also, because of its proximity to the Four Courts at Christ Church Cathedral, Castle Street was favoured as the offices of many attorneys and lawyers. For instance, at 40 Castle Street in 1774 we find William Fleming, Barrister. By 1823, probably due to the presence of the Irish Woollen Warehouse, we find than no less than twenty-five individuals with occupations related to the tailoring and drapery business. These include silk manufacturers, linen drapers, woollen drapers, silk and ribbon and trimming manufacturers and hat-makers.

With the leather-working tradition in nearby Skinner Row, it is not surprising that a great number of shoemakers occupied this street. In the middle of the nineteenth century there were still a half dozen shoemakers

Above top: Number 4 Castle Street, now the headqurters of the Dublin Civic Trust, was restored in the late 1990s. This is the oldest surviving house in Castle Street.

Above: A doorway on the top floor of the house prior to restoration.

in Castle Street; Thomas Barnwell's shoemaking establishment survived in Castle Street up until the 1980s. Harry Barnwell, a master cobbler specialising in making orthopaedic shoes, was still working at 4 Castle Street in 1983. His family had been in the business since 1881. He commented that up until the middle of the last century we had, in Ireland, the finest leather available. 'It was produced by Callaghan's of Limerick and it's to the shame of the government that they let the company collapse twenty years ago.' In his opinion the modern, chemically tanned leather isn't worth a damn!

Number 4 Castle Street is the last surviving old house in the street. It was purchased in 1996 by the Dublin Civic Trust, who secured funds from the Department of the Environment and the European Union to restore the house as its headquarters and exhibition centre. A planning application had been made to clear the site and replace the house with a block of apartments, but through the intervention of the Office of Public Works it was decided that it was of 'significant historical, architec-

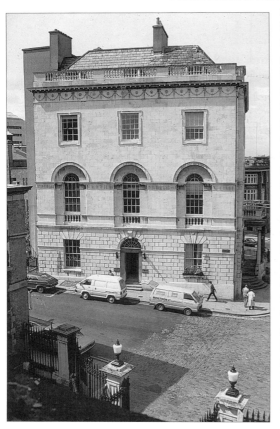

tural and heritage value', and was scheduled as a National Monument in 1995. This designation was made partly on the merits of the building itself, but also due to the survival of an earlier timber-framed house which was incorporated in the party wall to number 3. The four-storey, brick-fronted house with its attractive shopfront dates from about 1820. It was purpose-built as a shop-cum-residence, with separate doors for the shop and the residential accommodation overhead. There is a small flagged yard at the back of the house which is overshadowed by St Werburgh's Church. It is also unusual in that it is three rooms deep and once shared a narrow light well with its neighbouring building. The symmetrical shopfront, with its plain pilasters and small, attractive fanlight, has been carefully restored and the former shop is now used for exhibition purposes. To date, exhibitions have been mounted demonstrating the history and development in Dublin of windows, joinery, plaster-work and fanlights. Adjoining the Civic Trust building at the corner of Werburgh Street is a new apartment building, whose projecting upper floors make reference to the existence of the early timber-framed building on this site.

Aside from the presence of the various shoemakers, trunk manufacturers, tailors, hat-makers and taverns, nineteenth-century Castle Street was noteworthy chiefly for La Touche's Bank and Newcomen's Bank.

Newcomen's Bank was originally built in 1781. The site for the bank was acquired in the 1770s when a firm of bankers named Gleadowe operated in Castle Street. Thomas Gleadowe had taken over an older business called Swift's Bank. Gleadowe's son, William, married Charlotte Newcomen in 1772, and in the late 1770s the firm became Gleadowe & Newcomen. It then had premises at both Castle Street and at 19 St Mary's Abbey, across the river. Sir William Gleadowe Newcomen commissioned Thomas Ivory, one of the most distinguished architects in eighteenth-century Dublin, to construct the new bank building in 1781. Ivory's building, which is one of the most delicate and refined of its type in Dublin, continued to be used as Newcomen's Bank until 1831, when it was sold to the Hibernian Bank.

The main entrance to Newcomen's Bank was originally situated on Castle Street, in the centre of its symmetrical elevation. The proportions of this façade are in perfect harmony with the scale of the building, the positioning of the windows and the exquisite refinement of the carved stone ornamentation. In style, Thomas Ivory's elegant, palatial building has frequently been likened to the work of Robert Adam. The ground floor contains offices and an elegant curved staircase of a grand scale. It is ornamented by a delicate wrought-iron balustrade, and has a coved plasterwork ceiling with top lighting. The staircase, with its domed ceiling and top light, is not unlike the elegant pair of staircases across the street in the Royal Exchange. Even the plasterwork decoration bears a close resemblance. It leads to the principal rooms on the first floor and, by

Above: A fragment of the original frieze from Newcomen Bank.

Left: A rare example of a fan-shaped granite pavement, which has survived in front of Newcomen's Bank. Few pavements of this type now remain in the city.

Opposite top: The decorative lead fanlight of number 4 Castle Street, made in the early 1800s, before restoration.

Opposite bottom: The fine façade of Newcomen's bank, restored in 1995, which faces Dublin Castle.

Right: A cherub from the painted ceiling of the oval room in Newcomen's Bank. This is attributed to the artist Vincenzo Valdre, who also painted the ceiling in St Patrick's Hall in Dublin Castle.

means of a subtle curved corridor, to a magnificent oval room with an elegant fireplace.

In 1856 the façade facing Cork Hill was doubled in size and a new portico and entrance was added. The work was carried out with such care that the casual observer would scarcely notice the two different periods of workmanship. In 1884 the building was sold to Dublin Corporation as part of their scheme to create the new Lord Edward Street, and at this time a new stone front incorporating a small fountain was erected to face the new street. The Corporation initially used the building to house the City Accountant, Architect and Sanitary Officer, but later, became a public office for the payments of rates and water charges. This activity took place in the former banking hall of the building.

In 1995 a major project of refurbishment was undertaken, which involved significant repairs to the stonework and the careful cleaning of the building. In some areas the damaged masonry was replaced and rusted iron cramps were removed. The beautiful white Portland stone was cleaned using a calcium spray and various poultices. The work was carried out by the Dublin Corporation in conjunction with David Slattery as stone consultant. The painting on the ceiling of the oval room contains symbols of wine and plenty, with classical figures floating amid clouds of cherubs and garlands of flowers. The ceiling is thought to represent a spear-bearing Greek god of pleasure and plenty. A second oval room was later added on the north side of the building. The basement of the bank is also of some interest, having a series of small, vaulted chambers which were presumably once used as strong rooms. It contained a wine cellar and other cellars under the street for the storage of firewood and turf.

Newcomen appears to have been involved with the construction of the Royal Canal and indeed a bridge is named after him at North Strand. He lived at Killester House in north County Dublin. It has been suggested that the family lived far beyond their means and that when the bank went into liquidation in 1825, enormous debts were revealed.

Across the street from Newcomen's Bank once stood the large premises of the La Touche Bank, generating a favourite Dublin quip in the early nineteenth century: 'Why is Castle Street like a river?' 'Because it runs between two banks!'

David Digges de La Touche des Rompiers came to Ireland with King William III and fought at the Battle of the Boyne. He settled in Dublin and established a business in the Liberties, initially manufacturing cambric and silk poplins. La Touche handled large sums of money for his customers and through this his bank evolved, leading eventually to his business in Castle Street. One of his two sons was to manage Dublin's most successful

Below: An early nineteenth-century engraving, showing a busy scene at the entrance of Dublin Castle at Cork Hill.

Right: Part of the plasterwork ceiling from one of the main reception rooms in the La Touche Bank. Following the demolition of the bank, the ceiling was moved to the Bank of Ireland, College Green.

Below: The original design for the façade of the La Touche Bank in Castle Street by Joseph Jarratt.

Opposite top: A newspaper from 1945, showing the early demolition of one of Dublin's historic buildings.

Opposite bottom: The front elevation of St Werburgh's Church as depicted by Brooking in 1728.

private bank, while the other became an influential member of parliament and continued in the textile business.

By the end of the eighteenth century there was a proliferation of small private banks in Ireland, which were often no more than small businesses issuing notes – rather like a credit note from a shop. There were six banks in Dublin at this time, and due to a shortage of silver coins each of them began to produce their own notes, which flooded the marketplace, where they were traded and even pawned. Most surviving examples of these notes, some of which are in the Bank of Ireland's collection, have been endorsed many times by the signature of the bearer.

The La Touche Bank was built before 1735 and is one of the earliest recorded banks in the city. The building was erected by David La Touche and backed onto Dublin Castle. It was a magnificent five-bay, four-storey combined business premises and residence. Wings, slightly lower in height, were added to either side of the bank in the early nineteenth century. In 1870 the La Touche Bank was taken over by the Munster Bank, which occupied the building for some years until their new premises, now the AIB, in Dame Street were completed. In 1945 the building was dismantled, leaving only the arcaded ground floor, although a fine plasterwork ceiling representing 'Venus Wounded by Love' was dismantled and re-erected in

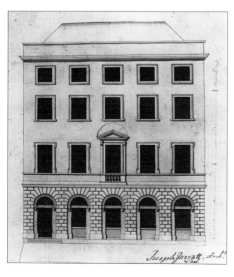

Joseph Jarratt, Arch.

the Directors' Dining Room in the Bank of Ireland, College Green. It is appropriate that at least one element of La Touche's old bank should have been salvaged and installed in the Bank of Ireland, as David La Touche was the first governor of the Bank of Ireland in College Green.

Castle Street was also the home of a third private bank, belonging to Benjamin Burton, a prominent figure in the late seventeenth century, who became Lord Mayor of Dublin in 1706. Burton was immensely wealthy and the expression 'as safe as Ben Burton' came into popular usage. Sadly, when Burton's partner Harrison died in 1725, the bank's liabilities amounted to over £65,000 – a massive sum in the eighteenth century.

Henry Shaw's *New City Pictorial Directory*, published in 1850, gives us an interesting impression of what Cork Hill looked like before the making of Lord Edward Street. A row of six or seven five-storey Georgian houses, with shops on the ground floor, stood across the path of the present Lord Edward Street, linking Exchange Street Upper with the Newcomen Bank in Cork Hill. Another group of houses and shops stood at a right angle to these, facing the main entrance to Dublin Castle. The line of these buildings is still preserved today between Parliament Street and Lower Exchange Street.

Prior to the creation of Lord Edward Street, all of the properties on the north side of Castle Street ran back to Copper Alley. Late eighteenth-century maps in the Dublin City Archives show the various long plots, including a variety of passageways, which led to internal courts, where other houses were situated. One of these large houses, with a court to the front and a yard to the rear at Copper Alley, was later occupied by the Irish Woollen warehouse. Another passageway led to Pembroke Court, while a third, named Peter's Alley, joined Castle Street with Copper Alley. The south side of Castle Street, as we have already noted, was originally held by the family of Sir James Ware and his descendants. It, too, was divided into a number of house plots, including the large forty-eight-foot frontage of the La Touche Bank. A map of 1769 notes a property on Castle Street, on 'the west corner of the steps to the new passage'.

St Werburgh's Church

The present St Werburgh's Church stands on the site of one of the oldest churches in Dublin. St Werburgh, or Werbergher, was the female patron saint of Chester, England, where a shrine was erected to her in AD 875. Although Dublin's St Werburgh's Church is mentioned in the twelfth

Former Dublin Banking Centre

La Touche Building, Castle Street, Dublin, which is being demolished, was once the head office of La Touche, one of the great Huguenot bankers.—*Irish Independent* Photo. (R.).

Right: The spacious mid-eighteenth-century interior of St Werburgh's, one of the last Georgian churches still in use in the city.

Below: Decorative plasterwork detail over the east window of St Werburgh's Church.

century, we have no description of it.

The church was, by all accounts, well kept and well frequented during the seventeenth century, and many prominent families were buried there. For example, Sir James Ware was buried here in 1666.

By the early eighteenth century the church was considered 'decayed and ruinous' and the then Archbishop of Dublin, William King, set about building a new church. In 1713 the old church was demolished. The cost of building the new church, which had been designed by Thomas Burgh, the Surveyor General, was estimated at about £6,000. An interesting, unpublished thesis by Lesley Kavanagh, written in 1992 for the Fine Art Department of Trinity College, reveals the background to the rebuilding of St Werburgh's Church. In a letter of 1717, written by Archbishop King to the Earl of Anglesey, King informs the earl that twenty-five churches have been built in Dublin, eighteen have been repaired and two remain to be rebuilt, these being St Werburgh's (which was demolished in 1713) and St Anne's in Dawson Street.

Archbishop King's letters, which survive in Trinity College, show that he was keen to inject new life into the Protestant parishes of Dublin by improving and repairing the various churches in his care. King was well aware of the undeveloped state of Irish architecture in the late

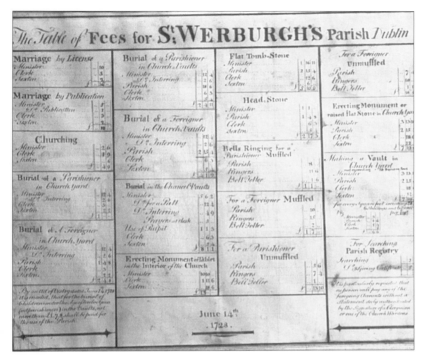

Left: An old schedule of fees from St Werburgh's Church, outlining the charges for various services, such as the 'muffling of bells' for a funeral.

Below: The façade of St Werburgh's as it is today. The steeple was removed in the nineteenth century at the request of the Dublin Castle authorities, who felt that it might be used by snipers.

seventeenth century, and he saw his church-building programme as a way of re-establishing the importance of the Church of Ireland in Dublin. Archbishop King's correspondence reveals that Robert Molesworth, a fellow member of his Board of Commissioners, was anxious to promote a much more exciting design for St Werburgh's Church. Many new churches were being erected in London at this time and the Archbishop was keen to show that Dublin was more than just a provincial city in the kingdom. In another letter, Archbishop King bemoaned the lack of steeples in the Dublin skyline; he must have been very pleased with the fine example that once made St Werburgh's a city landmark.

Above the columns, which enclose the apse at the east end of the church, is an elaborate entablature, surmounted by a series of large ornamental urns. Rich swags of stucco fruit and flowers surround the arched east window. Many interesting and famous people are buried in the crypt below St Werburgh's Church, including Lord Edward FitzGerald, one of the

Above: A rare example of medieval stone carving from the tomb and effigy of Thomas, the seventh Earl of Kildare.

leaders of the 1798 Rebellion. In an ironic twist of fate, Lord Edward's captor, Major Sirr, was buried in 1841 in the eastern corner of the churchyard. Even Gilbert, writing in the 1850s, noted that his stone, 'which is now broken, is shaded by a melancholy, stunted tree'. The steeple of St Werburgh's Church originally reached 160 feet in height and was topped by a gilt ball and vane. Gilbert mentioned it as 'one of the chief ornaments of Dublin', and noted that 'Francis Johnston the eminent Architect (had) offered to secure it in a permanent manner'. Gilbert also stated that a 'large stone monument, with some smaller figures preserved from the ancient building, has been inserted in the southern wall of the church'. It is widely believed that this monument was the tomb of Lord Thomas FitzGerald, better known as Silken Thomas.

St Werburgh's Church is essentially a plain, rectangular structure, but it is the internal joinery that really makes the interior so remarkable. The stained woodwork of the galleries and pews are enhanced by the rich carving of the organ case, the pulpit, the lectern, the glazed panelling at the back of the church and the large framed notices of Parish Benefactors, which are situated in the side aisles. The combined effect is one of great richness and antiquity. The spacious galleries are supported on plain pilasters, while the upper gallery at the back of the church, along with the organ case, is supported by exquisitely carved, fluted Ionic pillars. Decorative detail on the organ case is outstanding, including the openwork brackets at either side, the egg and dart moulding surrounding the organ console and even the tiny ironwork escutcheons which surround the keyholes of the doors to the console. Similarly, the gold-painted notices, which bear the names of Parish Benefactors since 1646, are displayed in beautifully carved timber frames. On these we learn that Robert Ware donated £5, Sir John Rogerson £10 and Francis Harrison £20 towards the rebuilding of the church in 1726.

The pulpit, which came originally from the chapel in Dublin Castle, is a most spectacular piece of woodcarving. A Gothic pillar which rests on a carved bible supports a capital which consists of carvings of the four evangelists' heads, and these in turn support the four gospels – four carved books which carry the intricately carved pulpit itself. Even the lectern, which is composed of a short Doric column, is a magnificent piece of joinery and complements the rest of the woodwork in the church. The floor of the church is entirely flagged in stone, although the diagonally laid slabs of the central aisle have been painted in black and white for many years. The mid-eighteenth-century windows, with their heavy glazing bars, survive throughout the church and conform to a pattern that would have been popular in the early eighteenth century.

There are many interesting memorials and marble tablets around the walls of St Werburgh's Church, but the oldest monument is the tomb and double effigy which is said to be that of Thomas, the seventh Earl of Kildare, and his wife. A tablet on the wall behind the tomb suggests that it was made in the fifteenth century and was originally erected in the Monastery of All Hallows, now Trinity College. It was moved to the outer wall of St Werburgh's Church in the seventeenth century and re-erected in its present position by the Duke of Leinster in 1914. Gilbert, however, tells us that the monument came from the medieval Church of St Maria del Dam near the Dame Gate on Dame Street. The worn effigy shows a knight and his wife supported on a plinth of Gothic-style carved stonework, including eight figures across the front.

The old graveyard of St Werburgh's Church is an oasis of grass, trees and crumbling gravestones in the midst of a busy urban area. The stone walls of the original Parochial School now form the garden of the present Deanery of Christ Church Cathedral.

Werburgh Street lies on a hill, sloping southwards towards the course of the River Poddle, which lay originally just outside the medieval city wall. St Werburgh's Church, Christ Church Cathedral and the buildings of High Street occupy the highest point in the medieval city. The medieval city wall, as we have already mentioned, ran between Hoey's Court and Ship Street Little, where it is still visible today. It crossed Werburgh Street and continued on its course through an eighteenth-century residential court known as Derby Square. Derby Square was approached by a narrow passage from the street and is shown on Rocque's map as containing seven houses.

The picturesque doorway on Werburgh Street, which bore the name of the square cut into the stone lintel, remained there up until the 1990s. Although much of the square had already disappeared, this writer naively thought that this historic doorway, which had so often been illustrated in books about Dublin, was safe from destruction. But no, another thread in the tapestry of our city was ripped out. It has been replaced by the Christ Church car park which is attached to Jury's Hotel.

Above top: The early nineteenth-century Castle Steps, which linked Ship Street and Castle Street, are a forgotten part of old Dublin.

Above: The unusual entrance to Derby Square, which was dismantled and removed by Dublin Corporation and remains in storage.

Gilbert tells us that Derby Square, which was about eighty feet long, was originally surrounded by about twelve houses and was erected by John Derby, a dealer in butter in the late seventeenth century. He also mentions that many eminent lawyers occupied buildings in Derby Square because of its proximity to the courts and the location of a Court of Chancery office

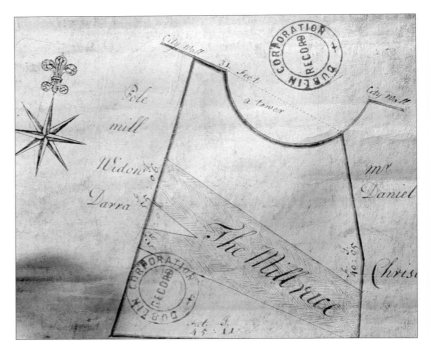

Right: An eighteenth-century map of part of today's Ship Street. It is from the Dublin City Archives and shows the site of the Pole Mill and the mill race adjoining the medieval city wall.

Below: The door and shop window of a long-vanished Ship Street house.

there. Part of this site was excavated by archaeologists in 1993, and another section of the medieval city wall was uncovered.

The long-vanished Kennedy's Lane and Ross Lane once joined Nicholas Street, which was inside the medieval city, to Bride Street, outside the city walls. Only the ground floor, with its plain limestone façade and Doric pilasters, remains of St Nicholas's Church. Kennedy's Lane must have passed through a gate in the city wall either in or close to Geneval's Tower, one of the defensive towers in the southern side of the wall.

Ship Street

Most motor traffic enters Dublin Castle by means of the Ship Street Gate, which is located to the southwest and originally lay just outside the medie-

val wall of the city. Ship Street Great and Ship Street Little have remained something of a backwater. The L-shaped street, with its perfectly intact surface of stone setts, is flanked by one office building, a number of warehouses and Dublin Castle itself. However, this was not always so; Ship Street was once filled with many houses and small businesses. Some of the houses were impressive, and the *Georgian Society Records* of 1909 contain an illustration of a magnificent double doorcase, carved in stone, at numbers 7–8 Ship Street. The early eighteenth-century doorcase was composed of blocks and scrolls, which supported a wide pediment. A pair of Venetian windows flanked the doors on either side. On the wall of one of the warehouses in Ship

Street Great is a stone plaque recording the existence here of the church of St Michael le Pole.

Ship Street Little lies on a gradual slope which finds its lowest point at the back entrance to Dublin Castle. Little Ship Street follows the course of the River Poddle, flowing as it does just outside the medieval city wall at this point. Several mills are known to have been powered by this stream but the positions of the Pole Mill and its mill race are recorded on a variety of maps as lying beside the city wall in Ship Street. The enclosed surface car park on Ship Street probably occupies the exact site of the mill. A map of 1756 in the Dublin City Archives shows the course of the mill race,

Above: The unique double doorcase of a pair of houses in Ship Street, from a photograph taken *c.*1900. All of these residences were eventually demolished.

Below: The modest houses and shops erected by the Wide Streets Commissioners in Ship Street in the early nineteenth century, on the site of the Pole mill race. They backed onto the old city wall.

which emerged from the mill to flow under five small houses, which, if standing today, would largely block the entrance to Dublin Castle in Ship Street. The old Pole Mill took its name from the church of St Michael Le Pole, which we shall discuss shortly. Maps of the street show us two houses

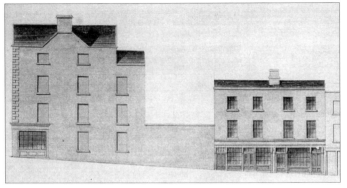

adjoining the old mill, which in 1762 were occupied by the Reverend Richard Challoner Cobbe, the minister of St Bridget's Church, and Arthur Shepherd, Notary. Both houses backed on to the remains of a tower, part of which projects from the medieval city wall and can still be seen today.

Ship Street stood in the Parish of St Bridget's or Bride's and the church itself stood nearby on the corner of the present Bride Road. The land on both sides of Ship Street Little belonged to the Dean and Chapter of Christ Church Cathedral, who received ground rents from the various property holders. One of the buildings in Ship Street Little served as an almshouse in 1819. It would appear that the Wide Streets Commissioners bought up properties in Ship Street in order to widen and improve the approaches to Dublin Castle. Whether it was a piece of city planning or a move to improve the security around the castle, a consistent effort was made between the years

1790 and 1820 to clear away all the small houses which backed on to the castle itself. These included houses on Castle Street, Cole Alley (which became Castle Steps), Ship Street, Stephen Street and George's Lane (later renamed Great George's Street South).

All of the old businesses on Ship Street, which once included a wide selection of timber merchants and dealers in hardware, have gone. The well-known firm of Smith and Pearson may have originated at 11–12 Ship Street, where in 1857 we find Thomas Pearson selling wire. Pearson was only one of eight wire workers listed in Ship Street in the 1850s.

All of the houses on the east side of Ship Street Great, which included numbers 30–44, were redeveloped in the early nineteenth century as an infantry barracks and thus became part of Dublin Castle. A separate stone arch gives access to the parade ground behind.

Opposite, between Ship Street and Chancery Lane, we have the site of the ancient church of St Michael Le Pole, which, eighteenth-century drawings inform us, housed what was probably Dublin's only round tower. The round tower and church stood until the year 1778. Although the fairly plain, rectangular structure of the church appeared to have been modernised, the loss of the early medieval round tower displayed a disregard for the history of the city even in the eighteenth century. The site of the church was later occupied by St Bride's School, a graveyard and an almshouse.

Concerns were expressed in 1980 that the archaeological site of the Church of St Michael Le Pole might be destroyed following the sale of a large tract of land for redevelopment. The importance of this site rests with the fact that it is an early ecclesiastical settlement in the context of an important medieval town. It was hoped that an archaeological dig would tell us something about Dublin's earliest religious settlement and, in particular, reveal the base or remains of the original round tower.

Chancery Lane

Chancery Lane is a short, L-shaped street, connecting Golden Lane with Bride Street. It is called Chancery Lane because of the number of lawyers and those of the Chancery (the lord chancellor's court) who lived there in the eighteenth century. The street is now devoid of any historic buildings of any kind, but Rocque's map of 1756 shows that both sides of the street were once lined with Georgian houses, many of which survived up until the

Above top: An early twentieth-century billhead from Pearson's, the wire manufacturers.

Above: An early nineteenth-century map of Ship Street, showing the now-cleared houses at the entrance of Dublin Castle.

Opposite top: A drawing from the Wide Street Commissioners for the new houses and shops on Little Ship Street.

Opposite bottom: An aerial photograph showing the western environs of Dublin Castle, including the line of buildings that constitute the former barracks of Great Ship Street.

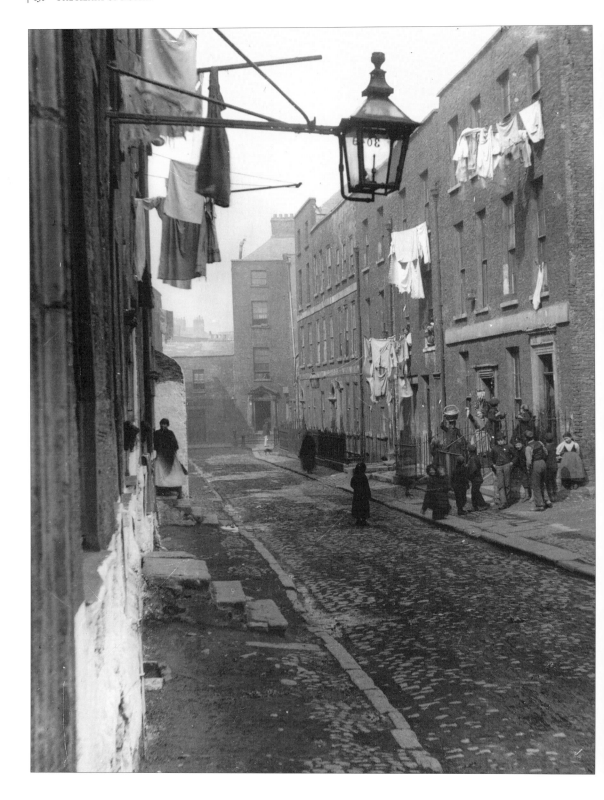

Left: A billhead from the the ironmonger Thomas Moffit. Nineteenth-century Chancery Lane was home to a number of such businesses.

Opposite: A nineteenth-century photograph of Chancery Lane, showing that tenement use of the eighteenth-century houses was well established. It is unusual to find a photograph showing the city's cobbled streets and footpaths. The crowd of children are standing outside the former Lord Chancellor's house.

mid-nineteenth century. Another sketch of Chancery Lane, illustrated in *Shaw's New City Pictorial Directory*, published in 1850, shows two impressive Georgian houses located at the corner where Chancery Lane Great met Chancery Lane Little. These four-storey-over-basement Georgian houses had fine stone doorcases with pillars and pediments. They were built on lands belonging to the Vicar's Choral of St Patrick's Cathedral, and in the early nineteenth century there was a racket court at the rear of number 37. Sadly, not a trace of a house remains in Chancery Lane today. The office block on Golden Lane, now the premises of the Woodchester Bank, occupies the site of some of the Chancery Lane houses.

Of particular interest is an illustration in *Shaw's New City Pictorial Directory* of a four-storey, Dutch gable-style house, described as 'the Lord Chancellor's Mansion; now in tenements'. This once magnificent house is shown with an elaborate stone doorcase, similar to one illustrated in the Georgian Society Records of 1910. The latter is a carved stone doorcase, whose segmental head is supported by a pair of elaborately carved ornamental scrolls. The tall doorway with its simple fanlight is typical of the very earliest years of the eighteenth century.

The Lord Chancellor's house adjoined the premises of Parkes & Company's ironmongery establishment at 25–27 Chancery Lane, which consisted of three houses. Parkes also had premises in the Coombe at this time. By the nineteenth century Chancery Lane had ceased to be a fashionable residence for lawyers and had instead developed a reputation for brassmongers and ironmongers. For instance, 30 Chancery Lane was occupied by Thomas Moffit, 'Wrought Iron Safe Manufacturer to the Bank of Ireland'. Moffit's label may still be discovered inside the doors of safes and strong boxes in old businesses in Dublin and elsewhere. Numbers 28–29 were occupied by William Curtis, Brass Founder and Gas Fitter, Pump and Water Closet Manufacturer.

A map of Chancery Lane in the Dublin City Archives shows other property leased from Dublin Corporation to Edward Slicer in 1722. The map, which probably dates from the early 1800s, suggests that the area was already

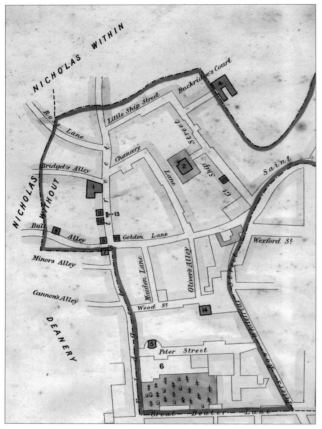

unfashionable as a residential district, as the rear of the houses contained a confusion of workshops, yards and sheds. This pattern is also confirmed by another map in the Longfield collection in the National Library, which shows Sherry's Court and Cummin's Court surrounded by a confusion of stables and kitchens, yards and small gardens. These various courts, which were so much a characteristic in Dublin in the eighteenth and nineteenth centuries, were approached from Bride Street through narrow, arched passageways that ran underneath the houses on the street. The map also shows a reasonably large house accessed by steps at the end of Sherry's Court.

Bride Street

Bride Street, or St Bridget's Street as it was called in Rocque's time, stretches southwards from Werburgh Street, past the back of St Patrick's Cathedral to Kevin Street. It was a residential street with its own parish church in the eighteenth century, and was then home to various industries in the nineteenth century. Bride Street suffered the indignity of being largely wiped out during the last

Above: A map of the defunct parish of St Bridget, which included Bride Street and stretched eastwards as far as South William Street.

Below: This map shows the rectangular plan of the now-vanished St Bridget's Church.

hundred years. A substantial piece of old Dublin disappeared in the 1890s when the Iveagh Trust redeveloped much of the tenement area between Patrick Street and Bride Street with housing and amenities for the poor. This included the creation of St Patrick's Park, adjacent to the cathedral.

Coupled with the complete eradication of every old house between Dublin Castle, Kevin Street and Patrick Street came the disappearance without trace of the Church and Parish of St Bride. This ancient parish lay just outside the city walls and incorporated a strange geographical area. As already mentioned, the church stood at the corner of Bridget's Alley on Bride Street, almost opposite Chancery Lane. The parish ran from here to the back of Dublin Castle, across to George's Street, including the present South City Markets, on to South William Street and even touched on Grafton Street. It ran back to Bishop Street in the south but skirted round the neighbouring Parish of St Peter, which included half of Stephen Street and most of the Aungier Street area. On the west the parish was bounded by the property of the Dean of St Patrick's Cathedral and the Parish of St Nicholas Without.

In 1660 Sir William Domville leased a block of land to the east of Bride Street from the Dean and Chapter of St Patrick's Cathedral. Sir Domville,

Left: Bride Street was the home of a famous bird market until recent times.

Below: The Aviary public house, which occupied the corner premises at Bride Street and Canon Street, has since completely disappeared.

who was the Attorney General at that time, constructed a dwelling house here that was surrounded by the orchards and gardens formerly belonging to the dean of the cathedral. Domville complained that he sustained large losses during the Civil War and that he had 'been indemnified about £1,000 by the waste and destruction of several buildings erected by said Gilbert Domville [his father] upon the premises which were all destroyed'.

St Bridget's, or Bride's, Church is known to have existed in the twelfth century and was amalgamated with the Church of St Michel Le Pole not long afterwards. Both churches were transferred from the jurisdiction of Christ Church Cathedral to that of St Patrick's Cathedral. In 1706 the Dean granted the ancient Church of St Michel Le Pole to be used as a schoolhouse but, interestingly, ordered that the round tower should be specifically preserved. A widows' almshouse stood adjacent to the national school and here, in the middle of the street, a new pair of stocks were erected in the year 1750 at a cost of £3.

St Bride's Church is depicted in an amateur sketch, made in about 1820 and preserved in the National Gallery of Ireland. It is shown as a simple rectangular building with a pair of arched east windows, above which, in the gable, was a public clock. The church had an internal

gallery not unlike St Werburgh's, and the organ, with its beautifully carved case, is in collection of the National Museum.

The parish derived an income from various properties which were let, including the Queen's Head Hotel in Bride Street, two houses in Great Ship Street, a house in Great Cuffe Street and a large house in Grafton Street which brought in £43 per annum. Other funds came from investments, including £6,000 worth of Grand Canal debentures, and donations, such as

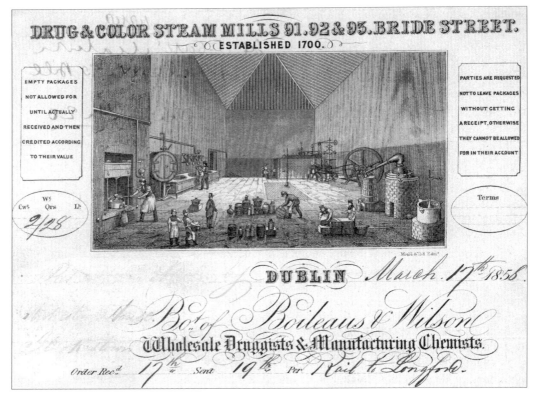

DRUG & COLOR STEAM MILLS 91.92 & 93.BRIDE STREET.
ESTABLISHED 1700.

EMPTY PACKAGES NOT ALLOWED FOR UNTIL ACTUALLY RECEIVED AND THEN CREDITED ACCORDING TO THEIR VALUE

PARTIES ARE REQUESTED NOT TO LEAVE PACKAGES WITHOUT GETTING A RECEIPT, OTHERWISE THEY CANNOT BE ALLOWED FOR IN THEIR ACCOUNT

Terms

DUBLIN *March. 17th 1856*

Bot of Boileaus & Wilson
Wholesale Druggists & Manufacturing Chemists.

Order Recd 17th Sent 19th Per Rail to Longford.

Above: This elaborate billhead from 1858 gives a rare view of a Victorian factory interior.

Below: Balusters from the oak staircase of number 36 Bride Street, now also demolished.

one of £300 from a Mr Bachelor. Fees for marriages amounted to £10/4/– and burials £17/6/–. All of these figures point to the financial difficulties the parish was facing in 1849. Even then, this once wealthy parish was in a state of decline. A map published in that year, complete with historical notes and remarks about the state of the parish, declares that, 'The full amount of Minister's money has not been paid for some time'. The map shows a thatched cottage in Great Ship Street, though this was probably long gone by 1849 when the map was printed. Photographs were taken by the Iveagh Trust of St Bride's Church before its demolition in 1899 to make way for the Trust's rebuilding projects. The new Edwardian street demanded a new identity, so the old name, Bride's Alley, was changed to the rather suburban sounding Bride Road.

The street directory for 1851 lists three bird cage makers in Bride Street in Flora Mitchell's treasured book *Vanishing Dublin*, she tells us that the birds were sold even in the 1960s in small wicker cages. A broad cross section of trades was represented in the street during the nineteenth century, including cabinet-makers, carvers and gilders, a pewterer and a tin plate worker. Numbers 10, 12 and 13 Bride Street were occupied by Loftus A Bryan's hardware and ironmongery warehouse. Bryan's sold a wide range of household goods and old-fashioned ranges are occasionally to be found bearing their nameplate. A bill of 1867 shows that they supplied a large country house with one dozen scavenger's brooms, one bell spring and bell, two dozen brass-headed nails, one draw-out china bell pull, copper wire, five dozen common cranks, eight brass cranks and seven house bells. These materials were used to install a system of servants' bells. In 1858, numbers 91–93 Bride Street were occupied by Boileau and Wilson, who advertised themselves as wholesale druggists and manufacturing chemists. The firm, which was established in 1700, manufactured and sold all the ingredients for producing paint and varnish, including white lead, linseed oil, drying oil, turpentine, dryers and pigments. Boileau and Wilson's drug and colour steam mills, beautifully illustrated on their billhead of 1858, show an impressive array of machines for grinding and mixing colours. Two hundredweight of best ground white lead cost 14 shillings, and four gallons of linseed oil cost 16 shillings and 4 pennies. A monument to the Boileau family is to be seen in St Werburgh's Church.

Above: A 1960s photograph which includes number 36 Bride Street (on the left). No old houses now survive in Bride Street.

One of the more important residences of Bride Street that has disappeared was that of George Dowdall at number 36, on the west side of Bride Street, backing on to Marsh's Library. Dowdall was a solicitor at the Court of the Exchequer, and the house, with its large, panelled rooms, was illustrated in the Georgian Society Records in the early 1900s. There was a fine staircase and compartmented plasterwork ceilings that date from the very early eighteenth century. The house, which measured five windows across and had a central doorcase, was illustrated in Flora Mitchell's *Vanishing Dublin*. She describes the staircase of number 36: 'a beautiful, wide, shallow oak staircase running up three sides of a spacious once panelled hall'. Her sketch of the east side of Bride Street shows a group of typical old Dublin houses with shops on the ground floor. A mother appears at an upstairs window and children are playing in the street – this is the Dublin of the 1960s.

Flora Mitchell's painting of Bride Street was done in 1963 and carries the note that the house was partially demolished. She records the existence of a pub called the Aviary, which stood at the corner of Bride Street and Canon Street. The pub was no doubt named in honour of the local bird market, held here every Sunday morning.

One of Dublin's most impressive early eighteenth-century houses, Molyneux House, stood on the corner of Bride Street and Peter Street. It was a wide, brick-fronted house, and its striking features included a bold

Above: Molyneux House was a
large detached mansion built
in 1711.
Below: An 1812 map showing
Peter Street, Molyneux House
and the amphitheatre. The
Adelaide Hospital was built on
the northern side of
Peter Street.

cornice and pediment, stone coigns and a handsome carved stone doorcase, which was approached from the street by a flight of steps. It was built in 1711 by Thomas Molyneux, an Army physician whose family had lived in the Liberties and become wealthy during the seventeenth century. Molyneux was born in 1661 and studied medicine in Leyden, the Netherlands, where he produced a study of herbs which is now among the records of the Botanic Gardens in Dublin. He became a distinguished doctor and was appointed Governor and Physician of Dr Steevens's Hospital.

The house was in some respects similar in style and size to the Mansion House in Dawson Street, which had been built a few years earlier. The windows of the house were unusual, being nearly flush with the façade. There was a finely carved coat of arms and a stone tablet, bearing an inscription, set in the broken pediment of the hall door. The tablet read: 'This house was erected in the year 1711 by Sir Thomas Molyneux, bart, descended from Sir Thomas Molyneux, Chancellor of the Exchequer in the

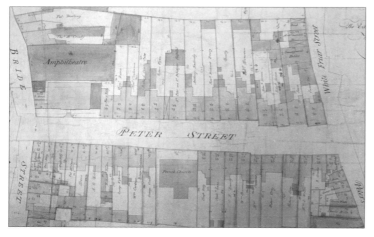

reign of Queen Elizabeth'. The house is recorded in the Georgian Society Records of 1910 and photographs show the wonderfully spacious staircase with its hand-carved balusters, brackets and newel post.

The Molyneux family occupied the house until the late 1770s when it came into the possession of an equestrian performer named Philip Astley. Astley erected a large amphitheatre behind the house, fronting onto Bride Street, and in it he arranged performances of musical pieces, dancing, tumbling and pantomimes, as well as providing entertainment with his own horsemanship. The theatre was opened in 1789 and is shown on a map of 1812 in the Dublin City Archives. The map also shows the French church in Peter Street, where today a plaque on the wall states that it was founded in 1711, and that the remains from the French Huguenot cemetery were removed and re-interred here in 1967.

Mr Astley's amphitheatre was apparently very successful for a number of years and was, for a while, considered to be 'the most fashionable place of entertainment in Dublin', according to the Georgian Society Records. It seems likely that it was Astley who had the walls of the drawing room in Molyneux House covered in old tapestries representing the story of Don Quixote. The *Georgian Society Records* state that there were large and spacious rooms in the house and that Astley used them for music practice and as dressing rooms, while the dining room was converted for use as a coffee house. The amphitheatre, which was entered from Bride Street, was equipped with a pit and gallery, though the theatre's boxes were entered via Molyneux House from Peter Street.

Astley sold his interest in the premises in 1809 and after a few unsuccessful years it eventually closed, becoming in 1815 an asylum for blind females. At this time the theatre was converted into a chapel. The asylum moved to Leeson Street in 1862, and Molyneux House was renamed Albert Hospital. In 1943 Molyneux House was demolished by Jacob's Biscuits in order to build garages on the site, although part of the chapel remains in the present office building, which was converted in 1974. The beautiful stone-carved coat of arms was rescued from the demolition and is now on display in the hall of the College of Physicians in Kildare Street. The site of Molyneux House is currently occupied by a warehouse.

New houses and apartments were built on Bride Street by Dublin Corporation in the 1970s and 1980s, and it is

Above: Interesting new houses, such as these built in the 1980s, were erected by Dublin Corporation in Bride Street.

Below: One of several ceramic roundels on the new houses, depicting a scene from Swift's *Gulliver's Travels*.

Above: A nineteenth-century impression of a high-ceilinged ward with a central stove in the Adelaide Hospital.

Below: The central Victorian blocks of the now-closed Adelaide Hospital have been incorporated into a new development.

generally held that the design and construction of these is far superior to those erected on private estates by speculative builders.

By the end of the eighteenth century Dublin had a fair number of hospitals. In 1839, when the Adelaide was founded, there was, in fact, already a small hospital in Peter Street, known as the Hospital of St Peter and St Bridget. This establishment was as much a private medical school as a hospital and in this it followed a long Dublin tradition. It later became the Ledwidge School of Anatomy, Medicine and Surgery, and was eventually taken over by the College of Surgeons. The fine Victorian premises of another medical institution, the Carmichael School, can still be seen at the corner of Aungier Street and Whitefriar Street, where it is now run as a hostel for tourists. The unusual Renaissance-style terracotta frontage of the Carmichael School was erected in 1879. It is recorded in David Mitchell's book *A Peculiar Place, a History of the Adelaide Hospital* that, during the building of a new wing to the Adelaide Hospital in 1968, workmen found an underground chamber, tightly packed with human bones. The bones had apparently come from the dissecting room of the Ledwidge School of Anatomy!

The Adelaide Hospital was established in Bride Street as 'a hospital for the exclusive use of Protestants', although it appears that this denominational bias was not strictly adhered to. There were, however, a significant number of poor Protestants in the city of Dublin in the nineteenth century, and the Adelaide Hospital was intended to cater for their needs, and thus it became known in the Liberties as the Protestant hospital. The hospital was named after Adelaide, the German wife of King William IV.

The hospital opened in Bride Street with only fourteen beds and room for expansion was clearly limited within the old house. In 1858 three houses were acquired in Peter Street, and the hospital was able to reopen with seventy-five beds. The nursing staff were organised by a Miss Bramwell, an English lady who had worked with Florence Nightingale in the Crimea. In 1861 Father John Spratt of Aungier Street crossed swords with his new neighbours in the Adelaide Hospital, objecting to the fact that 'although they admit Catholics as patients, yet no Catholic priest is allowed to enter the wards of that hospital', and he advised Catholics to keep away from it. Father Spratt had re-established the Carmelite Friars in Whitefriar Street and was the moving force behind many new Dublin charities. The Adelaide Hospital was built on land which had almost certainly belonged to the Whitefriars in medieval times. Even within the hospital there was dissension over the issue of admission of Catholics to the Dispensary, and in 1864 a vote by hospital subscribers ruled in favour of their admission.

In 1874 Lord and Lady Farnham of Cavan left a substantial legacy to the hospital to enable it to expand. Two years later the Madeleine Wing was added, following a donation in memory of Lady Madeleine Crichton. This was followed by the addition of a fever hospital and a new nurses' home during the 1880s. A nurse's uniform in the Adelaide Hospital consisted of three dresses (all six inches from the ground), fourteen aprons, twelve collars, twelve pairs of cuffs, six belts and six Sister Dora caps. In 1889 their day began with breakfast at 6.30am and ended at bedtime at 10.30pm. These were their hours for four days of the week, while on the other three they finished at 3pm. During training nurses received no salary and had to pay for their own uniforms. In 1894, numbers 28–30 Peter Street, which incorporated the old Ledwidge School, were brought into use by the hospital.

Another chapter in Dublin's history closed in 1999 when most of the buildings of the old Adelaide Hospital were demolished. The buildings in question were not of any great architectural interest and the two older portions of the hospital have been retained for conversion into apartments.

Below: Speed's map (1610) shows the close proximity of three ancient churches.

Below bottom: The substantial St Peter's Church, which was once a landmark in Aungier Street.

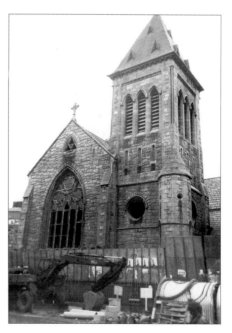

Peter Street

Peter Street, or more correctly St Peter's Street, was so named because it led from Bride Street to the ancient church of St Peter, which is first recorded in the fourteenth century. With the expansion of Dublin in the late seventeenth century, a new church was built on the site in 1685. The church was enlarged in 1773 and was then completely rebuilt in 1867. The Victorian church, a substantial building of cut stone, was demolished in 1982 by the YMCA, who redeveloped the site with a sports facility and meeting rooms. Though the Gothic-style church was of no extraordinary architectural interest, it was well built and could have been converted to the requirements of the YMCA. Few people looked on old buildings in that light in the early 1980s and the spacious cross-planned church was levelled. Meanwhile, the YMCA had vacated their premises in Lower Abbey Street, the famous Metropolitan Hall, which was sold to the Irish Life Insurance Company and was subsequently demolished. In one move two significant public buildings disappeared and while the YMCA was the catalyst for this, their intentions were simply to provide better facilities for their members and a hostel for visitors.

In 1980 the value of the St Peter's Church site in Aungier Street was put at £175,000, a figure which included the exhumation of bodies and the preparation of the site. The completion of the new Aungier Street buildings in the late 1980s was one of the first new developments in the street since the nineteenth century and gave encouragement to a number of other new shops and apartments in the immediate area. Part of their own plan included the erection of an office building with a frontage on Aungier Street, the rents from which would help to fund the YMCA development. By 1982 St Peter's Church, which was a listed building, had been vacant for several years and had been the victim of vandalism. According to Frank McDonald, writing in the *Irish Times* at that time, over half of the 44,000-square-foot building which the YMCA hoped to erect would consist of a four-storey office block.

The narrow street which runs between the YMCA and the present Dublin Institute of Technology is called Peter's Row, and here in 1851 stood the substantial premises of Thomas Palmer and Sons, coach-makers. These premises were rented by William Beale Jacob in the following year,

Above: The imposing granite entrance to the offices of Jacob's Biscuit Factory in Peter Street.

Below: A malicious fire brought about the ultimate destruction of Jacob's. The granite-built ground floor was incorporated into the new building of the Dublin Institute of Technology (DIT).

GENERAL VIEW OF WORKS
BISHOP ST., PETER'S ROW & PETER ST.
OFFICES:- 28 to 31. Bishop St. ·

LIVERPOOL OFFICES & WAREHOUSES
286 to 294 Scotland Road

MANCHESTER WAREHOUSES - 102 George St. Hulme
SALE ROOM 21 Fennel St

and so was established what would become one of Dublin's largest industrial concerns in the late nineteenth century, Jacob's Biscuit Factory. The Jacobs had already established a good business in baking ships' biscuits in Waterford. The Dublin business prospered and in the 1860s fellow Quaker William Frederick Bewley became a partner in the firm. In 1880 the biscuit factory was completely rebuilt following a fire which destroyed their old premises and machinery. The events were recorded in Jacob's book of dates, a fascinating volume, which was handed down from generation to generation. The 1880 fire began at the Bishop Street side of the bakery and quickly spread across the roofs so that the whole sky was ablaze. A detachment of the Seventy-seventh Foot from Ship Street Barracks in Dublin Castle was brought in to cordon off the area and a bystander commented that the flames reflected on their brass buttons and scarlet tunics.

By 1884 Jacob's was back in full production and introduced to Ireland for the first time the famous cream cracker! The business continued to expand, eventually taking in the entire block between Bride Street, Bishop Street and Peter Street. The former iron foundry of Tonge and Taggart in Bishop Street was acquired to extend the bakehouse and build a new power house. The new 1880s factory consisted of a massive five-storey structure on Peter's Row, of which only the granite arcade on the ground floor now survives.

The red-brick industrial buildings and offices erected by W & R Jacob in the 1880s were typical of their time. The main offices in Bishop Street were entered through a substantial granite doorway, flanked on either side by brick-arched windows. A large chimney occupied the centre of the site and there was a tower containing a reservoir of water for the factory. The huge site, covering some eighteen acres, became one of the largest industrial concerns in late nineteenth-century Dublin, coming second only to Guinness's. Apart from the baking hall and the packaging section,

Above: This illustration of Jacob's entire factory shows the massive extent of their premises. Illustrations such as this were often used on their packaging as a form of advertising.

Below: A coal-hole cover from the Bishop Street foundry of Tonge and Taggart.

Right: This trade card from Stephens' coach factory in Bishop Street represents just one of the prominent trades in the district.

Below: This unusual building in Aungier Street, which was once a medical school and later a cork factory, is now a hostel.

the complex included a substation, an engineers' shop, a carpenters' shop and a printing department which prepared all labels, posters, cartons, wrappers, cards, price lists and brochures. The tin-making department remained important up until the 1960s, and it is often forgotten that many of the large biscuit tins were actually returned as empties and were then steam cleaned and sterilised in the factory before being used again.

By 1905 Jacob's had offices in Manchester and Liverpool as well and their magnificent Dublin premises were illustrated in a coloured lithograph. Horse-drawn wagons are seen outside the arcaded openings on Peter Street, where they were prepared for making deliveries. In the 1960s, Jacob's electric delivery vans were a familiar site around the city.

In 1977 Jacob's moved their entire operation to Tallaght and the huge Bishop Street site became the subject of regular vandalism and arson attacks. Part of the site was acquired by the Office of Public Works for use as a government stationery store. These buildings, the most modern on the site and were no architectural beauties, were ultimately destined to become the new premises of the Public Records Office of Ireland. The rest of the site lay derelict for nearly ten years, with a major fire in 1987 bringing about the demolition of the fine 1880s building in Peter's Row.

CHAPTER SEVEN

Aungier Street to
South William Street

Aungier Street

Aungier Street, which dates from the second half of the seventeenth century, is named after Sir Francis Aungier. The buildings of Aungier Street, for so long a neglected thoroughfare, were completely disregarded until 1996 when four houses were discovered to contain their original seventeenth-century features. One of these houses, now fully restored and containing a coffee shop known as the Staircase, was about to be demolished when the Dublin Civic Trust intervened and Dublin Corporation acquired what was

Left: Aungier Street was laid out in the seventeenth century as a residential street.

then discovered to be one of the oldest surviving houses in the city. It dates from 1666. The Dublin Civic Trust arranged for the conservation of the remarkable staircase and the stabilisation of the structure of the building. The property was then sold on to a sensitive developer who has created a small bed-and-breakfast business in the building, whilst preserving the historic features. When so much of the fabric of Dublin's old streets has been lost, this was an excellent demonstration of how a partnership of public bodies and individuals could save a rare example of a seventeenth-century Dublin house.

The Whitefriars Church in Aungier Street is a foundation of the Carmelite Order, whose remarkable history stretches back to 1280, the year in which the Priory of St Mary was founded. The priory was established on land given by Sir Robert Bagot, a prominent figure in medieval Dublin whose name is recorded in Baggot Street, and consisted of an extensive religious establishment including a residence, houses, lands, orchards and a church. During the Reformation in 1539, all of this was confiscated by the English Crown, as part of the Dissolution of the Monasteries. After an absence of more than two centuries the Carmelites, or 'White Friars', returned to this part of Dublin and eventually re-established themselves in a small street off Aungier Street, which became known as Whitefriar Street. It was not until 1825 that Father John Spratt, a Carmelite friar, commenced building a new church on the present site.

George Papworth designed the original church, but it was greatly enlarged in 1856, and then trebled in size in 1868. The 1825 Whitefriars Church was entered from what is now the rear, in Whitefriars Street, and it consisted of a long, thin, rectangular structure without aisles. It was not until 1914 that the present entrance to the church on Aungier Street was built, with its unusual two-storey Italianate façade. Even then the altar remained located at the east end of the church and it was only in 1954 that this was moved to its present position at the opposite end. Whitefriars is now a large church and the nave's thin columns create a strange sense of lightness, supporting as they do outsized capitals with wide arches above. The vaulted plastered ceiling gives the impression of an Italian Byzantine or Romanesque church. The present altar is covered by a large domed *baldacchino*, supported by fluted marble columns.

Above top: Whitefriars Church, shown here with its western entrance (now closed), was built in 1825 close to the site of the medieval mother house.

Above: The beautifully sculpted statue Our Lady of Dublin in Whitefriars Church.

Father Spratt was a humanitarian and a most interesting figure in the life of Dublin in the early nineteenth century. He was Honorary Secretary to the Sick and Indigent Roomkeepers' Society and he helped to found many institutions to help the homeless and poor in Dublin. He was also instrumental in establishing a school in nearby Longford Street in 1822. It is said that the original deeds, dating from 1402 and establishing White

Left: This nineteenth-century drawing shows number 12 Aungier Street, the birthplace of composer Thomas Moore (1779–1852). The house, with its original 'Dutch Billy' gable, was probably of early eighteenth-century date.

Below: Rocque's map shows the street and church planned by Sir Francis Aungier in the late seventeenth century.

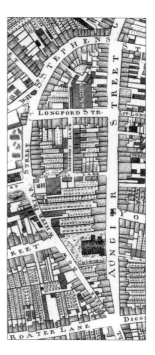

Friars in Aungier Street, survive, but unfortunately their whereabouts remain a mystery. One of the chief treasures of this church is the medieval statue known as Our Lady of Dublin. Once again it was Father Spratt who, whilst walking in Capel Street one day in 1824, saw the sculpted, whitewashed figure in a second-hand shop. Father Spratt bought the life-sized statue and had it cleaned, restored and erected in the Whitefriars Church. The statue is not unlike the sixteenth-century sculptures of the Henry VII Chapel at Westminster, and is the only surviving example of such sculpture in Dublin. It is thought that it may have come from St Mary's Cistercian Abbey, north of the Liffey, having been discarded after the Reformation and probably used as a pig trough in a nearby yard. The back of the timber statue is completely hollowed out. Our Lady of Dublin, as it is called, is a very beautiful sculpture. The drapery is extremely

Above: A photograph of York Street, taken in the 1960s, shows the scale and grandeur of the once intact eighteenth-century street.

Below: An elaborate eighteenth-century ceiling in Aungier Street. Surprisingly good craftsmanship was often to be found behind the façades of old houses in the area.

accomplished, the hair and face serene and she is holding the infant Jesus in her arms. In 1915 the statue was made the centrepiece of a beautiful shrine, with a gold mosaic background and an elaborate marble altar.

Numbers 63–65 Aungier Street also belong to the Carmelites and exhibit three of the most intact Victorian shopfronts remaining in the city. The shopfronts are decorated with carved brackets, a heavy cornice and bold fascia board. One of the premises is used as a charity shop, another is used by the Carmelite Travel Agency and the third is empty.

Across the street at number 12 is a pub currently known as 'JJ's', which bears a plaque that records the fact that Thomas Moore was born here in 1779. An early drawing that survives in the National Gallery shows that it was once a gabled house. However, the present public house was largely rebuilt.

Aungier Street and its surrounding district have lived through several incarnations as the fate of the area changed through the centuries. While Temple Bar and Dame Street developed in a more or less haphazard manner in the seventeenth century, Aungier Street would appear to have been planned by the owner of the estate, Sir Francis Aungier, who started to build here after 1660. The Aungiers were an important family who had already erected a mansion house somewhere near the site of Whitefriar's Monastery, in the early seventeenth century. Nuala Burke, in an article in *Geography Ireland*, has described the development of the Aungier estate and noted that in the early seventeenth century the house was described as a large residence with fourteen hearths. In 1616 it was occupied by Alderman Robert Ball.

The Monastery of Whitefriars was seized by the Crown in 1541, during the Reformation, and is recorded as having been demolished in that year. Later, the property was acquired by the Aungier family who added to it the old medieval parish church and graveyard of St Peter which was bordered by today's Stephen's Street, and other lands that ran as far as St Stephen's Green and Cuffe Street. The ancient Church of St Peter was situated on a small hill and indeed there is still a slight slope in Stephen's Street Upper. Sir Francis Aungier acquired the title of Earl of Longford and this name still exists in today's half-vacant Longford Street. Sir Francis Aungier, who was Master of Ordnance, was also a friend of, and distantly related to, the Duke of Ormonde, Ireland's influential Lord Lieutenant from the 1660s to 1680s.

Above: The heavy construction of the seventeenth-century timber floors at number 21 Aungier Street.

Below and below bottom: These two pictures show the same building, number 21 Aungier Street, before and after restoration, during which an ugly frontage was returned to its former elegance.

The new Aungier Street was opened in 1661 and was seventy feet in width. It was then considered to be the widest street in the city (or more correctly in the suburbs, as it was then outside the city proper). Most contemporary streets were only twenty or thirty feet wide, and some of the early medieval streets were even as narrow as twelve or fourteen feet in width. Twelve years later, in 1673, Aungier opened up York Street, which connected Aungier Street to St Stephen's Green.

Aungier was anxious to attract a wealthy and titled clientele to his area, and for a short time he succeeded in doing so. For example, the Bishop of Kilmore leased a large site with a 129-foot frontage onto Aungier Street and built himself a substantial house. It was this house that was eventually leased by Aungier's heir, Michael Cuffe, to Jacob Poole, the clothier who we will discuss in connection with Fumbally Lane. Poole in turn leased it to David Digges La Touche, a merchant. Other lanes were straightened and improved. Goat Alley became Digges Lane, after the aforementioned merchant, who in the eighteenth century developed the garden of an earlier house. The curiously named Beaux Lane was perhaps corrupted into Elbow Lane and subsequently Bow Lane, while Love Lane eventually became Mercer's Street.

Another resident of Aungier Street was Sir Robert Reading who built a mansion for himself, and went on to develop a further two houses in nearby York Street.

The house rescued by the Civic Trust at 21 Aungier Street did not at first look at all promising, as the exterior was rendered in shabby grey cement and the windows were blocked up. Inside most of the floors were missing and there was only a half-rotten flat roof to keep the rain out. Miraculously, within all of this, the original seventeenth-century staircase,

Above: A late seventeenth-century staircase in number 68 Aungier Street.

Below: Details from a schedule of fittings for the front room of an eighteenth-century house in Aungier Street.

Opposite top and middle: Two of the traditional shops that remain on Aungier Street – Kavanagh's sweetshop with its display of old sweet jars, and Coyle's, probably the only gents' hat shop left in Dublin.

Opposite bottom: Gabled houses in Longford Street.

with its wide handrail and chunky banisters, survived. The original central chimney stack, a unique feature of large houses of the 1660s, also survived and has been incorporated into the new structure. As the interior was opened up much of the original timber-framed structure became visible. The restoration work on the building was completed by Fionn MacCumhaill, the owner of many other converted old properties in Dublin.

Sir Francis Aungier borrowed heavily to develop his new estate and he also donated a site for the building of a new St Peter's Church in 1680. This church was finished five years later, and combined the old parishes of St Stephen, St Peter and St Kevin. The site was later occupied by the Victorian St Peter's Church, which was demolished in 1982. It is interesting to note that in the earlier years of the Aungier estate there was no industrial activity there, unlike the Earl of Meath's estate, which was full of breweries and tanneries.

In the 1660s sites on Aungier Street were leased out to various developers, who were usually artisans – such as builders, carpenters, plasterers or roofers. It is recorded that John Linegar, a slater, built eight houses in Aungier Street during the 1660s. John Herne, a bricklayer, built a house, 'three storeys high beside garrets and cellars', and by 1682 it was leased to Henry Mockler, an innkeeper. By 1667 other residents of Aungier Street included Sir Henry Ingoldsby, the Earl of Donegal, Robert Ware and the Countess of Mount Alexander, whose houses were valued at £50 each.

By the early eighteenth century, Dublin was changing again, with new houses being built in more pleasant areas such as St Stephen's Green and Dawson Street. As the gentry began to move out of the houses of the Aungier estate, they were replaced by merchants, tradesmen, the lower gentry and army officers. Many of the large plots, which had once been taken up with detached houses and their gardens, were divided up.

In the early eighteenth century the new occupant of the Earl of Rosse's townhouse in Aungier Street was William Fielding, a coach-maker. Another

In the Street Parlour one Marble Chimney Piece, one Stove Grate, and Two Brass Locks —

smaller house, formerly bearing the 'Sign of the White Swan', was leased to Ambrose Leet, a weaver, while a large stone house at the corner of Stephen's Street was leased at this time to a weaver called Richard Delaney, who sublet it to a cabinet-maker. Number 20 was once occupied by the noted eighteenth-century sculptor John Van Nost, and by the brass founder William King. King created the brasswork of the stairs at Castletown House, Celbridge.

In an interesting lease of a house in Aungier Street, made in 1788, we find a schedule of fittings that included:

> ... in the street kitchen one grate and one dresser, in the back kitchen one grate and some pantry shelves, in the street parlour one marble chimney piece, one stove grate and two brass locks, in the back parlour one marble chimney piece and one stove grate, and one brass lock, in the dining room one marble chimney piece one stove grate and two brass locks, in the bed chamber one wooden chimney piece and one grate, in the two pair of stairs room two wooden chimney pieces and two grates, in the garret one grate.

This lease was for a house on the east side of Aungier Street, with a frontage of eighteen feet six inches. It was being leased by Richard Eaton to Eleanor Mills, a widow, for thirty years.

Shortly after the discovery of the seventeenth-century staircase at 21 Aungier Street, several other houses in the street were examined and were found to have similar features. The old joists of the floors of Kavanagh's sweet shop, at number 10, have recently been exposed, showing heavy, square-profile timbers, which are typical of seventeenth-century construction.

As was the fashion of the early years of the eighteenth century, many of the new houses that were erected in this area were of the Dutch-gable type. A pair of such houses stood in Longford Street Great and remained intact until the 1950s, when a newspaper article announced that they were going to be preserved as the last remaining examples of their type in the city. Unfortunately they were demolished soon after that and the only trace of early houses now remaining in this street

is part of a Gibbs-style stone doorcase, which lies embedded in a half-demolished brick wall. Beside this doorway is the remains of a stone arch, which once led to the back of houses on Stephen Street and once gave access to the side of a large theatre that is shown on Rocque's map.

The theatre, which was partly situated on the site of St Peter's Churchyard, was opened in 1733 and was reputedly designed by Sir Edward Lovett Pearce. It faced Longford Street and had a large stone portico, consisting of eight Tuscan columns and a pediment. The theatre does not appear to have been very successful as it closed in 1746 and houses were later built on the site. A sale of the Portland-stone portico and other building materials took place in 1767 and was advertised in *Sleator's Public Gazette*.

A late eighteenth-century map of the houses on the north side of Stephen's Street (in the Longfield collection in the National Library) shows several paired Georgian houses which backed onto Dublin Castle. There was a half bow- or quadrant-shaped window on the return of one of the houses, a feature that was once commonplace on Dublin buildings. The house adjoining it was recorded as 'Mr Clegg's holding', and it is astonishing to note that several generations of shoemakers named Clegg occupied these premises for almost 200 years, until 1998, when they moved to Rathmines. This entire block, including the old houses of Stephen's Street and other premises on George's Street, is the subject of a planned development by Dunnes Stores, whose remarkably successful supermarket business actually originated in Stephen Street. It

Above top: Fanagan's, the undertaker's, beside the present YMCA.

Above: A staircase ceiling lantern from the eighteenth-century Leitrim House in Stephen Street.

Opposite top: Mercer's Hospital, founded in the early eighteenth century and closed in 1983.

Opposite bottom: Curved Stephen's Street, once noted for its toolmakers and saw sharpeners, was also the home of Dunlop's works, the makers of the world's first pneumatic tyre.

would indeed be a noble gesture on the part of Dunnes Stores if they were to give back to the City of Dublin one short street of restored buildings, instead of a bland reproduction.

John Speed's map of Dublin shows 'St Steven's Church', at the eastern end of Stephen Street, lying directly adjacent to St Peter's Church and graveyard. In 1610 these two churches were shown on the extremity of the suburbs of Dublin, with nothing but fields beyond them. Stephen Street was connected by George's Lane to Dame Street. St Stephen's Church and the Leper Hospital were reputedly founded in the thirteenth century.

Mary Mercer, the daughter of an English doctor who had studied medicine in Trinity College, founded a home for poor girls on this church site. A lease dated 1724 confirms that the old St Steven's Church was leased to her for the purpose of building a hospital. The hospital, containing ten beds, was opened in 1734, but it appears to have been rebuilt in 1756 when Parliament gave a grant of £500. The old hospital building whose façade may

be seen at the centre of the present Mercer's Clinic dates from this period. It was a three-storey building, four bays in width, to which a porch was later added.

In 1789 the College of Surgeons acquired a house in Mercer's Street, which was eventually incorporated into the hospital when the teaching of surgery and anatomy began there. The Mercer's Street façade was extensively remodelled in the nineteenth century and a handsome stone clock tower was added at that time.

By the middle of the nineteenth century Aungier Street encompassed a broad cross section of trades, including a number of window blind manufacturers and coach-builders, but no one trade or business character-ised the street. The premises of William Fanagan, undertakers, occupied the house directly adjacent to St Peter's Church. It is an eighteenth-century house which still retains some interesting features, such as a fine plasterwork ceiling at first floor level.

Great George's Street South

Great George's Street South, as it is correctly called, is an important and busy thoroughfare today, linking the southern districts of Camden Street, Rathmines and

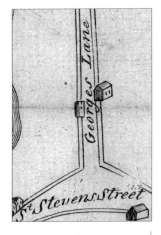

Above: Speed's map, showing George's Lane before it was built up with houses.

Below right: An 1879 photograph of the houses on Great George's Street South that were cleared to make way for the South City Markets.

Below: A docket from the calico department of Pim's in Great George's Street South.

Opposite top: A shopfront and footpath on Great George's Street South in 1879.

Opposite bottom: By the late nineteenth century Pim's had become one of the largest department stores in Dublin. It was demolished c.1970.

Ranelagh, to the city centre. George's Street, as it is commonly called, takes a gentle curve between Dame Street and Stephen's Street, and Speed's map shows that it was an established route as early as 1610.

In the eighteenth century George's Lane, as it was then known, was made up of many old houses of varying width and proportions. Those on the west side backed onto the gardens, artillery ground and stables of Dublin Castle. On the east side the street, which widened at the point where the present South City Market stands, was joined by Fade Street, Joseph's Lane and Exchequer Street. Exchequer Street was simply called Chequer Street in the eighteenth century. It was Joseph Fade, a successful Quaker banker, who built the houses on Fade Street and developed Joseph's Lane, naming them both after himself. Eighteenth-century George's Lane, or George's Street, was not a fashionable district, but it was a prosperous one, occupied by many artisans, such as felt-makers, bookbinders and clock-makers.

In 1780, 11 George's Lane was the site of Patrick Sweetman's Sugar House. He received more than £4000 from the Wide Streets Commissioners at about this time, when they acquired his property in order to widen the street. Various tradesmen, including a brazier, a plumber, a sugar baker and an iron founder, gave evidence as to the value of Mr Sweetman's molten pots, cisterns, lead syrup boxes, copper pans, cooling boxes and other utensils.

Today Great George's Street South is dominated by the massive Gothic-style South City Markets, which was begun in the late 1870s. This large Victorian building occupies the site bordered by Fade Street, Drury Street, Exchequer Street and George's Street.

In the nineteenth century George's Street boasted one of Dublin's first

and largest department stores: Pim Brothers'. Even by 1850 the Quaker Pim brothers, who were already prominent businessmen in Dublin, had acquired an entire row of houses, 75–83 Great George's Street South, and were then described as wholesale and retail woollen and linen drapers, hosiers, silk merchants, haberdashers and ribbon and fringe manufacturers.

By the 1870s Pims' premises had extended from the corner of Dame Lane all the way up George's Street and comprised a building twenty-five windows in length and five storeys in height. Their wares were displayed in a continuous run of ground-floor windows stretching the length of the street, and their billhead shows that they also had an extensive factory at Greenmount and large paper stores in South William Street. Pims' remained in business in George's Street for almost another 100 years, before the property was sold in 1969. It was then demolished and replaced by an office block of supreme dullness.

Another name that was to become very familiar in the line of builders, providers and hardware was that of Thomas Dockrell, who was based at 68 George's Street. Dockrell's had a large store and timber yard in Golden Lane nearby, and in the Victorian period they specialised in plate, crown and sheet glass, glaziers' diamonds, cement, plaster of Paris, paints, oils and colours, paper hangings and builders' ironmongery.

At this time there were several Wesleyan Methodist chapels in the George's Street area. These included the primitive Wesleyan Methodist Chapel at 63 Great George's Street South, a Methodist almshouse for aged widows at 15 Whitefriar Street and a Methodist tabernacle at the corner of Longford Street Little and Aungier Street. The Methodist church known as George's Hall survives to this day and its treble-

Above: The manager of Dockrell's in his office in 1895.

Below: An 1895 photograph of Dockrell's in Great George's Street South.

arched Gothic window overlooks Dublin Castle garden.

A great many well-known businesses have at one time or another occupied George's Street, including Findlater's and Woolworth's. It is often forgotten that Bewley's opened their first shop at number 13 South Great George's Street in the early 1870s. This shop, which became the first of three Bewley's Oriental Cafés, closed as recently as 1998. Joshua Bewley, as we have already seen, established his tea business in the 1840s in Sycamore Alley. The George's Street café was followed two years later by another café in Westmoreland Street.

Another business, occupying one of the last eighteenth-century houses in the street, is the pub known as the Long Hall. This building has a distinctive Georgian front with Victorian stucco embellishments, while the interior has remained virtually unchanged since the nineteenth century.

Whyte & Sons, cut-glass and china merchants, occupied a fine corner premises at the south end of the South City Markets. Whyte's business originated at 3–4 Marlborough Street.

A most historic event took place in George's Lane in 1745 when Bartholomew Mosse, the founder of the first ever maternity hospital in Ireland or Britain, opened his Lying-in Hospital there. Mosse leased a house that had previously been used by a celebrated rope-dancer named Madam Violante. He converted the house, which early engravings show was attached to a large courtyard, into a twenty-four-bed hospital. Here he accommodated the poor women of Dublin and provided a level of dignity and comfort which was hitherto unknown. A contemporary observer noted:

> The misery of the poor women of the city of Dublin, at the time of the lying-in, would scarcely be conceived by anyone who had not been an eye witness to their wretched circumstances; that their lodgings were generally in cold garrets open to every wind, or in damp cellars, subject to floods from excessive rains; destitute of attendance, medicine and often of proper food, by which hundreds perished with their little infants.

Mosse continued to run the hospital here in George's Street for almost twelve years, while at the same time he campaigned and raised funds to build an impressive new hospital across the city at Parnell Square, later to be known as the Rotunda. Four thousand and forty-nine children were born in Dr Mosse's Hospital in George's Lane. Ian Campbell Ross, in his *History of the Dublin Lying-in Hospital*, suggests that the hospital's first home lay nearly opposite Fade Street at 59 George's Lane, backing on to Dublin Castle.

Above: Bewley's shopfront on George's Street, refurbished in the 1980s and now closed.

Below: An 1890s Bewley's coffee tin (right), with instructions on how to make good coffee (left).

Following the completion of the Rotunda, the old hospital opposite Fade Street was converted to use as a 'lock hospital', which accommodated those with infectious diseases. Gilbert tells us that the house stood behind the street and was approached by a narrow passageway. It contained twelve rooms with various wards and closets for the nurses.

A disturbing description by the Reverend James Whitelaw, recorded in the 1790s, shows how some of the properties originally built by Joseph Fade in the early eighteenth century had fallen into ruin and were housing destitute families in quite inhumane conditions. Whitelaw was carrying out a census of the population and entered a 'ruinous' house in Joseph's Lane, near Castle Market, when he was 'interrupted in my progress, by an inundation of putrid blood, alive with maggots, which had from an adjacent slaughter yard, burst the backdoor'. Upstairs he found water pouring through the roof and in the garret the entire family of one poor shoemaker. The house contained a total of thirty-seven persons.

In 1876 a group of prominent businessmen from the George's Street area succeeded in getting an Act of Parliament passed that would allow them to develop a south city market. The South City Market Company was established, and two of

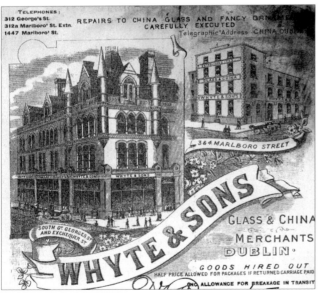

its main promoters were Pim and Dockrell, who already had the largest business interests in the street. In the clearance of the entire block, the old Castle Market and Joseph's Lane were swept away, along with a great number of old slaughterhouses and dwellings that had been described as unfit for human habitation.

The imposing new market building was opened in 1881 and incorporated a large, glass-covered market area. It was not a particularly successful commercial venture and some have suggested that there was resentment on the part of the citizens of Dublin because it was designed by English architects and built by English contractors.

The market was somewhat modified after a serious fire in 1892. In about 1970 proposals were put forward for the demolition of the entire market building and its redevelopment as offices. Fortunately these came to nothing. The central arcade experienced a commercial revival during the 1990s and is now home to some of the small businesses that originated in places like Temple Bar. The building is a remarkable Gothic extravaganza of the Victorian period, with deep-pitched roofs, decorative turrets and a grand Gothic entrance. Shops were incorporated all around the outside of the building at ground-floor level and most of these are still thriving today. Like the rest of George's Street and indeed most of the city east of Dublin Castle, Joseph Fade's lands were originally held under lease from the City of Dublin, in this case for £13 per annum.

As early as 1732 we find Joseph Fade leasing a plot to the Reverend John Daniel for

Above top: Dr Mosse's Lying-in Hospital on Great George's Street South, the first of its kind in Dublin.

Above: The elegant glass and china showrooms of Whyte & Sons.

the building of a house. Daniel sublet the property in 1747 to Richard Jones, a coach-maker. A yearly rent and a ground rent were payable to Joseph Fade, 'clear of all taxes including taxes, cesses, subsidies, assessments, military money, chimney and hearth tax, lamp money, etc, etc'. This house was joined on the south by another plot let by Fade to a carpenter named George Stuart, and had an eighteen-and-a-half-foot frontage onto George's Lane.

A deed concerning 84 Great George's Street South, premises on the west side of the street belonging to Robert Fanning, cabinetmaker, quoted an earlier lease from the Wide Streets Commissioners, which stated that a seven-foot pavement of mountain granite was to be constructed in front of the house. The deed, which dates from 1856, also mentions that number 83, the neighbouring property, was lately in the possession of officers of her majesty's ordinance (who were connected to Dublin Castle), and was now owned by Messrs Pim & Co.

Dockrell's premises occupied a large group of buildings standing between George's Street, Drury Lane, Lower Stephen's Street and Fade Street. The company had established an excellent reputation for the decoration and repair of private houses and businesses, and specialised in painting and decorating.

In 1800 the Wide Streets Commissioners surveyed all of the properties on the west side of George's Street with a view to improving the setting of Dublin Castle and regulating the street line. It would appear that many of the houses were rebuilt and that a lane, which ran between the stables of Dublin Castle and the houses, was provided to give access to the rear yards. Some of the houses on the west side of the street were acquired in 1798 to accommodate soldiers, who continued to use the buildings until the 1850s. A small gate, now blocked up, led to the 'informers' steps', which gave access to the old RIC yard in Dublin Castle.

A map from the 1850s in the Dublin City Archives shows 'intended warehouses' backing onto the wall of Dublin Castle. Various old photographs from 1879 show the typical 1730s houses, which had been erected on Fade's property. They were gable-fronted and the interiors were probably panelled throughout.

Gilbert tells us that the name George's Street or George's Lane originated from the presence of an early church, dedicated to St George, which stood in the vicinity. Richard Stanyhurst, writing in 1586, records that St George's Church had recently been demolished. Sir William Petty, the seventeenth-century inventor and author, lived in George's Lane. Petty experimented in shipbuilding and designed a type of early catamaran, which he tested in Dublin Bay.

Above top: Great George's Street South, a busy area by day and night, is dominated by the South City Markets.

Above: Castle Market, in a photograph from 1879. It was replaced by the South City Markets.

Exchequer Street / St Andrew's Church

The name Exchequer, or Chequer, Lane is derived from the presence of the old Exchequer on this site. It originally included the whole street as far as Grafton Street, but in the nineteenth century the name of the lower half of this street was changed to Wicklow Street.

The first serious development in this area seems to have occurred in the late seventeenth century with the building of the new St Andrew's

Right: The Central Hotel on
Exchequer Street.
Below: The International Bar at
the corner of Wicklow Street
and Andrew Street.

Church, the site of which is now occupied by a Victorian church and is
successfully used as the tourist information centre in St Andrew's Street.
In 1695 we learn that a plot of ground on the corner of Exchequer Street
and Clarendon Street was leased to William Digges, who it seems laid it out
for building five houses.

The pattern of development in Exchequer Street and Grafton Street
appear to have been similar. Building leases, which were granted in the
closing years of the seventeenth century, ran for ninety-nine years, so that
by 1798 the leases of many properties had reverted to the landlords and
presented an opportunity for rebuilding. These streets were largely rebuilt
in the early nineteenth century and this is the reason who so very few
eighteenth-century houses have survived in this district.

In about 1900, when the leases expired again, much of Wicklow Street
and Exchequer Street was completely rebuilt once more,
leaving us with today's predominantly Edwardian shops and
office buildings. An old photograph of Exchequer Street, taken
in about 1879, shows a now completely vanished streetscape of
Georgian-style brick houses with old-world shopfronts, all
probably dating from the early nineteenth century. The street
itself was cobbled and the pavement laid with granite slabs. The
south side of Exchequer Street, including the corner of South
William Street and what is now Wicklow Street, was redeveloped in 1803 by a Mr Drury Jones, whose ten properties were
leased out. Across the street two holdings of land, which had
been assigned to William Williams in 1671 and included the site
of St Andrew's Church, were built up and subsequently

redeveloped in a similar way. However, some early houses do survive in this block, for example the three houses adjoining St Andrew's churchyard, one of which houses Café Rouge.

The stretch of St Andrew's Street leading up to the junction with South William Street was originally called Hog Hill. Some of the land, including that on which Mr Jones built his houses in Exchequer Street, was originally granted to Thomas Pemberton in 1643. To the west of Williams's property holding in Hog Hill stood the old Trinity Hall, already mentioned as a residence for Trinity academics and students. The gardens of Trinity Hall stretched back to Exchequer Street and were eventually developed as well.

In more recent times the site of Trinity Hall will be better remembered as the Moira Hotel, a small establishment that was demolished in the late 1970s. The site is today occupied by the present Trinity Street multi-storey car park, with its various shops and a very popular café at street level. The present Andrew's Lane Theatre and adjoining laneway also stand on the site of the original gardens belonging to the seventeenth-century Trinity Hall.

The late nineteenth- or early twentieth-century rebuilding of Exchequer Street and much of Wicklow Street involved an increase in height for most of the buildings. Some of the old three-storey buildings became tall four-storey, red-brick-fronted buildings, many of them ornamented with terracotta window mullions or even urns and gables at the roofline. The result is one of Dublin's most intact, if not very ancient, streetscapes. The corner premises, which houses the International Bar, is a typical example. Where shopfronts had previously remained low, now they were tall and gave emphasis to the commercial premises within. The large red-brick structure that until recently accommodated the Wicklow Hotel was built in the 1880s. The Wicklow Hotel is recorded in Wicklow Street as early as 1850 and, like so many family-run hotels, it lasted right up until the middle of the 1980s. The building is now occupied by Tower Records. What a pity that these old city-centre hotels could not have held on for another ten years!

Mr John Gifford built two houses in Suffolk Street in 1781 'in such a manner which he deemed most advantageous'. While in the same year Alderman Rose erected a house at number 10, beside St Andrew's Church, which was 'altogether a very capital house'. This was leased to William and John Rigby, gunmakers. Dobbyn, a watch and clock manufacturer, occupied

Above: The Moira Hotel, which occupied two houses laid out by the Wide Streets Commissioners in the late eighteenth century. It was closed in 1977 and later demolished.

Below: An engraving from the nineteenth-century billhead of Callinan's, the china, glass and lamp merchants, showing the new St Andrew's Church.

number 13 Suffolk Street, which also accommodated an entrance to Rigby's shooting gallery, a long hall extending to the rear of the building. This site, extending from Suffolk Street to Wicklow Street, had been a bowling green in 1655. It had then belonged to Nathaniel Foulkes, who held a large tract of land east of St Andrew's Church. Rocque's map of 1756 shows a substantial house occupying the Suffolk Street side of the site, with an enclosed formal garden whose wall bounded Chequer Lane (now Wicklow Street). Number 7 Suffolk Street was occupied by Mr Walpole, a linen draper, who took a lease here in 1780. His son was Edward Walpole, a linen draper and damask manufacturer whose business became very well known at 9 Suffolk Street in the early nineteenth century. From these leases it would appear that much of Suffolk Street was rebuilt in the 1780s. Early eighteenth-century Dublin Corporation records suggest that there had been several cagework houses in the Suffolk Street/College Green area.

Part of Foulkes's holding, which touched the west side of Grafton Street, was leased in 1682 to Thomas Pooley, who we have already encountered in the Temple Bar area. (Pooley's holding will be discussed in the context of Grafton Street.)

The first St Andrew's Church was, as we have already seen, situated near Dublin Castle. The new church was erected in St Andrew's Street in 1670 and was most unusual, being oval in plan. It was generally known as the 'round church' and was used in the eighteenth century as an official church to the parliament, which was located in nearby College Green. The round church had plain, arched windows and double galleries within. It had a conical roof and a small belfry to one side. It would appear that it was substantially rebuilt in the late 1790s. The noted architect Francis Johnson

Above top: An engraving of the so-called Round Church of St Andrew's, from the early nineteenth-century trade card of James Trevor, tailor.

Above: This much-weathered statue of St Andrew once stood over the main entrance of the church.

Right: The trade card of James Trevor, showing his own premises and the Round Church of St Andrew's.

drew up plans, which included an elegant and very Gothic tower and spire. The interior was completed by 1807 but the tower remained unfinished. Unfortunately, the church was destroyed by a fire in 1860. Shortly afterwards, a competition to design a new church was held and, in accordance with Victorian tastes, it was won by the Gothic design of Charles Lanyon and William Henry Lynn.

The new church, opened in 1866, is indeed a very fine example of Victorian Gothic architecture, and the quality of its limestone masonry and carving are excellent. An examination of some of the buttresses and pinnacles of the church show that they remain uncarved, presumably due to a shortage of funds. A weather-beaten statue of St Andrew, which came from the church, stands rather sadly in a corner of the grounds, which have been used for car parking for many years. Following its closure around 1990, the church was purchased by Dublin Tourism who converted it, with great sensitivity, into a Tourist Information Office and their own headquarters.

South William Street

Georgian Dublin is considered by many people to consist of the famous eighteenth-century squares, such as Merrion Square, Parnell Square and Mountjoy Square, but of course there was once much more to it than that. Until some twenty-five or thirty years ago, Dublin was a relatively unspoilt and mainly Georgian city. Entire streets have since disappeared and the number that can claim to be intact Georgian streets are very few. South William Street is one whose streetscape is predominantly Georgian in character and, although it was mainly built as a residential area, the street has been a noted centre for trading over the last 200 years. South William Street is today known as the centre of the so-called 'rag trade' or fashion and clothing industry. This important street, which lies between Dublin Castle and Grafton Street, is dominated by two important eighteenth-century buildings: Powerscourt Townhouse, the city residence of the Wingfield family, and the City Assembly House, now the Dublin Civic Museum. The street runs parallel to Clarendon Street and George's Street, and looking west the vista is closed by what was once Mercer's Hospital, and is now a medical centre. In an important study of South William Street published by the Dublin Civic Trust in 1999, it has been pointed out that the original development of the street took place as early as 1685 when the land was leased to William Williams. Unfortunately all of the early houses have disappeared, but Rocque's map of 1756 gives a good impression of what the street may have looked like.

The lands of South William Street and Clarendon Street are described on a late seventeenth-century map as 'the whole land of Tib and Tom'. The derivation of this peculiar title remains a mystery, although a building called the House of Tib and Tom is

Above: The Egyptian-style knocker on the door of the Dublin Civic Museum.

Below: The attractive Dublin City Assembly House, South William Street, home to the Dublin Civic Museum and meeting place of the Old Dublin Society.

shown on an early map to have stood near Exchequer Street.

One of the most important developments that took place between South William Street and Drury Lane was the building of Castle Market there in 1785. It was called Castle Market because it replaced the old market, already discussed, which stood between Dame Lane and Dame Street. There is no known picture of this once very large market, which occupied the space running from the AIB on Dame Street up to the corner of Great South George's Street. Only the name, Castle Market, lives on today, in a plaque on the wall of South William Street opposite Powerscourt Townhouse. However, the eventual building of South City Markets between George's Street and Drury Street in 1878 was in a sense the continuation of this market tradition in the area.

One of the most interesting buildings in South William Street is the City Assembly House. This small but attractive house was erected in 1765 by Simon Vierpyl and Richard Cranfield. Vierpyl was an English sculptor and builder and he is known to have built a number of houses in South William Street and elsewhere in the city. The City Assembly House features an octagonal exhibition room originally used by the Society of Artists, of which Richard Cranfield, a wood carver, and Vierpyl were members. The activities of the Society do not appear to have lasted more than about fifteen years and by 1809 the building had become known as the City Assembly House. The front part of the building consists of three storeys over a basement, and it has a cut-granite façade and Doric entrance at ground-floor level. The interior is ornamented by a beautiful open-well staircase, and has a top-floor gallery, lit by an overhead octagonal lantern. The plasterwork and cornices throughout the Assembly House are typical of the 1760s – they are boldly modelled and exhibit freehand scrollwork and classical decoration. The Assembly Room, formerly used as the artist's exhibition room, is today principally used for lectures and exhibitions concerning the history of Dublin city. The space is lit by a large, glazed lantern and is furnished with a collection of James Malton's prints of Dublin and other important relics of Dublin city's history.

Powerscourt House, or Townhouse as it is presently known, is one of Dublin's great Georgian mansions. It is justly famed for its beautiful interiors and wonderful plasterwork ceilings. Since its conversion as part of Powerscourt Townhouse Shopping Centre in the early 1980s, it has become well known to Dubliners as it is open daily, free of charge, and some of the shops and galleries are located in the house itself. The house has a giant granite façade and is entered by means of a curved flight of steps, which leads to a beautifully proportioned hall and staircase. The hall, with its stone mantelpiece and marble floor, is exquisitely decorated with a bold plaster frieze and cornice. A pair of stained pine doors surmounted by a glazed Gothic fanlight leads to the stunning mahogany staircase. The beauty of the carving of this staircase and the scale and grandeur of this space make it one of the finest in Dublin city. The rusticated plasterwork of the staircase is designed to simulate stone and the rococo style here and in the outer hall is attributed to James McCullough. The exquisite ceilings of the main reception rooms are most likely the work of Michael Stapleton. Here the plasterwork is delicate and refined.

Powerscourt House was designed by Robert Mack, a stonemason and architect, for the Wingfields of Powerscourt, and was built in 1771. Robert Mack later submitted designs for the Royal Exchange and the Four Courts, but he was unsuccessful. The house is said to have cost £8,000 and it took three years to complete. Granite from the Powerscourt estate in County Wicklow was used in the construction of the building. In

Below: The magnificent façade of Powerscourt Townhouse, from an engraving by Pool and Cash.

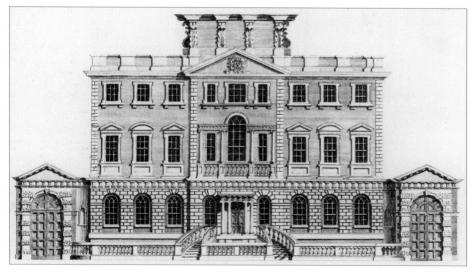

1807 Lord Powerscourt sold the property to the Government Commission for Stamp Duties for £15,000. This body constructed a very substantial courtyard at the rear of the house which now forms the Powerscourt Townhouse Shopping Centre. In 1832 the clothing wholesalers Ferrier and Pollock bought Powerscourt House and remained in business here until the 1970s.

In what appears to have been the complete rebuilding of South William Street in the latter half of the eighteenth century, many fine houses were constructed and a good number of these survive today. Quite a number of the houses feature the open-well staircase that was popular in the mid- to late eighteenth century. Such staircases were not particularly common in Dublin, but there are at least ten good examples remaining in this street. Most of these handsome staircases are constructed of timber, although there are some examples of stone cantilevered stairs, such as that at 16 South William Street. All of these staircases are characterised by solid wooden balusters and carved stair brackets. Many of the surviving Georgian houses in South William Street contain their original plaster cornices, which are similar to those in the Civic Museum. Such classical cornices usually feature scrolls of foliage interspersed with birds or baskets of fruit or flowers. Like the decorative plaster-work, much of the internal joinery, including doors, doorcases and chair rails, has survived quite well in South William Street. Many of the mid-eighteenth-century houses have shouldered doorcases, which was the fashion at the time.

Although there are few Victorian buildings on South William Street, the two-storey, Gothic-style buildings of Castle Market are a pleasant addition to the area. They were built around 1880, at the time of the development of the South City Markets, and they harmonise very satisfactorily with the fairy-tale Gothic style of the Market. Adjoining Cooke's restaurant at Castle Market is the imposing façade of the original offices of the Dublin Artisan

Opposite top: A delicate plasterwork medallion from one of the ceilings of Powerscourt, by Michael Stapleton.

Opposite bottom: The impressive staircase of Powerscourt, showing bold decorative plasterwork by James McCullough.

Left: The beautifully embellished, early nineteenth-century trade card of A&W Morrison, wholsesale merchants, at 6–7 South William Street.

Below: By the late nineteenth century, South William Street was renowned for its poulterers and fishmongers.

Dwelling Company, now Bruce College. A typical building of the early 1900s, it is constructed of red brick with granite detailing.

In 1795 James Malton depicted Powerscourt House and some of the smaller brick houses on the east side of the street. His beautifully coloured and very accurate print shows the original railings, Gibbsian doorcases and prominent chimney stacks of the neighbouring houses. By the early nineteenth century there were a considerable number of merchants and traders in South William Street. The predominant trades included wine merchants, tailors and drapers. By the 1880s the street was particularly well known for its provision dealers, fruiterers, poulterers and fishmongers. A noted firm of this time was John G Powell, fish, ice, poultry and game dealer. The wine merchants 'Bagots & Hutton' were located at numbers 27–28, while numbers 22–23 were owned by the Quaker Pim family, who were involved in various entrepreneurial developments such as railways, the South City Market and the large Victorian store in George's Street, which we have already discussed.

Thomas Street

*T*homas Street, or more correctly St Thomas Street, is one of the few late medieval streets of Dublin whose pattern and footprint have survived. The street has managed to maintain its character as an old Dublin street, with its mainly intact Georgian and Victorian business premises and daily street trading. Many of the Georgian houses in Thomas Street are still standing, though a great number of them are in a rundown condition with their upper floors lying vacant. Others were refronted in Victorian times, concealing their eighteenth-century origins.

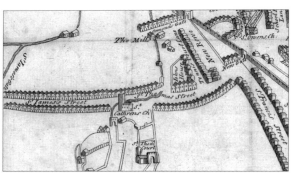

The name Thomas Street comes from the Abbey of St Thomas, founded in 1177, which was located on the site of today's Thomas Court, close to the present Pimlico. A recent archaeological dig has revealed part of a medieval tiled floor from the abbey, and the site has been occupied by Dublin Corporation, who plan to preserve it.

Thomas Street runs from today's Guinness's brewery eastwards as far as Francis Street, where a large building known as Corn Market House once occupied the middle of the thoroughfare. The street broadens in front of St Catherine's Church and narrows again near the National College of Art and Design. Speed's map of Dublin of 1610 shows the street arriving from the west and curving slightly towards the Liffey to arrive at Newgate, which was one of the entrances in the medieval city wall. Passing inside the gate, the visitor would have found himself standing almost directly in front of St Audoen's Church, and from there High Street would bring him to the centre of the medieval city.

In the mid-eighteenth century map-maker John Rocque gives us a picture of the western portion of Dublin city. Beyond Thomas Street and St James's Gate stretched St James's Street and Mount Brown towards Kilmainham, while to the south, Marrowbone Lane and Cork Street

gradually gave way to the open fields of the countryside. Basin Lane stands just to the south of St James's Street, not far from the present St James's Hospital, and is so called because of the existence of a huge city reservoir, a long thin container of water known as the city basin, made prior to 1720. Nearby stood the city workhouse which eventually became part of St James's Hospital but has now completely vanished. It stood beside the rather alarmingly named Cut Throat Lane. To the north stood three hospitals – the Royal Hospital in Kilmainham, St Patrick's Hospital and Dr Steevens's Hospital which stood at the bottom of Steevens's Lane.

It would be logical to expect the western approaches of the city to be the area where agricultural businesses and trades would most likely be found. Up until the early nineteenth century, Thomas Street was the gateway to the west, the route by which many farmers came to sell their corn and other produce, and to buy tea and other luxury items before returning home. The Corn Market, standing just outside the medieval city wall, was an important marketplace. Gilbert tells us that corn was exported from Dublin since the thirteenth century, and that it was traditionally sold in this area. Beside the Corn Market was an area known as the Bull Ring, so called after an iron ring that was fixed to the wall of the Corn Market, to which bulls were tied. There was a tradition in the Liberties of bringing the new bridegroom, on his return from church, to the marketplace, where he had to pay homage to the Bull Ring by kissing it. In such markets the control of weights and measures was always of great importance, but especially where corn, flour and bread were concerned. In 1310 some of the bakers of Dublin were humiliated by being dragged on hurdles through the

The Corn Market House in Thomas Street

The Corn Market House in Thomas Street

Right: The Corn Market House as depicted by Brooking in 1728.

Below: An eighteenth-century map of Thomas Street, showing the position of the long Corn Market House in the centre of the street.

streets for using false weights! The fourteenth-century Book of Ross records that one penny was equal in weight to thirty-two grains taken from the middle of an ear of corn. Twelve pence made one ounce and twelve ounces made one pound of twenty shillings. Then, as now, the price of wheat varied greatly, depending on the weather in a given year. When the weather was bad, the price of corn was high.

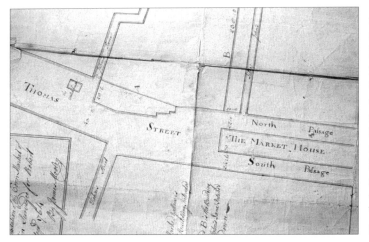

The Corn Market building, where these transactions took place, is shown on Brooking's map of 1728 – it had been completed in the previous year. It was a long, arcaded building, the bottom part of which was completely open to the street. Here, under the extensive shelter provided by the thirteen arches on each side, trade could be carried on during inclement weather. There were rooms on the upper floor and the roof was ornamented by a small cupola. When the building was removed in about 1800, and some of the business was relocated to the Corn Exchange on Burgh Quay, the Thomas Street traders objected strenuously. Thomas Street, as with much of the Liberties, had a long tradition of industries that were agriculture related, such as brewing, distilling and tanning. The people of the area relied on such business for their livelihood. In 1759 Arthur Guinness established his famous brewery at the west end of

Thomas Street, while two years earlier, Henry Roe had established a distillery that was to become one of the largest in the country. However, as we
shall see, there were many other breweries and distilleries in the area that
pre-date Guinness's.

One of Ireland's best-known brands of whiskey, Power's, had been
produced in Thomas Street since 1776. Power's Distillery, now occupied
by the National College of Art and Design, stood on a large site at John's
Lane, fronting onto Thomas Street. This distillery, which was taken over
by the college in 1976, will be discussed later.

George Roe's distillery is recorded in *Thom's Directory* of 1845 as occupying 157–159 Thomas Street. It was originally entered through an arched
gateway, not unlike that of Guinness's, which is preserved across the
street. The gate was flanked by two small pedestrian arches and the two
windows above suggest that there were small offices upstairs. Four-storey
Georgian houses adjoined the entrance to one side. George Roe's Old Malt
Whiskey was justly famous and the distillery boasted the largest pot-still in
the world. In 1890 the business became part of the Dublin Distillers'
Company, and remained so until 1955 when the property was taken over by
Arthur Guinness Sales Ltd. A massive windmill stood among the many tall
brick chimneys in Roe's Distillery. The windmill, which with its onion
dome, was erected in 1805 to grind corn for the distillery, and is believed to
be one of the tallest in Europe. Known locally as St Patrick's tower, it is a
smock windmill, a type where the dome, with the sails attached, rotates in
order to catch the wind. The date 1805 appears on a stone over the main
doorway and the sails of the windmill remained in working order until
about 1860. With the advent of steam power, the mill ceased to operate,
and the sails were then removed. The windmill may
still be seen among the warehouses of Guinness's.

Above: The windmill at Roe's
Distillery.

Below: A nineteenth-century
printed card showing Roe's
Distillery, later to be incorporated into the Guinness site,
where the impressive windmill
may still be seen.

Adjoining the former Roe's Distillery today is a
large building constructed between 1908 and 1920
for the Irish Agricultural Wholesale Society (IAWS).
In the late 1890s the Society occupied one of the old
Georgian houses of the street. Much rebuilding took
place in about 1909 following a major fire that
destroyed many of their warehouses. The Society
evolved out of the Agricultural Co-operative
Movement, which had been founded by Sir Horace
Plunkett in about 1889. It initially sold machinery to
its members but later dealt in eggs, poultry, pork and
honey. A dairy engineering department, a grocery
business and banking were also carried on here. The
early twentieth-century building is faced in red
Portmarnock brick and has a distinctive Mansard roof
with dormer windows. It contained showrooms for
agricultural machinery at the front of the premises
and extensive warehouses to the rear.

ESTAB 1757
GEO. ROE & CO
LIMITED.

THOMAS STREET
DISTILLERY.
DUBLIN.
TRADE GR MARK

A plaque on the front of number 151 Thomas Street records the tragic arrest of Lord Edward FitzGerald following his leading role in the uprising of 1798. A reward of £1,000 had been offered by Dublin Castle for information leading to FitzGerald's arrest, and it was known that he had been sheltered in a feather merchant's premises in Thomas Street. Murphy, in whose house he was found, describes how Major Sirr from Dublin Castle entered, followed by a soldier with a sword in his hand:

> I put myself before him and asked his business. He looked over me and saw Lord Edward in the bed. He pushed by me quickly and Lord Edward, seeing him, sprung up instantly like a tiger, and drew a dagger which he carried about him and wounded Major Sirr, slightly, I believe. Major Sirr had a pistol in his waistcoat pocket which he fired without effect. I was immediately taken away to the yard.

Right: Major Sirr, based in Dublin Castle, was a highly efficient but much-hated officer.

Below: Thwaites, later noted manufacturers of mineral waters, were important brewers in the eighteenth century.

Major Sirr's shots did, in fact, wound Lord Edward and after a fight in the house he was taken by sedan chair to Dublin Castle. He was imprisoned there and died soon afterwards from his injuries. Murphy was also imprisoned and his house ransacked by the military, who commandeered it as a barracks. A marble chimney piece that is said to have come from the room in which the arrest took place is now in the boardroom at the rear of number 151. The carved tablet of the mantelpiece bears the image of a reclining female figure, possibly Ceres, with a bunch of wheat and sickle at her feet. As one of the authors of the Thomas Street Architectural Survey noted, 'It was strangely appropriate that this mantelpiece should one day be in the headquarters of the Irish Agricultural Wholesale Society'.

The Thomas Street Architectural Survey was carried out in 1985 under the auspices of the Liberties Association. This valuable study, directed by Mairin Doddy, recorded every building in Thomas Street and is a valuable source of information about the buildings and their occupants.

A study of *Thom's Directories* over a period of 140 years shows that the businesses in Thomas Street had a steady base and did not change hands very frequently. Many of the occupants remained at their same address over several generations, from the mid-nineteenth century right up until the 1970s. Apart from the larger industries, of which we will hear more, there were many smaller soap and candle manufacturers, starch manufacturers, soda water makers, victuallers and bakers.

Thomas Street Breweries

The consumption of ale has been popular since the Middle Ages, and an
account of 1610 tells us that there were no fewer than 1,180 ale houses and
ninety-one public brew houses in the city of Dublin, whose population
then consisted of about 4,000 families! During the seventeenth century
many of the wealthier families brewed their own beer, but brewing as a
commercial enterprise came to prominence in Dublin during the eighteenth century. In 1763, Joseph Thwaites presented a petition to the Irish
House of Commons requesting aid to assist in the brewing of Irish porter.
At that time there was much competition from porters being imported
from England at favourable rates. By 1773 Mr George Thwaites, Master of
the Corporation of Brewers, stated that the number of breweries in Dublin
had declined from seventy to only thirty.

A brewery is known to have existed at St James's Gate since 1670, when
its owner acquired rights to water from the City of Dublin. These water
rights passed to Sir Mark Rainsford, brewer. In 1715 the Rainsford family
leased their business to Paul Espinasse and the whole property was eventually transferred to Arthur Guinness in 1759 at a rent of £45 per annum.

Arthur Guinness became actively involved in Dublin society and public
life. He was a member of the Wide Streets Commissioners, became a
governor of the Meath Hospital, and later became Master of the Corporation of Brewers. His own house in Thomas Street is said to have been built
during the 1770s. The house was probably refronted during the
mid-nineteenth century and has a large classical doorcase of Portland
stone. This four-storey-over-basement, seven-windows-wide house
stands just to the eastern side of the present main gate to the brewery. The
foundation date of the brewery, 1759, is inscribed on a plaque on the left

Above: The old cooperage at Guinness's, showing men preparing staves and barrels.

Below: This nineteenth-century carved frame, bearing the arms of Dublin Corporation, once held an illuminated address to the Guinness family.

Opposite top: One of the many maltings in the Liberties that supplied the breweries.

Opposite bottom: The curved warehouses that once adjoined the filled-in Grand Canal harbour.

hand side of the main gate's arch, while the date of the current year is inscribed annually on the right hand plaque. Passing the brewery on 1 January 2000, I was impressed to note that the date of the new century was already in place!

Brooking's map of Dublin in 1728 shows the city as it was thirty years before the time of Arthur Guinness. To the west lay the city basin, from which brewers drew their vital supplies of water. In front of Guinness's brewery, at the west end of Thomas Street, was the late medieval defence to the outer city of Dublin known as St James's Gate. The lease which Guinness had signed for the brewery in Thomas Street entitled him to the supply of water 'free of tax or pipe money'. Rocque's map of 1756 shows a stream running along the back of his premises. Guinness began to brew a new beer, which had already become popular with the porters at Covent Garden in London. This beer, known as porter, was made with roasted barley, which gave it a dark colour. By 1833 Guinness's was the largest brewery in Ireland and later in the nineteenth century the family were to become extraordinarily generous benefactors to the city of Dublin. The restoration of St Patrick's Cathedral, the construction of the Iveagh Baths and the Iveagh buildings, the building of the Iveagh markets and the restoration of St Stephen's Green are but a few of the Guinnesses' legacies to the people of Dublin. In 1939 Rupert Guinness donated Iveagh House in St Stephen's Green to the Irish government. This gracious mansion is now occupied by the Department of Foreign Affairs.

Throughout the nineteenth and twentieth centuries the brewery expanded and grew with ever larger storehouses, brew houses and malthouses. From about 1830 onwards, Guinness began to export 'the product', as porter was often called, especially to Britain. Until quite recently the product was brewed in enormous timber vats bound by iron hoops. The brewery was also equipped with a very large cooperage, where all the barrels were made, as well as a printing works, where bottle labels were printed, and engineers' workshops. A system of narrow-gauge railway tracks connected the various parts of the brewery and there was also a connection to the national railway network. The area between Thomas Street and Victoria Quay was known as 'the lower level' and was 'where are placed the cooperage shops, cask washing sheds, racking and filling stores and platforms for the dispatch of stout either by drays, motor lorries, boat or railway'. Down on the quays, from the nineteenth century onwards, barges and lighters were loaded with barrels that were ferried downriver to larger ships, which exported Guinness all over the world. The main ingredients of porter are malt, made from roasted barley, hops and water. Even in our sanitized age, the smell of roasted malt often permeates the entire city of Dublin when a west wind prevails.

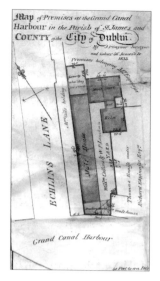

James's Street Harbour, at the back of Guinness's Brewery, was completed by the Grand Canal Company in 1785, and was once a very picturesque and busy part of the city. As the original Dublin terminus of the Grand Canal, it linked this heavily industrial part of the city with the rest of the country and with its agricultural suppliers. The docks were originally quite extensive and consisted of two rectangular basins and a third semicircular harbour around which various warehouses were ranged. Commercial traffic in the form of barges ceased in James's Street Harbour in 1960, and by the 1970s the canal was being referred to as 'a dirty and dangerous ditch' by residents. Unfortunately, instead of maintaining the canal by restoring and cleaning it, the whole canal and harbour were filled in and partially built over. The actual harbour site is now largely wasteland. A number of small industries there are making furniture and metalwork. Some of the impressive stone warehouse buildings survive, including the curved storehouse, which was built in the early nineteenth century. In 1833 Richard

Espinasse, a descendent of the family who had owned a brewery in this vicinity before the arrival of Arthur Guinness, sold an extensive malthouse and maltstore on Grand Canal Harbour to William Collins and William Lenihan. The buildings, which almost adjoined Echlin's Lane, included a malthouse, a malt-store, a kiln and a large yard.

In the early twentieth century, Guinness's was reckoned to be the largest brewery in the world. It still occupies more than fifty acres in the western part of Dublin city. Guinness's developed a well-earned reputa-tion for taking care of the welfare of their employees and many considered a job in the firm to be as secure as a job in the civil service or Dublin Corporation. A medical service, pensions, a savings bank, sports and leisure facilities, educational schemes and even housing were provided for employees. The Guinness museum, Ireland's first museum of industrial history, was opened in 1966. After almost 240 years, the Guinness family are now no longer connected in any way with the business.

At the back of the brewery, close to the Grand Canal Harbour, is the Market Street Fermenting House. This extraordinary eight-storey building is reminiscent of the New York skyscrapers built in about 1900. Although its height and scale are so modern, its finish is still Victorian. Equally impressive is the Robert Street Malt Store, which was erected on a site adjoining the Canal Harbour. The ground floor of the Malt Store, which is traversed by the narrow-gauge rail track of the brewery, is a forest of cast-iron columns that support the floors above.

In 1984 Guinness's completed a conversion of one of their old hop stores in Rainsford Street into a visitors' centre, museum and art gallery, where in that year it was planned to host an interna-tional art exhibition. The Guinness Hop Store became one of the largest exhibi-tion spaces in the city and provided a suitable venue for major art exhibitions at a time when Dublin had no museum of modern art. The word 'museum' would hardly be a correct description of the very lively and interesting presentation that showed the history of the brewery, the life of the Liberties area of Dublin and the various crafts and skills associated with the industry itself. The four-storey Hop Store was originally built in the 1860s and was cleverly converted by the provision of a large entrance lobby and staircase inside. The Hop Store had remarkable success as a tourist attraction and was a mecca for all Guinness-loving tourists who come to the capital. It is currently being relocated at the Market Street Fermenting House.

Thomas Street Traders

Much of the premises of Miller and Company, tea, wine and whiskey merchants, which adjoin Guinness's brewery may still be seen in Thomas Street. The distillery of Adam Miller is first recorded in 1854 at 12 Thomas Street, although they had been in business for some ten years before that. Their fine Victorian office premises, occupying 10–13 Thomas Street, are thought to have been erected in the 1890s. A vehicle entrance through the three-arched brick façade gives access to a large group of buildings, including a bottling house, a cooperage, a tea and wine store, stables, hay lofts and other outhouses. On a visit to these buildings during the middle of the 1980s, I was impressed by the survival of much of the old Victorian equipment associated with bottling. A bell still hangs in the corner of the yard, which was once used to announce tea breaks for the employees. Wine manufactured from grape pulp was produced in the wine stills of Miller's up until the 1980s, and during the First World War elderberry and rhubarb wines were made from the produce of their own farm. Many of the most interesting industrial antiques were donated to the Guinness museum, where they are now being restored.

Above: The former Thomas Street Library is now converted as a hostel for tourists.

Number 14 Thomas Street is a handsome, early nineteenth-century house, once occupied by John Murphy's, bellfounders. Murphy's bell foundry was responsible for casting bells for many famous churches, including Maynooth College Chapel, St Patrick's Cathedral, Christ Church Cathedral and St Audoen's Church. Murphy, also variously described as a coppersmith and plumber, flourished here between the years 1852 and 1888.

Wood's bacon factory was situated to the rear of houses at numbers 22 and 23 Thomas Street, later to become the Dublin Corporation Public Library. This five-bay house with its arched vehicle entrance is a fine merchant's house of around 1790. The façade was plastered and embellished probably in the 1880s, but the original Georgian-

Above: A giant sharpening stone stood in one of the outhouses of Miller's among old wooden vats and barrels.

Above: A nineteenth-century horse-drawn fire engine racing up Sackville Street, on the cover of a Victorian musical score.

style doorcase with its Ionic columns survives intact. An unusual feature is the use of such columns around the adjoining goods entrance as well. In 1884 the building was opened as one of the first public lending libraries, along with another Corporation library in Capel Street. These libraries remained in use until 1985. Following the closure of the Thomas Street Library in 1985, the building was left unoccupied and was subject to repeated acts of vandalism. An extremely important and rare marble mantlepiece made by Bossi, and possibly worth up to £20,000, was stolen at the time. In 1987 local residents and members of the Liberties Association were horrified to see the Corporation removing the roof from the old

Thomas Street Library. Mr Noel Carroll, the spokesman at the time for the Corporation said, 'The building had been dangerous for some time and it is effectively gone.' Under pressure from conservation bodies, who feared its demolition, the building was sold and was converted into a tourist hostel. The original interior of the former public library in Thomas Street was attractive, having a fine staircase and bow-ended reception rooms.

Many destructive fires took place throughout the city in the eighteenth and nineteenth centuries, and Thomas Street seems to have suffered more than its fair share of them. In 1892 twelve horses burned to death in a stable fire at number 18 and only the prompt action of the fire brigade saved the neighbouring Miller's wine and whiskey stores from destruction. Another devastating fire, in 1862, largely destroyed the premises of Messrs Abbot and Company at 61 Thomas Street. The horse-drawn fire engines, some of which were located at different parish churches and others belonging to the Corporation, came quickly, but were not able to save the extensive drapery stores. They were, however, able to prevent the fire from spreading to the east, into a distillery belonging to a Mr Mahalm. Another fire, in 1876, destroyed a ham and bacon factory belonging to a Mr Wood at 22 Thomas Street. The store, containing over 9,000 hams and over 100 barrels of pork, went on fire at about eleven o'clock in the evening and once again there was concern that the fire would spread to an adjoining whiskey store belonging to a Mr Gleeson. The fire was brought under control and firemen were able to save the belfry of St Catherine's Church, which had also caught fire.

Throughout the second half of the nineteenth century there was continued agitation for a proper fire service to be provided by the Corporation, and in 1907 a site was acquired in Thomas Street for a new fire station. This was to be one of four new stations, two of which were located south of the River Liffey at Tara Street and Thomas Street, while the others were located at Dorset Street and Buckingham Street on the north side of the city. Prior to the building of these fire stations by the Corporation, the responsibility for maintaining firefighting equipment rested with the various parishes, and fire engines and ladders were kept in parish churches and other public places, such as at Nelson's Pillar. Two old wooden fire engines may still be seen in the porch of St Werburgh's Church. Many businesses maintained their own firefighting equipment, including Guinness's and Power's Distillery.

The new Thomas Street fire station was erected in 1911 to the designs of architect Charles J McCarthy. It is a fine building, constructed of Donegal sandstone and Portmarnock brick. The arched ground floor allowed access for the various

Above: A pair of leather fire buckets from the Guinness Museum, used for fighting fires in the early nineteenth century.

Below: An eighteenth-century timber-built fire engine from St Werburgh's, showing the rectangular trough for water and the pump mechanism.

Above: Street traders in Thomas Street in the late nineteenth century. The licensed premises of Power's, which then formed part of the Georgian streetscape, may be seen in the background.

fire engines while the upper floors accommodated the firemen. At one time the firemen and their families lived overhead. The building, facing up Meath Street, fits well into the general streetscape but has lain vacant for many years now.

A dramatic improvement has been recently effected at the corner of Thomas Street and Thomas Court, just facing St Catherine's Church. This corner premises, built in brick in the late nineteenth century, was in recent years known as the Robert Emmet Inn. There had been a grocer at this address since the early 1800s and the present building was probably remodelled by Gleeson, a grocer, who took over these premises in 1868. The public house has recently been renamed The GF Handel, and its elegant appearance gives a great lift to this part of the street. Rogers' Pub, located at 60 Thomas Street, was one of the last traditional pubs remaining in the area and closed only during the late 1990s. The building, standing at the corner of Vicar Street, is of eighteenth-century date, while the pub front and interior probably date from the 1880s. There had been a tradition of grocers and spirit dealers in these premises dating back to before 1800. It became the property of J Rogers in 1930.

In an interview in 1985 Mr Rogers, the son of the original owner, said that in the old days all the pubs in the district sold groceries and served drink. Tea, sugar and groceries were sold at the front of the shop while the pub was located at the back. Mr Rogers said that in the early days they bottled their own ale and whiskey and that his usual working day was from ten in the morning to ten at night, closing at 9.30 on Saturday nights and opening from two to five on a Sunday. Commenting on how the street had changed, he said that, 'At one time the street was full of food shops, whereas now it's nearly all markets and stalls.' Mr Rogers said that, in the 1980s, crime was a real anxiety and that vandalism to property was very prevalent. He recalled the outstanding service that was provided by the trams and said that they had had a tram every three minutes down to College Green. There was a very large population in the area and the side streets were full of tenements:

All of the streets here were populated. Ah yes, there were a lot of games played on the streets. I mean, Meath Street, of course, it's a busy street still but it was a good street then. Francis Street was equally as good as Meath Street, you had High Street too, and you had Cornmarket, all that area. What do you think populated Ballyfermot, Kimmage and all those places, only moving people out from these areas ... There were a few streets around here where women of ill repute collected. The back of Guinness's was very famous for that, where there was few or no lights. That didn't start with this generation!

Below: Street trading is still popular in Dublin today.

When asked whether it was ever necessary to go outside this street to buy anything, he replied:

You see, Thomas Street to a great extent was working class and a provincial type of trade. Now if you wanted to get, say, a really good suit or something like that, you would go into town to some of the tailors ...

Regarding the street traders, Mr Rogers had this to say:

It mainly runs down through families, and some of the dealers now, I could have known their grandmothers. They sold outside. I suppose they're a breed unto themselves. You've got to be able to survive the elements. It's very hard. I mean you mightn't pay any rates or rent, but you've got to be able to take the rain when it comes. There's a good deal of money to be made in dealing now. In those years they were much more restricted and at one time they brought in a rule where they couldn't even put a basket on the street and they had to put a basket, just one basket, with a rope around it, around their neck and got what they called a crutch, a little wooden piece in the middle, that would take the weight off their neck … which meant they got to sell everything out of the one basket, nothing like stalls or anything like that … there was always a sale of fish 'round here and that went back for hundreds of years. Thomas Street was always a street for the dealers. I remember a time when George's Street was full of dealers and they put them off George's Street … so they got rid of the dealers and when they got rid of the dealers the shops suffered very badly because a lot of the business that came to the street came to the dealers as well as for the shops.

(This interview was carried out by members of the Thomas Street Heritage Project.)

Right: One of the last traditional shopfronts on Thomas Street was Seezer's. The gold-and-black lettering and the glass fascia were once commonplace.

There were quite a number of bakeries in the district and many butchers. Seezer's was one of the best-known pork butchers and had a very attractive shopfront, which was only taken down in 1985. The Seezer family came from Germany before the First World War and ran a very successful business in Thomas Street. Seezer's was sold in 1978 and included the entire house, shop, store and sausage factory. It was first leased in 1911.

Not far away, at the entrance to Vicar Street, stood a modest Georgian-style house which, together with its neighbour, was demolished in order to build the present glass-and-brick-fronted Vicar Street pub and music venue. Some see the new building as incongruous in the traditional street, but it has without doubt brought a new clientele into the area.

The two upper floors of a pair of houses adjoining Roger's pub were crudely hacked off in the 1980s. There are still several alleys running at right angles to Thomas Street; one in particular, known as Molyneux Yard, survives with its ancient cast-iron bollard still intact.

It was here in Thomas Street, just near the opening of Vicar Street, that Robert Emmet's aborted rebellion of 1803 went very wrong. Emmet had planned to infiltrate Dublin Castle by bringing six coaches with six men in each, which would drive into the upper castle yard as if going to a party, but a passing soldier became suspicious of the group. The coachmen became anxious and abandoned the plan and Emmet was forced to gather his men and try to take the castle on foot. In Thomas Street they were joined by a

Above: A thriving butcher's and grocer's in a 1930s photograph of Thomas Street at Molyneux Yard.

drunken rabble who grabbed pikes, knives and any sort of weapon. By coincidence, at that very moment the coach of Lord Kilwarden came by with his daughter and nephew in it. The mob stopped the carriage and the two men were taken out and savagely beaten to death. By this time the military had been alerted and Emmet made his escape into the countryside outside Dublin.

It was reported at the time that many of the mob in Thomas Street were armed with pikes and went along the street breaking lamps. At Vicar Street they attacked a watch house and seized the constables' poles. Other accounts stated that the men were not particularly drunk but were in a very violent mood and ready to take on the military and attack Dublin Castle. Late at night a detachment of troops under the command of Alderman Darley found Robert Emmet's depot, just off Thomas Street, which was full of printed proclamations, pikes, hand grenades and hundreds of cartridges. Behind false partitions they found more pikes, proclamations, rockets, pitch, explosive lights, scaling ladders, musket balls and chains

Above: Robert Emmet's secret depot of weapons at Mass Lane, which were to be used in 1803.

and grappling irons which were to be used to gain entry to Dublin Castle. They also found a green coat heavily laced with gold and a military cocked hat to go with it, along with banners of green and white for the new army. A detailed list of Emmet's military stores was drawn up by a colonel and shows just how much preparation had been done. There were about 150,000 musket balls, 156 grappling irons, 42,000 rounds of musket-ball cartridges and many other homemade bombs, including 104 champagne bottles filled with gunpowder. Robert Emmet was eventually captured and on 20 September 1803 he was hanged, drawn and quartered in front of St Catherine's Church.

Gordon & Thompson's and Frawley's represent two of the older-style drapery stores that were once commonplace in Dublin. Thompson's building had been occupied by one of the first cinemas in Dublin, 'the People's Picture Palace', in 1913. When the cinema opened, it was extremely popular and the crowds outnumbered the seating capacity. The cinema had vanished by 1926 and was incorporated into Thompson's drapery store. The manager of Thompson's described how he had served his time in Switzer's Department Store before coming to Thomas Street. He commented, 'In the old days when you started your apprenticeship it took a few days before you could learn to make up a parcel. Nowadays, you just throw the goods into a plastic bag. Parcel-making is now considered as an art. Most young shop assistants couldn't make a proper parcel now.' Describing the street traders, he said, 'They work really hard for a living, but yet they are always willing to do someone else a favour. Another thing is, they are all women. They are always friendly when you pass them on the street and you never hear them complain.'

Frawley's, still the principal drapers in Thomas Street, have occupied number 35 since 1891; they acquired the adjoining house in 1936. Number 36 had been the premises of Williams and Company, tea merchants, since 1886. It was in a house on this site that Joseph Fade, a quaker businessman, had established a bank in 1715. Frawley's was established in 1892 by

Below: Number 118 Thomas Street, incorporating the Victorian front of Gilbey's branch shop. The back of this premises was recently rebuilt.

Cornelius Frawley, who took over the business of another drapers named Kelly. Mr Lee, whose family have been associated with Frawley's since the 1920s, remarked that in the old days Christmas Eve was the busiest day of the year, with the business at its height at half-past eight at night. 'Now, of course, it's finished at half-past five and Christmas Eve is no longer the busy day here. I remember quite clearly going by Christ Church when the bells would be ringing at midnight.'

Among the grocers of Thomas Street two buildings stand out – the premises of Wardell's, tea merchants, at number 76, and the façade of number 38, the premises of Patterson's, tea merchants. The stucco-embellished façade of number 38 bears the inscription, *Established AD 1782*, which may be the year when Adam Calvert, a Quaker, set up his business here. It was Henry Patterson, a descendent of Calvert and also a Quaker, who erected the elegant frontage, which is now all that remains of the building. The building is now used as a type of indoor market, and goes under the name of the Bazaar.

Above: Blanchardstown Mills, the famous flour merchants', occupying numbers 119–122 Thomas Street.

The Wardells established themselves as tea merchants in Thomas Street in the 1840s and some twenty years later commissioned the popular Victorian architect, William Mitchell, to design an appropriate commercial frontage at number 76. The design made extensive use of Dalkey granite and polished stone, along with stone pilasters and decorative roundels. The façade is all that remains of this typical nineteenth-century commercial premises, which is unfortunate, as the interior was once very elaborate – as befitted one of the leading tea merchants of the day. The building ran back to a considerable depth, with a large two-storey ware room at the back, which contained an internal gallery and overhead light. A story was told by a descendant of the Wardells' to members of the Thomas Street Heritage Project in 1985: John Wardell, the founder of the firm, had a fondness for horse racing, but as a Quaker he could not be seen to indulge his passion. It was claimed that he won two Irish Derbys under the pseudonym of John Dennison, but that he was photographed in a newspaper leading his winner out of the Curragh and was subsequently censured by the Society of Friends. John Wardell became extremely wealthy and as a patron of the arts acquired a very large collection of paintings, which he housed in a special gallery in his own home.

Even as recently as 1985, Wardell's were selling 30,000 or 40,000 chests of tea a year, but in recent years the firm was taken over by Barry's tea merchants. Since the middle of the nineteenth century, Wardell's blended their own teas, importing it directly from various producers in India. Until the introduction of packet tea in the 1930s, all teas were sold loose and

Wardell's were one of the biggest suppliers to the many small shops and pubs around the country.

The last proprietor of Wardell's attributed the decline of the various tea merchants in Dublin to the influx of various large English concerns such as Lyons, who promoted the use and sale of tea bags. The Irish concerns were slow to advertise and resisted the change from loose tea to packet teas and tea bags. Much of the work in the packing room was done by women.

Tea was brought up from the bonded warehouses in the docks by horse-drawn carts and Wardell's had their own fleet of delivery vans, which were horse-drawn in the early days. Mr Wardell also commented on the smell of roasting coffee which emanated from their coffee warehouse off Francis Street. He added: 'There were lots of other smells in Francis Street, O'Keeffe's the knackers' yard where they melted down all the horses' and cows' hooves, and the smell, you could hardly have lived there. On a hot summer's day you had the contrast with the smell of coffee and the knacker's yard but the other thing that this area was famous for was pigs.' He also commented on the quantity of gin that was drunk, especially in working class areas: 'There was a lot of drunkenness, far more drunkenness in Dublin in those days than there is today, which not a lot of people realise. They didn't have drugs. Cheap gin was a penny. It was a relatively cheap drink and the old biddies used to have terrible fights on the streets.'

The still-vacant shop front of W & A Gilbey at 118 Thomas Street is in many respects similar to that of Wardell's. It has a handsome stucco frontage with a small polished red granite column in the centre of the shopfront window. The carving of the name and numbers on the fascia and on the capitals are of the finest quality. This Thomas Street outlet was one of several owned by Gilbey's and was opened in 1886. Next door stands the impressive façade of the Blanchardstown Mills, built in about 1900 and occupying numbers 119–122 Thomas Street. The grandiose frontage with its giant pilasters at first- and second-floor level disguises what was

Above: The Dublin Distillers' Company Ltd was an amalgamation of three large city distilleries at Thomas Street, Marrowbone Lane and Jones' Road.

Below: A whiskey bottle label from Power's Distillery.

basically a large grain warehouse. The company, which had operated in the street since the early 1890s, sold a wide variety of meal, flour, oatmeal, grain and chicken feed. A fire in the 1970s destroyed much of the buildings to the rear. Having lain idle for some time, a new development was erected behind the façade of the Blanchardstown Mills and Gilbey's and it now houses the Iceland store and a multi-storey car park. For many years, an old sub-post office stood at the corner of Thomas Street and Bridgefoot Street. It became derelict in 1975, following its acquisition for road-widening, and has since been demolished.

As we have seen, street trading has been a feature of Thomas Street for centuries and Rocque's map of 1756 marks the position of the Glib Market there, which was the centre of this activity. It was named after a small, now underground, stream called the Glib Water.

Power's Distillery – Thomas Street

In 1791 James Power converted his public house into a distillery, which grew to become one of the best-known producers of whiskey in Ireland. Power's Distillery was located at the rear of 109 Thomas Street in the 1790s, but by the early nineteenth century he had also acquired the adjoining property. This fine pair of Georgian houses were unified as 110 Thomas Street and contained an elegant licensed premises on the ground floor. There was a continuous Georgian-style balcony across the first floor windows and all of the upper floors also had balconies. By the middle of the nineteenth century the distillery covered several acres of land and incorporated a fine front office and counting house, a corn sampling room, grain stores, mills, kilns, brewing coppers, brew houses, a backhouse, an engine room, worm tubs, a cooperage and a special house for the stills. It was undoubtedly the presence of the Glib Water stream that allowed Power to create the distillery in this location in the first place. The stream, which

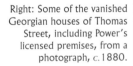

Right: Some of the vanished Georgian houses of Thomas Street, including Power's licensed premises, from a photograph, c. 1880.

now flows underground, passed through the distillery and once powered several mills.

Sir John Power, who was knighted in 1841, was a close friend of Daniel O'Connell and it was he who laid the first stone of the O'Connell monument in Sackville Street in 1854. The Powers came from Wexford, where they maintained a fine house at Edermine, just outside Enniscorthy. They had a reputation for favouring the employment of Wexford people in the distillery in Thomas Street. In 1884 James Talbot Power donated funds towards the completion of the Augustinian church that stood opposite the distillery in John's Lane. A major fire occurred in Power's Distillery in 1877 when the still house and the receiving house, which contained two huge vats of first proof whiskey, almost exploded:

> The flames of which reached fully over the high spire of St John's Chapel. The noise of the explosion of each of the receivers could be compared to nothing but to the shock of an earthquake.

By the late nineteenth century Power's was one of the largest whiskey producers in the world and in addition to their own warehouses in John's Lane the company had bonded warehouses under Westland Row railway station and beneath the Corporation Fruit and Vegetable Markets. Power's Grain Store, a large, five-storey brick building, was built in 1817 and has a handsome cupola with a weather vane on top. Corn was stored in this building, where it was dried and milled.

Above: A late nineteenth-century view of Power's Distillery, showing the impressive offices fronting onto Thomas Street.

Right: A Power's Distillery chimney stands alone during demolition in 1985.

In 1966 John Power and Son became part of the Irish Distillers' group and the distillery lay idle during the 1970s. When the art college took over in the 1980s, the distillery complex was virtually intact, although suffering from considerable decay and some vandalism.

Power's were famous for having the most up-to-date machinery in the distillery trade and much of it lay intact in the buildings when they were taken over by the National College of Art and Design. William Dick, an authority on industrial history, pointed out that the two stills, each with a capacity of twenty-five gallons, were said to be the largest pot stills ever made. The brewing coppers were the finest of their type and the brew houses contained two thirty-three-foot-wide mash tons which were dismantled in 1985. A very impressive 120-foot chimney stack was also demolished at this time although a smaller one, ninety-five feet in height, still stands. Two of the large copper stills remain *in situ*, but unfortunately all the surrounding buildings with their iron floors and associated machinery were removed in the 1980s.

Originally located in Kildare Street, the NCAD saw the buildings and the district of Thomas Street as stimulating and inspiring for their students. It was also clear that the creation of an art college was going to be, to some degree, in conflict with the preservation of such an important collection of nineteenth-century industrial equipment. It was proposed that a museum of industrial design could, in fact, be incorporated, to mutual benefit, into the new College of Art buildings. Unfortunately this did not happen and much was demolished, including the cooperage, the backhouse, the can pit room, the brewing house, the tallest of the chimneys and part of the still

Above: Power's Distillery during demolition in 1985, with the spire of the Augustinian church in the background.

Below: Three copper stills from Power's Distillery. Two now remain as objects of curiosity in the 'plaza' of the National College of Art and Design.

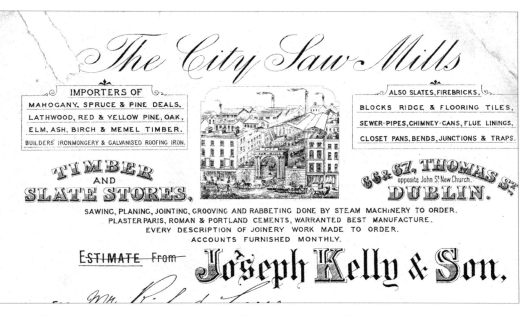

The City Saw Mills

IMPORTERS OF
MAHOGANY, SPRUCE & PINE DEALS, LATHWOOD, RED & YELLOW PINE, OAK, ELM, ASH, BIRCH & MEMEL TIMBER.
BUILDERS' IRONMONGERY & GALVANISED ROOFING IRON.

ALSO SLATES, FIREBRICKS,
BLOCKS RIDGE & FLOORING TILES, SEWER-PIPES, CHIMNEY-CANS, FLUE LININGS, CLOSET PANS, BENDS, JUNCTIONS & TRAPS.

TIMBER AND SLATE STORES,

66 & 67, THOMAS St
opposite John St. New Church.
DUBLIN.

SAWING, PLANING, JOINTING, GROOVING AND RABBETING DONE BY STEAM MACHINERY TO ORDER.
PLASTER PARIS, ROMAN & PORTLAND CEMENTS, WARRANTED BEST MANUFACTURE.
EVERY DESCRIPTION OF JOINERY WORK MADE TO ORDER.
ACCOUNTS FURNISHED MONTHLY.

ESTIMATE From **Joseph Kelly & Son,**

house. The engine house and two of the stills remain, along with the old grain store. It is perhaps not too late, at this stage, to consider the establishment of a small industrial design museum in the context of the college. By comparison with cities all over Europe, including many eastern European capitals, it is extraordinary that Dublin has no museum specifically devoted to the history of design and manufacture in the applied arts.

The Grain Store building has now been converted into studios and a library for the National College of Art and Design (NCAD). The present administration offices of the NCAD are housed in a group of granite and red-brick buildings, probably erected about 1876. The Victorian interiors were finished to a very high standard and include a fine panelled boardroom with a carved timber fireplace surround. The main part of this building was completed by 1878 and contained a counting house and office with mahogany counters and brass fittings and leaded lights.

The well-built stone goods entrance to the NCAD, at 109 Thomas Street, was constructed in the 1890s to the designs of WM Mitchell. This building stood on the site of Power's original goods entrance to their distillery behind, although their original licensed premises occupied the adjoining building, number 110, and was once known as a departure point for coaches leaving for the country.

Above: This billhead illustrates the extensive premises of Kelly's City Saw Mills in the late nineteenth century.

Below: Classical entrance gates and arches, such as these, were once commonplace at large industrial concerns.

Above: The new Vicar Street pub and music venue reflecting the Augustinian priory church at John's Lane.

The finely crafted granite archway is flanked by two smaller arched doorways, which gave access to internal offices. Power's original premises at 110–112 Thomas Street were rebuilt or refronted in the 1890s and are now occupied by a pub called the Clock. The ornamental brick window surrounds and cornice are very typical of the late nineteenth century.

The noble church of St Augustine and St John, facing on to Thomas Street, has a very ancient history, with records of a church having existed on this site since the twelfth century. It went through many different forms until it was finally rebuilt in its present configuration in the late nineteenth century. A hospital and priory were originally established on this site in the late twelfth century by a pilgrim returning from the Holy Land. The priory, which was dedicated to St John the Baptist, was occupied by the Canons Regular of St Augustine. In 1539 the priory was suppressed and it was really not until the early eighteenth century that a Roman Catholic chapel was again in regular use on this site. In 1748 a new but modest chapel was erected here, a rectangular building that was approached from John's Lane. It was typical of the eighteenth century that the erection of a Catholic chapel was tolerated but, like those of Quakers, had to be discreetly placed out of sight in a side street. On the east side of the chapel stood a large square tower, which is marked on Rocque's map of 1756 and was commonly known as St John's Castle. This eighty-foot tower was the only surviving portion of the original medieval hospital and priory and was eventually demolished in about 1800. An interesting event took place here in 1733 when,

> On Tuesday last, seventeenth November, the famous flying man lately arrived from England, flew twice from the top of King John's Castle in Thomas Street to a post fixed within a few doors of Meath Street. He performed it after a very surprising and extraordinary manner and the last time sounded a trumpet as he was coming down.
> [Dublin Evening Post]

The space between the old chapel and Thomas Street was occupied by a collection of irregularly built old houses, acquired in 1854 by Dr Dominic Corrigan and sold on to the Augustinian order for the purpose of building the new church. Sir Dominic Corrigan, as he later became, had grown up in one of these houses on Thomas Street and he became a distinguished surgeon, later building for himself a fine mansion overlooking Dalkey Island.

In 1781 the old John's Lane Chapel was extended northwards, incorporating a gallery in the north aisle. The style of early Roman Catholic chapels such as this was very similar to those churches of the Presbyterians and Quakers, being rectangular in plan, plain in style and often having a gallery. Few Catholic chapels of this age remain intact in Ireland today. The foundation stone of the present Augustinian church was laid in 1862, but the church was not considered completely finished until 1911 when the finishing touches were put to the interior. The roof and spire were completed by 1874, while the elaborate exterior was not finished until 1895. The bulk of the church was constructed from Dalkey granite with red sandstone dressings, and the greater part of the work was carried out by the noted builder Michael Meade. Much of the elaborate sculpture was executed by Earley and Powell of Camden Street. The church was designed in 1860 by the firm of Pugin and Ashlin, who specialised in the Gothic-revival style. The high altar was produced by sculptor Edward Sharpe in 1906 and cost £1,600. The interior of the church is greatly enriched by stained glass, some from the Harry Clarke studios and more from the German firm of Meyer. The bells of St Augustine's were cast in Thomas Street by Murphy's Bell Foundry in 1872, and the elaborate medieval-style hinges on the main doors were forged by Fagan of Brunswick Street. The fantastic Gothic pulpit is a remarkable piece of stonecarving.

The Augustinian church, with its characteristic Flemish-style spire in red sandstone, became a distinctive landmark on Thomas Street and the western portion of the city of Dublin. In 1937 the granite-built priory that adjoins the church on the western side was rebuilt to the designs of Ashlin and Coleman. During the late 1980s a programme of restoration work was begun at the church. Much of the decorative carved stonework, which had been carried out in red sandstone, had become eroded and in some places in danger of collapse. A very thorough scheme of work was initiated

Above: The streetscape in this part of Thomas Street has changed little since James Malton's engraving of St Catherine's Church (1795).

Below: A plan of St Catherine's, showing its symmetrical composition and the tower to the right, with a double staircase that gave access to the galleries.

whereby some of the damaged stone was replaced and other elements were carefully repaired with a matching stone mortar.

The Bank of Ireland, which occupies 84 Thomas Street, is another handsome granite building of the Victorian period. It was built originally for the Hibernian Bank and has characteristic segmental headed windows, decorative mouldings, collonettes and capitals. As one would expect from a building of this type, the quality of detail is good and includes a fine mosaic entrance hall, entrance door and good interior panelling. The bank is adjoined by another Victorian commercial premises built in about 1870 for Garret and Company, grocers. Here again we see the successful, but more restrained, use of brick and granite detailing.

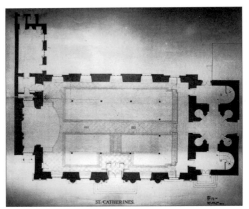

Number 141 Thomas Street, the premises of Patrick Massey, undertakers, is thought to be one of the oldest surviving houses on Thomas Street and certainly has one of the most unusual façades, with three wide relieving arches of brick in the first floor. Despite some alterations at ground floor level, much of the frontage and façade is original. The house contains an early staircase of great interest, featuring barley-sugar balusters and a heavy handrail. Some of the original corner fireplaces, dating from the 1740s, survive in the house.

The recent restoration of St Catherine's Church is now complete. This has involved the cleaning and renovation of the granite façade and tower that face Thomas Street and Thomas Court. When this work is finished, it is hoped that St Catherine's will enter into a new and more secure phase of its history, as the last thirty years have not been kind to it. Malton's print of the church shows it in its heyday, a sedate Palladian-style building facing onto Thomas Street, with an extensive graveyard to the rear. The present building, which succeeded an earlier St Catherine's, was begun in 1765 and, like most of its sister Church of Ireland churches in Dublin, was designed with a substantial gallery. The gallery is a magnificent work of joinery and woodcarving, including pilasters with finely carved Ionic capitals.

In 1969 the church was deconsecrated and handed over to Dublin Corporation. The Church of Ireland authorities auctioned off the church fittings, including the original box pews, an act of vandalism repeated in the 1980s at St Mary's Church. Fortunately for this historic building, an interested group, many coming from the Irish Georgian Society, formed the St Catherine's Trust in the 1960s and proceeded to painstakingly renovate the interior. However, by the mid-1980s, St Catherine's Church was again vacant and became the target of vandalism. The organ, which had survived and had been restored by Lord Moyne, was stolen around 1990. It was not until the late 1990s that a Christian Group, known as CORE, obtained a lease of the building and raised the necessary funds to restore it along with grants from the Heritage Council, Dublin Corporation and the Department of the Environment.

Below: The graceful interior of St Catherine's, now happily restored to use as a church.

Usher's Quay and Usher's Island

Below: Number 15 Usher's Quay was featured in James Joyce's story, 'The Dead'. The house is about to be restored.

Below bottom: Number 12, with its ornamental fanlight, reflects the quality of many of the houses that once stood on Usher's Quay.

The busy Liffeyside road known today as Usher's Quay and Usher's Island is a dusty thoroughfare for traffic speeding westwards out of the city. It is not pleasant to walk here because of the noise, traffic and pollution. However, it was not always so, as the quays were once lined with houses, built in the eighteenth century, of which only two or three now remain.

Usher's Quay is named after the family of Usher (sometimes spelt Ussher), who were prominent citizens in Dublin from the fifteenth century onwards. Various members of the family were mayors of Dublin during the sixteenth century, and their house was located beside the Liffey, close to the Bridge Gate. John Usher is credited with having published the first book ever printed in the Irish language, in 1571, and his son issued the first Irish edition of the New Testament, which was 'printed at the town of the ford of hurdles in the house of Master Usher, at the foot of the bridge of John Francke, 1602'. The Ushers of Bridge-Foot became a distinguished and well-known family in seventeenth-century Ireland. Usher's Island, a piece of ground sandwiched between the mill race of the River Camac on one side and the River Liffey on the other was held by Christopher Usher in the late seventeenth century.

Number 15 Usher's Island was the setting of the Joyce story 'The Dead'. Built in around 1805, it was once four stories high with elegant rooms and a handsome wrought-iron staircase. Although the top floor was removed, it was occupied for many years by Dardis and Dunn, seed merchants, who eventually sold it in 1983. It is now one of two remaining Georgian houses on Usher's Island, and it is currently in a semi-derelict condition, though a scheme for its restoration has been proposed by a new owner.

John Gilbert, in his *History of the City of Dublin*, tells us that the London Tavern on Usher's Quay was the starting point for the Athlone stage coach in 1737. There were also four public cranes for weighing butter on Usher's Quay in the middle of the eighteenth century.

Usher's Quay was developed with houses in the early eighteenth century. Of the several fine houses that once stood there, few now remain, but we know that in the eighteenth century it was a fashionable residential district. One of the houses, for instance, was

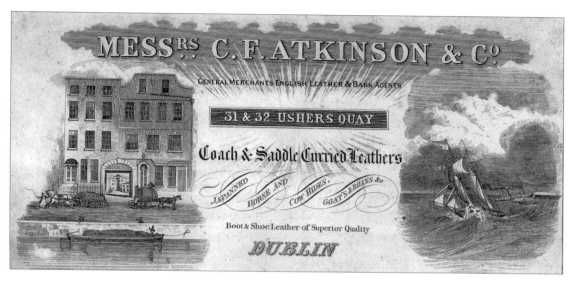

occupied by Theobald Taaffe, the Earl of Carlingford.

Number 34 Usher's Quay was equal in scale to those of Merrion Square. In the 1830s it was occupied by an educational institution called St Vincent's Academy. It later became the Seminary of St Laurence O'Toole. Next door, at 32 Usher's Quay, stood the double premises of Messrs Atkinson & Co., who describe themselves as 'hide, bark and leather factors'.

Bit by bit the old houses of the quays disappeared. In 1965, for instance, 20 Usher's Island, the home of an eccentric barrister and informer, Francis McGann, was demolished. In the early years of the nineteenth century it transpired that McGann, who was a devout Catholic, had been informing on various ringleaders of the 1798 rebellion and that it was his tip-off that lead to the ultimate arrest of Lord Edward FitzGerald in Thomas Street. For this information, McGann received a pension and other payments from the British government. His home was a typical eighteenth-century house, with an attractive Georgian doorcase and wrought-iron balconies. The bachelor McGann and his spinster sister were buried in the vaults of the Church of SS Michael and John, where a sum of money was left in his will for the saying of a perpetual mass for the repose of his soul.

In 1987 a fire destroyed a similar house on Usher's Quay, the premises of Birch Ltd, lift manufacturers. The building was subsequently inspected by the Dangerous Buildings Section of Dublin Corporation, who decided that it should be demolished. In 1985 a particularly fine cut-stone warehouse at 25–26 Usher's Island was also demolished, this time at the behest of Dublin Corporation's Road Engineering Department. The mills, constructed sometime prior to 1850, were known as the City of Dublin Flour Mills, and were owned by the Rainsfords, who at one time, occupied the Anna Liffey Mills in Lucan. Rainsford was also described as a barm brewer, and by 1911 there was also a bakery on the premises. The five-storey mill building was acquired as a hostel for the Simon

Above: A billhead from the mid-nineteenth century from Atkinson's, suppliers of leathers.

Below: A detail of the wrought-iron staircase at number 15 Usher's Quay.

Community, but planning permission was granted on the condition that over eight feet would be taken off the front of the building, thereby sealing its fate. Many years ago, Mr George Redmond, the Assistant City and County Manager at the time, told me that there were inadequate sight lines for traffic emerging from Watling Street because of the projection of the mill building. However, he omitted to point out that Watling Street only accommodated one-way traffic – in the opposite direction!

City of Dublin Flour Mills & Bakeries.

Above: This impressive mill on Usher's Island was demolished in 1985.

Below: The grandiose Victorian façade of Home's Hotel, which later became Ganly's auctioneers.

Another casualty of the Corporation's road-widening plans was Burke's pub, which stood at the corner of Bridge Street and Usher's Quay and was demolished in 1983. A four-storey redbrick corner premises, Burke's was a handsome Victorian building with a corner entrance of cut stone.

Ganly Walters, the well-known Dublin firm of auctioneers, had their origins as cattle salesmen, wool and corn brokers, auctioneers and valuers at 18–20 Usher's Quay. They were also represented in the cattle markets of Liverpool and Manchester. Ganly's is one of the longest established auctioneering firms still in business in Dublin today. Ganly's premises on Usher's Quay occupied the former Homes Hotel, an old coaching house for those travelling to the west. In the nineteenth century Ganly's chief trade was in cattle, wool and corn, and they were given much credit for having promoted the Irish woollen trade. Ganly's occupied the old hotel for almost a hundred years, having acquired it in 1878. The grandiose structure, which was constructed in 1826 by a Scottish developer named

George Homes, contained a cloth market on the ground floor known as the Wellesley Market. Homes spent £20,000 in erecting the structure, which had a grand portico of seven Doric columns that fronted the four-storey stucco-ornamented building. Unfortunately the building was demolished shortly after Ganly's moved to new premises in 1977.

A map, dated 1790, from the Dublin City Archives shows a large tannery situated at the bottom of Watling Street, on the west side near the quays. The tannery occupied land that is shown as the property of Charles Domville. Water was supplied to the works by means of two mill races, one from the River Camac, which we have already mentioned, while the other was powered by the River Liffey. The latter is labelled on the map 'one through which the tide flows' indicating that it was a tidal mill race. By the second half of the nineteenth century, the tannery was shown on an Ordnance map as a timber yard.

Among the terraced Georgian houses that once lined the quays at Usher's Island, one large house stood out – Moira House, built in 1752 by John Rawdon, the first earl of Moira. The family occupied and maintained the house until 1826, when it was sold to a charity who reconstructed it as the Mendicity Asylum. At that time the house was enlarged, and the original stone pediment and cornice were removed. It had been an attractive building, detached, with its own garden overlooking the River Liffey. Arched and pedimented carriage entrances leading to the stables stood on either side of the front courtyard. The Mendicity

Above: The still intact Usher's Quay as it was in the 1960s, showing Ganly's auctioneers at numbers 18–20 and other Georgian houses.

Below: Wool was once weighed at Ganly's wool crane at Usher's Quay.

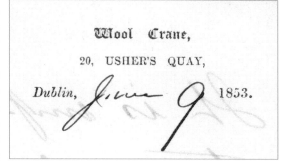

Institute was established in 1818, in an attempt to accommodate some of the many beggars who populated the streets of Dublin. Moira House continued to serve that purpose until the 1950s, when it became vacant and was eventually levelled in 1960.

To the south of the quays lie Bridgefoot Street, Usher Street and Island Street, now a desolate area crying out for redevelopment. Much of it, including a large site now owned by Guinness's, was, even in the eighteenth century, very industrialised and was the location of timber yards, breweries and tanneries. The mills were served by a mill race, a tributary of the River Camac, which flowed behind Steevens's Hospital and through the present Guinness property.

Various leases of the late eighteenth century show that there were several timber yards in the district. For instance, in 1767, Thomas Meade leased a yard to Thomas Bell, timber merchant, and in another lease for 23 Usher's Island, a Mr Davis retained to himself the right to store timber in the yard to the rear. In 1785 we find a Mr Edward Burrows giving a lease of a house and a warehouse to George Maquay. Most of the old warehouses of the district have now vanished and in 1986 one of the last large, stone-built warehouses, three stories in height and supported on cast-iron columns, was demolished in Bonham Street.

D'Arcy's Brewery, which boasted that it was the 'largest brewery in Ireland – but one', occupied a large site on Usher Street. D'Arcy's, which went under the name of the Anchor Brewery, was established in 1818 by John D'Arcy. His son, Matthew D'Arcy, was a magistrate and MP for County Wexford. Records of a brewery on this site go back to 1782 when it belonged to Messrs Kavanagh and Brett. In 1818 it was sold to Mr John D'Arcy for the huge sum of £35,000.

The Anchor Brewery covered an area of seven acres, including a very large maltstore. Like Guinness's, the brewery was equipped with an

Below: The Anchor Brewery, one of the largest breweries in Ireland, as it looked in the nineteenth century.

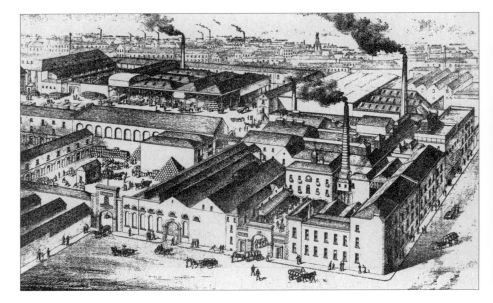

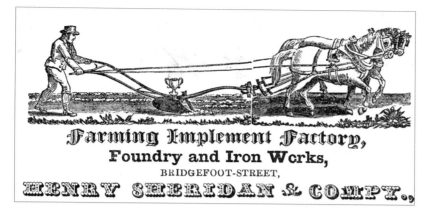

Left: The billhead of Sheridan's, one of the many ironworks in this part of the city.

Below: The Phoenix Brewery of Watling Street, which prospered in the late nineteenth century, was one of many such industries in Dublin.

extensive cooperage, stables, malthouses, kilns and brew houses. It was entered by two substantial arched gates, not unlike the present gate at Guinness's. The main gate led into a courtyard that was overlooked by a three-storey brick building, which housed the offices of the brewery. The offices were raised above an arcade that had a public clock and a sculpture of a nymph holding an anchor. A contemporary engraving of the brewery shows a myriad of brick and stone buildings, several chimney stacks and the office building with a cupola on its roof. Nothing now remains of this brewery.

At this time Marshalsea Lane was a narrow thoroughfare joining Thomas Street with Bonham Street and took its name from a group of buildings known as the Marshalsea. The original Marshalsea stood between Christ Church Cathedral and Wood Quay, but was demolished in the mid-eighteenth century. The Marshalsea Lane building was constructed as a type of debtors' prison where whole families were sometimes confined

Below: The Marshalsea, which later became a military barracks.

under extremely harsh conditions. The extensive buildings, which are thought to have been erected in the 1770s, were laid out around two courtyards that housed the prisoners' rooms, guard rooms, a chapel, an infirmary, a ball court, baths and privies. The marshal of the prison had his own quarters in the upper yard. This interesting structure, with its courtyards of three-storey brick buildings was demolished in 1975.

In the nineteenth century there was an iron

foundry in Bridgefoot Street that specialised in manufacturing farm implements. Henry Sheridan's ironworks produced everything from horseshoe nails, kitchen grates, ranges and ovens, spades, shovels, anvils, rainwater pipes and spouts, to farm rollers, threshing machines, straw- and hay-cutters and ploughs. A few doors away at 39 Bridgefoot Street was the rival firm of Classon Duggan & Co., who also dealt in all kinds of iron, steel and tin as well as supplying timber, steel and laths. The firm of James Fitzsimon & Sons, Timber and Slate Importers, was established at 15 Bridgefoot Street as early as 1780, but slowly expanded and eventually took over the premises of Classon Duggan as well. Fitzsimons also had their own sawmills and an extensive yard and wharf at the North Wall. The firm specialised in supplying timber for the manufacture of carriages, carts, floats, vans and jaunting carts.

The Brazen Head is situated at the bottom of Bridge Street, near the River Liffey. The Brazen Head is thought to be the oldest public house in Ireland – the present building is certainly of very early eighteenth-century date. It is hard to argue against the claim that a pub stood on this site since medieval times and the records certainly show that the Brazen Head existed in 1668. It has been much modernised in recent years, though the ancient windows on the staircase in the back of the house, which may date

Below: Some very old glass remains in the early eighteenth-century staircase window of the Brazen Head pub, off Bridge Street.

Below bottom: A passageway still leads to the Brazen Head.

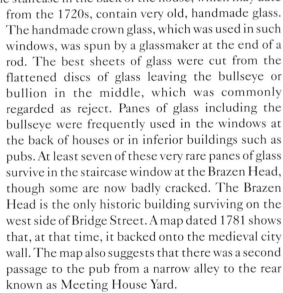

from the 1720s, contain very old, handmade glass. The handmade crown glass, which was used in such windows, was spun by a glassmaker at the end of a rod. The best sheets of glass were cut from the flattened discs of glass leaving the bullseye or bullion in the middle, which was commonly regarded as reject. Panes of glass including the bullseye were frequently used in the windows at the back of houses or in inferior buildings such as pubs. At least seven of these very rare panes of glass survive in the staircase window at the Brazen Head, though some are now badly cracked. The Brazen Head is the only historic building surviving on the west side of Bridge Street. A map dated 1781 shows that, at that time, it backed onto the medieval city wall. The map also suggests that there was a second passage to the pub from a narrow alley to the rear known as Meeting House Yard.

This point, at the Meeting House Yard, marked the western extremity of the medieval city wall of Dublin. The wall was defended in this area by several towers, including Harbard's Tower, Usher's Tower and a defensive gate at the bottom of Bridge Street. Harbard's Tower stood at the back of the Brazen Head Hotel and was once occupied by a man of that name in the late sixteenth century. The

tower was still standing in 1781, when the map describes a property let to James King as 'situated at the rear of the houses on the west side of Bridge Street, together with the tower there unto adjoining'.

It is a well recorded fact that the United Irishmen often held meetings in an upstairs room in the Brazen Head prior to 1798, and that Oliver Bond, one of the leaders, lived in a house across the street.

In 1982 the then owner of the Brazen Head, Mrs Mary Cooney, expressed concern over the Corporation's plans to widen the street and demolish the historic archway that led into the pub. Nonetheless, the arch was removed and a ridiculous parody of a medieval arch was reconstructed, complete with false brick battlements. Even now it would be more appropriate to build a new structure on the site with, at the very least, a faithful reproduction of what was there originally, as the present street frontage of this historic pub is an unfortunate combination of sham history and an ugly parking lot with a palisade fence. Fortunately the original courtyard, with its old doorway and plaster sign on the wall, survives.

Mrs Cooney recalled Bridge Street when it was still full of houses, people and children, 'but the houses are gone now – slowly but surely the Corporation knocked them down and I miss them sorely'. Bridge Street is now part of the inner tangent route, a road conceived many decades ago to connect the north and south city centres. It is a soulless thoroughfare, but the construction of several new apartment blocks has at least banished the many derelict sites that blighted the area for so long.

Above left: Bridge Street, near the Brazen Head, in the 1960s.

Above right: The Baker's Hall at number 6 Bridge Street with its elaborate coat of arms, which now stands outside the National Museum on Kildare Street.

Above: This large warehouse, once belonging to Power's Distillery, lies behind Usher's Quay and is remarkable for its rooftop meadow. It is shortly to be demolished.

Below: Part of Strangways' map of 1904, showing the original medieval city wall in the bottom right-hand corner, onto which the Brazen Head once backed.

Many of the stables and backhouses that adjoined the city wall were, like the Brazen Head, approached by means of long passages from Bridge Street. Another unusually located pub was 'The Sign of the Jolly Drayman', which stood beside the bridge on the site of the present road at Merchants' Quay. The pub, owned by a Mr P Wogan in the late eighteenth century, was surrounded by various small buildings, including a tap room. A map in the National Library shows a passage from the kitchen to the yard that ran under Mr Wogan's tap room! Part of the pub appears to have sat directly overlooking the River Liffey.

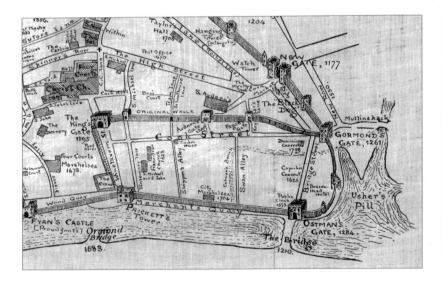

CHAPTER NINE

The Coombe and Ardee Street Area

*T*he greater part of the Liberties stretching from Cork Street down to Blackpitts and across to the Coombe was once a densely occupied area that was both residential and industrial. Rocque's map of 1756 provides plenty of evidence of this and also shows a number of narrow alleys, such as Cuckolds Row and Mutton Lane, connecting the Coombe with Newmarket and Ardee Street. A small mill race, a tributary of the River Poddle, running parallel to Cork Street, powered a group of mills on the western side of Ardee Street, the site today of Strahan's timber store.

To the west, Ormond Street and Chamber Street gave access to the Weaver's Square, a forgotten part of old Dublin that was once lined with gable-fronted houses of early eighteenth-century date. As the name

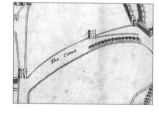

Above: Speed's map, showing the Coombe, which then lay well outside the medieval city.

Left: A view of the Coombe in the 1930s, showing the Coombe Maternity Hospital, of which only the porch and portico remain.

Right: The Victorian façade of number 10 Mill Street is still standing. Later alterations disguise the building's early origins.

Below: One of the most beautifully carved early eighteenth-century staircases in Dublin was located at number 10 Mill Street.

Opposite: The stones of this remarkable doorcase, *c*.1720, await reassembly.

implies, these houses were erected mainly by Huguenot weavers who lived and worked in this area. Chamber Street ran southwards into Newmarket, which was a long narrow square laid out in the late 1670s and lined on both sides with houses. A few industries still operate there now, though new apartments are being built, especially at the eastern end. A short street named Ward's Hill connected Newmarket with Blackpitts, where there were many tanneries.

Mill Street, which lies to the south of Newmarket, is now a quiet backwater, but it took its name from the presence of a number of mills in this area which were powered by the River Poddle. It must then have been a busy and industrious district. A large, early house still stands in Mill Street, though its beautiful front, which consisted of a pair of Dutch gables and a magnificent carved doorcase, were replaced by a clumsy Victorian façade in the late nineteenth century. The house, with its remarkable carved and panelled staircase along with a sequence of panelled rooms, was also vandalised in the 1980s, though many of the original fittings were salvaged. The magnificent doorcase, with its engaged fluted columns and highly carved Corinthian capitals, was moved to the yard behind the house, but in more recent times was stored for safety at the Guinness Hopstore. Here it was possible to see the enormous stones which comprised the great scrolls or swan necks and their carved rosettes. Peter

Above: The wrought-iron lamp brackets of the cut-stone entrance to Ardee House were constructed *c*.1720.

Below: The beautiful panelled staircase of Ardee House.

Walsh, in his comprehensive article on the early houses of the Liberties (*The Liberties of Dublin*, The O'Brien Press, 1973), suggests that this doorway may have been carved by William Kidwell, a sculptor of monuments who came to Dublin in 1711. He also points out that the remains of one of the mill ponds which gave the street its name was still to be seen in 1973 at the back of the house.

Number 10 Mill Street was a large house, five windows wide, consisting of three storeys over a basement. As the building still stands and currently belongs to Eircom, there are strong hopes that it may yet be restored to its original condition, especially as many of its decorative features still exist. The alterations to the façade, including a new gable and a porch, were carried out in 1891 when the building was converted for use as a mission hall and school. The stone of the doorcase has deteriorated over the years, but with careful restoration could still be pieced together.

It has been suggested that number 10 Mill Street was a dower house belonging to the Brabazon family who were the Earls of Meath. The name Ardee Street is derived from the Earl of Meath's early connections with the town of Ardee in County Louth. The street was formerly known as 'the Crooked Staff'. It was here that the Brabazons erected a townhouse – Ardee House. The old house has a tall cut-stone doorcase, echoed by its tall façade. Ardee House was attached to the former Coombe Maternity Hospital, where it served as a nurses' home in the 1930s, some years before its demolition.

The Earls of Meath have left their name on many surrounding streets, including Meath Street, Grey Square, Reginald Street, Brabazon Street, Earl Street and, of course, Ardee Street. The Liberties of this part of Dublin had been granted to the Earls of Meath, who still retain title to some of its lands.

Another large house of similar vintage once stood on Ward's Hill just around the corner from number 10 Mill Street. Ward's Hill was the home of a wealthy brewer named Richard Ward, who established his business in this area in the late seventeenth century. It is thought that this house may once have had a similar gable treatment to that at Marrowbone Lane. An engraving from the *Dublin Penny Journal* shows a similar merchant's house, also built in the early 1700s, but which was composed of one massive gable which contained just one window at third-floor level, three at second-floor level and seven at first-floor level. Early photographs show that the more modest houses which adjoined Ward's Hill also had

Dutch gables and were of similar age. All of these houses suggest that great prosperity was produced by the industries of the area. Sadly they were swept away in the early twentieth century.

The terraced houses of Weavers' Square and Chamber Street were fronted with triangular gables and were generally three windows wide. Most of these weavers' houses disappeared in the 1950s, although one of them (minus its gable) may still be seen in the street. The very attractive houses of Sweeney's Lane, which were built in 1721, survived until 1932.

The Coombe, which may be seen on Speed's map of Dublin (1610), is a street of great antiquity. Unfortunately, several of its most important historic buildings have now vanished, including the Weavers' Hall, the Coombe Lying-in Hospital and St Luke's Church, which now remains only as a burnt-out shell.

It is no surprise, given the prominence of weavers in the area, that the weavers' guild hall was built in the Coombe in 1745. The Weavers' Hall is marked with a WH on Rocque's map, and it stood almost opposite the entrance to St Luke's Church. The hall occupied a frontage of forty-seven feet, and was joined on either side by the Weavers' Charity School at number 15 and the Weavers' Alms House at number 17. The front of their hall, which stood directly on the Coombe, was ornamented by a gilded lead statue of King George II, which stood there until 1937. Some fragments of

Above: Ward's Hill House, one of the vanished mansions of the Liberties.

Below: Gable-fronted houses in Poole Street off Pimlico, *c.*1900.

the statue are said to remain in the Dublin Civic Museum. An important tapestry that once hung in the Weavers' Hall was for many years preserved by Messrs Atkinson & Co., the noted Dublin Poplin manufacturers. However, it is now in the Metropolitan Museum of Art in New York. The tapestry was the work of John Van Beaver and was dated 1758.

A grand staircase gave access to the upstairs meeting room of the weavers, which was ornamented by elaborate woodwork. This room featured a large fireplace with an unusual timber-carved overmantel. The overmantel was composed of a circular panel, surmounted by a richly carved semicircular pediment. This woodwork, along with a magnificent doorcase from the entrance to the hall, was salvaged, shortly before the demolition in 1956. Photographs taken by the Office of Public Works in 1954 show that the building was in poor condition, but it is surprising that no efforts were made to prevent the destruction of such a historic landmark in the Liberties of Dublin.

This side of the street was let to Richard Faulkner in 1726 and laid out in twenty-five lots for building. The houses were of modest proportion, as the plots were laid out in widths ranging from fifteen to twenty-one feet. John Gallagher, a noted resident of this area and recently elected City Alderman, was born in the Weavers' Alms House on the Coombe. He recalled that in his youth the street in front of the Weavers' Hall was paved

Above: An internal door in Weavers' Hall. It was salvaged and is now awaiting a suitable home in a museum of Dublin.

Right: The vanished Weavers' Hall in the Coombe. The statue of George II by Van Nost is shown holding shuttles and weaving implements.

with wooden blocks, in order to reduce the level of noise from passing horses and carts. John Gallagher has worked unceasingly for the preservation of old Dublin and for the living communities, especially of his own area. He was one of those who, along with Deirdre Kelly, stood in front of the bulldozers in the early 1970s when the Inner Tangent road was being forced through Kevin Street.

The impressive premises of John C Parkes & Sons occupied 109 to 111 the Coombe for over 100 years. An advertisement for Parkes of the Coombe from the 1880s lists their comprehensive stock of goods, including all manner of hardware, plumbing equipment, domestic appliances and paints. Japanned goods, saddlery, ropes and twines, along with brushes, combs and spoons were also available. Parkes was destroyed by fire in 1984,

Above: The Coombe in the mid-1980s, showing the buildings of Parkes on the right.

Below left: JC Parkes' substantial premises, which incorporated several Georgian houses, were destroyed by fire in 1984, shortly after closure.

Below: A customised toilet chain pull from Parkes.

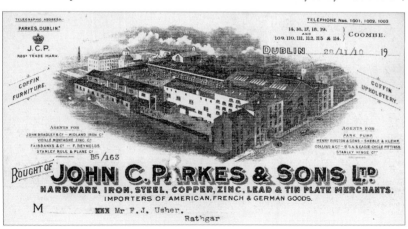

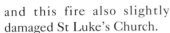

Above: St Nicholas Without and St Luke's was destroyed by fire in 1986.

Below: The 'barley-sugar' balusters of the staircase in St Luke's Church.

and this fire also slightly damaged St Luke's Church.

St Nicholas Without and St Luke's was described in an article in the *Irish Times* by Pat Liddy in 1986, but within weeks of this was completely gutted by a malicious fire. Many of the refugee French Huguenots, who were weavers in this district, were allowed to use the Lady Chapel of St Patrick's Cathedral in the late seventeenth century. But in 1707 a new parish church of St Luke was erected. This long rectangular church, with its handsome Georgian gallery, was closed in 1976. The church was originally approached by an avenue of trees from an entrance on the Coombe, but this old avenue and adjoining graveyard will soon become part of a new highway connecting the Inner Tangent route to Crumlin. The final service before its closure was recorded by John Bates:

> The church was filled to capacity, the interior as lovely as ever. Some hand or hands had lovingly cleaned and garnished here. Every brass gleamed from the painted walls. A tiled aisle shone, as did the blackened Victorian floor grilles that covered the central heating pipes. The old organ sounded as throaty as ever ... What woodcarver here in the Liberties wrought these gild cherubs that smiled down from the organ case?

The church was officially known as St Nicholas Without and St Luke's, and now only the derelict shell of the Widows' House of the Parish of St Nicholas Without and St Luke's remains to recall this name in the Coombe. Across from it is the Holy Faith School, which was opened in 1887.

The Coombe and its Industries

A map in the National Library of Ireland dated 1793 shows a brewery in Ardee Street. This brewery was situated on the corner of Cork Street and Ardee Street, on the west side, and depicts a large corner house that projected into the street at Cork Bridge. This house, which is also shown on Rocque's map, belonged to a Mr Thwaites and was attached to the brewery. The largest part of the site was taken up by a malthouse, while the neighbouring properties to the west were in use as tanyards – one of them was equipped with drying lofts where new leather was left to dry. The map also shows a small water course, which ran partly underground and partly open along the front of the brewery in Ardee Street, passing under Cork Bridge at the point where Cork Street takes a sharp turn into Ardee Street.

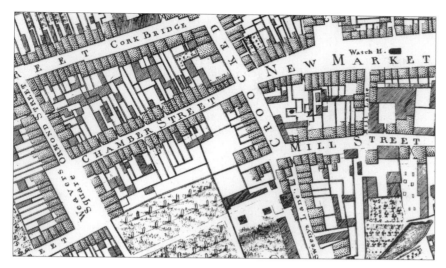

One of the few attractive old buildings which has survived in the Ardee Street area is the old house and brewery offices of Watkins & Co., brewers and maltsters, at 8–12 Ardee Street. Watkins Brewery was established in the early nineteenth century by an Englishman, Joseph Watkins, and it is said that his brewery was located on the site of the former brew house of the monastery of St Thomas and that the old crypts were, at one time, used as cellars. The Ardee Street brewery covered a site of about five acres. Watkins had a large clientele in Ireland and also exported their beers. They were one of the last small breweries to stay in business well into the twentieth century.

The building is of interest not least because it is one of the few surviving grand houses of the Liberties. It has a fine Georgian-style doorcase and elaborate fanlight, and retains all its original features, including its brick façade and sash windows. The rooms of the interior are generously proportioned, and the staircase with its rounded corners and niches is typical of the early 1800s. A fine cut-granite archway leads into the original brewery yard while to the right are the former offices, which also date from about 1800. A large safe with a Gothic-style door once stood in this building and bore testimony to the valuable trade that was carried on there. In about 1900 the amalgamated firm of Watkins, Jameson and Pim also controlled a large brewery at

Above: The many weavers' houses, now all gone, are shown in the streets of the Liberties in this map by Rocque (1756).

Below: The goods entrance and residence of the Ardee Street Brewery.

Bray, which stood by the River Dargle.

The late Georgian house and offices, which face up Cork Street, were defended in 1916 by Eamonn Ceannt and there is a plaque on the building to record this fact. However, not even this historical association was enough to prevent road engineers planning a dual carriageway from Crumlin to run down Cork Street right through the middle of it. The threat of demolition hung over this and the adjoining house until the late 1980s, when the Corporation's road was realigned. Due to the persistence of the present owners, the Maguire family, and to the efforts of An Taisce during the 1980s, the future of these buildings now looks more positive.

Another late eighteenth-century map in the National Library illustrates a nearby section of Ardee Street, between Newmarket and Mill Street. Once again the industrial nature of the area is in evidence, with two limekilns and a forge, attached to a large yard. Rocque's map also shows the limekiln and nearby Sweeney's Lane, which in his time (1756) stood at the very fringe of the city looking out onto the fields and countryside of County Dublin. The brick gabled houses of Sweeney's Lane have been described in several publications and were attractive brick houses of the 'Dutch Billy' type, built by weavers in 1721.

Above: The Georgian staircase in the Brewers' House in Ardee Street.

Right: An early nineteenth-century map, showing a tannery in Mill Street, with a bark mill and sheds.

The Mill Street and adjoining Blackpitts area was at one time the site of several tanneries. The name Blackpitts comes from the black stained pits or vats in which leather was cured by the various tanners in the district. In 1973 one of these vats remained to be seen in the back garden of a house in the district. In the tanning process, the bark of oak trees was used to cure the leather. The bark was milled into a pulp and then placed in a tank with the leather, where it was immersed in water for several weeks or months. One such tannery occupied a site beside Mill Street and Newmarket, and incorporated two houses, a tanyard and a bark house. A lease map of 1799 shows that the property almost opposite number 10 belonged to Robert Cope Gibton and was leased to John Stoyte. A water pipe and a mill are shown adjoining it. The bark house is described in the deed as a bark mill, situated 'on the south side of Newmarket in the Liberties of Thomas Court and Donore … with … the full use and privileges of the piped water which runs through Newmarket aforesaid'.

The tannery at 32 and 33 Mill Street remained in the possession of Molloy and Company, tanners, in the late nineteenth century. At this time there was a second tannery in the street, at number 8, belonging to Hayes Brothers, who became one of the leading firms in the late nineteenth century. Hayes's principal tannery occupies 44–49 New Row South. In 1659 it came to the attention of the Guild of Tanners that some were 'imboldened to putt for sale theire deceiptfull leather in theire houses, yards, back sides and other obscure places, not dareinge to adventure theire said leather to the viewe of the markette', and ordered that leather should be sold only in the Corn Market on certain days and that all leather offered for sale should be assayed or marked. Some dubious tanners had 'putt theire keeves or fatts in tan hills, whereby leather doth receave unnaturall heates, and doe use hott woozes in tanninge of leather'! In 1616 a reference to the Tanners' Hall tells us that it was situated over St Audeon's Arch by the old city wall. The tanners of Dublin were granted a charter by King Edward I in 1289 and as such formed one of the oldest guilds in the city.

The process of tanning leather was a dirty and lengthy one. First the hair was removed from the animal hides by soaking them in a mixture of lime and water. The hides were then transferred to a tanpit, into which layers of crushed oak barks and water were added to make tannin. The longer they were left in the pit, the better the quality of leather. While much leather was exported from Dublin over the centuries, there was also a substantial demand in the city for making shoes, bags and saddles and many other articles.

In 1884 number 10 Mill Street was occupied by the ragged school, while number 3 was the notorious premises of O'Keeffe, horse slaughterer and manure manufacturer. The smells that emanated from O'Keeffe's are remembered by people to this day. O'Keeffe's premises was in use until recently as a scrapyard, and part of it was once occupied by the City of Dublin Brewery Company.

The Blackpitts River, the local name for the River Poddle, is shown on a map of about 1800, flowing under the street at the bottom of Fumbally Lane. The name Fumbally Lane has given rise to various theories as to its origin.

Above top: A row of 'Dutch Billy' houses, c.1720, in Sweeney's Lane, now demolished.

Above: A delivery docket from the Ardee Street Brewery.

Right: The unusual compartmented plasterwork ceiling of number 12 Fumbally Lane.

Below: The gutted ruin of number 12 Fumbally Lane after the fire in the 1980s.

One theory is that 'bum bailiffs', or hired thugs, lived here and that the lane became known as Bum Bailiffs' Lane! In his excellent study of the houses of the Liberties, Peter Walsh suggests that it is derived from the French family name of Fomboilie, and points to the fact that a lease was given in 1741 for 'two houses in a lane called Fombily's Lane leading from Blackpits to Newe Street, by David Fombily, skinner, to Anthony Fombily, skinner'.

It would appear that Fumbally Lane was originally laid out in 1721 by Jacob Poole, a brewer who had property interests in Blackpitts. The new land, which subsequently became known as Fumbally Lane, connected

Blackpitts with New Street. In her unpublished thesis on the old detached house at 12 Fumbally Lane, Rachel MacRory was uncertain as to who built this house or first occupied it, but was able to show that relations of Jacob Poole, the Taylor family, had brewing interests here since 1740 and may have built it.

The house, which lasted up until the 1980s, retained many original features including its panelled rooms, corner fireplaces and the early plasterwork ceilings. The compartmented ceilings were a rare surviving example of a style once popular in the 1720s. The ceiling of the principal room, which was on the first floor, was ornamented by a circular centrepiece framed in a square, surrounded in turn by twelve smaller squares. This geometrical design was formed with bolection mouldings while the centrepiece was decorated with boldly modelled rosettes, acanthus and oak leaves, garlands, branches, bands and ribbons. A smaller room at the back of the house was similarly ornamented. The top floor landing was once lit by a most unusual octagonal overhead lantern, which suggests that it once had a rooftop cupola, similar to that at Woodlands House in Santry.

The plan of the house was very unusual, containing a large hall, a parlour and several offices on the ground floor, which suggests that it may have been designed originally as the offices and residence of the brewery owner. The staircase was placed in a most unusual way at the side of the house. Though the house was rendered in more recent times, it seems certain that it was originally faced in red brick.

Rachel McRory established that Jacob Poole and his brother-in-law, Samuel Taylor, were Quakers and had brewing interests in Marrowbone Lane and Fumbally Lane. A deed of 1789 connects the house with the nearby brew house, malthouse and storehouses. These brewery buildings, which lay to the north of Fumbally Lane, passed from James Farrell, brewer, in 1779, to Samuel Madder, a brewer of porter from James Street, in 1820. Madder then operated the Blackpitts Porter Company here for some years,

Above top: The unusual roof structure and rear of number 12 Fumbally Lane.

Above: Detail from the main ceiling of number 12.

Left: A nineteenth-century photograph of a group of houses known as Brass Castle.

until the premises were converted into a distillery in the 1820s. It was later sold in 1828 for £5,000, complete with its steam engine and machinery.

By 1830 the distillery had passed into the ownership of John Busby and we find his initials, JB, and the date, 1836, embossed on a large water tank that may still be seen on the roof of the adjoining distillery building. John Busby, who owned a mill in Mill Street, also had a malt-house in nearby Newmarket. Between 1867 and 1883 the buildings, which incorporated a still house, a spirit store and a brew house, were taken over by the City of Dublin Brewery Company, who had other premises at the corner of Fumbally's Lane and Blackpitts. Some of their old stone buildings have been converted in recent years as offices. The River Poddle flows through the distillery site and once powered its machinery, which included mill engines.

The square, three-storey house is shown on the map in the Dublin City Archives as having a central flight of steps up to the hall door but these were probably removed when the house was converted into a textile factory in the late nineteenth century. In 1979 the house was occupied by Blair's Fancy Linens. In the early 1980s various individuals tried to acquire the building for restoration. In the meantime, it was burnt down and subsequently demolished. The loss of this house was indeed unfortunate, as it was a rare example of such an early house in Ireland, only paralleled by the recently restored Kildrought House in Celbridge. The surrounding yard with its tall stone distillery building is now about to be redeveloped. Across the road lies a terrace of six two-storey houses, three of which are possibly of late eighteenth-century date. They also appear on the early map.

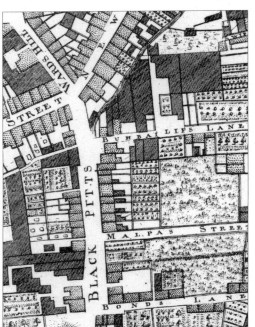

Above: Rocque's map, showing the Blackpitts area of the Coombe.

Blackpitts in the nineteenth century was noted for its dairies, one of which, though now closed and boarded up, still stands in the street.

The Blackpitts River is still visible in the grounds of the nearby convent at Warrenmount, where it finally disappears from open view and goes through a series of underground brick culverts on its journey to the River Liffey. Warrenmount was the eighteenth-century home of Nathaniel Warren, Lord Mayor of Dublin in 1782.

The Tenter Fields described an area that lay behind Blackpitts and stretched westwards towards Donore Avenue. The Tenters was a bleaching green where linen was stretched out on tenterhooks to be bleached by the sun.

The general squalor and unsanitary state of much of the housing in the Liberties was the subject of frequent comment throughout the nineteenth century. However, by the end of the century serious efforts were being made to address the problem. One of the first real improvements was made when the Dublin Artisans' Dwelling Company was established in 1876.

Under the new Public Health Act, many sites were cleared and houses began to be built. One hundred and twenty houses were completed by about 1900 in the Blackpitts area. They had also built 210 houses in the Coombe area by 1882. A separate organisation, the Dublin and Suburban Workmen's Dwelling Company, had erected about 250 houses in Cork Street by 1890, while the Guinness-funded Iveagh Trust had built 250 flats in the Bull Alley area by 1901.

Prior to the completion of these houses and Dublin Corporation's own developments, the poor of the city simply had to make do with the existing building stock. There was no profit in building houses for a poor working class who could not pay the rent, so the Victorian developers turned their

Above: This most unusual pair of gable-fronted houses, at the corner of New Row and Blackpitts, have long vanished.

Right: Children playing with dolls in the 1940s.

Below: This old house accommodated the offices of the maltsters, Minch Norton, in Newmarket until it was burnt down in the late 1980s.

attentions to the suburbs instead. Statistics for the middle of the nineteenth century show that one-third of the entire population of the city lived in one-roomed accommodation or tenements. Add to this the effects of the famine, an inadequate sewerage system and a poor water supply along with massive unemployment and it is not difficult to imagine the miserable lives suffered by many in areas such as the Liberties and parts of the north city centre.

The public baths erected by the Iveagh Trust in Bride Road, known as the Iveagh Baths, and the Tara Street Baths erected by the Corporation were part of an attempt to improve cleanliness and sanitation amongst the poor. The arrival of the Vartry water supply from County Wicklow in the late 1860s was also to improve the situation, but the provision of a proper sewerage system for the city was not really completed until about 1900. Now, a century later, we continue to evolve from a situation where such living conditions are still alive in older people's experience and memory. With it comes, even now, a lingering prejudice against anything old that might serve as a reminder of 'the bad old

days'. This understandable resentment of the past was often used, even as recently as twenty years ago, as a justification for getting rid of old buildings, whether or not they had any historic or architectural interest. The two great wars of the twentieth century caused little or no damage to Dublin, but the last forty years of the twentieth century made up for that with a vengeance!

We have already discussed the considerable number of breweries and distilleries located in Dublin's Liberties, and both the brewing and the distilling process required great quantities of malt. As a result, various malthouses, also known as maltings, were situated around the district. The old stone malthouses, with their distinctive hat-shaped roofs and ventilators, were once a feature of this district.

The last operational maltings belonged to Minch Norton in Newmarket, much of which was destroyed by a malicious fire in the 1980s. Many of the old malthouses, with their special floors of perforated tiles, fell into disuse during the last twenty years as new technology became available.

The best-known maltsters in Dublin were the Plunkett family. Their business was established in 1819 by two cousins who set up in Belview Street, just behind Guinness's brewery. By the middle of the nineteenth century, the Plunketts of Belview had become the leading maltsters in

Above: An 1890s billhead of Plunkett's, whose maltings were the largest in the city.

Below: Gable-fronted houses in Marrowbone Lane in a 1950s photograph.

Above: Part of the Belview maltings, which supplied Guinness's brewery.

Below: A circular malthouse at Plunkett's Belview maltings.

Ireland and in 1880 acquired a patent for their special method of roasting malt. (It is interesting to speculate as to whether the Guinness we drink today has anything like the flavour that must have been provided by the golden-brown malt once supplied to Guinness's by the Plunketts.)

The Belview maltings were very extensive and included a wide variety of buildings, including a circular malthouse. The maltings were eventually taken over by Guinness's, and the Plunketts moved their operation to premises at Islandbridge, which they also called Belview. The Islandbridge maltings continued to produce malt until 1970, and the whole complex remained intact for another ten years. Through vandalism and neglect many of the old buildings have been destroyed. An apartment development is now planned for the site.

The Marrowbone Lane distillery once stood close by the Belview maltings, at the back of the Guinness brewery. A plan of this distillery in the National Library shows that it was held by Mr Roe, under a lease from J&R Phepoe. Though long vanished, the most interesting feature of this distillery was a large windmill, which is clearly shown on the plan.

A distiller's house and offices fronted onto Marrowbone Lane, while various outbuildings and stables ran back along Phepoe's Lane as far as School Street. A mill race and watercourse are also shown, along with various stores and a still house.

The distillery later became known as Jameson's, although, confusingly, it was not in any way connected to the famous Jameson's Distillery, which lay across the river in Smithfield. The Marrowbone Lane distillery eventually amalgamated with the Jones Road distillery to form a new brand of whiskey known as DWD, Dublin Whiskey Distillery.

Left: The Iveagh Market was
built in 1902 and paid for by
the Earl of Iveagh.

Below: The carved stonework
heads represent the trading
nations of the world.

Francis Street

Today the name of Francis Street calls to mind the many antique shops that
line the street, but it has changed greatly in the last ten years. It was probably the cheap rents and availability of large store houses which first
attracted the antique dealers to the district some twenty
years ago, when it was also the home of many skilled craftsmen, such as french polishers and upholsterers. From
being a seedy street with derelict sites and broken-down
sheds, it has now become a fashionable residential street
with many apartment buildings.

Francis Street has a long history. It owes its name to the
existence there of a Franciscan friary, founded during the
thirteenth century.

In the eighteenth century over half of the population of
Francis Street was engaged in the textile industry, mostly
producing wool, silk and poplin. A century later the street
was largely given over to grocers, tea, wine and spirit
merchants, and there were no less than six tobacco pipe
manufacturers here in the 1880s. Tobacco smoking had
become very popular, especially among the working class,
but as there were then no cigarettes all tobacco was
smoked in clay pipes. The pipes were made from white
purbeck clay and were turned out in their thousands,
using moulds to shape the barrel and the stem. These
brittle pipes, which often bore historical images or nation-
alistic slogans, such as 'Éireann go Bráth', were finished by hand and sold
very cheaply. The remains of such pipes are often found in fields and
ditches where they were discarded when they broke.

Francis Street and Meath Street were also home to a large number of shoemakers and saddlers, who got their supplies of leather from the many tanneries of the district. Dairies too were scattered throughout the streets of this district and some of them lasted right up until the middle of the twentieth century, when the availability of bottled milk and stricter standards in hygiene put them out of business.

Above: A billhead from one of the many grocery shops in Francis Street.

Below: The Iveagh Market, which sold second-hand clothes, was built on the site of Sweetman's Brewery.

The street has always attracted traders in second-hand goods and the Iveagh Market was, until a few years ago, the centre of a thriving second-hand clothes trade. But with a great number of charity shops now selling second-hand clothes and a general increase in the standard of living, the business of the market has declined. A major restoration project for the Iveagh Market was proposed by Dublin Corporation and the building has now been leased to a developer. The market itself is a fine piece of architecture, with its Queen Anne-style façade on Francis Street and spacious galleried interior. The keystones of the several arches at the front of the building are ornamented with carved heads, which represent the various trading nations of the world. The Portland stone carvings are very striking and create a memorable feature of the building. Designed by Frederick Hicks and built in 1902, the market makes clever use of cast-iron columns to support the gallery and iron roof structure.

The market stands on a site that had once been taken up by an important brewery belonging to the Sweetman family. The eastern side of

the brewery abutted onto the old city wall, adjoining the back of what was, until recently, Mother Redcap's market. Recent archaelogical excavations underneath the old Iveagh Market have revealed parts of the brewery walls and foundations of several early eighteenth-century houses which fronted onto Francis Street.

The Church of St Nicholas and St Myra, which is pleasantly tucked away between Francis Street and John Dillon Street, was begun in 1829 and was one of the first churches to be built after Catholic Emanicipation. As such, it is unashamedly classical and owes much of its inspiration to Roman architecture. The design is attributed to the architects John Leeson and Patrick Byrne. A marble sculpture of the *Pietà* is situated above the altar and was sculpted by John Hogan. The portico and belfry were not completed until about 1860.

The Tivoli Theatre, or 'Tivo' as it was locally known, was opened in 1934 as a cinema, and continued in business until 1963. It could seat up to 1400 people and was the third largest cinema in the city. In 1987 the premises were reopened as a theatre and music venue and it remains popular today.

CHAPTER TEN

Christ Church Cathedral
and its Environs

The traditional date given for the construction of Christ Church Cathedral is the late twelfth century and it is usually stated that Laurence O'Toole, Archbishop of Dublin, founded the cathedral. However, it has been suggested by Roger Stalley that a more likely builder of this cathedral was John Comyn, the succeeding Archbishop of Dublin who came here from western England in 1181. Many architectural features of the cathedral are to be found in the twelfth-century abbeys and cathedrals of western England, so it is likely that Comyn may have brought stone masons from the Bristol area to direct the construction.

This was a building of ambitious scale by Irish standards, although small by English ones. When the cathedral was completed, it was probably the

Below: A mid-eighteenth-century engraving of Christ Church Cathedral.

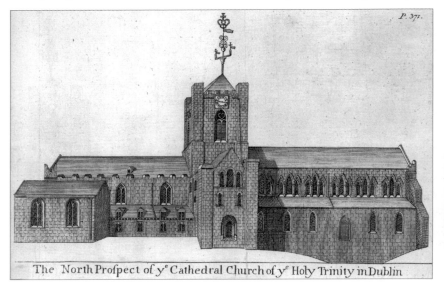

P. 371.

The North Prospect of yᵉ Cathedral Church of yᵉ Holy Trinity in Dublin

Left: The restored 1870 profile of Christ Church Cathedral, showing how it dominated the surrounding area, including Winetavern Street and the Irish House pub.

largest church ever built in Ireland at that time and it had many remarkable features. Stalley points out that it was the first Irish church to have a crypt, the first church to have an ambulatory surrounding the high altar, and the first to have a three-stage elevation, which included an arcade at ground level, a triforium (a Gothic passageway) at first-floor level and a clerestory (the windows high up in the side of the nave), which lit the church.

Nineteenth-century engravings and early photographs show the medieval cathedral as a somewhat grim and very plain structure, nothing at all like today's imposing Christ Church Cathedral. Clearly the decayed and shabby state of the cathedral in the late nineteenth century was an embarrassment to the Church, which recognised that urgent restoration and repairs were required to prevent collapse. As a result, the cathedral was almost completely rebuilt at this time to the designs of the architect George Edmund Street, and the work was paid for by the Dublin distiller Henry Roe. In his Victorian rebuilding work Street followed the medieval use of stone – limestone walls with yellow sandstone used for the moulded Gothic windows.

While it is currently the fashion to criticise restorations and rebuildings of this type, it is certain that the cathedral was in need of urgent repairs and that Street's work, so thorough and well-executed, has ensured the cathedral's survival for a few more centuries. However, it is true that much of the historic fabric of the ancient building was lost at this time, including the moulded stonework of many of the Romanesque arches, much original carved detail on the capitals and a good deal of the early Gothic features of the nave. Critics of Street's work find unacceptable the cavalier way in which the choir was completely rebuilt, doorways were moved about and stone turrets, flying buttresses and even chimney stacks were added to the cathedral.

During the restoration work, a hall was built on the site of St Michael's Church to accommodate the synods of the Church of Ireland, and the old medieval tower of St Michael's was incorporated into the new building. A dramatic bridge was constructed across Winetavern Street to link the hall to the cathedral. A mid-eighteenth-century engraving entitled 'The north prospect of ye cathedral church of ye Holy Trinity in Dublin' shows the unadorned cathedral devoid of battlements except for the chancel and tower, but having a large public clock, rather clumsily placed above the main belfry opening, along with a large weather vane surmounted by a crown and a cross. The print also shows the massive buttress that supported the northwest corner of the nave – it would appear that there was an ongoing problem with the stability of the north wall of the nave, which even today is some eighteen inches out of plumb. Photographs taken prior to Street's restoration of 1870 show the Georgian houses of Winetavern Street dwarfed by the great buttressed wall that ran along John's Lane on the north side.

Below: This nineteenth-century billhead shows how the buildings erected by the Wide Streets Commissioners on Skinner Row in the early nineteenth century backed onto cathedral property.

Opposite: A photograph taken in 1916 of part of the cathedral's choir, showing the reconstruction of the 1870s.

24 & 25, CHRIST CHURCH PLACE,
LATE SKINNER ROW,
Dublin.

An interesting bill from the firm of MacBirney and Collis, the fore-runners of MacBirney's of Aston Quay, shows a four-storey Georgian premises with their shop occupying the ground floor, where the main entrance to the cathedral lies today. The bill is dated 1838 with the address 24–25 Christ Church Place (later Skinner Row), and gives as much prominence to the cathedral as to their own premises. Once again it depicts the cathedral in its 'primitive' state, although a fine set of railings and Gothic gate piers had been erected on the new street frontage. The current railing with its limestone wall and piers is far more elaborate than this earlier one. The present ornamental railings are supported between limestone piers, sporting octagonal caps.

The names of the various narrow streets surrounding the cathedral are significant. Skinner Row suggests an early and important leather industry in the city, while Fishamble Street reminds us that this was the street where fish were once exclusively sold. Winetavern Street was so called because of the presence of so many taverns and wine stores. Even the name Cook Street is said to be derived from the many bakers and cooks who must once have worked in the medieval city.

The work of opening up the southern aspect of the cathedral and of widening Skinner Row was initiated by the Wide Streets Commissioners in the late eighteenth century, and maps of the period show the interesting collection of cathedral buildings that had been swept away by 1820. The present street at Christ Church Place covers the site of the following buildings: the Chantor, a building connected with the church choir; the Oeconomy, which had to do with the day-to-day economics of the cathedral; and the Office of the Chancellor. Other vanished buildings which would have stood in the cathedral precinct included that of the Treasurer and Colfabius, and the Prebendary of St John. The Prebendary was an old building that stood over the present Chapter House ruins and which was described as an 'arched passage with school room above'. There were also the Four Courts – the Common Pleas (for small claims), the King's Bench, the Chancery and the Exchequer, all of which occupied the yard at the present entrance to the cathedral. Apart from the Four Courts, many of these buildings had disappeared by the mid-eighteenth century and maps such as Rocque's show the many small houses of Skinner Row, which backed onto cathedral property.

Below: A plan of Christ Church Cathedral, showing the old Four Courts and other cathedral properties, which were closed during the eighteenth century.

Opposite top: The ancient crypt of the cathedral has recently been renovated and carefully lit to show off its late-medieval vaulting.

Opposite middle: An Ordnance Survey map shows Christ Church prior to its restoration.

Opposite bottom: The plan adopted by George Edmund Street for the restoration.

Prior to the widening of Skinner Row, the old Four Courts were entered via a passage from Christ Church Lane. A building called the Old Exchequer Chamber stood between the courts and Skinner Row. A sketch map of 1727, which survives in the National Library, states that: 'The cellar belonging to the Dean of Christ Church is under part of the High Court of Chancery' and 'the way from the little courthouse to the Four Courts'. The map also shows the site of the Vicar's Choral, a place of residence and practice of the choir, which by the eighteenth century had several houses built upon it.

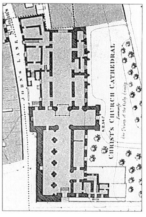

The twelfth-century crypt of the cathedral is unusual because it extends almost the full length of the church. The dryness of the crypt was always noticeable and many will remember the dusty floor, half concrete and half clay, which has recently been paved with new flagstones. The massive vaulted structure of the crypt supports the church above and was simply built of rough stones and lime mortar. This space, which was once leased out for the storage of wine, had become in more recent times a dumping ground for unwanted statuary and other artefacts, such as the fine pair of medieval stocks and a cat that had become mummified in an organ pipe! The stocks, which were made in 1670, are believed to have belonged to the courts of the cathedral. Those found guilty of certain minor offences would have their legs locked in the stocks for a period of time laid down by the court.

Approaching from the hill of Lord Edward Street, the view of Christ Church Cathedral is majestic, dominated by the immense size of the tower with its slated roof and large weather cock. The stone carving of the 1870s is of a uniformly high quality, as can be seen on the several gargoyles that

Above: The well-preserved stocks that remain in the crypt.

Below: Some of the replica medieval tiles that make up the nineteenth-century cathedral floor.

Below bottom: Delicately coloured medieval tiles, which survive in the Chapel of St Laud.

ornament the Chapter House, although they do not possess the character of the early Romanesque carving that survives here and there within the cathedral. It is pleasing to note that the replica cast-iron rainwater pipes in the Chapter House bear the embossed date 1999, a feature that appears on the earlier hoppers and downpipes, which are dated 1875.

The medieval Chapter House must originally have been a very beautiful building but all that now remains can be seen in the garden in front of the south transept. The shafts and bases of the original columns, which once supported a vault, still survive, as do the stones at the base of the elaborate west entrance and the east window.

One of the most attractive features of the present cathedral is the richly coloured tile floor, most of which dates from the late nineteenth century. Many of the tiles are replicas of medieval patterns, including rampant lions, marching foxes and *fleurs-de-lis*. Street's internal remodelling of the cathedral involved many substantial changes, including the removal of the old robing rooms from the south aisle of the nave, and the dismantling of solid walls between the aisles and transepts. In this respect, the changes that Street made were not unlike the present restoration of City Hall, which involves removal of later partitions and walls to bring the building back to its 'original' plan and create more satisfactory circulation. However, the changes Street made to the east end of the cathedral were quite drastic and involved the demolition of the long medieval choir. Quite a number of genuine medieval tiles were found during the work of the 1870s and these can now be seen in the Chapel of St Laud at the east end of the cathedral.

Long ago, the various officials and dignitaries had certain rights and held various properties in the cathedral's vicinity, but today the most valuable privilege may be the specially allotted car-parking spaces for the dean, archbishop and canons of the cathedral. These are not easy times for those entrusted with the care and management of such complex and historic buildings, as congregations dwindle and building and maintainance costs continue to rise. Today an outrageous price, which amounts to a ransom, is demanded just for the erection of scaffolding. On a building of this scale these preliminary necessities often cost far more than the actual repair work.

The Romanesque doorway on the south transept, which like the principal west door is always kept closed, has several beautifully carved birds on its capitals, but is unfortunately very weathered. The cathedral was always traditionally entered through the south door, while the main doors were kept closed.

On the continent you pay to enter museums, while most churches and cathedrals are free, but in Dublin, and it is to our credit, our museums are free but you pay to enter the cathedrals! This is not to begrudge the cathedrals their very necessary income, but perhaps the State should take a greater role in giving financial support to these national monuments. After all, the State spends a significant amount maintaining monuments and archaeological sites and running visitor centres, so the fact that these are

still in use is a bonus. It should, however, be recognised that small amounts of State aid have, in fact, been given to Christ Church Cathedral through such bodies as the Heritage Council, who some years ago assisted in the repair of the Chapter House.

Above: The former Synod Hall now houses the Dublinia exhibition. The romantic bridge was erected in the 1870s to provide access to and from the cathedral.

The Synod Hall, which stands across from the cathedral on St Michael's Hill (previously known as Christ Church Lane), is a Gothic-style structure, incorporating the medieval tower of St Michael's Church. A map of 1810 shows the entire site of the Synod Hall surrounded by High Street, Christ Church Lane, Cock Hill and Michael's Lane. St Michael's Church was then described as being in ruins and was adjoined on the north side by a school house and a church yard. The rest of the site was taken up with some sixteen or seventeen small houses, all of which were cleared away by the Wide Street Commissioners.

The Synod Hall displays a multiplicity of gables, roofs and chimney stacks, and presents an interesting profile from most angles. It, too, was erected by Roe, who, in 1875, offered to build a Synod Hall 'at his sole expense'.

The Synod Hall is connected to Christ Church Cathedral by means of a bridge, a great stone structure supported on four ribs. The Synod of the Church of Ireland sold the hall and it was bought by a private company, which offers visitors a journey through Dublin's medieval past by use of a series of life-size reconstructions, models and audio-visual presentations. Some of the artefacts discovered in the archaeological dig at Wood Quay reside in the hall, on loan from the National Museum of Ireland. Visitors to the Dublinia exhibition may cross the bridge and visit the cathedral.

Below the Synod Hall stands a small, Tudor-style house, with red sandstone, mullioned windows and leaded panes. This house, once occupied by the Verger of Christ Church Cathedral, became derelict in the 1980s, but has happily been restored since.

In 1882 a large and elaborate book was published describing the history of Christ Church Cathedral and giving George Edmund Street's justification for, and account of, the complete restoration of the cathedral. The book is dedicated to Henry Roe, the philanthropic distiller who rescued the cathedral from its state of neglect. Roe not only paid for the entire restoration and rebuilding of the cathedral, but he also donated five new bells and left a very substantial endowment fund to cover salaries and other expenses.

Seventeen years earlier, in 1865, St Patrick's Cathedral had been completely restored, through the generosity of Benjamin Lee Guinness. It is tempting to think that his fellow businessman and neighbour in Thomas Street, Henry Roe, simply wanted to 'keep up with the Guinnesses'. But such a judgement would be unkind, as Roe states in the book that his financial contribution is 'a thank offering … for mercies granted me, and for prosperity far greater than I have desired or deserved'.

Above: Two of the magnificent bells of Christ Church Cathedral. The bells of Christ Church continue to ring on a regular basis.

In many respects the book is a celebration of the restoration of Christ Church Cathedral, but on another level it is Street's justification for the work carried out. It describes how, by the mid-nineteenth century, the cathedral had lost much of its original significance and was a gloomy, run-down, mediocre building, surrounded by 'narrow lanes of mean and dingy houses'. Photographs of the period support this view.

Street very convincingly justified the restoration of 1875 by describing the architectural mess that the cathedral had been reduced to, in addition to a general state of neglect, where masonry in the nave was cracked and bulging. He was well aware of the various arguments of the anti-restorers, but he concluded that, 'Never could the word "restoration" be better applied than here.' He showed how the cathedral had decreased in importance since the Act of Union of 1800; how the completion of the Chapel Royal in Dublin Castle in 1814 had taken away the patronage of the Lord Lieutenant; how the moving of the courts to the new Four Courts in 1796 and the moving of the Corn Market to Burgh Quay had greatly diminished the importance of this part of Dublin. He described how the Irish Church Act of 1869 had deprived the cathedral of its regular funding, and that there was even a suggestion that Christ Church should cease to have the status of a cathedral.

A long sequence of events had brought Christ Church to this sorry situation, starting with the collapse of the nave in 1562. After this event, only

Above: This photograph, taken from the top of Winetavern Street, shows the pre-1875 cathedral in its early, unadorned state. Note the massive buttress at the corner.

the north side of the nave was left intact and a timber roof was installed instead of stone vaulting. A solid wall was erected instead of an arcade on the south side. This meant that an important part of the church – a third of the nave – was actually blocked up and remained so until the nineteenth century. Again and again, Street reiterates his statement of principle to which the restoration was carried out. It was to respect 'the reverend solicitude with which every intention of the original design was followed out, and every fragment of good old work preserved'. Elsewhere, Street wrote: 'The marks of age on every stone ought to be held sacred.'

The basis of Street's restoration lay in his study of the plan of the crypt, the east end of which was considered to be the original twelfth-century structure. The plan of the crypt became the template of the entire restoration project and the reconstruction of the east end, with its choir, chancel and ambulatory, is based on it. He recommended that the building contract be given to Gilbert Cockburn & Son of Dublin, but curiously all of the decorative ironwork, brass rails and even the liturgical vessels such as flagons and chalices were made in England. So too were the oak stalls in the choir. The magnificent tiled floor, which closely followed the pattern and colours of medieval examples found in the cathedral, were made by Craven, Dunhill and Company of Jackfield, Ironbridge in England.

The Environs of Christ Church

Some of the cathedral's surrounding streets remained partially intact until the 1960s. At that time the view of the cathedral from across the Liffey was framed by the remains of buildings at the bottom of Winetavern Street, which included a collection of four-storey houses. The most eye-catching building was the famous Irish House, a distinctive public house that stood at the corner with Wood Quay.

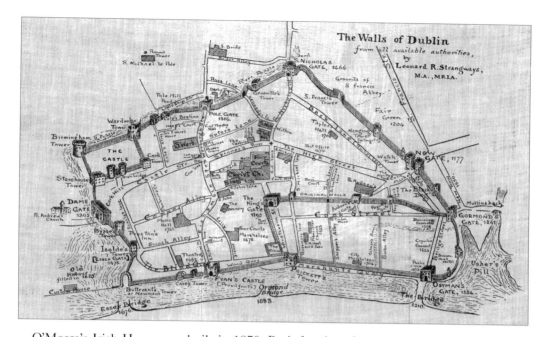

The Walls of Dublin
from all available authorities,
by
Leonard R.Strangways,
M.A., M.R.I.A.

O'Meara's Irish House was built in 1870. Both façades of the corner premises were elaborately ornamented with plasterwork figures representing: Grattan Addressing the Irish Parliament; The Maid of Erin; Daniel O'Connell and a variety of Irish wolfhounds. The parapet was decorated with ironwork and six enormous Irish round towers made of plaster. The figure of Erin is depicted weeping over her stringless harp and Grattan is addressing the last Irish Parliament. The symbolism of this nationalist-inspired ornamentation is fairly clear, but in 1870 the *Irish Builder* wrote sarcastically about the 'genius who designed the unsightly structure now in the process of erection at the corner of Winetavern Street on the quays'. The long story of the acquisition of the entire Wood Quay site by Dublin Corporation included, in 1965, the proposed demolition of the Irish House. Fortunately, Guinness's purchased all of the figures and had plaster casts made of them, but so far no opportunity has arisen to display the unique collection of statuary.

Winetavern Street

The Wide Streets Commissioners had erected a number of terraces of three-storey houses at Michael's Hill, at the top of Winetavern Street, in the early 1800s. These interesting old houses, which were designed with simple shopfronts and unusually large Wyatt windows, were pleasantly stepped down to match the gradient of the hill. Similar houses, with the more usual sash windows, were also built in Michael's Lane, just below the present Synod Hall. The new houses on St Michael's Hill were laid out in a gentle curve in order to create space around the west end of the cathedral. Just as the Wide Streets Commissioners dictated the renewal of this area in the 1800s, in our time the government's 'Designated Areas' programme

Above: Strangways' conjectural map of the wall of Dublin (1904) shows the central position occupied by Christ Church in the 'medieval city'.

Below: A plaster figure of Daniel O'Connell from the Irish House.

Opposite: Winetavern Street in the 1930s was still a residential and shopping area.

brought about the construction of new apartments in the 1980s, though without the same architectural guidance.

An Ordnance Survey map of 1866 shows a large fire station located just off Winetavern Street, on the site of the present park. The eighteenth-century Deanery of Christ Church Cathedral stood just to the north of St John's Church, almost exactly on the site of one of the first Wood Quay office blocks. The Deanery, said to have been designed by Edward Lovett Pearce, is shown on eighteenth-century maps as a large, almost square building, with a double flight of steps at its entrance. A map of 1799, in the possession of the National Library, shows that the Deanery was then sandwiched between the City Turf and Coal Yard, which later became the aforementioned fire station on Winetavern Street, and the Chancellor's House, which lay between it and Fishamble Street. The entrance to the Deanery was by means of a passageway at ground level, through the middle of the Chancellor's house, and there was a yard fronting Fishamble Street that later became known as Deanery Court.

Fishamble Street

It is difficult to believe that almost a third of Fishamble Street has disappeared as a result of the opening of Lord Edward Street in 1886. The construction of this new street, which was to link Dame Street to Christ Church Place, brought about the clearance of all of the buildings on the west side at the top of Fishamble Street, including the Church of St John. The Wide Street Commissioners had, in the early nineteenth century, examined all of the old houses between the present Kinlay House and the corner of Castle Street. As we have already seen, it was they who

Left: Rocque's map shows the pleasant curve of Fishamble Street before the top half of the street vanished.

Below: An engraving of the imposing façade of St John's Church in Fishamble Street, c.1820.

rebuilt the houses on the opposite side of the street, just east of the choir of Christ Church Cathedral.

Fishamble Street is unusual among Dublin streets, in having been allowed to hold on to its pleasing curved route down to the River Liffey. It was, no doubt, this proximity to the river that led it to become the principal street for the sale of fish in the medieval city. It became known as the fish-shambles, meaning a place for the butchering and sale of fish.

There are very few good drawings or photographs of Dublin's smaller vanished churches such as the old Fransiscan Church at Merchants' Quay, St Michael's at High Street, St Nicholas Within, the remains of which now stand on Nicholas Street, and the Church of St John the Evangelist, which once stood at the top of Fishamble Street. An old photograph of St John's Church shows that it had an impressive Palladian façade. Four large engaged columns and a pediment ornamented the front of this plain, rectangular church. It was designed by the very competent Dublin architect George Ensor, and built in stone in the late 1760s. As previously mentioned, it had a small graveyard attached to it. The records suggest that a church dedicated to St John had stood on this site as early as 1178. An interesting parish record mentions that £30 was paid to Thomas Newman, a clock-maker, in 1704 for maintaining 'one watch with two dyalls' that he had set up on the seventeenth-century tower on the east side of St John's Church. Henry Grattan, whose family had lived in Fishamble Street for almost a hundred years, was baptised in St John's Church in 1746. The tower of the church was probably dismantled in the 1760s. The church closed in 1877 and was demolished some seven years later by the Corporation in preparation for a proposed new street which would link the environs of Christ Church directly with Dame Street. Nothing now remains of the Church of St John or its graveyard except for six flat gravestones, which are preserved in the park beside the Civic Offices.

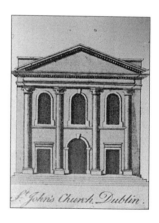

St John's Church, Dublin.

Towards the bottom of the street, on the west side, stood the house of another well-known Dublin family, the Molesworths. Molesworth's Court was a detached house in Fishamble Street, erected in the middle of the seventeenth century. The first Robert Molesworth, who built Molesworth Court, died in 1656 and was buried in St Audoen's Church. It is said that Molesworth made his money by winning the contract to supply cloth

and materials to make a thousand tents for the government. Robert Molesworth Junior, was appointed Envoy Extraordinary to the Court of Denmark in 1692, and this prosperous family went on to develop many property interests in Dublin, especially around Essex Street. Robert became Viscount Molesworth in 1716 and Molesworth Street was later developed on fields belonging to his family.

A narrow passageway known as Fleece Ally was entered almost directly opposite the present George Frederick Handel Hotel on Fishamble Street, and was one of three similar passageways that led to the Four Courts Marshalsea. This building, which is clearly shown on Rocque's map of 1756, was a type of debtors' prison and consisted of four large buildings ranged around a courtyard. It was situated at the back of the houses of Wood Quay. Leonard Strangways' historical map of the walls of medieval Dublin dates the Four Courts Marshalsea to 1678. It was replaced in the 1770s by the new Marshalsea Barracks, which we have already come across in Bridgefoot Street.

William Townsend, one of Dublin's leading silversmiths and goldsmiths in the eighteenth century, was also resident in Fishamble Street. An example of his delicate rococo-style silverwork may be seen in the National Museum of Ireland. Among other things, he is known to have made a number of very fine silver dish rings – useful and ornamental objects used to prevent hot dishes from burning a dining-room table. Townsend specialised in the free-flowing rococo style, which we have already seen in the plasterwork of the period houses in nearby Parliament Street. Townsend died in 1775.

Gilbert tells us that in the eighteenth century Fishamble Street was noted for the manufacture of wicker baskets – perhaps to cater for the fish trade and the many fruit sellers who also frequented the music houses and theatres. The tradition of basket-making in the street survived well into the nineteenth century: the street directory of 1851 indicates five basket-makers and seven trunk-makers occupying the various houses in Fishamble Street.

Several timber-frame or cagework houses survived in the street until the eighteenth century. One of these, known as the London Tavern, was destroyed by a fire in 1729.

Gilbert states that the greater part of the buildings in and around Fishamble Street and Copper Alley at that time were in fact timber-frame structures. One such house in Fishamble Street belonged to the Plunkett family and was said to date from 1563. It bore two coats of arms on its front, one of the Plunkett family and one incorporating his wife's family arms. In the eighteenth century it was converted into the Bull's Head Tavern. This tavern stood on property belonging to Christ Church Cathedral and was a popular venue for dinners and banquets held by various city guilds.

By the 1850s quite a few properties in Fishamble Street had fallen into tenement use, but numbers 18 and 19 were occupied by the 'Artists and Mechanics Warehouse' of Thomas Kennan & Son, Lathe and Tool Manufacturers. Next door, at number 20, stood the Fishamble Street Theatre, which incorporated the walls of the eighteenth-century Musick Hall. Thirty years later, Kennan's had expanded their activities to include a horticultural building and steam joinery works, but they continued their unrivalled reputation for manufacturing fences, gates and roofs alongside the sale of tools and other implements. Even today, hay barns with the Kennan nameplate can be found in old farmyards around the country.

Apart from the Kennan's building, only one other old house survives in Fishamble Street, and this thanks only to the perseverance and courage of the Casey family, who have lived there since 1870. The house, which is believed to date from the late seventeenth century, once incorporated a Victorian 'off licence' or shop on the ground floor. The appearance of the present four-storey house, which stands on the corner of Fishamble Street and Smock Alley, suggests that it may have been refronted in the nineteenth century. However, the presence of large beams running through the centre of the ceilings of the principal rooms, along with the corner fireplaces, hints at a late seventeenth- or early eighteenth-century date for the original house.

Above: Kennan's, before recent refurbishment, and the archway that led to their factory – once the site of the famous Musick Hall.

Above: A vignette from Kennan's notepaper, showing their factory on Fishamble Street.

Left: A late nineteenth-century billhead, recording the fact that Kennan's was established in 1780.

The Fishamble Street Musick Hall

Fishamble Street is best-known today for its long-vanished Musick Hall, where Handel first performed his *Messiah* in 1742. The Musick Hall, which opened in 1741 for the first time, could accommodate about six hundred people and was elaborately decorated throughout. A contemporary description, quoted by Gilbert, sets the scene:

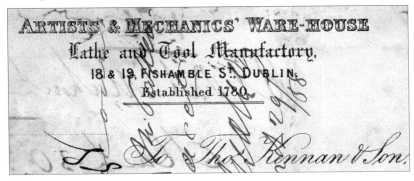

Right: An early photograph, c.1870, showing the parish fire ladders in front of the gable-fronted houses that stood between Essex Quay and Blind Quay, at the bottom of Fishamble Street.

The interior of the house formed an ellipse, and was divided into three compartments – pit, boxes, and lattices which were without division, the seats were covered with rich scarlet, and fringed to match, while a stuffed handrail carried round gave them the form of couches, and rendered them particularly agreeable for any attitude of repose or attention. The pilasters which supported the front of the boxes were cased with mirror, and displayed various figures on a white ground, relieved with gold. The festoons were fringed with gold, and drawn up with golden cords and tassels. The ceiling was exquisitely painted. In the front was a drop curtain on which was depicted an azure sky with fleeting clouds from the centre of which was Apollo's lyre emerging in vivid glory …

A plan of the Musick Hall from 1804, held in the City Archives, shows a large stage with the pit and boxes on either side. There was a gallery at the Fishamble Street end, under which a passage opened on to the street. On the south side of the theatre, overlooking Copper Alley, there was a large coffee room and a room called the Green Room. A hall and stairs standing adjacent to what later became Kennan's House gave access to the gallery and boxes. To the east of the theatre, behind the stage, stood a house that fronted on to Copper Alley.

Gilbert tells us that Ridotto Balls – masquerades with music and dancing – were held in the Musick Hall in 1773 and 1774. On these occasions carriages and sedan chairs entered Fishamble Street from Castle Street, turning into Copper Alley where the passengers were admitted to the Musick Hall. After the performance, carriages waited for their passengers in nearby Smock Alley, while sedan chairs attended in Copper Alley. Gilbert noted that the inhabitants of the neighbourhood often complained that they were deprived of sleep by the great and incessant clamour of the chair carriers and servants after various popular events in the Musick Hall. Little has changed in 200 years – late-night revellers from the nearby Olympia Theatre continue the tradition!

Many of the concerts and performances at the Musick Hall were held for the benefit of various charities, such as Mercer's Hospital, which received funds from the first performance of Handel's *Messiah*. In 1769 a concert was held in aid of the Lock Hospital in Townsend Street, and in 1780 the first Irish State lottery took place in the Musick Hall in Fishamble Street.

A tall archway of Victorian date was built on the site of the entrance to the original Musick Hall. Along with the neighbouring eighteenth-century house, this miraculously survived until this year. The archway, though carefully propped up by a steel frame, was unfortunately destabilised. It was literally hanging off the steel frame and had to be dismantled. During the 1980s there had been considerable doubt as to whether the arch and the adjoining house, which was used as the offices of Kennan's Iron Works, would survive at all, despite their historic significance. Both, however, have now been restored, and for the first time since the eighteenth century, major redevelopment has taken place in this entire quarter, mainly consisting of apartment blocks with some shops in the nearby streets.

Wood Quay Area

The presence of the City Turf and Coal Yards in the late eighteenth century on a site near Wood Quay is significant, because in the early part of that century Wood Quay was actually known as the Coal Quay. The ownership and use of property in this area by Dublin Corporation is not a recent thing – the Ordnance Survey map of 1866 shows two substantial Corporation yards located just off Fishamble Street, on the site of the present Civic Offices.

Eighteenth-century Winetavern Street was narrow and clustered with small houses, becoming almost a lane at the end near Christ Church Cathedral. A lease of one of these old houses, at the top of Winetavern Street facing Cock Hill, was let by Valentine Challenor and his wife Maria to John Merle in 1791. It was described as 'one small shop with a small room over it'. As a result of the demolition by the Wide Streets Commissioners of most of the west side and part of the east side, the street was turned into an unusually wide thoroughfare in the early nineteenth century. Drawings and photographs of the period depict the various houses at the top end of the street,

Below: A photograph taken in 1963 of Dublin Corporation's old fire brigade yard at Wood Quay, off Winetavern Street.

which, on the east side, boasted Dublin's narrowest shop – a tall, thin premises measuring only seven feet across! It was demolished in 1949 and the rest of the houses on this side of Winetavern Street were cleared away in the mid-1960s to prepare a site for Dublin's Civic Offices.

It is well known that the Civic Offices were a long time in coming. An eventual archaeological dig on the entire site uncovered part of the medieval city wall and much of the old Viking city of Dublin. The ensuing confrontation between officialdom and the public will has been well documented, but the 1990s erection of a quayfront office building went some way towards reconstructing the streetscape of the area.

We know that large quantities of wine were imported through Dublin and that the sovereign of England or his agents were entitled to select two hogsheads of wine from any cargo. Since medieval times taverns were obliged to display a sign over the door and the owner's measures were checked against the official gallon, quart and pint measures. Among the names of some of the early seventeenth-century taverns or pubs in Winetavern Street we find the Black Boy Cellar, the Golden Lyon, the Common Cellar, the Spread Eagle, the King's Head and the Golden Dragon. In the seventeenth century one Barnaby Rych made the following observations about the city's numerous watering holes:

There is no merchandise so vendable, it is the very marrow of the common wealth in Dublin: the

whole profit of the towne stands upon ale houses and selling of ale ...
There are whole streates of taverns, and it is a rare thing to finde a
house in Dubline without a taverne, as to find a tavern without a
strumpet.

Mr Rych went on to say that 'every other woman in the city was brewing
their own beer which they sold at a high price'. He lamented the fact that
they bought their malt in Dublin at half the price that it was sold for in
London – but that they sold the drink in Dublin at double the rate they did
in London! He concluded that the beer sold in these 'filthy ale houses' was
mere 'hogges wash', and is 'unfit for any man's drinking but for common
drunkards'. Most of these early taverns would have been accommodated in
timber-frame houses, and a few of them survived into the eighteenth century when they were considered very old-fashioned and a considerable fire
hazard. Gilbert, writing in 1854, described a large brick house in Winetavern street with the date 1641 displayed on the façade and a coat of arms
with the letters RM. The lower part of this house was used as an inn known
as the Pyed House.

It is said that the wealth of the Byrne family, who in the eighteenth cen-
tury built Cabinteely House, originated in Winetavern Street. Daniel
Byrne, a tailor, won the contract for clothing some forty thousand men for
Cromwell, from which he made his fortune.

Skinner Row

Few Dublin streets have vanished so completely as Skinner Row, a narrow
but important medieval street that linked Dublin Castle to Christ Church
Cathedral and High Street. Prior to the clearance of Skinner Row by the
Wide Street Commissioners in 1821, the irregular line of houses and shopfronts presented, according to Gilbert, 'the appearance of a narrow and
sombre alley'. This street, the name of which is recorded since medieval
times, was the traditional home for skinners, curriers (Curryers Lane
joined Skinner Row on the south side) and leather merchants.

Skinner Row was also the location for the city Tholsel, a building used
for the gathering of market taxes and for public meetings. It occupied a
prominent site on the corner of Skinner Row and Nicholas Street, where it
adjoined the Church of St Nicholas Within.

In the eighteenth century many wealthy traders, jewellers, goldsmiths
and silversmiths had their shops in this street, along with booksellers, publishers and at least two noted coffee houses. A substantial timber-frame
house survived there until 1780, when it was replaced by 6–8 Christ
Church Place. Gilbert informs us that this house, known as 'The Great
House', was converted into a coffee house by Richard Pue, a printer, after
which it became known as 'Dick's Coffee House'. In 1699 John Dunton, an
English publisher, commented on Dick's Coffee House and its proprietor,
who he described as 'a witty and ingenious man, [who] makes the best
coffee in Dublin'. Gilbert goes on to tell us that 'like most other coffee

Opposite: A century of change:
these photographs show Wood
Quay as it was in the nineteenth
century (top); the site in the
1970s (middle), cleared of
buildings and looking almost
rural; and as it is today
(bottom), with the new Civic
Offices fronting the river.

houses in Dublin, Dick's was located on the Drawing Room floor' (meaning the first floor), while the ground floor was occupied by various shops, in this case a bookseller and a publisher.

Richard Pue's premises were described in 1703 as 'a moyety of timber houses divided into two tenements. One hath two cellars and in the first floor two shops and two kitchens. On the second floor three rooms (two of them wainscoted). On the third two rooms, and on the fourth, two garrets'. This description would suggest that this was a large house, consisting of four storeys over a basement or cellar.

Pue's premises became famous for its auctions of books, lands and other goods. An auction was advertised in 1711 of an important collection of chimney pieces from Kilruddery Estate near Bray, to be held in Dick's Coffee House at Skinner Row. The auction included 'seven chimney pieces, pillars and hearths, seventeen window plates and a large sideboard table, all of pure marble of different colours'. The tradition of selling valuable items by auction is kept alive in this district by the firm of Reilly, who have now moved to Francis Street.

Below: Only the ground floor remains of the façade of a forgotten Dublin church, St Nicholas Within (the city walls).

Despite the renown of his coffee house and auctions, Richard Pue is best remembered for the publication of his 'newspaper' in the early 1700s entitled *Pue's Occurrences*.

Among the many interesting names of shops and premises in Skinner Row, Gilbert records a sword cutler at the Old Dolphin, a goldsmith at the Kinge's Head, a bookseller at the Sign of the Leather Bottle, a publisher at the Sign of Mercury, next to the Tholsel, and another premises called the Sign of the Pestle and Mortar.

Sir Patrick Dun, who was an army doctor in the late seventeenth century, lived in Skinner Row in 1690, and left a large sum of money for the founding of what was to become Sir Patrick Dun's Hospital, a noted hospital on Grand Canal Street, then called Artichoke Road, which survived until the 1980s.

The first Tholsel in Skinner Row is known to have existed in medieval times. The Tholsel was the venue for the collection of tolls or duties at markets or fairs. It became a place where public meetings were held and where punishments were meted out – the stocks or the pillory were the usual sentences for the convicted. Libellous publications and fraudulent goods seized by the lord mayor were publicly burned at the Tholsel, and public notices were erected there. In the latter part of the eighteenth century the Wide Streets Commissioners frequently met in the Tholsel.

The building was also used for the elections and meetings of Dublin Corporation, but these were transferred to the City Assembly House in

South William Street in the late 1790s when the Tholsel became delapidated. Similarly, it had been used as 'a Sessions House' until the erection of new courthouse facilities in Green Street, which opened in 1797. The seventeenth-century building was erected in 1683 on the same site as earlier Tholsels. It was an almost square structure, with a frontage of sixty-two feet, two storeys high and displaying a cut-stone façade. Malton's engravings of 1795 give us the best record of its appearance. The upper floor was raised above three massive arches, which originally gave access to a kind of covered market area, while the front was embellished with two large Tuscan columns surmounted by statues of King Charles II and King James II, which stood in niches. The statues were carved by William de Keysar in 1684 and cost £29. With the eventual demolition of the Tholsel in 1807, the statues were moved into Christ Church Cathedral. They have lain in the cathedral's crypt ever since. Inside the Tholsel there was a spacious hall, ornamented by four massive columns. This chamber, with its stone-flagged floor and open balustrades on each street frontage, was used as an exchange by merchants.

Above: Malton's engraving of the Tholsel illustrates a vanished Dublin Street known as Skinner Row.

Below: The timber-carved coat of arms that once graced the Tholsel now rests in the crypt of Christ Church Cathedral.

High Street and St Audoen's

To the casual observer, High Street is just another busy and unremarkable thoroughfare, with its modern buildings and its six lanes always full of traffic. The visitor could be forgiven for not realising that this was one of the oldest and most important streets in medieval Dublin. As the name implies, High Street was once the main thoroughfare, linking the western approaches to the city at the medieval entrance called Newgate, with Christ Church Cathedral at Skinner Row and Dublin Castle at the bottom of Castle Street.

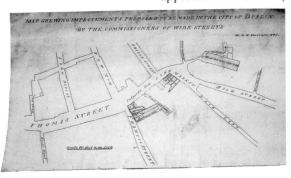

Today's Cornmarket is a large and shapeless traffic junction, but it was once a tight and narrow twisting entrance to the medieval city. This street pattern, dictated by the medieval walls of the city, was still in evidence at the time of Rocque. He showed, in 1756, the approach from Thomas Street past the old Cornmarket building, through the narrow Cutpurse Row, under Newgate and into Cornmarket, off which a series of narrow courts and alleys radiated.

Above: An early nineteenth-century map, showing the properties at Cornmarket and the corner of Francis Street, which the Wide Streets Commissioners acquired in order to widen the street.

The New Hall Market stood on the sloping ground between Cornmarket and Cook Street and its site is now covered by the wide slope of Bridge Street. In the late eighteenth century this market accommodated some thirty stalls, which were laid out around a narrow triangular court. Nearby stood the Black Dog tavern and prison, along with the medieval gatehouse or tower of the Newgate itself. To the east lay St Audoen's Church, with a narrow passage leading down through the city wall at St Audoen's Arch and into Cook Street. Back Lane branched southwards off Cornmarket and, like High Street, was once thickly populated with old houses, the backlands of which accommodated various industrial activities, such as tanning and brewing.

The line of a remaining section of city wall is evident on Rocque's map, forming the back wall of the yards behind the houses on the south side of Back Lane. Extensive industrial buildings stood on the other side of the city wall, and these were later to become Sweetman's Brewery, which were entered from Francis Street. On the opposite side of Back Lane, tucked in behind old houses and reached by a narrow passageway, was the Tailors' Guild Hall, which is one of the few old buildings to have survived in this part of the medieval city. One shop, which sells prams, is the only building left on High Street that recalls the original street line, but it now seems curiously out of place, standing on the edge of a highway and sandwiched between the giant classical portico of the Catholic St Audoen's Church and the ancient Protestant St Audoen's.

Leaving aside the complete eradication of the buildings, the homes and the businesses that once made this a street, the achievement of the last twenty years has been the reconstruction of the entire area with apartments and some offices and shops. The clearance of High Street also presented the opportunity of allowing the archaeological excavation of various sites in the vicinity. One area close to the city wall at Back Lane revealed traces of the post-and-wattle houses of the twelfth century. The remains of other timber-frame houses of the medieval period have also been found. Further evidence was uncovered to show that stone buildings replaced the earlier timber structures, and the discovery of kilns for producing roof tiles suggests that many roofs may have been tiled rather than slated or thatched. Evidence of thirteenth-century cagework houses and of medieval leather-working 'factories' was also discovered in High Street.

The excavations in High Street, which began in 1967, were completed in 1972. They demonstrated that, interestingly, the tradition of tanning and leather working survived in Back Lane well into the nineteenth century. In 1813, for instance, Henry Luttrell, the Earl of Carhampton of Luttrellstown, granted a lease of premises in Back Lane to James Dixon, a tanner of Kilmainham.

A map of properties on the south side of Back Lane, from the National Library, shows the estate of the prebendaries and vicars of Christ Church. This map illustrates the old city wall, with Sweetman's Brewery lying to the south and a turret or tower, half-octagonal in shape, projecting from the

Below: Handkerchief Alley was one of many narrow passages that once stood between Francis Street, Back Lane and Cornmarket. These areas were densely populated in the nineteenth century.

city wall. The map also illustrates the complex juxtaposition of houses alongside various commercial enterprises, such as Gannon's Gurrying House, Hyland's Leather Store, a saw pit, a shambles and a horse-mill.

Another map of the same area in 1816 shows that various workshops and stables had been replaced by a starch manufactory. A narrow passage named Blackhall Row gave direct access from Back Lane to the city wall turret. In the early nineteenth century, Blackhall Row was extended into Binns Court and Plunkett Street, the whole area being redeveloped in the late nineteenth century as John Dillon Street. Sweetman's Brewery was demolished to clear the site for the Iveagh Markets. The gurrying house off Back Lane was a place where leather was beaten and softened ready for use. It is likely that those engaged in this task were tough individuals who may have acquired the uniquely Dublin name of gurriers!

The National Library map, which appears to be of late eighteenth-century date, also indicates the existence of a 'tay

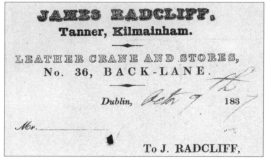

Right: An eighteenth-century plan of the south side of Back Lane, showing the line of the city wall (below Sweetman's Brewery). It also shows Blackhall Row and various sheds and buildings, which were mostly used by leather manufacturers.

Below: An 1830s trade card of one of the many tanners in Back Lane.

Opposite top: This photograph shows the chronic state of dilapidation of the Tailors' Hall before its restoration.

Opposite bottom: The magnificent early eighteenth-century entrance to the Tailors' Hall in Back Lane was incorporated into a street of houses and shops.

room', or tea room, close to Blackhall Row. The map shows that the Hyland family were tenants of a number of properties here and operated a leather business. Off Back Lane we find a number of residential courts including Fagan's Court, Byrne's Court, Busby's Court, Fletcher's Court, McCullough's Court and Angel Alley. Lamb Alley and Handkerchief Alley were other decaying residential enclaves which were approached from Francis Street and Cornmarket. The passage called Lamb Alley was referred to in an early nineteenth-century lease as 'Mr Cuddy's holding under Christchurch, formerly known by the name of the Holy Lamb'.

Mid-nineteenth-century street directories show that tanning and its associated industries, including leather stores and shoemaking still occupied most of the street. There were numerous curriers and leather sellers, including, for instance, John Mulligan, tanner, skinner and leather merchant, with tanneries at Watling Street and Mill Street; Richard Dowling, a bellows maker, at number 50; Andrew Murray, a last maker; William and Samuel Parker, who were wholesale leather merchants; and Thomas and Richard White, tanners and curriers who also had a property at 35 High Street. Lamb Alley was recorded as consisting of ten houses in tenements with one dairy.

The Sun Taverne is shown on a map of 1682 occupying an important corner position at Back Lane and St Nicholas Street. Nineteenth-century street directories show that Robert Quaile, a wholesale leather merchant, was in business at 47 Back Lane. A deed of 1781 tells us that premises in Back Lane were in that year let to Alderman William Quaile.

JAMES RADCLIFF,
Tanner, Kilmainham.

LEATHER CRANE AND STORES,
No. 36, BACK-LANE.

Dublin, _Octr 9th_ 183_7_

Mr. _____

To J. RADCLIFF,

The Tailors' Hall, which was erected in 1706 as a meeting place for the tailoring fraternity, is the only surviving guildhall in Dublin. The tailors were an ancient guild and had had several other halls or meeting places before this. The Tailors' Hall is a large, plain building, incorporating various meeting rooms with a large hall, which could be rented out for public meetings as a way of generating income for the guild. The guild, which was exclusively Protestant until 1793, had considerable powers and was influential in matters of trade. They had the right, for instance, to seize the cloths of tailors who were not members of the guild but were selling in the city of Dublin. They also voiced their strong objections to the proposed Act of Union in 1800.

The Tailors' Hall has been restored twice in its recent past – first by a voluntary committee who set up the Tailors' Hall fund in 1966, some time after the building was declared unsafe by Dublin Corporation, and again in the 1980s when it was taken over by An Taisce as its national headquarters. The large rectangular space which comprises the Great Hall is lit on the south side by four large arched windows. A magnificent marble mantelpiece records in an inscription that it was 'the gift of Christopher Neary, Master: Alexander Bell and Hugh Craigg, wardens, 1784'. The magnificent carved tablet at the centre of the

Above: The stone monogram of Winstanley's boot and shoe factory in Back Lane.

Below: Nineteenth-century High Street developed a reputation for high-class tailors and drapers.

mantelpiece, which features a female head, has in the recent past been stolen three times and has been recovered twice through various antique dealers. Sadly, it was again stolen in 1998 but has not yet been recovered. This hall has witnessed all sorts of momentous occasions in Irish history and has been used by different groups which would never have seen eye to eye on political matters. In the eighteenth century the Grand Lodge of Freemasons used the hall, while in 1792 a Catholic convention, led by the Protestant Wolfe Tone, became known as the Back Lane Parliament, and presented a petition to King George III seeking the right to take part in elections and the right of trial by jury.

The hall contains a semi-circular minstrel's gallery, which has a delicate wrought-iron balustrade and, at the opposite end, a series of panels which carry the names of the masters of the Tailors' Guild since 1419. An interesting feature of the Tailors' Hall is the open-well staircase with its barley-sugar balusters, which itself leads to the Wolfe Tone room on the first floor, a pleasant meeting place with a corner fireplace fashioned out of Kilkenny marble. The large gateway with its broken pediment, through which the Tailors' Hall is entered from Back Lane, once stood between a pair of old Georgian shopfronts, which were part of a terrace of three-storey houses. The Tailors' Hall, which was also a meeting place for the United Irishmen, served as a school in the nineteenth century and more recently as a hostel for the homeless.

Nineteenth-century High Street gained a reputation for its wholesale woollen drapers, cotton and linen warehouses, leather merchants and other businesses associated with the clothing industry. For instance, we find Sigismund S Moss, candlewick manufacturer at 37 High Street with his cotton-mills located at Kilternan in County Dublin. Clare and James Egan's 'wholesale woollen, linen and cotton warehouse' was located at number 14 and 15 High Street and Walsh and Keely's 'wholesale and retail blanket, flannel and counterpain warehouse' was situated at number 9. Richard Allen, a noted tailor, had his West of England woollen hall and general warehouse located at 52 and owned another premises at 28 Sackville Street Lower. By the 1890s Allen had been succeeded by Pearson & Company, run by a grandfather of this writer, and the premises had been extended to incorporate two houses, 51 and 52 High Street. Richard Allen, a Quaker businessman, was described in *The Industries of Dublin* as 'a philanthropist and temperance reformer'. The book went on to describe the tailoring business of 'Messrs Pearson & Co. ... a very large and valuable one, and comprises a select variety of patterns in tweed, serges, cheviots, homespuns and fancy coatings of the best Irish, Scotch and West of England makers.' Their business

O'HARA'S

OLD ESTABLISHED

SHIRT MART,

STOCK, GLOVE, AND HOSIERY

ESTABLISHMENT,

No. 27, HIGH-STREET,

(Near Corn Market,)

DUBLIN.

premises, which extended back some 120 feet and were lit by a glass roof, displayed a large stock of goods, arranged on tiers of shelving. There were also two large workshops, which accommodated a cutting department and the work area of a large number of tailors employed in putting together the garments.

In the early 1800s the Wide Streets Commissioners initiated various plans to widen the street at Cornmarket. One of their first actions was to remove the block of houses at the corner of Francis Street, which created the extraordinarily narrow Cutpurse Row. The drawing prepared in 1811 by the draftsman Thomas Sherrard was approved by three of the Commissioners – Nathaniel Hone, Jeremiah D'Olier and Frederick Darley. Further improvements to the width of the street were considered in 1845 when houses at the bottom of Francis Street and Back Lane were earmarked for demolition. It was only in the early nineteenth century that Bridge Street Upper was formed by cutting through the old New Hall market. This left two pedestrian alleys or passageways connecting Cornmarket with Cook Street – Keysars Lane and St Audoen's Arch.

In the nineteenth century a Parochial School and a Widows' Alms House stood in front of St Audoen's Church, quite close to the city wall. There is no trace of any buildings on this site today, as it forms part of a small park. The city wall, which now stands in isolation with none of the old dwellings and houses which once clustered around it, is an interesting relic of medieval Dublin. But somehow it fails to inspire much more that a passing glance, perhaps because it has been sanitised and stripped of its original context and meaning. If there were old houses in and near it, and if perhaps it were possible to walk along the top of the wall, as one can in Chester or Clonmel, it might allow the visitor to better understand the reason for the wall as a defence for the small medieval city.

St Audoen's Arch is the only medieval gateway which survives in the city of Dublin. It is a substantial structure – the archway is some twelve feet wide and twelve feet high, and though it was reconstructed in the 1880s following the demolition of a tower or room above it, much of the masonry is original. In 1602 the room above the tower was leased out to the Tanners' Guild who used it as a meeting place until the middle of the eighteenth century. Even in the 1880s the Corporation were entertaining the possibility of demolishing the arch completely. Following considerable public protest, it was somewhat heavily restored in a mock-medieval style and flights of steps were inserted into the surface of the old narrow street. Today St Audoen's finds itself in a strange setting, with a highway on one side and a small, attractive park on the other. For most of its existence, the church has been enclosed by houses and other buildings.

Three-quarters of the original Gothic church, the only surviving medieval church in Dublin, has for centuries lain roofless, with the church itself occupying the remaining section. It must once have been a very unusual church, with its large Gothic arcade running down the middle, its chancel twisted slightly to orientate it towards the east.

A church was first built on this site in 1172, dedicated to St Audoen who was bishop and patron saint of Rouen, in Northern France. The oldest roofed section, which is still in use as a church, is thought to date from the twelfth century, while the south aisle, or Portlester Chapel as it is called, was added in the middle of the fifteenth century.

Above: A pair of plasterwork plaques, rescued from a house in Cornmarket.

Right: The houses of Cornmarket were completely cleared to facilitate the making of the dual carriageway from High Street to the Liffey.

Left: This engraving of St
Audoen's by George Petrie
shows the Portlester Chapel.

The interior of the present church would be greatly improved if the
walls were replastered, as there is at present an unhappy clash between the
ancient walls, which have been stripped and cement pointed, the modern
brick surrounding the east window and the shallow, coved ceiling which is
plastered. It would be tempting to imagine the entire church roofed, as it
must once have been, with an open timber structure. In the meantime,
Dúchas have re-roofed part of the south aisle and provided a new entrance
for visitors to the church. The recent works have been carried out in what is
currently the approved style, a somewhat clinical intervention using steel
and glass, but not in any way altering the original fabric of the building. I
would have preferred to have seen timber used rather than steel; the
manufactured uniformity of steel does not sit well in the context of medieval stonework. While the re-roofing is to be welcomed, one is left wishing
that the remaining two-thirds would also be covered in this way. A gallery,
which provides a new exhibition area, has been erected here in the guild
chapel of St Anne, in the same modern idiom, and an excellent display has
been mounted, tracing the history of the church.

The Seagrave monument, which occupies part of the north wall in the
St Audoen's Church, is a striking sixteenth-century memorial and it has
been carefully cleaned and restored in recent years. As the size and prominent position of the monument suggests, the Seagraves were an important
family in early sixteenth-century Dublin. The monument was erected in
1553 and depicts the husband, wife and family kneeling at their prayer
desks. The monument has lasted extraordinarily well considering it is
made from plaster.

Napper Tandy and Oliver Bond were both church wardens of the
Church of Ireland St Audoen's Church in the late eighteenth century, as
was Henry Grattan's uncle. Many other noted families were associated St
Audoen's, and some were buried here, including Robert Challenor's family,

Above: A nineteenth-century photograph of St Audoen's Church with its pinnacles, which have since been removed.

Opposite top: St Audoen's Arch before it was reconstructed in the 1880s. The cobbled street led through to the tenement houses of Cook Street.

Opposite bottom: Cook Street was once famous for its coffin-makers and French polishers. It was comprehensively cleared in 1932.

buried in the church since the 1490s. The names of Plunkett, Chamberlain, Loftus, Luttrell, Seagrave, St George, Jervis, Molesworth, Barnewall, Netterville and Trimbleston could also be mentioned. In 1820 the Wide Streets Commissioners, in their proposals for improving the whole area, considered the removal of an old almshouse and a group of buildings that directly abutted the tower of St Audoen's Church. This was eventually done and a new almshouse built opposite.

The medieval tower of St Audoen's Church contains three bells, dated 1423, which were rung continuously up until 1898. Three more bells were added in the seventeenth century, the largest of which, called the Old Cow, was hung in the tower in 1694. The church bell was rung every day at 6am to call people to their work. It was rung again at midday, and finally at 6pm to let the populace know that they could down tools. The bells of St Audoen's had been made safe by the 1980s, due mainly to the efforts of

Alex Donovan, who had been a trustee of St Audoen's since 1925. Donovan generously established a trust fund to ensure the maintenance of this, Dublin's oldest church.

The chapels of Portlester and St Anne and the chancel of the church have been without a roof since the late eighteenth century. A well-known engraving by George Petrie illustrates the church with a local woman hanging out her washing to dry amid the Gothic arches. The print was made before the construction of the 'modern' Catholic church of St Audoen, which lies hard up against the east wall.

St Audoen's Catholic Church, designed by Patrick Byrne, was built between 1841 and 1847, but the giant portico was not added until its closing years of the nineteenth century. The great bulk of this massive church, which is set back from the street, can be seen from many angles, but is almost overpowering when viewed from Cook Street. The interior is ornamented with fluted Corinthian pilasters and lit only by a series of arched windows

placed high up on the walls. An attractive feature at the entrance is the giant clam shell, frequently seen in Italian churches, which is used here as a holy water stoop.

Cook Street

Below St Audoen's and the city wall lies Cook Street, which in the nineteenth century and even more recently was famous for its undertakers and coffin-makers. In 1850 there were at least twelve coffin-makers and undertakers, and a great number of rag dealers or paper brokers occupied warehouses here. An old bill from 1913, from John Keogh Hendrick, 'under-taker and proprietor of job coaches' based at 3 Cook Street, tells us that a polished oak coffin then cost £7, a mourning coach £2/15s/–, three carriages £1/19s/–, a hearse and removal to the church £1, while other sundries brought the total bill to £18/1s/6d.

In 1850 we find Michael McGarry's copper, lead and oil business. The manufacturing was carried on at 10 and 11 Cook Street, at his copper and lead mills at Palmerstown and at Ashtown in west County Dublin. The old oil and dye wood mills are still standing at the bottom of Mill Lane in Palmerstown.

It has already been noted that no timber-frame or cagework houses have survived in Dublin, but an interesting example is recorded in Cook Street. The house, which was demolished in 1745, bore the following inscription on an oak beam running across the front of

Above: The elegant trade card of John Keogh, Hendrick, undertakers, of Cook Street.

the building: 'thow who madest the heaven and earth bless this house which John and Joan Luttrell caused to be built in the year of our Lord 1580 in the 22nd year of the reign of Elizabeth.' The eighteenth-century traveller Austin Cooper noted that several similar houses were being taken down on the west side of St Audoen's Arch at the time of his visit in 1782.

CHAPTER ELEVEN

St Patrick's Cathedral
and its Environs

*S*t Patrick's Cathedral is one of Dublin's largest public buildings, and the imposing bulk of its masonry structures cannot fail to impress the passer-by. Though not large by English standards, St Patrick's Cathedral must have always dominated the Dublin skyline, especially when surrounded by the lower and more modest buildings of the past. Malton's famous print of 1795, which is based on a watercolour, shows the west front surrounded by the humble houses of a terrace called Cross Poddle, and to the north a group of Dutch Billys on Patrick Street to which a series of lean-to structures had been added which housed the merchandise of various stallholders, mainly butchers. In this picture – which, from comparison with contemporary maps, can be taken as an accurate view of the cathedral in the late eighteenth century – two cattle are being driven up Patrick Street, perhaps on their way to the slaughterhouse.

Left: Malton's view of the west front of St Patrick's Cathedral shows a small house in Cross Poddle, one of many in the area which were cleared by the Wide Streets Commissioners in the early nineteenth century.

The site of St Patrick's Cathedral had always been considered a poor one, situated as it is on low-lying ground made damp by its proximity to the River Poddle. But the cathedral builders did not choose the site at random,

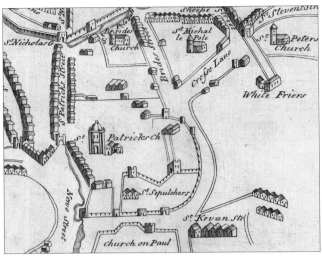

they came here because of the location of the venerated St Patrick's Well, the site of which was discovered during excavation works in 1901. The church was dedicated on St Patrick's Day in 1192, but was rebuilt as a cathedral in the middle of the thirteenth century. The tower of the cathedral blew down in 1316 and Archbishop Thomas Minot later wrote to the Pope seeking financial support to rebuild the tower and reinstate the bells. As a result, the tower later became known as the Minot Tower.

During the Reformation the cathedral was taken over and on the orders of King Henry VIII all the statues of saints and religious images were destroyed. The minor canons' or petty canons' hall was converted into an almshouse. In 1560 a public clock, the first of its type, was erected on the tower. Even in the seventeenth century the cathedral was in a poor state of repair, and reports continued to be made that suggested that its structure and fabric were in need of major work.

The cathedral was re-roofed in the late seventeenth century, using oak from the Coolatin estates in County Wicklow. Although some further work was carried out on the cathedral in the eighteenth century – such as the addition of the spire in 1749 – the cathedral was in such bad shape by the beginning of the nineteenth century that serious consideration was given to a complete rebuilding. In 1812 the roof of the nave was rebuilt at a cost of £1,500, but an early nineteenth-century engraving shows it as a plain open-truss timber roof, whose beams cut across the top of the west window. The north transept had been on the point of collapse until its rebuilding in the 1820s.

Henry Pakenham, the Dean of the cathedral in 1844, said: 'The whole exterior of the cathedral bore marks of unheeded dilapidation for 600 years' and added that 'the stone minarets are so honeycombed that the old mortar alone keeps them together.' In 1860 Sir Benjamin Lee Guinness came to the rescue and proposed to fully restore the cathedral on condition that he could personally oversee the work and not be bound by any committee or advisors. He wrote to the Dean:

> No deviation from the original design (however slight) shall be permitted and I shall hold myself personally responsible to the Dean and Chapter that those parts of the cathedral with which I may interfere shall be restored by me to a state of perfect and permanent repair.

During the next five years, Guinness spent over £150,000 restoring the cathedral. Guinness's son, Lord Iveagh, rebuilt the vault of the choir during the period 1899 to 1904. However, many contemporary commentators felt that the work carried out by Guinness was excessive. They felt that he had strayed beyond the simple restoration of the original fabric into a conjectural reconstruction of a more idealised Gothic building. Despite such quibbles, most people would agree that Guinness saved the cathedral and guaranteed its survival for many centuries to come. This view is supported when one considers the state of the cathedral prior to restoration, as described in a contemporary account:

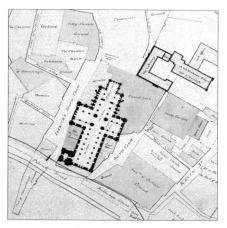

> The nave and south transept were a wilderness, the shafts and mouldings gone or mutilated, the south wall of the nave and end of the south transept alarmingly out of the perpendicular. The original stone vaulting had disappeared except in the aisles of the south transept. On the exterior of the Church most of the window dressing had gone to decay. The flying buttresses on the south side were ruins and those on the north side even more decayed.

In a recent detailed study of the various nineteenth-century restorations carried out on the cathedral, Michael O'Neill catalogued the extent to which the original fabric of the cathedral was replaced. For instance, between the years 1844 and 1852 the Lady Chapel or Chapter House was almost completely rebuilt. This reconstruction was designed by the architect Richard Cromwell Carpenter. The Lady Chapel was used during the seventeenth and eighteenth centuries as a French church by the Huguenot refugees who had come to Dublin. The Huguenots of the French Chapel were also given their own burial ground, which stood adjacent to the Dean's own garden – the so-called Cabbage Patch. The burial ground had been laid out in 1666 to relieve pressure on the graveyard that immediately surrounded St Patrick's Cathedral. That graveyard was 'over much burdened with multitudes of corpse interred there'. The cabbage garden, which

Above top: Detail from Malton's engraving, showing cattle being driven to the butchers' slaughterhouses and stalls on Patrick Street.

Above: An eighteenth-century map, showing the plan of the cathedral with surrounding properties, including the Oeconomy to the north and Vicar's Close to the south.

Opposite top: Speed's map shows the position of St Patrick's Cathedral – outside and to the south of the medieval walled city.

Opposite bottom: Inside St Patrick's Cathedral, looking towards the chancel.

stood on the opposite side of Kevin Street, may have been used by the Cromwellians for the cultivation of cabbage, a vegetable which, they claimed, they first introduced into this country some few years previously.

By the nineteenth century the original stone vaulted roof of the choir had been replaced by a flat plaster ceiling and some of the delicate Gothic windows had been blocked up. The walls of the cathedral were stripped of plaster in 1902.

St Patrick's Close

Rocque's map (1756) reinforces the impression of an ancient and majestic cathedral surrounded by many small houses and alleys, including St Patrick's Close North and St Patrick's Close South. The southern St Patrick's Close did not in any way resemble today's pleasant curving street where visitors are dropped off by coach. In 1845 the Wide Streets Commissioners proposed the construction of such a street, though it would have been built to the west of the Deanery rather than in its present position.

A late eighteenth-century map of the cathedral and its surroundings shows all its associated properties and gives an impression of just how influential it was in medieval times. The Treasurer's Ground ran south to Bride Street, while the archdeacon of Glendalough's lot bordered on Bull Alley to the north. To the south, along Kevin Street, stood the grounds belonging to the Vicar's Choral and opposite the Archbishop's Palace, now Kevin Street Garda Station, stood the Chancellor's Garden. The Palace of St Sepulchre, which belonged to the archbishop, stood to the southeast of the cathedral, adjoining the library later to be known as Marsh's Library. The Dean's house and garden remain in the same location today, but the map shows that there was once an impressive double entrance from Kevin Street.

Above top: A stone-carved corbel of Dean Swift from the 1860s.

Above: St Patrick's Cathedral's strongbox.

Right: The gentle curve of St Patrick's Close is a pleasant oasis, and in the early twentieth century was full of trees.

Opposite top: Mitre Alley, shown on this map, is now occupied by St Patrick's Cathedral Grammar School.

Opposite middle: This old house on Kevin Street is now used as the cathedral office.

Opposite bottom: Patrick Street was famous for its market, seen in this nineteenth-century photograph.

The Vicar's Choral and the Archbishop of Dublin's yard adjoined the Deanery on the west side – much of this site is now taken up by St Patrick's Cathedral Grammar School. It is the oldest school in Ireland, having been founded in the fifteenth century. Records show that six choristers began their education in the robing room of the cathedral in 1431. For nearly 500 years the school provided an education exclusively for choristers in the cathedral, but this changed towards the end of the nineteenth century, and the school now provides an education for boys and girls of all religions.

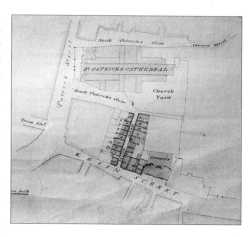

A lonely Dutch-gabled house, which survives on Kevin Street, backs onto the grounds of the Cathedral School. The house was largely reconstructed in the twentieth century, though some of the original structure was retained. The late eighteenth-century map also shows the existence of a courthouse directly adjacent to the nave of the cathedral on the south side.

To the north, in the area now covered by St Patrick's Park, stood three large properties belonging to the Cathedral Oeconomy. A narrow passageway called Glendalough Lane connected Bride Street with the now-vanished St Patrick's Close North. The Petty Canons' Ground, which later in the nineteenth century became Canon Street, also connected Bride Street with St Patrick's Close North.

The eventual construction of the present St Patrick's Close in the middle of the nineteenth century allowed for the erection of a low wall with railings around the cathedral precinct. Late nineteenth-century photographs show how the Victorians had completely changed the setting of the cathedral. It was no longer surrounded by small and often decaying ancient houses; the cathedral was now viewed in the romantic setting of trees and railings. The laying out of St Patrick's Park to the north of the cathedral further improved its environs.

Patrick Street

There are many impressions of Dublin left to us by different artists, but Walter Osborne's late nineteenth-century painting of Patrick Street relates a different story. His view shows the street, with its old eighteenth-century houses still intact, as a crowded market-place with stalls of fish and vegetables and various lean-tos and awnings jutting out from the houses into a street filled with people, horses and carts. Three children occupy the foreground of the painting as if to remind us that in Dublin's overcrowded streets large, poor families were commonplace.

Patrick Street was famous for its street market, selling meat and fish, fruit and vegetables and a map of 1797 shows the area immediately adjacent to Walker's Alley, containing several slaughterhouses and a butcher's stall on the corner

of Patrick Street and Walker's Alley. Photographs of the period show the cobbled street and the tall Georgian houses jostling each other as they make their way uphill towards Nicholas Street to the north. The large-scale planning and rebuilding of the east side of Patrick Street, which was undertaken by the Iveagh Trust, involved the clearance of old houses and the laying of St Patrick's Park and the Iveagh Buildings. St Patrick's Park was laid out in 1903 and brought about the demolition of many small houses and several lanes and alleys, including Mylers Alley, Walkers Alley, Goodman's Lane, Verschoyle Court, Baldam's Court and Canon Street.

Across the road the last vestiges of the old Patrick Street were swept away in 1983 as plans for a dual carriageway proceeded apace. The new road has again changed the setting of the historic cathedral. The planned roadway was intended to run past the west door of the cathedral, but thanks to the persistence of Dean Victor Griffin of St Patrick's Cathedral, it was reduced from a planned width of ninety feet to forty feet at this point.

An eighteenth-century map in Marsh's Library shows the original Deanery with two flights of sweeping steps both from the front and back of the building. An earlier Deanery, which was erected in 1713, was burnt in 1781. The present, late eighteenth-century replacement contains a

Above: Patrick Street in the 1980s, before the controversial road-widening took place.

Below: Patrick Street in a photograph from the 1890s.

magnificent open-well staircase with an attractive plasterwork ceiling overhead. The kitchens below are vaulted.

Mitre Alley was a small narrow passage connecting St Patrick's Close South with Kevin Street. It passed to the west side of the Deanery stables, which are today incorporated into buildings used by St Patrick's Grammar School. Mitre Alley, which was also known as Chapter Lane, was a narrow cobbled street bounded on the west side by a row of 'Dutch Billy'-style houses. In 1845 the Wide Streets Commissioners proposed to acquire some twelve houses that occupied Mitre Alley in order to create a more fitting approach to the cathedral.

In the Deanery there is a large painting of Dean Swift by Francis Bindon, showing him in his simple black robes with St Patrick's Cathedral in the background. The carved frame is an outstanding example of eighteenth-century Dublin craftsmanship, and it was made by John Haughton, who was paid £18/30s for it. There is also a carving of the Dean's head, which may be seen in one of the corbels, executed in the 1860s, on the exterior of the cathedral.

Naboth's Vineyard was the name given to a garden that was laid out and tended by Dean Swift, and was his favourite place of recreation. The garden, formed in 1724, was planted with fruit trees and the whole enclosed with a high stone wall. In 1822 the Meath Hospital and County Dublin Infirmary were erected on the site of Naboth's Vineyard.

The original Palace of St Sepulchre was erected by Archbishop Comyn at the time of the foundation of the Cathedral Church. The buildings now occupied by Kevin Street Garda Station contain several elements of the old Palace, including a sixteenth-century arched entrance, on the side closest to the cathedral, with some carved tablets above it, the original

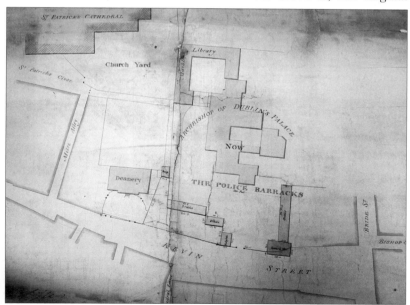

Above top: Part of the original seventeenth-century staircase of the Archbishop's Palace in Kevin Street.

Above: An elaborate internal pair of doors on the first floor in the Palace.

Left: An eighteenth-century map, showing the Palace of the former Archbishop of Dublin, now Kevin Street Garda Station, with the Deanery on the left and Marsh's Library above.

Above: This sixteenth-century cut-stone entrance to the Archbishop's Palace, with the carved tablets above, lies neglected at the side of Kevin Street Garda Station, and deserves to be opened up as the focal point of the building.

seventeenth-century staircase and a remarkable panelled door. The wide doorway is framed by shouldered architraves and decorated with Tudor roses and large swags of fruit that hang from a lion's mask.

It has been suggested that the name St Sepulchre may have been adopted in the late twelfth century to mark the activity of the crusaders in their attempt to recover the Holy Sepulchre – the tomb in which Jesus was laid – from the so-called Infidels. The massive entrance gates and brick wall, which front onto Kevin Street, were erected in the early eighteenth century.

Marsh's Library is one of Dublin's greatest treasures and yet it is relatively unknown to many Dubliners, who perhaps think that it is not open to the public. It was built in 1701 by Archbishop Narcissis Marsh in the grounds of his Palace of St Sepulchre. Designed by Sir William Robinson, the architect of the Royal Hospital Kilmainham, it is distinguished by its tall windows, steep roofs and mellow red-brick façades. The library is attractively ranged around three sides of a courtyard, part of which is linked to a modern paper conservation workshop that was established by the generosity of Mr and Mrs Jean-Paul Delmas.

The library, which is situated on the upper floor, away from any dampness and making the best use of natural light, is fitted out with a magnificent sequence of panelled bookcases, which are filled with a highly important collection of early published books. The dark oak panelling of the bookshelves is ornamented by carved, white-painted plaques, which bear the number of each bookcase. These are carved in imitation of drapery and swags and are accompanied by the most delicate of Gothic screens, also painted white, which are topped by carved foliage and a bishop's mitre. These screens and doors protect some of the rarer books in the library's collection, while others were actually chained to wooden rods to prevent their removal from the library! The ground floor contains the apartment of the curator Ms Muriel McCarthy, who has zealously minded and promoted the library over the last forty years.

The Iveagh Trust was set up by Sir Edward Cecil Guinness in 1890 for the purpose of providing housing and amenities for the poor of both Dublin and London. Guinness had become immensely wealthy through the flotation of his company in 1886, and through the establishment of this

Philanthropic Trust the lives of thousands of people were immeasurably improved. His initial endowment of £200,000 led to the building of 10,000 dwellings in England. In Ireland, £50,000 was dedicated to the construction of 800 dwellings in Dublin and the provision of 130 hostel beds in the city. The main concentration of the Trust's building work was in Kevin Street and in the area between St Patrick's Cathedral and Bride's Alley.

The wholesale reconstruction of the area was begun in the 1890s and was completed by about 1915. It consisted of two five-storey residential complexes, a baths, a hostel and a play centre. The Iveagh Baths, built in 1904, are perhaps the most remarkable of these buildings, although now only the façade remains unaltered. The façade is striking and is in some respects reminiscent of an English seventeenth-century mansion. The arched entranceway with its portcullis-type feature is emphasised by a large decorative escutcheon proclaiming the name Iveagh Trust Public Baths, above which is a room surmounted by a small copper dome. A long glazed roof allowed the pool itself to be lit with natural light. The brick, sandstone and terracotta façade is raised on a granite plinth, all of which was somewhat damaged by water penetration and inappropriate chemical cleaning. The baths were equipped with a large pool, surrounded by a gallery with a wrought-iron balustrade. They were erected for the dual purpose of providing recreational facilities and improving basic hygiene amongst the poor, many of whom had no running water in their houses.

Above: The Iveagh Baths, with its richly ornamented entrance, is one of Dublin's very few Art Nouveau buildings.

Below: The sumptuous classical style of the Iveagh Buildings on Bull Alley, now used as a community school.

Unfortunately, following the closure of the pool in 1987, the baths were considerably vandalised and much of the wrought-iron decorative balustrade was stolen. The Corporation decided to close the baths, because they were faced with a considerable bill to make good various structural defects. Following the closure of the baths, many were concerned about the fate of what is Dublin's only Art Nouveau building. After lying derelict for some eight years, rescue finally came when it was taken over by a private company. The building has now been restored as the Iveagh Fitness Centre and has a small, scaled-down pool and a gymnasium.

The new buildings erected by the Iveagh Trust completely changed the character of both Patrick Street and Nicholas Street as all the old and reportedly very decrepit eighteenth-century houses were swept away. Some of the new residential buildings on Patrick Street were provided with shops on the

Above: A four-foot-high carved wooden figure, now in the Dublin Civic Museum, which once stood above a shop in Patrick Street.

ground floor, which are still in use today. The building work in Kevin Street began in 1894 and also swept away many small houses, which had been built around courtyards. The site backed onto the former cabbage garden or graveyard and covered a large open area where ropes had been manufactured.

One of the earliest developments initiated by the trust was the construction in 1892 of two blocks of red-brick houses or apartments at Thomas Court. These three-storey apartment buildings were erected by the Dublin Artisans' Dwelling Company for the Iveagh Trust and were located near the Guinness Brewery.

As we have already mentioned, the Wide Streets Commissioners carried out various improvements to Patrick's Street, St Patrick's Close, Kevin Street and the bottom of the Coombe (later to be called Dean Street). In 1813 seven houses in front of the cathedral, called Cross Poddle, were acquired and were subsequently cleared away. This work was followed, in 1836, by the acquisition of small houses at the bottom of the Coombe, between New Row and Kevin Street. At the same time a triangle of properties was acquired between Free Stone Alley, Kevin Street and New Street. This attractive, but no doubt dense and jumbled, network of streets was realigned to form a clear passage from Dean Street through to Kevin Street Upper.

In the twentieth century another massive street clearance took place in this area, sweeping away all of the reconstructed buildings of the early nineteenth century. Even now the urban landscape at this sprawling road junction is unsatisfactory, and only a few apartment developments have so far been erected in an attempt to recreate the sense of a street. Nothing now remains of the new houses that were built in accordance with the Wide Streets Commissioners' plans, except perhaps for some houses on Dean Street and the corner building on the west side of Francis Street, which is currently used as an antique shop.

CHAPTER TWELVE

St Stephen's Green

St Stephen's Green is both the largest and oldest square in the city of Dublin. The twenty-seven-acre park provides Dubliners with a relaxing green oasis amid the traffic and noise of the city. The buildings that adorn the four sides of the green include some of the finest Georgian architecture in Dublin, as well as being a repository of a long and colourful history. The area became known as St Stephen's Green because of its proximity to the Church of St Stephen, which once stood on the site of the present Mercer's Hospital building. In late medieval times the lands at St Stephen's Green were used as commonage, where the citizens of Dublin could graze their sheep and cattle free of charge.

In the 1660s Dublin Corporation, who, as we have already seen, claimed all the lands east of the medieval city, began to plan the development of the green, reserving some twenty-seven acres as an open space for the benefit of its citizens. In 1664, ninety building lots were laid out on the four sides of the green. St Stephen's Green has undergone many changes since, to the

Left: The elegant north side of St Stephen's Green is as fashionable today as it was in the 1890s. The great Georgian mansions (centre) were adapted to become gentlemen's clubs.

Right and below: Malton's engraving (right) and Rocque's map (below) show the fashionable park in its eighteenth-century form, symmetrically laid out around the statue of King George II.

Above: St Stephen's Green was a focus for the building of many fine Georgian houses.

extent that none of these late seventeenth-century houses survive. Brooking's map of St Stephen's Green made in 1728 shows it as a large empty space, simply a green surrounded by a double row of trees, with a collection of large houses on three sides. Rocque's map, made some thirty years later, shows the green divided into four quadrants, with a central feature or mound that was at that time ornamented with an equestrian statue of King George II. (The statue, by Van Nost, was blown up in 1937.) The map shows that the building of the four sides of the square was more or less complete, apart from some of the larger plots on the east side. He also shows the Quaker burial ground, in the centre of the west side, which was later the site of the College of Surgeons' building, built in 1806. The map shows a variety of large detached houses with gables and tall chimney stacks, some of them standing on St Stephen's Green North.

James Malton's print of St Stephen's Green, published in 1796, gives an impression of the orderly layout of the square and the central statue of George II. The empty green is given over to the grazing of some horses, and there is a double line of elm trees, providing shade for the fashionable ladies and gentlemen who walked along the gravel paths.

The buildings of St Stephen's Green have always been the province of the fashionable and wealthy of Dublin society. The building of 9 St Stephen's Green, now the St Stephen's Green Club, in 1756, heralded the latest fashions in interior decoration, having elaborate plasterwork by the La Francini brothers. The St Stephen's Green Club has one of the most outstanding interiors of any house on the green. The two ceilings of the dining room on the ground floor and those of the reading room on the floor above are very beautiful. The former two ceilings feature a complex arrangement of birds, swags, foliage and putti (or cherubs), one of whom is portrayed as Vulcan hammering on an anvil. On the reading-room ceilings an image of Minerva, with her sword and shield, floats against the background plasterwork, surrounded by a lion and more putti. The plasterwork panels of the staircase feature Juno, the metamorphosis of Antigione into a stork, and other classical figures such as Mercury and Minerva. The three panels are framed by highly elaborate stucco frames, in the form of swags and scrolls intertwined with foliage and other motifs. The staircase itself is an outstanding example of a timber construction, its Doric pillar-style balustrade similar to that in Castletown House in Celbridge, County Kildare.

In the 1840s the house became the property of the Reform Club, of which Daniel O'Connell was a prominent early member. The façade was rebuilt in 1844 by the architect Michael Mullins, one of the first Roman Catholic architects to make a successful career in Dublin. He was responsible, it is believed, for the design of the elegant card room to the rear of the present-day club. The card room is a rectangular structure with a domed light in the roof and the walls are decorated with plaster panels in the Georgian classical style. Other additions at this time included extra bedrooms, two billiard rooms and various meeting rooms.

In 1984 the club considered selling their premises for use as a banking hall and offices, and accordingly applied for planning permission to demolish the Victorian card room, which would have been necessary to accommodate a three-storey office extension to the rear. Fortunately, the club did not proceed with this plan and has instead gradually refurbished the entire building, whose elegant rooms are in daily use and are hired out for special events and dinners.

In the late eighteenth century Samuel Hutchinson, the Bishop of Killala, lived in number 8. This late eighteenth-century house replaced an earlier residence, the one-time home of Viscount Castlecomer, which was described as 'the very convenient large house, with two coach-houses, three large stables and other convenient out-offices and a large garden, very fit for a nobleman or private gentleman'. The Georgian house was heavily remodelled in Victorian times and the present grand flight of steps with its bold ironwork, the elaborate entrance and the bay windows all date from this period. The Hibernian United Services Club, to give it its full title, took over the mansion in 1848.

Twenty years after the construction of numbers 8 and 9, more palatial houses were being built between Dawson Street and Kildare Street, including numbers 14–17 St Stephen's Green. Number 15 was built by Gustavus Hume, who was involved in much property development and speculation,

Below: Large sections of St Stephen's Green have disappeared, including, for example, every house in this photograph of the attractive and varied streetscape of St Stephen's Green West, taken in 1978.

and who is remembered in the name Hume Street on the east side of the square. Hume's new house was subsequently let to Richard Cox, the son of the Archbishop of Cashel, who had recently erected a magnificent house for himself in County Kilkenny known as Castletown Cox. Numbers 14 and 15 were let to Ambrose Leet in 1778 at £80 per annum, 'excluding of his buildings a coach house, and stables, estimated to be worth £105'.

The site of numbers 16 and 17 was once occupied by a large square mansion with a forecourt and curved flanking walls. An old map in the Dublin City Archives shows the layout of the house and ground, with an extensive bowling green lying between it and the lord mayor's residence. The kitchens, beer cellar and stables were all located away from the house on the Dawson Street side. The house was identified, by the architectural historian Frederick O'Dwyer, as the residence of Thomas Wyndham, the Lord Chancellor from 1726 to 1739, and Brooking's map suggests that it was very imposing and may have had a tower on the roof. Numbers 14 and 15 have most of their original features intact, including fine plasterwork ceilings in the principal rooms. Dublin Corporation, who are the present owners of the two houses and the early Gothic-style mews to the rear, are currently planning their full restoration.

In 1976 two gentlemen's clubs, the Kildare Street Club and the University Club, amalgamated and moved into one building – number 17 St Stephen's Green, a house originally built for Lord Milltown in 1776 and bought by the University Club in 1815. The hall and stairs, and indeed all the main reception rooms, of number 17 are of an outstanding quality and were decorated in the delicate Robert Adam style by the stuccadore Michael Stapleton.

The firm of James Adam, noted auctioneers since 1887, was first established in Merrion Row, and later at 19 St Stephen's Green where furniture and fine art sales were originally held. In 1969 they moved to 26 St Stephen's Green. James Adam came from Paisley in Scotland and was apprenticed to Arthur Jones and Company, home furnishers and auctioneers. The Adam company undertook much government work and also acted as valuers to many public companies.

Their old building, and 18–21 St Stephen's Green, were demolished to make way for Stephen Court, a large, brown-coloured office block with tinted glass. The windows of number 19 and of the Presbyterian Association, amongst dozens of others, had been blown in by a bomb, in 1958, which destroyed a statue of Lord Eglinton. The two adjoining properties, numbers 20 and 21, were two fine four-storey-over-basement Georgian houses, typical of the sixty houses demolished around St Stephen's Green between 1965 and 1985.

Above: The offices and sales rooms of James Adam and Sons are a landmark on St Stephen's Green.

Below: The Shelbourne Hotel in the 1890s.

The north side has been recently improved by the refacing of the old Scottish Provident office block near the Shelbourne Hotel, and it has to be admitted that, with the passing of time, the Stephen Court office block has mellowed somewhat.

The Shelbourne Hotel, one of Dublin's best-known establishments, occupies what is arguably the finest location in Dublin, looking out over St Stephen's Green towards the Dublin Mountains. Taking up numbers 27–34, it has for many years held the reputation of being the finest hotel in the city. It was founded in 1824 by Martin Burke when three houses were joined together to form what was then called Burke's Hotel, which quickly became the most fashionable place to stay in Dublin for the gentry and the well-to-do. The three houses that comprised the original structure replaced a much older residence known as Carey House. The hotel was named after the Earl of Shelbourne in recognition of the fact that Carey House was once his home. The use of this titled name undoubtedly helped to build up the superior cachet of the hotel, which it still maintains to this day. William Thackeray, who stayed there in 1842, gave a good account of it and thought the daily charge of 6s/8d was good value as it included a lavish breakfast, luncheon and dinner.

When William Jury and Charles Cotton took over the hotel in 1865, it was completely rebuilt in its present Victorian manner. The sumptuous new hotel, designed by John McCurdy, was fitted out with all the latest Victorian comforts. The

Above: Old houses, sold for small sums by today's standards, were acquired for redevelopment as office blocks.

Below: Number 52 has one of the finest stone doorcases of St Stephen's Green, seen here complete with its original panelled door and brass fittings.

Shelbourne has been part of the Trust House Forte Group since 1960, and is rated as one of the finest hotels in the world.

Despite its importance and beauty as an urban space, many depredations were made on the fine Georgian architecture of the green over the last thirty years. One of the earliest twentieth-century demolitions on St Stephen's Green was that of Tracton House, which stood on the corner of Baggot Street facing the Shelbourne Hotel. The house, which was believed to have been built in the 1740s and was later occupied by James Dennis, Baron Tracton, was demolished in 1912 to make way for the construction of the Bank of Ireland on that site. The drawing-room fittings and the magnificent ceiling were carefully taken down and re-erected in the National Museum, where they lay until the 1960s when they were installed in the State Apartments in Dublin Castle.

The row over the demolition of four houses at the east corner of St Stephen's Green and Hume Street in the late 1960s came to a head when architecture students from UCD and Bolton Street occupied the buildings. The debate raged on for several months with the Royal Institute of Architects of Ireland and all the major conservation bodies trying to persuade the developers not to demolish the houses. They were demolished anyway in the early 1970s and replaced with office blocks with neo-Georgian façades. Over the same period, a further twelve houses were demolished at the southeast corner of St Stephen's Green, adjoining Earlsfort Terrace.

Fortunately, several important buildings on the east side survive, including number 51, the present headquarters of the Office of Public Works, a much remodelled Georgian house. The collection of Irish marble samples in the entrance hall of this house is all that remains of the Museum of Irish Industry, which once occupied the building. Number 52, the elegant eighteenth-century home of the banker David La Touche, contains a series of very fine rooms with painted murals and good plasterwork dating from the 1770s. A unique survivor in the hall of this house is a pair of brass holders for the poles that once carried the sedan chairs of Dublin's Georgian citizens.

The Loreto College at 53 St Stephen's Green is a fine Georgian house with plasterwork by Michael Stapleton. The remaining buildings leading up to the corner of Leeson Street, with the exception of number 60, were occupied by St Vincent's Hospital. The hospital, founded in 1834, encased a mid-eighteenth-century house with stunning plasterwork by Robert West. The remarkable staircase of this house, now owned by the Irish Permanent Building Society, positively drips with the elaborate rococo stucco work of West. The hospital vacated the buildings in the early 1970s when it moved to a new site at Elm Park in Donnybrook.

Number 60 St Stephen's Green stands at the corner of Leeson Street and though it appeared to have been almost abandoned for many years, it contained three of the finest ceilings on the green. After many legal difficulties, the house was eventually acquired by the Irish Permanent, and following a major reconstruction the three ceilings were meticulously copied and put back in the reconstructed building. Excellent though the reproductions are, the unfortunate result of the copying process is that the original ceilings were destroyed.

Further large chunks of Georgian Dublin disappeared with the building of the Sugar Company headquarters at the bottom of Leeson Street. This entailed the demolition of the former Magdelene Asylum and its chapel, and was followed in the early 1980s by the outrageous demolition of twelve houses on the same side of Leeson Street. These houses included some early, panelled houses with Dutch-gabled façades and the magnificent townhouse of Lord Ardilaun, once belonging to the Sacred Heart Convent. The site formed part of the massive site belonging to the Gallagher Group, which extended back to Earlsfort Terrace.

Probably the two best-known houses in St Stephen's Green are Newman House and Iveagh House, both located on the south side. Newman House and its neighbour Clanwilliam House, at numbers 85 and 86, are two outstanding Georgian townhouses, both of which have been beautifully restored over the past ten years. The earlier house, number 85, dates from 1738 and exhibits some of the finest Baroque plasterwork in Dublin, the work of the La Francini brothers. The chief glories of the house, which is now open to the public, are the beautifully proportioned

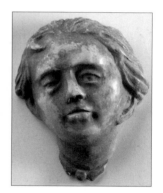

and richly decorated Apollo Room on the ground floor and the saloon on the first floor.

The dignified Portland-stone façade of Iveagh House disguises the existence of two earlier houses, numbers 80 and 81. These two houses were thrown together in 1863 by Sir Benjamin Lee Guinness to create a sumptuous palace with a grand staircase whose walls are faced with marble. Both houses had impressive lists of occupants. These included Robert Clayton, Bishop of Kilalla, who lived in number 80 in the 1730s, Lord Mount Cashel and, in the early nineteenth century, John Philpott Curran.

In 1939 the Earl of Iveagh presented the house to the Irish nation and since that time it has been used as the headquarters of the Department of Foreign Affairs. In that year a major auction was held on the instructions of the Earl of Iveagh, and an extraordinary collection of antique furniture, mirrors, ornaments, portraits and paintings, carpets, rugs and the furnishings of some sixty bedrooms were sold. The lush gardens that lie behind Newman House and Iveagh House and connect Harcourt Street to the back of the National Concert Hall are called the Iveagh Gardens – they were named in honour of Lord Iveagh.

Above: Iveagh House, gracefully rebuilt by Sir Benjamin Lee Guinness in the 1860s.

St Stephen's Green South possesses a church which is one of the great architectural gems of the nineteenth century, and is well worthy of close scrutiny – the University Church. A neat, arched entrance in the Byzantine style leads the visitor through a somewhat barren vestibule and into a small rectangular church of stunning beauty, passing through a forest of short Byzantine columns which support the gallery. The visitor is transported back in time into the marble-clad church, which could almost be on an island in the Venetian Lagoon. Every surface is decorated, including the open roof structure, painted by John Hungerford Pollen, who was also the architect for the church. This unique church was commissioned by Dr Newman in 1856 and was erected for the benefit of the students attending the new university. It operates today as a normal parish church, but is also very popular as a venue for fashionable weddings.

Above: From Newman House, a unique lead hopper, part of a drainpipe, dated 1766.

Of the four houses which stood on the corner of St Stephen's Green South and Earlsfort Terrace, later replaced by Canada House, Karl Jones, the property correspondent of the *Irish Times*, wrote in 1969: 'It would be difficult to envisage any final outcome other than the ultimate demolition of the four houses, and the redevelopment of the site. They look particularly out of place, tucked disconsolately against the disapproving shoulder of the neighbouring

development.' The neighbour referred to was, of course, a new office block belonging to the City Bank.

The trend had already been well established by the demolition, some three years earlier, of three very fine houses, numbers 47–49, which stood on Stephen's Green East near the corner of Hume Street.

In a quite illogical way, several intact Georgian streets, such as Harcourt Street, Hatch Street Lower, Leeson Street Lower and St Stephen's Green West, were considered unworthy of preservation, while Hume Street, Ely Place, and Clare Street, along with the main Georgian squares, were all listed.

In 1969 a petition was drawn up, with a plea to allow no further demolitions until an assessment of the merits of the area and any proposed planning applications had been given a public airing. The names of the signatories are interesting – they included Maurice Gorham, Marie Comerford, Desmond Guinness, Sheila Carden, Kevin B Nolan, Mícheál Mac Liammóir, Fergus O'Donoghue, James Plunkett, Peadar O'Donnell, T Desmond Williams, MJ Tutty, Niall Sheridan, TP Conneally, Evelyn Shiels, Francis J Byrne, Austin Dunphy and Seán O'Faoláin. Over the next fifteen years, many excellent articles were to be written by people such as Vivien Igoe, Helen Connolly and John Mulcahy about the demise of St Stephen's Green. Frank McDonald and other writers took up the cause again in the 1980s, all to little avail. Maureen Concannon O'Brien, who lived at 99 St Stephen's Green and formed the St Stephen's Green Protection Association, succeeded in reclaiming some half a dozen houses from the major Irish Life development near the corner of Harcourt Street.

In 1963 three fine Georgian houses, 74–76 St Stephen's Green, were advertised in the national newspapers as 'ripe for immediate

Above: Remarkably, St Stephen's Green South retains its Georgian character.

Above: The Russell Hotel was replaced by an office block in the 1970s.
Below: St Stephen's Green West as it was in the late nineteenth century. The low building was occupied by May's Music Shop.

redevelopment'. The group, which were replaced by an office block, included the former Skerries College with its beautiful cut-stone doorcase and wide entrance hall. The drawing room ceiling of Skerries College was salvaged by the Office of Public Works. Not all of the houses of St Stephen's Green were as grand as these, and some of those lying between Newman House and Harcourt Street, such as number 82, were of a more modest scale, and had smaller panelled rooms and corner fireplaces.

Wesley College, founded in 1845 at number 79, once comprised an interesting collection of Victorian school buildings. The college stood behind the Methodist Centenary Church (so called because it commemorated the founding of the first Methodist church in Ireland a hundred years earlier.), whose façade was incorporated into another office development. Wesley College moved to Ballinteer in South county Dublin in 1972 and sold the St Stephen's Green properties to Irish Life for redevelopment. A few years later, in 1975, the Russell Hotel, which stood on the corner of Harcourt Street, closed its doors and was eventually replaced by the office block now known as Russell Court. The Russell, which incorporated three houses, was originally opened as a temperance hotel by Thomas W Russell, and it developed an excellent reputation as one of Dublin's leading hotels. A lengthy ten-year battle, which came to a head in about 1980, was fought

Left: A group of soldiers in the early twentieth century march past numbers 119 and 120 – the only pair of houses still remaining on St Stephen's Green West.

Below: A pair of birds from the cornice of number 129 St Stephen's Green, which was destroyed in 1989.

over the fate of the remaining Georgian houses between the Russell Hotel site and the old Centenary Church, and some of them were saved.

As we have already noted, the west side of St Stephen's Green has suffered most at the hands of property speculators, and retains a small degree of dignity thanks only to the survival of the Royal College of Surgeons, the Unitarian Church and a pair of Georgian houses. The remaining buildings are very representative of dreary late twentieth-century commercial construction and the streetscape is not helped by the fact that a major derelict site, once occupied by the house in which Robert Emmet was born, has still not been developed after almost twenty years.

A huge site, now partially occupied by the Stephen's Green Shopping Centre, was gradually assembled in the 1970s on this side of the square. The properties, including all of South King Street, the old Dandelion Market and Gaiety Green, a shopping arcade, were cleared of tenants by 1980. Most of it was owned by the Slazenger family, the owners of Powerscourt House in Enniskerry. The Dandelion Market, which flourished during the 1970s, had occupied what was once the extensive premises of Taylor Keith, manufacturers of mineral waters, whose premises ran back towards Mercer Street. They in turn had taken over from Hovenden and Orr, who at one time were noted Dublin brewers.

Some of the houses demolished contained Georgian features, such as number 129, whose lavishly decorated staircase was illustrated in the Georgian Society Records. The stairwell possessed a large plaster niche

Above: An unusual early nineteenth-century engraving of the Royal College of Surgeons, which was designed in 1806 by Edward Parke.

Below: The Metropolitan Laundry, which flourished in the 1920s, was one of several commercial enterprises to be found on St Stephen's Green West.

Below bottom: One of the hand-carved wooden brackets from number 127 St Stephen's Green West.

and elaborately ornamented cornices decorated with life-sized birds, flowers and fruit. Its neighbour, number 130, was well known to Dubliners as May's Music Shop. May's, the 'Pianoforte and Music Sellers', had been in existence since 1900 at this location. This house had late seventeenth-century features and some of the upstairs rooms had boldly modelled cornices of mid-eighteenth-century date. The Green Cinema, which came into existence about 1940, occupied number 127, which in the early 1900s had been a famous Turkish baths. Since the nineteenth century, due to the presence of the College of Surgeons, there were several medical suppliers and makers of surgical instruments in buildings nearby.

Arthur Jones, upholsters and cabinetmakers, had occupied number 135 since about 1850. The well-known Dublin firm of Strahans, who were in the same line of business but became noted removal and storage contractors, succeeded them. Two well-known Dublin booksellers, Books Upstairs and Cathair, originated as stall holders in the Dandelion Market, which was for many years prior to 1980 a popular market for antiques and jewellery.

Much of the initial acquisition of property on these sites was carried out by the Lambert Jones company in the 1960s and 1970s. The last buildings to succumb to the pressure to sell out were those at the corner of King Street South, including the attractive Victorian shopfront of Brown's the Chemist, Rice's Pub and its neighbour, Sinnott's in South King Street. Sinnott's was a particularly attractive pub, with its old-world bar and beautiful late Victorian frontage. Despite promises from the developers to retain the carved wooden façade and its polished marble uprights, it was completely smashed by mechanical diggers.

The once fashionable York Street, which was laid out on axis with the centre of St Stephen's Green West, declined into tenements in the twentieth century, and even today provides a startling contrast to the opulent life that is lived in parts of nearby St Stephen's Green. Many of the inhabitants of York Street were very poor and made a living as street dealers, selling fruit and other merchandise.

The forerunner of the College of Surgeons was founded in 1780 when the Dublin Society of Surgeons was formed, but it was not until 1806 that the foundation stone was laid for the present building at the corner of York Street. The building was completed in 1809, but was further enlarged in the 1820s due to its enhanced status and the growing number of students.

Of the seventeen houses that once ranged from York Street to the corner of Cuffe Street, only the handsome pair at 119–120 St Stephen's Green remain. The centre of the building is ornamented by a partially blind Venetian window, a circular niche and a bold cornice above the second floor.

Number 124 was a modest four-storey Georgian house bearing a plaque identifying it as the 1778 birthplace of Robert Emmet. The entire block of houses that lay between the College of Surgeons and the corner at South King Street was deliberately neglected over a long period of time, resulting, in 1984, in the partial collapse of the Emmet house and its neighbour. Despite persistent appeals from An Taisce in the preceding years to have the house restored, and the fact that it was a listed building, nothing had been done by Dublin Corporation. Across the road stands a statue of Emmet, gesturing hopelessly towards the still vacant site of his demolished birthplace. The statue of Robert Emmet is a replica of one made by Jerome O'Connor for a group of Irish Americans. It was presented to the Irish people by Mr and Mrs Francis Kane of Washington DC and it was unveiled in 1968 across from the house where Emmet was born.

St Stephen's Green West is still a disappointment, despite the arrival of a new hotel and the existence of an elegant restaurant at number 119. By contrast, the general quality of the streetscape on the south side is good and, apart from the office blocks at either end, its Georgian appearance is still intact between Loreto Hall and Russell Court. While the east side presents a unified façade of Georgian-style frontages, many, on close examination, are merely a disguise for office blocks.

It could be argued that the Green has been the least fortunate of all the Dublin squares as large sections of it were demolished in the 1970s and 1980s to make way, for the most part, for bland office blocks. No side has come through unscathed, and major conservation battles were fought over the houses at the Hume Street junction, and at the corner between the Methodist Centenary Church and Harcourt Street, and on the site of the present St Stephen's Green Shopping Centre. The devastation visited on St Stephen's Green has been terrible, with losses of landmarks such as the birthplace of Robert Emmet and dozens of fine interiors on all four sides of the Green. Repeated newspaper articles in the early 1980s were entitled 'The Spoiling of St Stephen's Green', 'The Rape of St Stephen's Green' and 'The Sterilisation of St Stephen's Green', and they documented the average Dubliner's sense of helplessness as we watched house after house of one of Dublin's best-loved streetscapes vanish.

Above top and above: Even Robert Emmet's birthplace, at number 124 St Stephen's Green, was not safe from destruction and was eventually knocked down in 1984.

What happened to St Stephen's Green between 1965 and 1985 was well expressed by John Mulcahy in an article in 'Hibernia' in 1978: 'Fundamentally what is happening on the Green is that high-rent office buildings are squeezing out every other form of occupation, and in the process killing off the living inner city.'

The staggering number of houses – over sixty – lost around St Stephen's Green is hard to comprehend, especially as they disappeared in a piecemeal fashion, a few here and a few there. Singly, such houses might have been dismissed as having structural problems and not really having sufficient architectural merit to be worth saving, but collectively the whole Georgian assemblage of the four sides of St Stephen's Green presented a unique urban streetscape. As late as 1982, when An Taisce produced a map indicating what buildings should be protected in the Georgian core of Dublin's south city centre, only a fraction of those remaining on St Stephen's Green were actually included.

It is interesting to note the slow progression from the 1960s and 1970s, when total demolition was favoured, to the policy of retaining façades and some internal features in the 1980s, up to the current position some twenty years later where we are beginning to think about retaining the whole building. For example, in 1982, numbers 89–91 St Stephen's Green were scheduled for redevelopment, but this time at least the houses was not demolished because An Taisce and various conservation groups made clear their concerns.

The demolitions of twenty and thirty years ago have meant that there are parts of St Stephen's Green, particularly on the west side, which have never recovered their previous character. It is ironic that some of the office blocks, which were built to replace the 'obsolete houses', have had to be refaced or, in some cases, completely overhauled after such a short time.

Above top: The site of houses at St Stephen's Green West and South King Street is now occupied by the St Stephen's Green Shopping Centre.

Above: The backs of these houses prior to demolition in 1986.

Harcourt Street

The Georgian profile of Harcourt Street, its gentle curve connecting St Stephen's Green with the old Harcourt Street Railway Station, has survived, despite many attempts to destroy it. Several office blocks with Georgian façades were erected here in the 1970s.

Harcourt Street was laid out in the mid 1770s by John Hatch, who was responsible for many developments in this area, stretching from Camden Street across to Harcourt Terrace, and including, of course, Hatch Street.

The recent controversy over the proposed demolition of 3 and 4 Harcourt Street, two fine Georgian houses, one of which was the home of the Unionist leader Edward Carson, merely underlines the fact that the process of education to prevent the destruction of Dublin's historic

streetscapes will never be completed. Though the façades were well restored, the interiors (one with an attractive ceiling) were clumsily renovated as part of a hotel.

Fortunately, many fine interiors may still be seen in Harcourt Street, including those of Clonmel House, the offices at number 9 and the upstairs rooms of the Kennedy Art Gallery. Kennedy's artists' suppliers originated in South William Street in the mid-nineteenth century as brush manufacturers, moving to Harcourt Street in 1918.

Clonmel House was built in 1778 for John Scott, Lord Clonmel, and was once, before its subdivision, one of the largest houses on the street. The gardens of Clonmel House, where at one time it was proposed to develop a residential street, were eventually to be donated to the public as the present Iveagh Gardens. In 1907 Clonmel House had the distinction of being the first home of the Hugh Lane Gallery of Modern Art.

The National Children's Hospital served the young people of Dublin for well over a century, having brought together several smaller hospitals on this site in 1887. Following its relocation to Tallaght, the hospital closed in 1997, and the buildings still remain vacant.

Above top: Many attempts have been made to erode the graceful Georgian streetscape of Harcourt Street.

Above: One of the original stone brackets on the doorcases of numbers 3 and 4 Harcourt Street, all of which were lost during reconstruction.

CHAPTER THIRTEEN

Grafton Street
and Dawson Street

*F*or more than a century and a half, Grafton Street has been considered Ireland's most fashionable shopping district. Until recently it was a magnet for leading Irish firms such as Brown Thomas, Switzer's, Arnott's and Callaghan's, and their attendant legion of fashion devotees. Grafton Street is home to several long-established specialist shops such as Weir's the jewellers, Fox's the tobacconists and Thomas Cook's travel agency. It is also home to the most famous Bewley's café in the city.

Grafton Street may still claim to be the most fashionable shopping street in Dublin, but it is also a place for buskers and street performers, who carry on their business amongst flower sellers, billboard holders and chattering groups of foreign students. It has a powerful draw for Dubliners and tourists alike. The paving of the street, and its complete pedestrianisation, was carried out in the 1980s and has reinforced its image as the place in Dublin where people go to meet or to be seen. It is the place to parade, to linger, to gossip or to window shop. American journalist George Whitmore described it in 1983 as follows:

Dublin's street life, particularly during the lunch hour, is bustling and fast paced. On a sunny afternoon Grafton Street is vibrant with pedestrians, pavement artists, mimes, musicians and flower sellers. In the midst of it all sit men holding signs to advertise businesses further off the beaten track – a Dublin institution which has outlasted many colonial monuments.

Below: Rocque's map of 1756 shows the irregular line of Grafton Street, contrasting with the planned straightness of Dawson Street.

The origins of Grafton Street can be traced back to the early seventeenth century when Speed's map indicates a route or track running south from Trinity College. The street was first laid out in the seventeenth century, and was later named after a Lord Lieutenant of Ireland, Henry FitzRoy, illegitimate son of Charles II, who was the first Duke of Grafton. Joining Trinity College with St Stephen's Green, Grafton Street follows a gentle S-shaped curve, and stands in contrast to the grid-like straight lines of nearby Dawson Street and Kildare Street.

Above: There is rarely a moment when Grafton Street, which was fully pedestrianised in the 1980s, is not thronged with people.

We have already mentioned that Nathaniel Fowlkes held property adjoining Grafton Street as early as 1655. Fowlkes's property extended from 'the waste ground of Hoggen Green to Grafton Street (on the west side) to the lands of Tib and Tom'. In about 1671 an avenue was opened from Grafton Street to the Round Church, which would later be called Suffolk Street. St Andrew's Church was built on part of the ground known as the Bowling Alley.

On the east side of Grafton Street we know that a seventeenth-century house belonging to a Mr Burnyates was standing by 1680. Burnyates's property was bounded by 11 and 12 Grafton Street and by the road leading to St Patrick's Well, now Nassau Street. A map of 1680 features a sketch of Mr Burnyates's house, which was three windows wide, with the hall door set to one side. The windows are shown as having mullions with lattice glazing, probably in lead. The house was two storeys high with a third floor incorporated into the attic where there were three dormer windows. There was one central chimney stack. Houses of such age are very rare in Ireland, and there are few drawings or pictures of them.

This land was granted to the Church of Ireland primate, Archbishop Usher. Usher's holding, which consisted of a large field described as 'waste ground in the Parish of St Andrew's', was leased to Thomas Pooley in 1699 for a term of ninety-nine years. The houses at numbers 1–12 Grafton Street were subsequently built on this land and involved the demolition of Burnyates's house. In the early nineteenth century the Wide Streets Commissioners acquired the property and realigned this lower portion of Grafton Street.

The Pooley Estate included the part of Grafton Street that now faces the Provost's House in Trinity College. In 1764 this large garden site was leased to Lord Mornington, the Honourable Richard Wesley (later spelt Wellesley). Lord Mornington was an ancestor of the Marquis of Wellesley, who became the Duke of Wellington.

In the lease from the Pooley estate, Mornington pledged 'also to build an ornamental house thereon, for his own dwelling, and lay out on the said

house the sum of £3,000 sterling'. Mornington's plot had a frontage of 151 feet, and is now occupied by a group of buildings including the present Trustee Savings Bank. These fine bank premises were erected for the Northern Bank.

Nassau Street was then known as the St Patrick's Well Road. It formed part of the site of Lord Mornington's house and was part of Hoggen Green. It is curious that Rocque's map, which pre-dates the lease of Lord Mornington, already shows the house and garden on the site. The house and garden were later occupied by numbers 112–116 Grafton Street, which in the nineteenth century were occupied by several notable publishing houses.

The character of Grafton street is now predominantly Victorian, but during the early years of the eighteenth century it was a residential area and had amongst its inhabitants Lord Kinsale, the Earl of Dunsany and the Marquis Wellesley, who was born there in 1760.

The site occupied today by Weir's, the jeweller's, formed part of a block which was laid out in sites for building in 1780. Nine houses were to be built between Suffolk Street and Weir's Corner. Similar plots were planned for seven houses on Suffolk Street and twelve on Exchequer Street, now Wicklow Street. The conditions laid down by the Wide Streets Commissioners were quite strict and stated that they were:

Above: The top of Grafton Street, showing the run of houses on the right which were rebuilt to the designs of the Wide Street Commissioners in the early nineteenth century.

1. To build in uniformity, *viz* all the houses to be of one height and equal number of storeys.
2. That they are to have stock brick fronts and mountain stone coping and window stools.
3. That the front and rear walls are not to be less than fourteen inches thick.
4. That the party wall is not to be less than nine inches thick and to continue up to the top of the roof in each.
5. That, if possible, all do build together and that the City Surveyor do stake out the several lots of ground.

Other examples of the orderly planning of the Grafton Street area occurred as early as 1752, when the City Surveyor laid out what are now Chatham

Street, Harry Street and the adjoining part of Grafton Street in regular plots. This proposal was not carried through, as later maps show Harry Street in its present configuration. A similar plan was mooted in 1773, for the same parcel of ground, which was known as Flint's Croft, and houses were proposed for Grafton Street with twenty-three-foot frontages while smaller sites were allocated to the back streets.

During the latter half of the eighteenth century Grafton Street began to acquire a name for literary and cultural pursuits. The street became renowned for its publishers and booksellers, which included important names of the day such as Exshaw and Watson, publishers of the street directories. Also in 1766 the Dublin Society, later the Royal Dublin Society (RDS), erected a house as their headquarters at numbers 112–113, and at the rear of these premises free instruction in figure drawing was given to promising artists. This institution was the early precursor of today's National College of Art and Design. The Royal Irish Academy, now located in a fine house in Dawson Street, held its first meeting, in 1785, in Navigation House, which was situated in Grafton Street, next door to the RDS.

Above: The trade card of Bellew, one of the many booksellers that were once to be found on Grafton Street.

Below: This plaque, originally on the front of Bewley's café, records the existence of Whyte's Academy.

In 1758 Samuel Whyte established his famous English Grammar School at 75 Grafton Street, and it extended to the side of Johnson's Court – the site of one of the entrances to Bewley's Café. Many of Whyte's students were outstanding in literature and drama. One of them was Thomas Moore, whose recollections are worth repeating here:

> As soon as I was old enough to encounter the crowd of a large school, it was determined that I should go to the best then in Dublin – the grammar school of the well-known Samuel Whyte, who had a reputation of more than thirty years standing and was, at that time, at the head of his profession.

Samuel Whyte encouraged Moore's talent for recitation and acting. Whyte, through his connection and friendship with the family of Brinsley Sheridan, became devoted to drama, and his pupils often put on their own theatrical performances. He promoted male and female actors alike and gave lessons in elocution.

Others who attended the Academy included Richard Brinsley and Alicia Sheridan, the children of his close friends. Their father Thomas Sheridan was the manager of the famous Smock Alley Theatre. Robert Emmet, George Petrie and the Duke of Wellington were also pupils at the Academy. Whyte himself wrote many plays, texts on grammar and a treatise on educational principles for 'Respecting Young Ladies as well as Gentlemen'. Prizes for exams included copies of Whyte's collected poems, published in 1792. One of Samuel Whyte's several publications, *The Principal of the English Grammar School*, was printed by Marchbank, in Cole Alley, off Castle Street. After the Act of Union in 1800, Whyte's Academy slowly declined as many of his rich clientele, members of the nobility, began to leave Dublin city.

Samuel Whyte's father was the Deputy Governor of the Tower of London. His mother tragically died while giving birth to Samuel in 1733. In consequence, Whyte was cared for by his aunt and was educated in Dublin by an eminent schoolmaster in an academy in Golden Lane.

At almost exactly the same time as Lord Mornington was building his house in Grafton Street, the Commissioners of Inland Navigation (who oversaw the building of canals in Ireland) were building their own headquarters almost beside him – a building that sadly no longer exists. Their offices consisted of a three-storey, three-bay building in the classical style. The upper floors were built of brick while the ground floor and window surrounds were finished in stone. The offices became known as Navigation House.

The RDS acquired the site next door to Navigation House and built an exact copy, following the design of Christopher Myers. This was an attractive but confined building, with meeting rooms to the front, drawing schools to the rear and a gallery for a collection of plaster casts over the stables. The RDS stayed in Grafton Street until 1796, when they sold their premises and moved to a larger site in Hawkins Street. Lord Mornington's lease of 1764 may have coincided with the building of a new house, as Gilbert suggests that the family already lived in Grafton Street and that the first Lord Mornington died here in 1758.

Commercial Life

Though Grafton Street was originally a residential area, it gradually succumbed to commercial enterprises during the progress of the eighteenth century. There were various inns to be found in the district, such as the Black Lyon Inn, which was located at the corner of Anne Street in 1762. The Guild of the Tallow Chandlers, or Guild of St George, had a hall or meeting place in Grafton Street in 1783. The Royal Dublin Society, which has already been mentioned, operated from Grafton Street and under their auspices the Irish Woollen Warehouse was established in Castle Street and the Irish Silk Warehouse in Parliament Street, both of which had the aim of promoting these native industries. Gilbert states that, following the

Above: Grafton Street has attracted fashionable crowds since the nineteenth century.

Below: The billhead of a noted house-furnishing and furniture-removal company.

opening of Carlisle (now O'Connell) Bridge, the private residences in Grafton Street became gradually converted into shops.

In the nineteenth century the businesses of 112–116 Grafton Street, that part facing the Provost's House, included Samuel James Piggot, musical instrument seller and publisher, Henry James Dudgeon's stock-brokers, The Royal Irish Academy, Thomas Cranfield's print-sellers, publishers and frame-makers and Edward Ponsonby's printers and book-sellers. Cranfield published many fine prints, including for example a view of Queen Victoria leaving Kingstown Harbour in 1849, while Ponsonby's were publishers to Trinity College.

The firm of Piggot was originally estab-lished in 1834 in Westmoreland Street by Samuel Piggot, who was the owner of a cele-brated cello made by Antonio Stradivarius in 1720. In the nineteenth century, Piggot's were the sole agents of Steinway and Beck-stein pianos.

After 150 years, Piggot's is still a household name where music is concerned. In 1850 Pig-got's was only four doors away from McCullough's 'music and musical instrument warehouse pianoforte and harp ware rooms', which extended around the corner into Suffolk Street.

In 1802 we find Hodges and Smith booksellers at 21 St Andrew's Street.

Above: Lambert's Grafton Street shop, founded in 1798, occupied a Georgian house at the corner of Chatham Street.

Below: The new Edwardian premises of Lambert, Brien & Company. This fine red-brick building is now a branch of the AIB.

Not long afterwards they moved into Grafton Street, where they adver-tised themselves as 'Booksellers and Publishers to the University and the Royal Dublin Society and agents for the sale of the Ordnance Survey of Ire-land.' The firm was the predecessor of the well-known Dublin booksellers and publishers, Hodges, Figgis and Company.

Hodges and Smith occupied a house in the block between Suffolk Street and Wicklow Street. In 1781 the corner site here, now occupied by a building society, was leased to Nugent Booker and the building was occu-pied by a confectioner and a shoemaker. Number 21 Suffolk Street was also leased to Nugent Booker in 1784, and in the same year Mr McCullough, the pianoforte maker, was in occupation of number 22, which was described as 'a good house, three storeys above the shop'.

Lambert Brien & Company Limited were one of Grafton Street's most important businesses in the sale of household goods, which included lamps, brushes, etc. An early billhead shows the Georgian house with a plain shopfront. Small fanlights decorated each of the entrance doors and the royal coat of arms stood between the windows of the first floor. Lam-bert's were awarded their first Royal Warrant in 1849, on the occasion of Queen Victoria's visit to Ireland (probably through supplying Dublin Castle with candles or oil for lamps).

Lambert's, as it then was, placed a large advertisement on the Chatham Street wall of their premises, for the sale of wax spermaceti, tallow candles, soap and oil. Wax spermaceti were manufactured from sperm whale oil and were used as tapers for lighting oil lamps. Under the name of Lambert Brien & Company Limited, the firm expanded in the late nineteenth century and erected large-gabled, red-brick premises on the corner of the street.

Another noted premises in Grafton Street, which now alas has vanished, were Anderson, Stanford and Ridgeway's, a large furniture store, which was situated at the corner of Grafton Street and Lemon Street. In their large warehouse they stocked carpets, curtains and furniture, and they undertook carpet cleaning and 'carpet shaking' at their works in Westland Row. This firm flourished in the 1890s and continued in business right through the twentieth century.

The present Bewley's Café in Grafton Street occupies part of the site of Whyte's Academy and its ball alley. Bewley's has for a long time been regarded as the flagship of Dublin's café society and, like Grafton Street

itself, is a magnet that draws people from all over the city and suburbs. The most striking aspect of Bewley's throughout the twentieth century was the cross section of customers who were attracted there. Politicians, famous television personalities, journalists, writers, entrepreneurs, punks, clergy, fashion models, the horsey set, babies ... all were to be found in Bewley's, regardless of age or class. As one journalist commented: 'Bewley's is classless, ageless, timeless. Look on the floor beside the occupied tables and you will see rucksacks, briefcases, school bags, leather bags, plastic bags ...' Another writer, in the *Sunday Independent*, commented that, 'In a unique way Bewley's spells eternal hope: a trysting place where fusty old-fashioned gentility gave an extra edge to countless assignations.'

Ernest Bewley's first project was the establishment of a shop at 13 South Great George's Street in the 1870s, where he sold tea, sugar and coffee. A café, called Bewley's Oriental Café, was opened there in 1894; it unfortunately closed in 1999. In 1896 Ernest Bewley established a second café at 10 Westmoreland Street, which was enlarged in 1900 into Fleet Street. His crowning achievement was the Bewley's café erected at 97–98 Grafton Street in 1927. Bewley was involved in public life too and was elected to the Dublin City Council in 1907. He was a successful exhibitor

Above top: The Egyptian-inspired façade of Bewley's was completed in 1927.

Above: One of the famous Harry Clarke windows in Bewley's.

at agricultural shows and won many prizes with his Jersey cattle, with Bewley's butter and for showing Bewley's delivery vans and horses.

The oriental or Egyptian-style façade that ornaments the lower floors was designed by A Miller. Harry Clarke was commissioned in 1928 to design a series of windows for the café. One of Ireland's foremost stained-glass artists, Clarke produced six large windows which light the back room. An exotic atmosphere is created by the rich kaleidoscopic glow of colour – tropical birds with long curling tails, bright-petalled flowers and butterflies are bordered by swirling vines, while in between the birds and butterflies are flashes of cobalt blue and brilliant orange against a muted yellow-grey background. Harry Clarke was a prolific artist and left behind a rich collection of beautiful windows and many fascinating book illustrations. The Grafton Street windows were some of his last works; he died in 1931. His work was highly original and quite Irish, full of mystery, delicacy and colour, and in sharp contrast to the very stylised glass that was often imported from Britain and Germany to fill Ireland's church windows.

However, in 1985 the Bewley's cafés were very nearly lost for good, as the firm floundered with heavy debts and a large sum of money owing to the Revenue Commissioners. The two principal cafés, on Grafton Street and Westmoreland Street, were taken over by Patrick and Veronica Campbell and were refurbished in 1987 and 1989 respectively. This refurbishment represented an important act of faith in preserving something that was best about Dublin's city life. The buildings, with their handsome interiors and stained glass, had by the early 1980s become worn and tired in appearance, and the kitchens and service areas needed a complete overhaul.

The houses of Chatham Street, off Grafton Street, backed onto Tangier Lane. In the nineteenth century the street gained a reputation for its victuallers, poulterers and fish merchants. In 1851 there were nine victuallers and one poulterer here, including the well-known name of William Hanlon. This tradition remains alive today, with Sawers still trading in the street, though sadly FX Buckley has lately closed down. An interesting butcher's shop, possibly McDonagh's of Chatham Street, was demolished in 1980, the walls of which were decorated with tilework pictures representing sheep, cattle and calves in a rural setting. In the nineteenth century the Enniskerry coach office was also located in Chatham Street.

A late eighteenth-century map, in the National Library, indicates that there was a large complex, including a coach house, stables and forge, on the site of the present Westbury Hotel. Mr Beggs's stableyard and Mr Smith's coach house were entered from Harry Street, while another stable lane, roughly on the site of the present Westbury Mall, gave access to plumbers' workshops, a forge and other stables. The back of Bewley's in Grafton Street is indicated as the only Swan Yard and Livery Stables, while the site of Samuel Whyte's school is also shown, adjoining Johnson's Court.

John Sproule, who, with his brother Samuel Sproule, was an important builder and developer in the late eighteenth century, held part of

Below: The Little Midshipman, a plaster statue that stood above the Duke Street premises of Murray McGrath.

Clarendon Street. The site of the present College of Music in Chatham Street originally housed the Clarendon Market, which was mainly occupied by victuallers.

By the early nineteenth century the effects of the Industrial Revolution were beginning to take their toll on small self-employed artisans, especially those in the textile industry such as weavers and silk workers. The Liberties of Dublin, as we have already seen, was heavily populated with such people who relied on these trades for their livelihood. Many eked out a living while others made use of their commercial skills or were perhaps just lucky. John Wright Switzer was one of the successful ones. His family had come to Ireland as Palatine refugees from Germany. Like the French Huguenots, many of the Palatines were skilled craftsmen, and they settled in Dublin and Limerick. Switzer began his commercial career in the Liberties of Dublin as a cloth trader and by 1832 was trading as a military tailor and draper on Cork Hill. Six years later he moved to 91 Grafton Street, where he opened attractive premises with an arched Victorian shopfront, in which he could display his fine clothes. Switzer's business expanded and by 1860 his premises, which were now called the Commercial Hall Company, had enlarged into Wicklow Street.

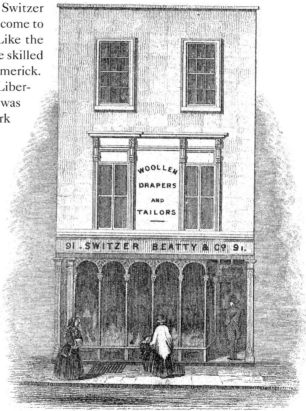

John Switzer died in 1891, but not before he had seen the name Switzer and Company emblazoned across the front of his great enterprise, a shop which then covered almost an entire block of Grafton Street and Wicklow Street. The magnificent pediment and mosaic nameplate remained over the once-spectacular Wicklow Street entrance.

In 1848 another draper established himself in Grafton Street just across from Switzer's. This was the small firm of Hugh Brown, formerly a buyer at Todd Burns of Mary Street. The following year he joined with James Thomas, another ex-employee of Todd Burns, and they formed the company of Brown Thomas. By the middle of the 1850s they had acquired three houses at numbers 15–17 and converted them into one shop.

Above: The elegant frontage of Switzer's first Grafton Street shop, shown here on a billhead of c.1850.

The three Brown Thomas buildings were unified behind an elaborate stucco façade. The architect William Caldbeck prepared the designs, which included pilasters at first- and second-floor level, a generous cornice and an ornamental parapet with urns. The firm of Brown Thomas and

Above: The Brown Thomas 1990s shopfront is simple but stylish – the essence of contemporary Dublin.

Below: The imposing premises of Manning's show that they were one of the leading drapery and tailoring establishments on Grafton Street.

Company, silk mercers, linen drapers, haberdashers and milliners, became one of the most popular in the city. In the 1880s it was described as follows:

> The premises, which are enormous in extent, present a very striking appearance to the visitor to Grafton Street, its many and handsome plate glass windows, stocked with articles of dress or millinery, proving an attractive object of interest, especially to members of the fair sex …
> The spacious shops, ware rooms, and showrooms of the establishment may, all through the year, be seen constantly being filled with a throng of fashionable costumers, buying or inspecting the varied treasures collected from all the principal continental markets.

Brown Thomas also stocked a wide variety of Irish linens, poplins, silks, lace and hosiery, and employed up to 250 local needlewomen and cutters. The fact that Brown Thomas continued to thrive right through the twentieth century is a testimony to the type of shop that it was and remains to be to this day.

In 1991 Brown Thomas bought Switzer's and began to plan the sale of their own 150-year-old premises and the move across the street. Their shop, with its distinctive open floors ornamented by fluted Corinthian columns, was sold to Marks and Spencer's. The building was demolished except for the façade and in the reconstruction Marks and Spencer's somewhat crudely replicated the old columns. The result, however practical, is a rather sanitised version of

INTEREST AT THE RATE OF SIX PERCENT PR ANNUM
CHARGED ON ALL ACCOUNTS OVER SIX MONTHS' DUE.

what was there before – gone are the thick, bouncy carpets which once covered Brown Thomas's squeaky floorboards.

The recent refurbishment and marriage of Switzer's with Brown Thomas has been carried out with great taste, and part of the original Switzer's balcony with its delicate swirling ironwork survives at the back of the store. The white marble 1960s façade was replaced by a simple stone frontage during recent renovations.

There was competition for Brown Thomas and Switzer's in the dressmaking and tailoring field in Grafton Street – businesses such as Manning's, who in Victorian times occupied numbers 102–103. Manning's, which was established in the early nineteenth century specialised in ladies' dresses and costumes and was one of the leading suppliers of court dresses. Manning's were allowed to display the royal coat of arms over their doorway because they had been appointed court dressmaker to various members of the royal family. Although royal appointments were scattered fairly liberally during the nineteenth century to different businesses, the recipients were very proud of these titles and usually displayed them prominently on their shopfronts and incorporated them into their billheads.

In 1876 Manning's supplied a Mrs Fitzgerald of Marley, Rathfarnham, with one widow's dress made of crêpe and a black cashmere dress which together cost eleven guineas. They also supplied a widow's cloak, silk hose, thread hose, a silk tie, a widow's bonnet, a black cashmere dress and other garments, all of which came to nearly forty pounds.

Above: Up until 1920 the acquisition of a royal coat of arms, as shown on this billhead from Morgan's the hatter, was much sought after by a wide variety of trades.

Below: Grafton Street was the leading address for the clothing and fashion trade.

Taaffe and Cauldwell were a prominent gentlemen's outfitters at 81 Grafton Street in the early twentieth century. They advertised themselves as shirt cutters, hosiers, hatters, tailors and general outfitters. They also supplied Indian and colonial outfits. Joseph Morgan, hatter, was another shopkeeper who proudly displayed the royal arms on his billhead, as he supplied hats to his Excellency the Lord Lieutenant. His premises were at 9 Grafton Street. In 1838 his bill describes him as hatter 'in-ordinary' to his Majesty and his Excellency the Lord Lieutenant. A good hat could then cost anything from 10/– to £1 5/–.

James Forest and Sons, neighbours of Manning's at 100–101 Grafton Street, offered a similar range of goods and declared themselves as 'silk mercers and lace manufacturers to her Majesty the Queen, the Prince and Princess of Wales, and the Irish court. Shawls, mantles, millinery, flowers hosiery and linens, family mourning for ready money.' By the second half of the nineteenth century there was little doubt that Grafton Street was the most fashionable commercial street in the city. It boasted a wide variety of shops dealing mainly in what would today be called the luxury end of the market.

Along with the many top-class drapers and tailors, we find some of Dublin's leading jewellers and watch- and clock-makers. These include Topham and White at 33 Grafton Street, Weir's at number 5, and West's and later Stoker's at number 22. The firm of Edmund Johnson should also be mentioned among the many noted goldsmiths and silversmiths in Grafton Street. In the middle of the nineteenth century a curious establishment, the Polytechnic Museum or Gallery of Art, Science, Mechanism and Amusement, offered for sale everything from croquet balls to chemical sets. One of Dublin's leading chemists, Hayes, Conyngham and Robinson, came to 12 Grafton Street in 1897, though the property had belonged to Mr William Hayes for some thirty years before that. Number 107 was occupied by the long-established firm of Hamilton and Long. It was founded in 1826 by Samuel Bewley and later became Bewley and Evans, then Bewley and Hamilton, and finally Hamilton and Long. Yeates and Sons, 'Opticians and Makers of Mathematical Instruments to the University of Dublin and the

Above: Topham & White was one of several high-class goldsmiths and jewellers in Grafton Street.

Right: This painting of North's premises, at the bottom of Grafton Street, shows 1880s costume and a horse-drawn tram.

Port of Dublin Corporation', were also situated in Grafton Street. Fannin and Company, makers of surgical instruments and suppliers of books to the medical profession, occupied number 41.

Above: The luxurious offices of North's of Grafton Street, depicted here on a blotter of *c.*1880.

Francis Faulkner's, one of the city's leading tea, coffee and wine importers, were to be found at 83 Grafton Street and 36 Dawson Street and were one of the most prestigious suppliers of wine in Dublin. In Victorian times Faulkner's wine was sold in their own bottles, embossed with their name. Mitchell and Sons were noted confectioners and their restaurant at number 10 Grafton Street survived up until the 1950s. The family business continued to thrive in Kildare Street where today they are successful wine merchants. In the twentieth century various firms stand out, such as Tyson's, 'practical shirt cutter and military outfitter', which was located at 57 Grafton Street. JM Barnardo and Son, the furriers, still trade at number 108 Grafton Street. Tobacconists were also present in the street and Kapp and Peterson, who originally occupied 53–55

Grafton Street, have now moved to number 107, nearly opposite Trinity College. The firm of James J Fox, tobacconist, has been known as one of the city's leading cigar and tobacco merchants for over a hundred years, and are located at 199 Grafton Street, also opposite Trinity College.

Above: This extravagant trade card shows that tobacco merchants were among the trades found in Grafton Street – the focus of luxury shopping.

Several of the leading businesses in Grafton Street have published histories giving details of the origins and foundation of their business. These include Hayes, Conyngham and Robinson in 1997; Weir and Sons in 1994; Brown Thomas in 1995; and Fox in 1981. While the format of these publications varies widely, the content is uniformly excellent and provides much useful information, including business records and personal recollections. It is also interesting to note how many of these successful and enduring businesses were founded by people who did not come from Dublin. Conyngham and Robinson (of Hayes, Conyngham and Robinson), came from Derry and Limerick respectively and were apprenticed to various apothecaries before going out on their own. Thomas Weir came from Glasgow in 1865 and went to work for West's, the successful College Green firm of jewellers.

Above: The last of the old family-owned businesses in Grafton Street, Weir's the jeweller and silversmith, was established in 1869.

James Fox migrated from London to Dublin in the 1860s and opened his own tobacco shop in 1881. Fox took over the well-established tobacco business of James Madden, which was established here in 1837. Madden was well known for his own blends of pipe tobacco, cigars and snuff. One of his blends was known as the Provost's Mixture and was especially prepared for one of the provosts of Trinity College. Among Fox's early clients were various members of the gentry, including for example Lord Powerscourt, but clergymen, lawyers and doctors were also regular customers. Orders were regularly sent to Dublin hotels, clubs, barracks and police stations. The shop cash book records the fact that the events of Easter 1916 caused no damage to the stock and it reopened as usual on the following Tuesday. The sale of American, English and Egyptian cigarettes began in a small way in the 1930s, and during the Second World War American cigarettes became very popular. In 1944 a hundred million American cigarettes were imported into Dublin, indicating that the craze for cigarette smoking had begun in earnest. Fox's shop occupies an interesting nineteenth-century building, erected on land which was first developed in the middle of the seventeenth century. Fox's neighbours once included the twin buildings of the Commissioners of Inland Waterways and the RDS, designed by the English architect Christopher Myers. The four-storey Georgian houses built by Myers can been seen in Malton's print of the front of Trinity College, made in 1796.

This lower stretch of Grafton Street is also illustrated in Shaw's *New City Pictorial Directory* of 1850, which shows the surviving Royal Irish Academy building at number 114 and Madden's tobacconist shop at the corner of Grafton Street and College Green. The house was rebuilt in 1880 in its present Gothic style with a striking stone turret, gable and chimney stacks. Fox's retains an interesting collection of old tobacco jars and snuffboxes, many of which may well have come from Madden's original establishment. (And now, to celebrate the continuity of such an old Dublin business, this writer is going to light up one of Fox's Number 11 cigars!)

The firm of Thomas Weir and Sons, jewellers, was not established until 1869. Their extensive and gracious shopfront extends around their corner premises from Grafton Street into Wicklow Street. It is one of the few stylish shopfronts of the traditional type to remain in Grafton Street or indeed anywhere else in the city.

The original glazed door of 5 Grafton Street, with its beautifully engraved glass bearing the name Weir and Sons, survives, although it has been moved to the Wicklow Street frontage. Inside the silver and watch department, some of the most magnificent display cases in Dublin can be seen. The cases, which have curved ends and domed tops, are entirely glazed. Weir's is today managed by David Andrews, the great-grandson of Thomas Weir.

This writer's grand-uncle, Percy Pearson, joined Weir's in 1920 and worked there for over sixty years. When he joined the firm, aged sixteen, the shop consisted of one building on Grafton Street at number 96, and three on Wicklow Street. The taking in of the corner premises, he recalled, made a great difference to business. The present unified shopfront dates from that time, probably the 1920s. As with all businesses long ago, hours were long and holidays were few. There was no such thing as coffee breaks, but there was usually an hour for lunch. Percy remembered that bicycles could be left in Grafton Street unlocked. He specialised in watches and jewellery and was, for many years, Company Secretary. He died in 1999 at the age of ninety-five.

Hayes, Conyngham and Robinson stands almost directly across the street from Weir's and followed in the long tradition of Dublin apothecaries and chemists. At the turn of the century they sold such items as talcum powder, hair tonic, cold cream, toothpaste, curing tablets and a variety of medicines, pills and tablets, many of which were compounded on the premises. Today's pharmacists have little in common with their forbears of 100 years ago, when many of the raw ingredients would be stored in the chemist's shop and made up as required. Chemists then prepared their own syrups, tinctures, extracts, medicated waters and even perfumes – very different to the present day multi-million-pound pharmaceutical industry. Even up to the middle of the twentieth century the old glass storage jars, the weighing scales and the pestle and mortar were vital accoutrements for every chemist.

Above: A knife blade from Weir's, who also produced a wide range of cutlery.

Dawson Street

The origins of Dawson Street date back to the year 1705, when Joshua Dawson, who was then Secretary to the Lord Lieutenant of Ireland, purchased a large holding of land between St Stephen's Green and Nassau Street. Here Dawson laid out a broad, straight street and on the east side erected a fine mansion for himself. Since 1715, this beautiful residence has served as Dublin's Mansion House – the residence of the Lord Mayor of the city.

Right: Little has changed since this early twentieth-century photograph of the Mansion House was taken.

Brooking depicts the house built by Dawson in a small vignette attached to his map of Dublin of 1728. Its appearance differs in many respects from that of the present-day Mansion House – it had neither a pediment nor a porch, and none of the other Victorian embellishments. As built, it was a large house, two storeys over a basement, with prominent coigns, a doorcase with a broken pediment, and a substantial parapet, which was ornamented by seven panels, decorated with figures.

Three eighteenth-century maps in the Dublin City Archives add to our knowledge of the Mansion House in its earlier years. The earliest (undated) map shows the square layout of the Mansion House, with a symmetrical forecourt flanked by curved gravel walks and lawns, and fronting onto Dawson Street. To the south lay the stables, yard and offices of the house, while to the north was a garden bounded by the holding of a Mr Knox. There was a bowling green to the east of the Mansion House, joining Stable Lane on one side and Mr Hume's holding on the other. Long thin sites were pencilled in for all of the property adjoining the Mansion House, except the forecourt, suggesting a possible development of houses on the Corporation property. This of course did not occur, except for the building of Northland House, now the home of the Royal Irish Academy.

A later map, dated 1776, shows that the immediate surroundings of the Mansion House were not developed, but that the ground between it and the back of the houses of St Stephen's Green was occupied by coach houses, yards and stables. Yet another map indicates that these buildings included a kitchen, a bakehouse, stables, a cow-house, a dairy to the rear and further yards. There was, at that time, a suggestion to remove these buildings and create a formal garden in their place, with steps leading from the side of the Mansion House, but this plan never materialised.

The house was purchased in 1715 by the City of Dublin as a permanent residence for the Lord Mayor. Dawson was paid £3,500 for the house and most of its contents, and there was a condition that he and his heirs were to be paid a symbolic 'loaf of double refined sugar, of six pounds weight' every Christmas yearly, if demanded! Dawson also agreed to erect a large room, thirty-three feet long, which was to be panelled. This subsequently became known as the Oak Room. The original lease contained an interesting inventory, which included:

> 24 brass locks, 6 marble chimney pieces; the tapestry hangings, silk window curtains and window seats, and chimney glass in the great bed chambers; the gilt leather hangings; four pair of scarlet calamanco window curtains; and chimney glass, in the Dantzick Oak parlour; the Indian calico window curtains and seats, and chimney glass, in the Dantzick Oak parlour; the window curtains and chimney glass in the large eating room.

Dawson was clearly pleased that the City of Dublin had taken his magnificent house as the residence of the Lord Mayor – it would enhance the prestige of his street and attract a high class of tenant, who would build houses of quality. As one would expect, the Lord Mayor's residence was not only well maintained but frequently improved and updated, as fashions changed. During the late nineteenth century, for example, all of the

Below: A late nineteenth-century photograph of the drawing room in the Mansion House, showing the Victorian taste for lavish ornament and cluttered opulence.

principal reception rooms in the Mansion House were wallpapered and the rooms were furnished with the kind of sumptuous clutter that late Victorian taste demanded. Photographs taken around 1900 by Sibthorpes, the decorators, show the drawing room, which they had been responsible for decorating. Today the principal rooms, including the drawing room and the dining room, exhibit a rather restrained décor, typical of the late Georgian period.

The staircase and hall are probably the least altered parts of the original building, and both areas retain most of their original panelling. The staircase itself is typical of the early eighteenth century and has carved brackets and handsome, barley-sugar banisters that support the handrail. The hall appears to have been modernised in Edwardian times by the addition of a Tudor-style ceiling and a screen. The marble mantelpiece in the dining room is a very remarkable piece. It is ornamented with caryatid figures, which support the shelf.

The great Round Room at the rear of the mansion house was erected in 1821, specifically for the purpose of entertaining King George IV on his visit to Ireland. This circular, brick-built structure, with its great timber roof, has served generations of Dubliners very well, and has been used for a wide variety of purposes, including exhibitions, formal occasions, theatre productions and fairs.

The entire structure was substantially refurbished in 1998 and is now back in use. The original roof was replaced in its entirety with a new steel frame. Building work has also just commenced on the south side of the Mansion House, on a plot of ground that has for many years served as a surface car park.

The Parish of St Anne

Joshua Dawson followed the example of an earlier Dublin developer, Sir Francis Aungier, by offering a site on Dawson Street for a new parish church in 1707. This gesture did not automatically indicate great religious zeal on the part of the donor, as the acquisition of a new parish and a parish church not only enhanced the status of his street and its development but had a practical benefit too. The parish was responsible for such functions as lighting, paving and policing in its own area, and this would naturally have been of great interest to would-be investors in Dawson's property development. The parish church was also part of the social and political structure of the day – being Anglican and loyal to the Crown, these churches were an essential part of the ruling class's culture and power. Such churches were generally sited in prominent locations where they would create an impact on their surroundings.

The new parish was named in 1707 'St Anne's Parish' by statute of Queen Anne, and was situated between Grafton Street and Merrion Street, in the suburbs of the city. Initially Joshua Dawson donated a site on the western side of Dawson Street for the building of a church. It appears that building was already well advanced when Dawson decided that he

Below: The intended elevation of St Anne's Church on Dawson Street, from Brooking's map (1728).

would prefer the church to be located on the east side of the street, where it would be aligned with South Anne Street. Dawson got his way and the present handsome church was erected on the east side of the street. It is a pity that the original planned façade was not built, as it has been identified as being inspired by the elegant Church of St Giacomo Degli Incurabili in Rome which the architect Isaac Wills appears to have closely followed. It was to consist of two massive storeys decorated with paired pilasters in the Corinthian and Doric style with a delicate open spire topped by a crown and orb. Brooking's map gives us an illustration of what the intended façade and tower might have looked like – somewhat similar to the remaining front of St Werburgh's Church. Behind it stood the large gaunt structure of the church, which, of course, was intended to be concealed.

The interior of the church, which was significantly more lofty than that of St Werburgh's, focused on an apsidal east end with three round, arched windows. Like the other major churches in eighteenth-century Dublin, it has a gallery, which runs around the interior on three sides. A large coved ceiling springs from an elaborately rich cornice, and long drops of plasterwork or carved wood representing fruit and flowers ornament the empty wall spaces between the windows.

In 1723 a benefactor named Lord Newton left the sum of £13 a year for the distribution of bread to the poor. The specially built shelves were until recently supplied with bread on a weekly basis, available to anyone in need!

It was, no doubt, the unfinished nature of the old façade that prompted the erection of the present Romanesque frontage, with its twin towers, in the nineteenth century. A new façade was first proposed in the 1850s, and plans, prepared by Sir Thomas Newenham Deane, were agreed in 1868. Although it is a fine piece of Victorian craftsmanship in its own right, it bears little relation to the interior of the eighteenth-century church. While everything in the original design is symmetrical, the Victorian front is deliberately asymmetrical, with towers of differing proportions. Unfortunately the larger of Thomas Deane's twin towers was never completed. Sir Thomas also took the opportunity to close the gap between the church and the Royal Irish Academy building by erecting an elaborate stone-fronted rectory in the same style.

Some ten years earlier, Sir Thomas Deane and his partner, Benjamin Woodward, had designed St Anne's school and church hall, which faced onto Molesworth Street. These two buildings, which were demolished in 1978, will be discussed in the context of Molesworth Street.

Above: The early nineteenth-century trade card of Murray, a carver and gilder in Dawson Street.

The Houses of Dawson Street

In the early decades of the eighteenth century, Dawson proceeded to build houses himself and grant leases to others for the purpose of erecting fine residences. In his leases, Joshua Dawson laid down conditions that there would be no commercial or manufacturing activity in the street, such as brewing or soap-making, and that there would be no businesses such as butchers or spirit dealers. The result was that Dawson Street became the residence of the well-heeled gentry. It is interesting to note that until recent years there was only one small pub – Dublin's smallest lounge – in a basement in the street, and that Dawson Street has always been free of dirty or noisy businesses.

Dawson was successful in attracting a wealthy and titled class of resident to his new street, and so in 1734 we find James, the third Viscount Charlemont, living there, with the Earl of Antrim moving in two years later. Other residents included Admiral Rowley, Lord Desart, Josiah Hort, the Archbishop of Tuam and the Honourable Richard Tighe. Among the residents who came to the street after 1750 were General Bligh, Lord Castlecomer, the Earl of Westmeath, the Bishop of Dromore, the Earl of Lanesborough, Lord Naas, Henry Grattan, Viscount Mayo and Viscount Strabane. Many of these names mean little today, but they were people of wealth and position in their time who could afford to fit out and furnish their houses with the best that money could buy.

Above: The drawing-room ceiling at number 15 Dawson Street being carefully dismantled in 1977.

Below: A 1970s drinks mat from the Royal Hibernian Hotel.

One such house was 15 Dawson Street, whose reception rooms on the ground floor and first floor were elaborately decorated with beautiful plasterwork. It was a house of remarkable quality with rooms of fine proportions, good fireplaces and panelled dados. A reconstructed ceiling, in the foyer of the office block on this site, shows that the plasterwork was of exceptional quality, featuring sculptured heads, musical instruments and scrolls all arranged in the rococo manner and divided into compartments. The ceiling in the dining room at the ground floor rear of the house was equally fine, with boldly modelled heads, flowers and roses. The house was demolished in 1977, along with the rest of the block, to make way for a dreary office block now occupied by Sun Alliance, the insurance group. Fortunately, the ceilings were expertly removed and one of them has been reinstated. During demolition the plasterwork was carefully sawn into odd shapes like a jigsaw and dismantled. The largest ceiling on the first floor was sawn up into fifteen neat squares and the pieces of ceiling, complete with plaster laths and joists, were carefully and expertly lowered with block and tackle onto a waiting scaffold.

The façades and some interiors of many fine Georgian houses still remain on Dawson Street, although most were modified in the nineteenth century by the insertion of shopfronts at ground-floor level. Good examples of such shopfronts include the fine bow-fronted shop window at 37 Dawson Street, for many years occupied by the APCK Bookshop, and its neighbour, the arcaded, stone shopfront of Morgan's, the wine merchants.

The Royal Hibernian Hotel
Dawson Street, Dublin 2
Telephone 772991 Telex 25220

The building that houses the Hibernian Bible Society is another example of a re-fronted eighteenth-century house. The early twentieth-century front, with its Egyptian-style columns, curved glass shopfront and projecting bay window at first-floor level, adds to the variety and character of the street – although doubtless a good Georgian doorcase was destroyed in the process.

Number 8 Dawson Street, which is situated on the east side, is a large house similar in scale to Royal Irish Academy House, further up the street. It is four storeys high and four bays wide, with a handsome stone doorcase. The interiors, though not very elaborate, are finished with good eighteenth-century cornices and joinery throughout.

As happened in O'Connell Street and elsewhere in the city, the Act of Union brought about an exodus of the gentry from the many Georgian houses. This in turn created opportunities for the opening of hotels and the creation of shops on the ground floors.

An early example of such a conversion may be seen in the trade card of Murray's, a looking-glass dealer who erected an elegant Gothic-style shop front at 62 Dawson Street in about 1820.

In the nineteenth century the street attracted at least one insurance company, many solicitors, a variety of charitable and religious organisations, merchant tailors, several ironmongers, seed merchants such as Drummond's and the plumbing and sanitary suppliers Maguire and Gatchell. There were also three hotels – Morrison's, Macken's and, of course, the Royal Hibernian. Morrison's Hotel stood at the corner with Nassau Street, facing Trinity College, and in 1900 was replaced by the very grand offices of the North British Mercantile Insurance Company. Macken's Hotel stood at the corner of Dawson Lane, on the site of the present New Ireland Insurance Offices.

The Royal Hibernian, which began at 48 Dawson Street, eventually expanded to occupy four houses. The Royal Hibernian was a renowned coaching hotel, and was associated with Bianconi's famous stage coach service, the name of which was taken for the 'Bianconi Grill'. In the twentieth century the hotel had its own orchestra and an excellent reputation for good food.

One of Dublin's best-loved and reputedly one its oldest hotels, it closed down in 1983 to make way for an office development and a shopping arcade. Although the buildings were listed for preservation, and though, contrary to popular belief, many of the original eighteenth-century features were still intact, the

DUBLIN BRANCH OFFICE

Above: The branch office of the North British Mercantile Insurance Company has recently been converted into a bookshop for Eason's.

Below: The Royal Hibernian Hotel, reputedly the oldest hotel in Dublin, was a landmark on Dawson Street.

Above: The shopfront of
Maguire and Gatchell with its
window display of plumbing
apparatus, c.1900.

Below: This impressive
building, erected by
Drummond's at 58 Dawson
Street, is now occupied by the
Hodges Figgis bookshop.

famous hotel was demolished. The Georgian ceiling from the staircase and most of
the fine woodwork was salvaged and is still
in storage, perhaps awaiting the construction, someday, of another Hibernian Hotel.
The hotel, which dated from 1751, represented only a small part of the whole site,
and could have been incorporated into the
new development.

Although the hotel had been modernised
and much of the ground floor was remodelled in a replica Georgian style, the upstairs
rooms of number 51 still retained their original Georgian fireplaces. Trust House Forte,
the owners of the hotel, had spent over £1
million on the buildings in 1980. In 1983, following its sale for £4.5 million,
this writer argued that while the whole hotel was not then making money,
it might 'in thirty years time be a lucrative proposition'.

In 1884 the firms of Maguire & Son and Robert Gatchell & Son were
still separate businesses, located respectively at 10 and 7 Dawson Street.
Both dealt in ironmongery and sold gas fittings, kitchen ranges and acted as
plumbers, though Gatchell was originally an ironfounder, specialising in
weighing scales, and was an agent for Chubbs of London.

W Drummond & Sons, seed merchants and
nurserymen, were established in the early nineteenth century and were in occupation of 58
Dawson Street by the 1850s. By the end of the
century they had acquired the adjoining house
and had erected magnificent new premises,
boasting a large projecting shopfront of plate glass
windows, which still stands today as Hodges
Figgis bookshop. The new façade of red brick and
yellow terracotta was an elaborate exercise in the
Flemish Renaissance style. It is crowned by a tall
gable, ornamented with scrolls and pinnacles.
Drummond's were one of the leading seed merchants in Ireland, and supplied many large
estates, farms and gardens with seeds, fertilisers
and tools. The firm, which had Scottish Presbyterian origins, had their own agricultural museum in
Stirling in 1855. In the middle of the nineteenth
century they stocked as many as twenty-two
varieties of peas, sixteen varieties of beans, ten
varieties of onion, fourteen varieties of cabbage
and nine varieties of lettuce! Even up to the 1960s

their shop contained hundreds of small drawers and pigeonholes in which seeds were stored.

Dawson Street has managed to retain its somewhat genteel air of dignity right to the present day, and one cannot help feeling that Joshua Dawson would be pleased about this if he were around today! The generous width of the street and the regular four-storey height of its buildings contribute greatly to the noble aspect of the street. This quality, however, has only just been maintained, for despite being designated as a conservation area since the 1980s, many of its older buildings were demolished and several office blocks of no great architectural distinction were erected in their place.

The first office blocks were erected in the 1950s and 60s by the Irish National Insurance Company and the New Ireland Assurance Company. The Norwich Union Insurance Company erected a large block on the west side of the street at the junction with Nassau Street. Following the purchase and demolition by the Gallagher Group of St Anne's School, the parochial hall and three Georgian houses on the corner of Dawson Street, two ungainly redbrick office blocks were erected. These buildings, which are more akin to industrial structures, have since been occupied by the European Parliament and its offices.

The Royal Irish Academy, which as we have already mentioned was founded in 1785, moved into its present home in 1852. The Academy, whose principal work in the field of scientific and historical research continues today, contains a fine library, which houses early Irish manuscripts of international importance. The Academy's activities, which are supported financially to a large extent by government, still embrace a wide range of studies, including physics, mathematics, astronomy, geography, history, chemistry, natural history, archaeology and languages.

The large house occupied by the Academy was built for Lord Northland, and has a magnificent staircase and reception rooms, ornamented with elaborate plasterwork. The library and meeting room, which were added to the rear by the Academy in 1854, are impressive spaces in their own right. The library was built as a museum to house the collection, which was to become the nucleus of that in the National Museum. It was transferred to Kildare Street in 1890.

Above: This spacious meeting room was added to the Royal Irish Academy in 1854.

Below: Plasterwork ornament from the staircase wall of the Royal Irish Academy.

CHAPTER FOURTEEN

Merrion and Fitzwilliam Squares

*M*errion Square has long been considered the epitome of Georgian elegance in Dublin. The owner of this previously undeveloped tract of land was Lord Fitzwilliam, whose family estates ran eastwards from Leinster House as far as Blackrock and Ringsend on the shore of Dublin Bay. The very large Fitzwilliam Estate included most of present day Roebuck and Dundrum and ran up to the Dublin mountains, where the family operated a quarry that provided granite for their various building projects.

The development of the estate got into full swing during the second half of the eighteenth century, partly because the idea of building a square of residential houses with a large ornamental park at its centre had already been proven a success, with the building of St Stephen's Green south of the Liffey and Rutland Square to the north. While the Fitzwilliam quarries supplied stone for walls, window sills, coping and steps, their extensive brickworks at Merrion Gates and Sandymount produced tens of thousands of bricks for the walls.

Following the construction of Kildare House, later called Leinster House, in the 1740s, and in keeping with the spirit of the time that saw great building projects spreading east of Dawson Street across Molesworth Street, Kildare Street, South Fredrick Street and Clare Street, the Fitzwilliams decided to lay out Merrion Square. The layout of the square itself is usually attributed to John Ensor, an architect who had worked with the very distinguished and prolific architect Richard Castle, and was later responsible for building several houses on Merrion Square itself. The first houses to be erected on Merrion Square were those on the west side. Dating from 1751, they were contemporary with those built in Merrion Street Lower. The construction of Clare Street in the 1750s was to dictate the line of the north side of the

Below: The scale, variety and delicate quality of fanlights and doorcases in Merrion Square is internationally recognised.

new square, where houses first began to be erected in 1762. The progress in constructing the square was slow, as separate houses and groups of houses were erected by different individuals at different times, and it was not until the early nineteenth century that the four sides were fully completed.

Some of the houses of Merrion Square took as long as two years to finish. The leases granted by Lord Fitzwilliam specified that each house had to be three-and-a-half storeys high above the cellars, have an eight foot area in front and that the whole street had to be paved. Strict conditions applied: commercial activities – ale houses, soap boilers and so forth – were banned.

Among those who first took leases and actually built the houses we find an interesting variety of bricklayers, carpenters, builders, architects, a painter and a plumber. Most of these men built houses as speculative operations and quickly sold them on or leased them to 'good' tenants.

Most of the stone supplied to the building work in Merrion Square came from the Fitzwilliam quarry at Ticknock. In 1779 the supply of stone decreased due to the fact that the quarries were flooded with water and Mr Ensor complained to Lord Fitzwilliam's agent, Mrs Verschoyle, that he needed stones from the quarry in order to fulfil the obligations of his building lease. The correspondence of Barbara Verschoyle and her mother, Elizabeth Fagan, survives in the Pembroke Estate papers and gives us an interesting insight into the workings and

development of Merrion Square. Barbara Verschoyle's predecessors as agents were, in fact, her mother and father. In 1764 Mrs Fagan wrote confidently to her employer: 'See how your plans for Merrion Square fixed some years ago are now going on with great success.' For her own part Mrs Verschoyle does not conform to the eighteenth-century female stereotype of the elegant but helpless widow, for to have overseen the entire development of Merrion Square – dealing with legal matters, builders, tenants and

Above: The view from a top floor window looking down on the Wilde home at number 1 Merrion Square North.

Below: Barker's plan of 1762, showing the planned layout of Merrion Square.

all the financial affairs of the Fitzwilliam Estate – she must have been extremely able. In her letters to Lord Fitzwilliam, Mrs Verschoyle makes frequent complaints about a Mr Sproule (the architect and speculator who laid out and developed the east side of Merrion Square and Holles Street), who was being difficult and rude. Mrs Verschoyle says 'has a law suit for almost every tail of ground he has' and she was clearly fed up with 'the unpleasant language I am forced to listen to'!

Jonathan Barker's plan of the square, made in 1762, shows a double row of trees to be laid out on the

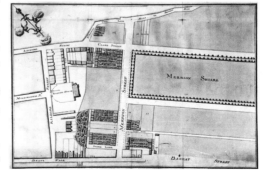

perimeter of the park. It also shows the completed houses of Merrion Street, including the seven houses adjoining the National Gallery. Four houses on the west side of Merrion Street were demolished to make way for the construction of what is now Government Buildings.

It could hardly be said that Leinster House dominates Merrion Square, as it is situated so far back from Merrion Street itself. The extensive garden between Leinster House and Merrion Square is known as Leinster Lawn and was laid out on land leased from the Fitzwilliam Estate. The left and right flanks of Leinster Lawn were developed in the nineteenth century by the construction of the Natural History Museum and the National Gallery respectively.

Upper Mount Street was developed along the axis of Merrion Square South and most of its houses were completed by the 1820s. St Stephen's Church, known fondly as the Pepper Canister, closes the vista down Mount Street and was consecrated in 1824. In the 1790s the west side of Merrion Square was ornamented by the addition of the Rutland Fountain, an elegant classical structure made of granite and Portland stone.

In her thesis of 1977, Siobhán Barry showed that several grandiose houses planned for Merrion Square were never actually built. Lord Mornington was refused the lease for a large site with a 100-foot frontage in

1765, while Lord Belvedere sought a 140-foot frontage for two houses for himself and his son, also never built. In 1770 Lord Louth sought a site with an eighty-foot frontage, on which he hoped to build a large house with a cut-stone frontage costing £6,000, but this was never undertaken either. We also learn that Barbara Verschoyle's house cost her £4,000 to build, 'excluding painting, except the first coat'.

The completed square originally contained ninety-one houses: thirty-two on the north side, seventeen on the east, thirty-five on the south and seven on the west. Most of the houses occupied a frontage of some twenty-six to thirty feet and were three windows in width. The most common type of house on Merrion Square is that in which the hall and staircase run straight from front to back and have two fine reception rooms on each of the principal floors. However, there is considerable variety in the type and width of the houses in Merrion Square, and this variety within the overall uniformity is to a large extent what creates the special harmony of the square. Some of the larger houses, which were four bays (or four windows) wide, have a forty-foot frontage. Most of the houses consist of three storeys over a basement and a popular feature is a bow-shaped projection to the rear. The houses of the north side make particular use of rusticated granite at ground-floor level and throughout the square there is a rich variety of doorcases, many of which incorporate some of the most beautiful fanlights in Dublin.

While there is great variety in the opulent interior decoration of the houses, the graceful proportions of the principal reception rooms on the ground and first floors is always evident. The Merrion Square houses exhibit some of the most refined decorative plasterwork and some of the most elegant marble mantelpieces in the city. An unfortunate trend of the last fifteen years has been the persistent theft of whole mantelpieces and, more particularly, of the carved tablets which formed their centrepieces. Almost every house in Merrion Square has been robbed of one or more of these important works of art, and it is worrying to note that almost none of them have been recovered. It has been suggested that these beautifully carved antique artefacts are being stolen to order and find a ready market in London and elsewhere. Fortunately, most of the houses have been spared the worst excesses of twentieth-century 'improvements' in the form of lifts or subdivision of rooms, but sadly only a handful of gardens and original mews buildings still remain intact around the square.

In the nineteenth and early twentieth centuries several of the houses of Merrion Square were occupied by notable artists and writers, including the mystic painter George W Russell, known as AE, who lived at number 84. A plaque on the front of this building records the efforts of Sir Horace Plunkett to promote cooperation and trade within Ireland. WB Yeats lived at number 82 from 1922 to 1928.

Merrion Square around this time was also the favourite place of residence for doctors and other professionals, who usually also had their consulting rooms on the premises. For example, Sir William Wilde (the

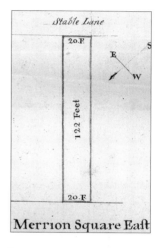

Above: A lease for a house on Merrion Square East, showing the unusually narrow twenty-foot frontage.

father of Oscar Wilde), lived at 1 Merrion Square, the prominent corner house now occupied by the American College. This house, standing on the corner opposite Clare Street, exhibits all the typical features of the 1760s, with its central staircase, pleasantly proportioned rooms and boldly modelled cornices. The house was greatly embellished by Sir William Wilde, who in the late nineteenth century added a large glazed conservatory or gallery to the Merrion Street side, where he also incorporated a small consulting room. During the recent restoration of this house by the American College, the consulting room, with its old glazed cabinets, has been carefully conserved and a collection of surgical instruments are now displayed there.

The Wildes also added several interesting nineteenth-century plaster casts of classical subjects, such as *The Age of Love*, *Cupid and Anacreon*, *The Dance of the Muses of Helicon*, and other plaques representing youth, old age, childhood and manhood. A balcony to the front of the house acted as a viewpoint, accessed through the first-floor drawing-room windows, from which the inhabitants could watch the world go by. Many houses of the square have either individual or continuous ornamental cast-iron balconies at first-floor level, which were added in the early nineteenth century.

The north side of Merrion Square was always considered a fashionable place for rich and aspiring types to promenade themselves. In 1791 a bill was passed in the House of Lords allowing for the centre of the square to be enclosed and planted. The streets about the square were gravelled and paved at the expense of the tenants. In 1795 John Ferrar wrote that he thought Merrion Square better than any in London, and that it was 'improved greatly this year by making a good gravel walk and planting with various trees a shrubbery within the iron balustrade'. A Victorian commentator noted in 1859 that 'a few ladies take within its railings their solitary constitutional walk; and a occasional gentleman is seen crossing it, producing his key at the gate and locking it after him as he would a wine cellar'. The ironwork of Merrion Square is still worthy of attention, in particular the fine railings and ornamental lamp holders, one or two of which survive.

Above and top: Details from the Italianate murals in number 49 Merrion Square.

Of the many remarkable houses in Merrion Square, number 35, is one of the most unusual, having a semi-spiral staircase and an elegant curved drawing room. The inner hall is ornamented with niches and there is an Adam-style ceiling of great beauty. This house, erected in about 1780, contains one of the most elegant ceilings of this period, displaying great variety and refinement within a strictly controlled and elegant design. Semi-circular fans, sphinxes and intricate garlands are woven into the designs of the ceiling to create a great work of art.

Number 49 is another house which was remarkably embellished by a later owner, in this case Robert Way-Harty, who, in 1831, became Lord Mayor of Dublin. Way-Harty commissioned an artist to decorate the walls of the principal drawing room of his house with murals in the Italianate manner. The walls of the first-floor rooms are covered with romantic landscapes in the style of Claude Lorraine and Salvadore Rosa. The house now

belongs to the National University of Ireland, and these most unusual rooms are used as a meeting place of the Senate.

As we have already noted, there is great variety in the houses of Merrion Square, although all conform to certain consistent features, for example, the use of russet red brick in the façades. Features found inside the houses include the stone floors of the hallways, the mahogany doors with their brass handles and the fine brass-bound locks of the hall doors themselves. The stone floors were usually laid in a honey-coloured Portland stone, although sometimes marble was used. In the earlier houses on the north side of the square, the staircases tended to have timber balusters and hand-carved brackets featuring floral motifs. In the later houses of the east and south sides, delicate and ornamental wrought iron is more frequently used to support the hand rail, and the stair brackets are more commonly made of gesso on wood and feature such details as pineapples and delicate spirals of leaves.

Many of the original Georgian-style windows of Merrion Square were replaced in the Victorian period with plate glass. The delicate glazing bars of the massively tall windows were

Above: Most of the staircases in Merrion Square have hand-carved brackets such as this.

Below: The white-painted Georgian windows, contrasting with the russet brickwork, in this Fitzwilliam Street house are typical of the whole area.

removed in favour of single sheets of plate glass, which in the second half of the nineteenth century were considered to be more fashionable. It would also appear that the windows of most of the houses of the square were given white-painted reveals at this time, which enliven the long expanse of brick-fronted houses.

The decorative plasterwork of the houses of the north side, built in the 1760s, is sometimes only confined to the cornice, but where the full ceiling is decorated, as in the cases of numbers 9 and 26, the style is rococo and more freely and boldly modelled than the ceilings of the later houses. In houses of the south side, such as numbers 63 and 84, the decorative plasterwork almost has the delicacy of jewellery and is contained within strict geometric rectangles and circles of the ceiling. These later ceilings of the 1780s and 1790s reflect the influence of the work of Robert Adam on the taste of the period and the preference for neo-classical symbols and figures.

At least seventy percent of the houses in Merrion Square are highly ornamented and that, apart from the recent thefts of mantelpieces, which has been fostered by unscrupulous dealers, the architectural legacy remains largely intact. There have been some losses, such as the burning of 39 Merrion Square, the former British Embassy, in 1972 following the events of Bloody Sunday in Derry (number 39 was later carefully restored by the Electricity Supply Board under the supervision of architect Austin Dunphy) and the demolition of Antrim House at 33–34 Merrion Square to make way for the building of Holles Street Hospital.

Antrim House, designed by John Ensor and completed in the 1770s, was once the largest house on Merrion Square (aside from Leinster House), being seven windows wide. It closed the vista on the south side of Merrion Square and enjoyed a magnificent view of the Dublin mountains. This mansion was the townhouse of the Earl of Antrim, owner of a large desmesne in the Glens of Antrim. It was bought by Holles Street Hospital in 1930 with a view to rebuilding the old hospital and expanding its capacity from sixty beds to 143. A small lying-in hospital had been established in Holles Street in 1884 and ten years later the National Maternity Hospital was opened on the same site. From that time until 1936, when the new building was completed, the hospital operated out of three houses in Holles Street. Holles Street, along with Clare Street and Denzille Lane, was named after Denzille Holles, the Earl of Clare. Many of the original features of

Left: The rococo-style
plasterwork ceiling at
number 26 Merrion Square.

Antrim House were reinstated in the new Holles Street Hospital, including the mahogany doors, decorative joinery and mantelpieces. Although a very fine eighteenth-century ceiling was lost, a fine Georgian-style room was recreated as a new boardroom.

The style of doorcase and door surround varied greatly in Merrion Square. The earliest, erected in the 1760s, favoured the simple addition of a pair of pillars, usually Doric in style and mostly topped by a broken pediment, which accommodated a small fanlight giving light to the hall. Scrolls or brackets were sometimes used instead of pillars and capitals. Fanlights got larger and larger as the eighteenth century progressed, and evolved from a small curved window into a full semicircle filled with delicate leaded glass. The fanlights of Dublin are famous throughout the world of Georgian architecture and nowhere are they more stunning than in Merrion Square. By the 1780s the doorways were becoming larger and sidelights were added to allow more light into the hallway. The addition of sidelights meant that the doorcase could now consist of four columns, often with pilasters attached, giving an even more elaborate overall effect.

The image of Merrion Square is inseparable from that of the National Gallery, which was opened in 1864, largely thanks to the efforts of one man – William Dargan. It was Dargan who organised and underwrote the great exhibition held in Dublin in 1853. The construction of a massive timber

and glass exhibition hall on the lawn at Leinster House created a great deal of public interest and began a series of large nineteenth-century industrial exhibitions in the capital city. The 1853 exhibition resulted in a financial loss for William Dargan, but did lead to the founding of the National Gallery of Ireland in 1854. Dargan's statue stands overlooking Merrion Square as a monument to his entrepreneurial spirit.

Merrion Square itself was purchased by the Archbishop of Dublin in 1930 for the sum of £100,000 for the purpose of building a Catholic cathedral for Dublin on the site. The project was never realised and in 1974 Archbishop Ryan handed the square over to Dublin Corporation who spent a considerable sum on improvements and landscaping prior to its opening as a public park.

In recent years a number of houses have been returned to private ownership and these include number 82, belonging to Michael Roden, and number 14, the premises of Photo Images, owned by Seamus Daly. Such houses have been meticulously restored and are used as a combination of private residences and discreet office use. The value of the properties on the square has rocketed over the last two years. Number 17 Merrion Square sold for £1.7m in 1999.

Fitzwilliam Square

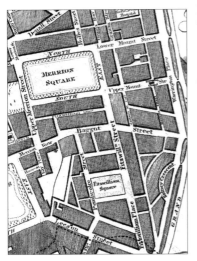

Above top: Brass bell pulls from a Merrion Square house.

Above: An early nineteenth-century map, showing the relationship of Merrion Square to Fitzwilliam Square.

The street that forms the east side of Merrion Square and runs in a southerly direction into Fitzwilliam Street was conceived as early as 1762, as Barker's map shows. The formation of Fitzwilliam Street was to lead, in 1789, to a plan to create another residential square somewhat to the south of Merrion Square. This would be called Fitzwilliam Square. Further away, the first houses of Leeson Street had already appeared in the early eighteenth century, and it was between here and the rather erratic line of Baggot Street that Fitzwilliam Square was planned. The Fitzwilliam Estate first granted leases for building on Fitzwilliam Square in 1791, and the first buildings to be completed were four houses on the north side. These houses, numbers 56–59, are shown on the map of Dublin made in 1797 by William Faden.

Although Fitzwilliam Square is small in terms of other Dublin squares – it is a quarter of the size of Merrion Square, half the size of Mountjoy Square and an eighth the size of St Stephen's Green – the progress in building the houses was slow. Work proceeded gradually through the early 1800s and was not really completed until about 1830. This, however, was quite normal – Merrion Square and Mountjoy Square had each taken similar lengths of time to complete, and various events, such as the Troubles of 1798 and the subsequent timber shortage during the Napoleonic Wars in the early 1800s, caused further delays.

Fitzwilliam Square consists of sixty-nine houses laid out around four sides of a well-planted central park. Mary Bryan, in her excellent unpublished study of Fitzwilliam Square (1995), has established the actual year of building for each house on the square through a close examination of the

Left: This aerial view of Fitzwilliam Square shows the methodical planning of the Fitzwilliam Estate in the early 1800s.

leases in the Fitzwilliam Estate papers. As we have already mentioned, the first houses were constructed on the north side by a variety of merchant developers. This was followed by the granting of building leases for the west side in 1805 and subsequent years, although one plot of ground had been leased since 1791. The houses on the east side of Fitzwilliam Square came next, with the first leases being made in 1814. The last side to be developed was the south side, where building work got under way between the years 1819 and 1824. Most of the plots were subdivided into twenty-five-foot or twenty-seven-foot widths and the developers were obliged to build their houses within four years, using a red stock brick for the façade and conforming to the general building instructions as laid down by the Fitzwilliam Estate.

Most lease holders built at least two houses, usually one for themselves and one to sell on, but some built several houses, such as William Dixon, a timber merchant from City Quay, who developed nine plots on the west side of Fitzwilliam Square. Another major builder was the firm of Henry Mullin and McMahon, who were successful contractors in major civil engineering projects of harbours and railways, and who built nine houses on the south side. Clement Codd, who came from a Wexford family of brewers, built two houses on the north side and four on the east side. Through his agent, Barbara Verschoyle, whom we have already met, Lord Fitzwilliam was able to keep a close eye on the development of his estate. His descendants continue to do so down to the present day, through the offices of the Pembroke Estate. As Mary Bryan commented, 'They appear to have combined practicality and aesthetic principles with notable success'.

In practical terms the houses were very well laid out, complete with broad streets, lanes to the stables and access to the rear. Issues relating to water supply, sewerage and lighting were also carefully addressed, and a committee or group of commissioners was eventually appointed to manage the affairs of the square and to look after the ornamental garden in the park. The result, which is still with us almost 200 years later, is that Fitzwilliam Square is a wonderful example of late-Georgian house building, and the square is as prestigious and as impressive today as it was back in the early nineteenth century.

The interior plasterwork decoration in Fitzwilliam Square is far less ambitious than it was in earlier houses and is mainly confined to cornices and ceiling centrepieces. The fashion for covering entire ceilings with elaborate decorative schemes had passed and elements from the Greek revival style, such as the Greek key pattern, were now common in the plasterwork friezes and cornices. There is a new boldness in the style of the work, although this may lack the refinement of late eighteenth-century craftsmanship. All of the houses have fine stone doorcases, usually incorporating Doric or Ionic columns, and many are decorated internally with mahogany doors and fine marble fireplaces.

The scale of the houses on Fitzwilliam Square is slightly smaller than those on Merrion Square, but many have a feature that is not so usual in the latter: a fine vestibule at the first-floor level in the return. In other words, at the head of the first flight of stairs there is an elegant hall or room, often ornamented by a pair of columns and lit by a row of stained-glass windows or sometimes by a rooftop lantern.

The typical Fitzwilliam Square house is a tall, dignified building, and in cases where the ground floor is treated with rusticated granite stonework, the brickwork of the upper two thirds of the façade stands out in elegant contrast. The most significant attribute of these houses is their elegant proportions, with the windows diminishing in height in the first, second and third storeys.

Right: Fitzwilliam Square was the original home of the Fitzwilliam Lawn Tennis Club.

A particular feature of the houses of both Merrion Square and Fitzwilliam Square is the brass rail situated just inside the hall door. This rail, which is usually kept beautifully polished and is unique to Dublin, has an unknown purpose, although some suggest that it was to aid gentlemen in taking off their boots on arrival in the hall.

It is a testimony to the skill of the builders and their overseers that most of the houses of the square are still in such excellent condition today. Though many of the original gardens of the houses have been turned into car parks, Mary Bryan noted in 1995 that twenty-six of the original mews buildings remained intact. Also remaining are many of the original stone walls, with their arches which gave access to the stables and mews buildings. A good example of this may be seen in Kingram Place, off Fitzwilliam Place.

The square, which was enclosed by a railing in 1805, was managed by a group of commissioners who were elected from the various residences. Funds were collected to maintain the park and to pay gardeners and lamplighters. The commissioners raised money to maintain the 'railing, gateways, locks, keys, chains, lamps and lampposts'. It was noted that in 1846 the gardener was equipped with a green cloth waistcoat, embellished with twelve special Fitzwilliam Square gold buttons. Rough games, such as croquet and cricket, were not permitted! (Nonetheless, in 1877 what was to become the famous Fitzwilliam Lawn Tennis Club was established here.) The noted twentieth-century resident Bay Jellett, leader of the Gaiety Orchestra, recalled her childhood memories of, 'the nannies in their starched uniform chatting and watching their charges'.

Fitzwilliam Square had many distinguished residents, such as Andrew Jameson, whose successful distillery allowed him to purchase a house in the square in the 1890s and have the hall completely redecorated in the baronial style, with oak panelling and a carved chimney piece with his family crest above. This house, once owned by Thomas Crosthwaite, a governor of the Bank of Ireland, was altered for Jameson by the architect Ambrose Derbyshire, who also enlarged and altered Sutton House for him.

Above: The demolition of sixteen houses on Fitzwilliam Street Lower in 1963 was the first serious attack on the city's heritage in modern times.

Above: Very few of the Fitzwilliam Square houses, with their elegant rooms, are still used as family residences.

Number 19 Fitzwilliam Square was the home of Lloyd Praeger, who was the founder of An Taisce in 1949 and wrote the fascinating book *The Way that I Went*, an all-encompassing tour of the natural and man-made heritage of Ireland. Number 2 Fitzwilliam Square was originally the home of Henry Roe, the distiller, who so generously underwrote the restoration of Christ Church Cathedral, and it was later the residence of William Dargan. The family of the painter Nathanial Hone has long been associated with 1 Fitzwilliam Square. Today two cultural institutions – the Goethe Institute and the Italian Cultural Institute – are both located in Fitzwilliam Square, from where they operate programmes of German and Italian cultural events.

It has often been assumed that the two major Georgian squares of Dublin's south city were somehow sacrosanct and safe from any attempts at demolition or inappropriate development. There were, however, a number of attempts to demolish groups of buildings, particularly in the Fitzwilliam Square area.

By far the most significant demolition proposal made at the expense of the Georgian fabric of this area was lodged by the ESB in 1962. A broad cross-section of the inhabitants of Dublin were shocked at the proposal to demolish an entire streetscape of sixteen late eighteenth-century houses in one of the most intact Georgian areas of the city, which incorporated an outstanding vista of the Dublin Mountains. The arguments went on for some three years, with many distinguished individuals contributing to the debate and various so-called experts from across the water justifying their fees by walking the tightrope of public opinion. At the time when the controversy was at its height, a new planning and development bill was being discussed and came into force in 1963. The new Planning Act was aimed at facilitating development and securing the preservation of amenities, both natural and man-made, for the common good, while protecting the rights of private ownership of property. In spite of this, the buildings were demolished, to be replaced by a new office block of modest height but with a relentlessly monotonous elevation.

Following the demolition of the Fitzwilliam Street houses by the ESB, an auction was held of a variety of interesting Adam-style marble mantelpieces, including several remarkable Bossi fireplaces. These beautiful white mantelpieces were inlaid with a coloured paste and were the unique creation of the Bossi family of artists from Florence. Many other mantelpieces, doors, fanlights, architraves, shutters and panelling were also sold at this auction, which took place in Midleton in County Cork.

A house on Lower Fitzwilliam Street, dating from the early 1800s, has been opened to the public by the ESB. The house is one of ten which the ESB renovated and rebuilt in the early 1990s, and Number 29, as it is known, is open to the public as a fully furnished late-Georgian townhouse. It was built in 1794 by an apothecary and developer named John Usher. In the kitchen the original range, complete with its maker's name and ornamental panels, has been beautifully restored and is the focal point of a fully furnished kitchen of the 1800s. The drawing room and dining room

Left: The stone-flagged hallway at number 25 Fitzwilliam Street, with part of the remarkable collection of furnishings of the Murnihan family, prior to its auction in 1999.

upstairs, along with the bedrooms, are also fully furnished with authentic pieces of the time.

The plan to restore the ten houses was initiated in 1988 and was welcomed by many as a vote of confidence in the historic city. It also signalled a new level of awareness concerning the importance of these houses and their location at the corner of Merrion Square.

In 1969 an application was made to demolish three houses – 5, 6 and 7 Fitzwilliam Square – and some debate ensued concerning the rights to redevelop solely for profit and the question of preserving one of the most intact and beautiful parts of Georgian Dublin. Even then, an *Irish Times* editorial pointed out that: 'It seems necessary, once and for all, to say what is to be preserved in Dublin. That done, it will be necessary to see that it is preserved.' As we have learned over the last thirty years, it is one thing to call for the protection of a building, and quite another to ensure that it actually happens. The houses were, in fact, already incorporated on the Dublin draft development plan as List B, and in the end it was only through the efforts of An Taisce, the Dublin Civic Group, and individuals like Uinseann MacEoin that the proposed office block was fought off.

In 1975 a semi-state body, Bord na Móna, provoked great controversy when it announced its intention to demolish five Georgian houses in Upper Pembroke Street and build a modern office block with a replica Georgian façade. Much public debate followed and total demolition was avoided although the houses were converted to offices.

A fascinating house in Fitzwilliam Square was in the process of being restored by Senator Edward Haughey in 1996 when a remarkable series of murals was discovered beneath later layers of wallpaper. The paintings, which have now been fully restored, depict classical scenes from antiquity, and feature idealised landscapes and panels representing Roman charioteers and dancing women. They are bordered by decorative panels and lavish Italian arabesques.

In 1999 the home of Justice James A Murnihan was sold and an auction of his extraordinary collection of antique furniture and paintings was held. This house, decorated and furnished with great taste, had an atmosphere of timeless elegance, but its well-worn and lived-in quality made it a unique representation of what most of the houses of Fitzwilliam Square must once have been like. Murnihan, who was involved in framing the Constitution of Ireland and became a Supreme Court judge, was a fanatical collector of art. He was a member of the Bord of Governors of the National Gallery of Ireland from 1925 till the 1970s, and he and his wife amassed a collection of over 1,200 important paintings.

Below: These modest houses on the corner of Molesworth Street and Kildare Street once had fine early eighteenth-century interiors.

Molesworth Street

Molesworth Street, by virtue of the fact that it still possesses just enough of its original Georgian buildings to maintain an air of grace, is chiefly known as the dignified thoroughfare leading to Leinster House. The street was laid out by Lord Molesworth in the early eighteenth century, and soon became a fashionable residential district. Up until about 1970 it was lined on either side with early eighteenth-century houses, most of which had panelled rooms and beautiful staircases. Sadly, various office developments in the street during the 1970s brought about the destruction of at least half of these houses along with St Anne's Parochial Hall and School.

Several houses did exist on the Molesworth lands prior to the laying out of the street in the 1720s. The land east of Dawson Street and the line of the new street was simply known as Molesworth Fields. The lands of Molesworth Fields had been purchased by the Earl of Kildare, and from the 1750s onwards he granted leases for the building of impressive houses on what would become Kildare Street. Gilbert informs us that the inhabitants of Molesworth Street were 'people of the highest rank in the city', such as Richard Parsons, the first Earl of Rosse, who died in his house there in 1741 and was later buried in St Anne's Church. Other noted early inhabitants of the street were Speaker Foster, who lived at number 27, and the Right Honourable James Fitzgerald, whose house at number 13 was demolished in 1972.

Examples of joinery from various demolished Molesworth Street houses.

Above left: A beautifully proportioned section of a staircase.

Above: panelled hall and stairs, once commonplace in this area.

Below: Exquisite woodcarving.

Above: Protesters at the demolition of St Anne's schools, Molesworth Street.

Below: The principal meeting room in the Masonic Hall, Molesworth Street.

St Anne's School and adjoining Parochial Hall were designed by Sir Thomas Deane and Benjamin Woodward, and were considered to be two of the finest examples of Gothic revival architecture in the city. The façade of the school building was constructed of alternate bands of granite and limestone, while the windows and string courses were ornamented with brick and Portland stone. The profile of its steep roof was broken with an asymmetrical arrangement of Gothic dormer windows. The resulting style was about as different as the Victorian architects could get from the regular symmetry of the Georgian surroundings. The well-documented destruction of these buildings in 1978, despite a great public outcry and the occupation of part of them by architectural students, was a disgraceful event.

The destruction of the old houses of Molesworth Street, many of which were timber panelled, had begun with one of the oldest in 1974. In that year one of the finest houses on the street, number 33, also known as Lisle House, was demolished, although its staircase was saved. This large house, which had a carved and panelled staircase of grand scale and featured exquisite woodcarving representing birds and flowers, was better known in the twentieth century as the premises of Sibthorpe's, the noted decorators and suppliers of paints and wallpapers. Fortunately, part of the carved staircase has now been incorporated into number 13 Henrietta Street, a building of similar period.

The destruction of Molesworth Street continued in 1978 on the two corner sites at the Dawson Street end and, in the early 1980s, on another three separate locations in the street. A block of houses, including numbers 10–14, were cleared to make way for the Setanta Centre. Those cleared included some fine houses, such as number 23, which had an elegant carved staircase and panelled rooms. Number 22, which stood on the corner of Kildare Street facing Buswell's Hotel, had a hallway with a paved marble floor and decorated with fluted Corinthian pilasters. This, along with other buildings on Kildare Street, was swept away and replaced by an office block named Kildare House, the corner of which is dressed up as several fake Georgian buildings.

The gradual conversion of Buswell's into a modern hotel also brought about, unfortunately, the complete gutting of several more houses, including the former Truman's art shop and Jane Williams's antiques shop, which stood at the corner of Kildare Street.

Frederick O'Dwyer, in his invaluable book *Lost Dublin*, points out that of the original twenty-three Georgian houses on the north side of the street only four now survive. These stand on either side of the Masonic Hall. The Masonic Hall, with its Italianate façade and Doric portico, is a remarkable building of the 1860s. The interior contains an impressive variety of meeting rooms and halls, each lavishly fitted out in a different architectural style, including Egyptian, Gothic and classical. It is the headquarters of the Freemasons in Ireland which can trace its history back to the 1720s. The hall was erected on the site of the townhouse of the first Grand Master, Richard Parsons, the first Earl of Rosse.

A number of the remaining houses that survive in Molesworth Street have their original features intact, such as number 15, now in office use, and number 29, the beautifully restored house belonging to Ib Jorgenson, which accommodates a fine art gallery. Molesworth Street can also claim what are possibly the two oldest Georgian shopfronts in Dublin. These have original rectangular fanlights and old-style glazed shop windows, and stand at the corner of Molesworth Place. Numbers 15 and 16, which were built as a pair, exhibit fine cut-stone doorcases with semicircular pediments. The doorcase of number 20 is even more elaborate, with its Gibbs-style blockwork on either side and prominent keystone. At the rear of number 20 are the elegant Georgian galleries of Gorry & Sons, picture dealers and restorers.

Above: This pair of Georgian shopfronts is a rare survivor in Dublin.

Below: Restoration work by the Dublin Civic Trust at number 11 South Frederick Street.

South Frederick Street

South Frederick Street runs between Molesworth Street and Nassau Street and, although less than half of its original houses still stand, it is an attractive small street. Its Georgian houses, dating from the 1740s and 1750s, were gently stepped down the gradually sloping street.

From about 1930, the New Ireland Assurance Company, which had offices on Dawson Street, set about acquiring all of the houses on the western side of the street. The company succeeded in buying all of the property except for one house, number 12, occupied by Miley & Miley, solicitors. It was due to the fact that the owners of number 12 refused to sell out in the 1970s and 1980s that numbers 10 and 11, built in 1756, were also eventually saved. These two houses were to become the first restoration project of the Dublin Civic Trust, which commenced in the early 1990s. The houses, which were acquired from New Ireland Assurance Company at a rock-bottom price on condition that they would be restored, were to fetch high prices when they were sold on a few years later. These houses stand today as models of good restoration work, but unfortunately all of the

houses on both sides of the upper part of the street were replaced by particularly dull office blocks.

The Dublin Civic Trust was founded in 1991 by a group of people including Ian Lumley, Geraldine Walsh and this writer. Like civic trusts in England and the Limerick Civic Trust in Ireland, it aimed to work in partnership with Dublin Corporation to secure the protection and enhancement of old buildings in the city of Dublin. When the project to restore 11 South Frederick Street got under way, the trust expanded to include Kevin B Nowlan, an experienced campaigner for Dublin's heritage, John O'Sullivan as administrator, and businessmen Michael Norris and David Willis.

President Mary Robinson formally opened 11 South Frederick Street in its fully restored state in 1995. The impressive staircase with its historic columned balusters forms part of the entrance hall and is the most striking feature of the house. The principal rooms, which lie to the rear, are half-octagonal in plan and have a projecting bay.

The house next door, number 10, is less elaborate but has a sequence of attractive, panelled rooms and a half-panelled staircase. The restoration of this house has been completed to an impeccable standard by the Hogan family who now live there.

Further down the street, the demolition of the entire block in the early 1980s resulted in the loss of several fine houses, including numbers 15 and 16, whose interiors were quite remarkable. The drawing room of number 15 featured a large and elaborate ceiling of rococo plasterwork, which was dismantled in 1984. Many years earlier, similar ceilings had been destroyed in numbers 5 and 6 at the top of the street. Number 14 was also an attractive house, with a bow to the rear and a fine open-well staircase.

Kildare Street

Kildare Street has a certain sombre quality, perhaps due to the presence of the various government offices and cultural and educational institutions and the formal nature of the architecture. It was originally laid out as residential area and, in the latter half of the eighteenth century, was home to a considerable number of titled families. This proved the Earl of Kildare right when he claimed that, having built Leinster House, fashion 'will follow me wherever I go'.

When it was built in 1745, Leinster House was the largest private mansion in the city. Originally known as Kildare House, it was built by James FitzGerald, the twentieth Earl of Kildare. When, in 1766, he was created Duke of Leinster, the present name came into existence. Leinster House was approached by Molesworth Street and entered originally by means of a giant gatehouse. This gatehouse, which took the form of a triumphal arch, was removed in the early twentieth century.

Above top: Numbers 11 and 12 South Frederick Street were rescued by the Dublin Civic Trust and are now fully restored.

Above: The once-attractive hallway of a South Frederick Street house.

This wide, imposing house, built entirely of cut stone, was constructed on undeveloped ground belonging to Lord Molesworth, lying at the eastern extremity of the expanding Georgian city. There are many magnificent rooms in Leinster House, including the two-storey entrance hall, the spacious picture gallery, which was converted into the present Senate chamber, and the boldly modelled library on the ground floor. The delicate plasterwork of the barrel-vaulted ceiling of the Senate Chamber was designed by James Wyatt.

Leinster House has undergone various changes of use since that time, becoming the headquarters of the Royal Dublin Society (RDS) in 1815, the centre of a museum complex in the late nineteenth century and the seat of government of the newly independent Ireland in 1924.

The RDS carried on valuable work promoting Irish industry, agriculture and manufacturing. It was through the RDS, for instance, that the National College of Art and Design and the Veterinary College of Ireland were both founded. The founding of the four major cultural institutions close to Leinster House – the National Museum, the Natural History Museum, the National Gallery and the National Library – was also due to the activities in the RDS.

Two large houses, 2 and 3 Kildare Place, were demolished in 1957. There was considerable controversy over the proposed demolition. These palatial houses, along with two others which had been demolished much earlier, are said to have been designed by Richard Castle and completed by his associate, architect John Ensor. A strongly worded article in the *Irish Times* of 24 June 1957 pointed out that there were no plans to develop the

Above: This sketch of the 1880s from *The Irish Builder* shows the proposed National Library and National Gallery with a modified Leinster House at its centre.

Below: John Rocque's map of 1756 shows the dominant position of Leinster House (then Kildare House) in Kildare Street.

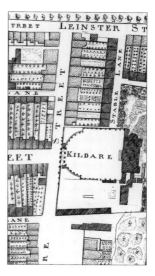

site and that the value of the property in terms of historic and architectural heritage, not to mention tourism, far outweighed the doubtful utility of a cleared site. It went on: 'Let no one imagine that there is anything seriously wrong or unstable about the two houses in Kildare Place. Is this not the beginning of the end for Georgian Dublin?' At this time the Irish Georgian Society was re-established by Desmond and Mariga Guinness who embarked on a mission to save Dublin's eighteenth-century heritage.

This event may well have heralded a new era of destruction, but it was not the first major change to take place in Kildare Street. A significant number of old houses had been replaced during the nineteenth century by the building of the Kildare Street Club, the College of Physicians and the National Library. One of the original houses was replaced in 1861 by William Murray's new building for the College of Physicians. Again built in the popular Italianate style of the 1860s, this elegant stone-fronted building possesses a fine interior with a grand entrance hall and staircase, and several magnificent reception rooms.

Three large Georgian houses were demolished to make way for the National Library in 1885. The twin 'palaces of culture', as Jeremy Williams described them, the National Library and the National Museum, were intended to frame Leinster House and proclaim Ireland's 'provincial yet imperialistic' heritage. The buildings were designed by Sir Thomas Newenham Deane, once a leading designer and exponent of the medieval revival movement. Here, however, he created an elegant but somewhat prosaic design in the Italian Renaissance tradition. The sandstone detailing of the Library and the Museum has weathered very badly and much of it has had to be replaced. The restoration of the stonework of the National Museum was only completed within the last few years and was achieved by the use of repair mortar and some stone replacement.

Another significant change in Kildare Street took place when a fire destroyed the four houses that comprised Maples Hotel. The site was then taken for the new Department of Industry and Commerce building. Maples Hotel occupied 25–28 Kildare Street until its closure in 1918. These four houses stood at the corner of Schoolhouse Lane, facing Kildare Place, a small public square that is seldom used by anybody. Between the Department of Industry and Commerce building and James Adam's premises on the corner of St Stephen's Green stands a row of some nine Georgian houses. This intact block of houses, along with a group of more modest ones, adjoined Buswell's Hotel and the few which stand at the bottom of the street are the only remaining elements of the eighteenth-century street.

Number 16, occupied by the Taylor Gallery, and number 22, occupied by Keane, Mahony and Smyth, possess most of their original features, including spacious staircases with wide handrails and chunky timber balusters. The rooms are large and have the usual heavy, classical cornices. Number 21, occupied by Mitchell and Son, wine merchants, is entered by means of a grand tripartite doorway of cut stone. Its neighbour, number 20,

Above: A carved timber newel post from a demolished house on Kildare Street.

now serving as a parking lot for the Shelbourne Hotel, has a most unusual façade, with Venetian windows on three of the upper floors. The original columns from the front door of the house were used on either side of the garage entrance, which was made through the bottom of the house.

The office block that now houses the Department of Agriculture replaced a large Tudor-style structure, which once housed the Church of Ireland Teacher Training College.

One of the largest houses to remain on Kildare Street is number 45, the original residence of Lord Doneraile. This house, four bays wide and four storeys over a basement, is entered by a magnificent doorcase of grand proportions. The walls of the fine staircase are ornamented with plasterwork frames, not unlike those in Leinster House, and several of the spacious rooms are panelled. The three adjoining houses at the corner of Nassau Street form part of Power's Hotel, but these have been heavily altered, especially at ground-floor level where several rooms have been converted into a pub.

The bottom of Kildare Street is dominated by the Kildare Street Club, a large Victorian building, designed in the style of an Italian Renaissance palace. A huge portico, which consists of three twenty-foot-high arches, stands over the street and now provides the entrances to the premises of the Alliance Française and the Heraldic Museum of the National Museum. This remarkable building was completed in 1861 and replaced their original clubhouse, which had been largely destroyed by fire in 1861. This house, erected by Sir Henry Cavendish, had been 'left in trust and for the use of the gentlemen of the Kildare Street Club' in 1782. The loss of the sensational carved stone staircase and entrance hall of the Kildare Street Club in 1971 has deprived Dublin of one of its finest nineteenth-century monuments. This half-Italian, half-oriental staircase, with its pierced stone balustrade, was set amid a magnificent hall of arches and pillars. It is fortunate, however, that the rest of the building escaped modernisation of this sort. Most of the major rooms are still intact and the richly textured façade, with its carvings of billiard-playing monkeys, can still be seen.

Above: The crest of the Royal Dublin Society, which moved to Leinster House in 1815.

Below: The Kildare Street Club was rehoused in 1861 in this Italianate palace, designed by Thomas N Deane and Benjamin Woodward.

South Leinster Street and Clare Street

The short range of houses that makes up South Leinster Street was erected in the 1750s on property once owned by the Earl of Kildare. Number 6 South Leinster Street was restored in 1970 by the company now known as Tegral, who still maintain it as their headquarters. Although originally acquired for

demolition, the company directors were persuaded by the Dublin Civic Group and the Irish Georgian Society to restore the house. Its stunning interiors, which can be seen today, are a tribute to their enlightened decision. It has a striking staircase with boldly modelled plasterwork, which is attributed to Robert West.

In 1997 there was widespread satisfaction amongst those who care for historic buildings when An Bord Pleanála ruled that 6 South Leinster

Street could not be demolished. This once elegant house, built between 1758 and 1760, had been acquired by the National Gallery for demolition in order to make way for a new purpose-built gallery extension. While many welcomed the much needed gallery extension, it was felt that the house and its ballroom mews building could be restored.

Number 6 had been the residence of Lord Kilwarden for the last two decades of the eighteenth century, until his murder on 23 July 1803, during the Robert Emmet insurrection. The ballroom was added by a subsequent inhabitant, Archibald Hamilton Rowan, a member of the United Irishmen, who lived there in the 1820s. The noted firm of Thomas Panter & Sons, painters, builders and decorators, occupied the building from the 1870s onwards, and were probably responsible for the ceiling paintings on the ground floor, which had been converted into a showroom. A statue of Hibernia with an Irish wolfhound was a well-known feature outside their premises and it survived there until the late 1950s. It is likely that Panter's was responsible for various alterations on the ground floor, including the removal of the original staircase and the addition of cast-iron Egyptian-style columns to the rear of the building. The magnificent rococo ceiling was removed from the original staircase hall and was reinstated in Ballyorney House, Enniskerry. One of the most pleasant surviving features of this large house are the large double bows which project to the rear.

The design and decoration of the staircase of 6 South Leinster Street was similar to that which was destroyed in the nearby 29 Clare Street. Both houses featured fine plasterwork panels that adorned the staircase and that were probably designed to frame a painting. The plasterwork on the main staircase in Leinster House is almost identical and it is possible that the same architect and craftsmen were involved. The magnificent staircase of 29 Clare Street, with its cantilevered stone construction and wrought-iron balustrade, was demolished some time after 1989 when the building passed into the ownership of the National Gallery. The interior was laid out with a spacious hall, a grand inner hall and staircase and a large ground-floor drawing room. Planning permission was granted in 1990 for a startling glass-fronted office block on the site of 27 and 29 Clare Street, but fortunately this development did not proceed. The design for the National Gallery extension has been modified and work is now in progress.

By the time of the demolition of number 29, the large and once beautiful four-storey house had been reduced to a wreck and its elegant wrought-iron staircase had been stolen. Even though it had inherited the situation from its previous owner, James Stafford, it is a matter of some shame that a body such as the National Gallery of Ireland did not seize the opportunity to rescue this building. It is ironic too that a body which leads the field in the restoration of other artworks, such as paintings and sculptures, could not have rescued this important house. Minor alterations had been made to the building, first by the Leinster Club, who added a cut-stone bay window at ground-floor level, and later on its conversion into offices by Michael Scott, when glass partitions were added on the first floor. In 1987 the Corporation ordered that the top two floors be removed for safety reasons.

Above: This once magnificent house, number 29 Clare Street, was finally demolished shortly after 1989.

Below: Part of a Vitruvian scroll from the staircase of this house.

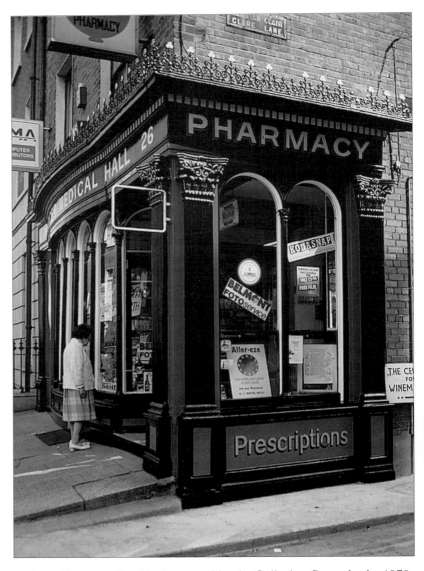

Right: Price's Medical Hall, the finest Victorian shopfront in Dublin.

Apart from an office block erected by the Gallagher Group in the 1970s at 22–25 Clare Street, the rest of the street is remarkably intact. Clare Street is the home of Price's Medical Hall, which boasts what is probably Dublin's finest Victorian shopfront. Richly carved Corinthian columns and capitals and a delicate arcade of windows support the elaborate frontage. Price's, which occupies 26 Clare Street, dates from the 1860s.

Perhaps more famous than Price's is Greene's Bookshop, which, with its ornate wrought-iron sign, canopy and stalls outside, is a Dublin landmark. Greene's, situated just around the corner from Merrion Square, was founded in 1843 by the Greene family, but since 1912 has been run by Herbert Pembery and his descendants. The bookshop occupies a curious

Georgian building, probably erected in the 1760s. Original cornices may still be seen in the ground-floor bookshop and in the second-hand department upstairs, where there is also an unusual oval room. It is a narrow building, located directly behind the larger Apothecaries Hall which stands on the corner of Merrion Square. The Guild of Apothecaries still occupy this house, where they have a fine boardroom on the first floor. The northern and most intact side of Clare Street also appears to date from about 1760 and includes the now much-altered Mont Clare Hotel.

Greene's was originally founded as a lending library, which was a popular type of institution before the advent of public libraries. Country subscribers could have books posted out, while boys on messenger bikes made deliveries throughout Dublin and the county. This writer has fond memories of early forays into Greene's, where Mr Pembery and the knowledgeable Ms Rochford maintained a remarkable supply of books of Irish interest. As one of the few old Dublin bookshops to survive today, it does a large trade in school books and also incorporates a small post office.

In the twentieth century there was a move away from using these large houses as private residences, but there is once again a trend towards residential occupancy, and some half dozen houses are now in private ownership again. Some of the houses are still occupied by educational institutions, libraries and archives but most of them are in use as offices.

Above: The main entrance (left) and (right) the wrought-iron staircase of number 29 Clare Street with Mr Daniel Gillman, ninety-year-old historian and authority on old Dublin.

CHAPTER FIFTEEN

St Mary's Abbey
and Capel Street

St Mary's Abbey

*J*ohn Speed's map of Dublin, made in 1610, clearly shows the isolated
position of St Mary's Abbey in relation to the rest of Dublin. The half-
sketch, half-plan of the actual buildings of the abbey is somewhat vague,
but a large wall, not unlike the medieval city wall itself, is shown encircling
the substantial demesne or park of the abbey. The stream known as the
Bradogue flowed along the wall's western boundary, close to a large defensive gate. The northern banks of the River Liffey are shown by Speed to be
as nature intended them, with the exception of one part where the abbey's
boundary wall touched the river.

At the time of the Dissolution of the Monasteries in
1539, St Mary's Abbey was considered to be the richest
Cistercian monastery in Ireland. Not only was it the
richest, but, apart from Mellifont Abbey in County
Meath, it was also probably the oldest Cistercian foundation in the country, having been established in 1139.

It is remarkable that much of St Mary's Abbey appears
to have survived until the late seventeenth century. At
that point, with the intensive development of these
lands by Sir Humphrey Jervis and Sir Richard Reynell, all
traces of the abbey, except for the Chapter House, were
obliterated. As Roger Stalley commented in *The Cistercian
Monasteries of Ireland* (1987): 'There is little doubt that St
Mary's Abbey was one of the finest medieval buildings in Ireland and,
located beside the port of Dublin, it was open to strong architectural influ-
ences from England. Of all Cistercian monuments in Ireland, this is the
one most in need of excavation.'

Above: Speed's map of 1610,
showing St Mary's Abbey and
precincts in their medieval,
undeveloped state.

During the 1880s part of the site was excavated to make way for a new building for Boland's Bakery. A conjectural plan of the layout and extent of the original abbey was made at that time. It is thought that a large church lay to the north of the Chapter House, its west end stretching back towards the present fruit markets. A large, square cloister, which would have adjoined the church, may have stood directly in front of the Chapter House. During the excavation work, numerous tiles and some of the structural walls were uncovered. One of the tiles found on the site depicts a monastery or church with a tall tower, and is possibly a representation of St Mary's Abbey itself.

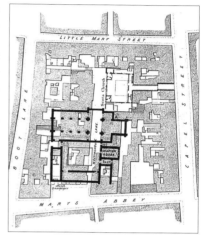

The survival of the Chapter House is indeed remarkable, and it is fortunate that it is preserved in such an intact state. The rectangular, vaulted space is quite large and was once lit by three windows at the east end, but these are now blocked up, as the Chapter House lies substantially below ground level. The medieval vaults of the Chapter House are carefully accentuated by the cut-stone ribs which support the roof.

The surrounding district was heavily populated with butter and herring merchants, dairies, fish dealers, corn chandlers and basket-makers, many of who occupied premises in Boot Lane. As we have already noted, the old fish market stood on the site of the present fruit and vegetable market and was entered by a narrow passage from Boot Lane, which is still in use today.

A public notice of 1820 proclaimed that Samuel Bewley was selling a large consignment of lemons and nuts on the quay at the Custom House. By the 1850s there were a number of foreign fruit merchants in the St Mary's Abbey area, hinting perhaps at the growing demand for a regular supply of foreign fruit and fresh vegetables and foreshadowing the Fruit and Vegetable Market, which was erected in the 1890s.

Above: A well-known conjectural plan, showing the possible layout of St Mary's Abbey in the context of Capel Street.

Below: The substantial vaulted Chapter House of St Mary's Abbey is all that remains.

St Mary's Abbey was also the base of some larger enterprises, such as builders' providers, seedsmen and rope and twine manufacturers. For instance, a wholesale china and glass merchant named Higginbotham was located in St Mary's Abbey and Pill Lane in the early nineteenth century. Street directories of that time give a fair indication of the poverty that existed in the streets of this area. Literally dozens of clothes brokers, dealing in cheap and second-hand clothes, existed in Mary's Lane, alongside shoemakers and one or two herring merchants.

Above: An early nineteenth-century trade card, showing the Georgian shopfront of Higginbotham's at the corner of St Mary's Abbey and Pill Lane.

Below: The imposing entrance to the Fruit and Vegetable Market on St Mary's Lane, which is surmounted by the full coat of arms of the city.

The Markets

When Dublin Corporation opened the Fruit and Vegetable Market in 1892 on the large rectangular site between St Mary's Lane and the old Pill Lane, it was following a long-standing tradition. The sale of meat and vegetables has been carried on here since medieval times when St Mary's Abbey held fairs on the green, an area now occupied by Green Street Courthouse.

The first edition of the Ordnance Survey map of Dublin city, made in the late 1830s, shows potato markets, egg and poultry markets and butter markets lying between Green Street and St Mary's Lane. A fish market

stood in the middle of the site of the present Fruit and Vegetable Market, while the Ormonde Market, which stood just behind Ormond Quay, was occupied by butchers. Not far off there was another vegetable market adjoining St Michan's Church, while Smithfield was the most important centre for the sale of livestock, horses and hay.

The present fine fruit and vegetable market building is in essence a large warehouse with a roof of cast iron and glass, supported on pillars. Today, it accommodates twenty-seven fruit and vegetable wholesalers. The business of the market begins at six o'clock in the morning and continues until three o'clock in the afternoon. The noise and the colourful array of produce from all over the world are testament to the market's role as a national centre for the distribution of fruit, vegetables and flowers. Many of the traders' hand-painted wooden signs, some of them in Gaelic script, are still hanging from the ironwork structure of the roof, and some archaic but fascinating notices, giving details of the market by-laws, are still to be seen.

While the problems of access, especially for large trucks and trailers making deliveries, could threaten the market's long-term existence in the city centre, any plans to move it away would represent a tragic loss for the city. Dublin is one of the few European capitals which has not so far relegated this important business, which supplies so many nearby shops and restaurants, to far-flung suburbs. In Paris, the ancient Les Halles was moved to the distant and featureless sheds of Rungis. In London Covent Garden was moved to New Covent Garden in Battersea. The future of the urban Fruit and Vegetable Market may well lie in the combination of the wholesale business with an all-day retail market, where the general public are encouraged to shop.

Dublin Corporation has recently embarked on the restoration of the market building, and work on the two main façades, including cleaning and some repairs, is nearly completed. The elaborate main entrance, facing onto St Mary's Lane, consists of a tall arch flanked by four stone columns and surmounted by a large sculpture of the arms of the City of Dublin. The two principal façades, with their long arcades of red- and yellow-brick arches, are embellished with decorative terracotta panels and a collection of attractive carvings in red sandstone, featuring details of fish, celery, leeks and turnips. Jeremy Williams aptly described the building as 'elegant, functional sheds screened by characterful façades that unite the monumental with the light hearted'. Across the street is the fish market, which was opened in 1897 and still carries on a limited business.

Many interesting and unusual street names were once to be found in the area surrounding the present Fruit and Vegetable Markets. A few, such as Cuckoo Lane, survive, but others, such as Petticoat Lane and Boot Lane, which ran along the eastern side of the market, have disappeared. Petticoat Lane was renamed Little Green Street, while Boot Lane became an extension of Arran Street East. Three more lanes that ran parallel to Capel Street and Church Street were Cow Lane, Bull Lane and Fisher's Lane, the latter joining the western side of the markets. Pill Lane, which once connected St Mary's Abbey with the Four Courts and ran along the southern side of the markets, is said to have derived its name from the Pole or Pill, a sort of inlet that stood at the junction of the River Bradogue and the River Liffey, where boats could be drawn up. Pill Lane was renamed Chancery Street after the Courts of Chancery, which form part of the Four Courts complex.

An interesting map of the Green Street area was prepared in 1753 by Kendrick, the City Surveyor, and showed a site intended for a new church in the middle of 'the Little Green' in Oxmantown. No church was built and instead the site was later taken for a new courthouse. The map also indicates the course of Braddock's Brook, otherwise called the Bradogue, flowing southwards beneath Halston Street, then called Hartstrong Street. In 1753 the root market was situated in Green Street, but Kendrick indicated that a better site for a new root market would be on Halston Street. The eventual site of Newgate Jail was indicated as being in the possession of a Mr Kennin, and some time later was described as the Dung Hills.

Above top: Lightfoot's is one of the many fruit and vegetable traders whose names live on in the market today.

Above: One of the beautiful carved stone finials on the Fruit and Vegetable Market.

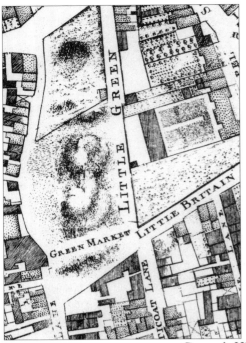

A large stone doorcase, with an arched entrance and Tuscan pillars of granite, still stands on the southern side of Little Britain Street, facing St Michan's Park. Whether this doorcase once formed part of an entrance to a grand property in the area is hard to say. A 1753 map indicates that St Thomas Bramball's house occupied this site, but Rocque's map of a few years later shows only modest buildings. The doorcase bears the Dublin city coat of arms, a possible later adaptation, and may simply have been an entrance to one of the many market buildings in the district.

The Ormonde Market once stood nearby, in the area between Pill Lane and the River Liffey. Rocque's map shows that it was laid out in a rectangular plan around a central courtyard, with an alley running through it. He also indicates that it was the site of a fish market. The Ordnance Survey map of almost a century later shows the Ormonde Market rebuilt on a circular plan and surrounded by a collection of small alleys named Royal Row, Dawson Row, Narrow Row and Beef Row. The Ormonde Market and surrounding area were swept away in the late nineteenth century to make way for new artisans' houses.

Above: Rocque (1756) shows the original Market Green area, now occupied by the Debtors' Prison, Green Street Courthouse and adjoining park.

Below: A stone doorcase in Little Britain Street, bearing the arms of Dublin Corporation.

George's Hill Presentation Convent and Primary School occupies most of the block between Mary's Lane, George's Hill and Cuckoo Lane, just north of the present fruit and vegetable markets. In the mid-nineteenth century, George's Hill was home to a variety of trades, including a victualler, an oil and pickle manufacturer and a poulterer, all of whom operated out of the Ormonde Market. Most of the original convent buildings, erected in 1794, remain intact, facing onto the narrow street called George's Hill. George's Hill Presentation Convent incorporated a large convent building, adjoined by a rectangular-shaped chapel and ornamental gardens. The original national school stood to the north of the convent, on George's Hill, but was replaced by a modern school building in the 1960s. It was here, in the Convent of George's Hill, that Catherine McAuley took her vows and later went on to create a new religious order – the Sisters of Mercy. She established her first convent in Baggot Street in 1826, and by the time she died, twenty-five years later, there were some 3,000 Sisters of Mercy all over the world, running schools for the poor, orphanages, homes for the deaf and blind and other charitable institutions.

Rocque's 1756 map indicates a large circular glasshouse, or glass manufactory, at the corner of the Bradogue, on the site now occupied by the George's Hill Primary School. Situated at the corner of St Mary's Lane and Bradogue Lane, now Halston Street, it was known as 'the Round Glass House'. In the late seventeenth century it belonged to a Captain Philip Roache, who had learned the skill of glassmaking in Europe. Mary Boydell, in her researches on Dublin

Left: A 1950s photograph of Little Britain Street, looking towards Capel Street and showing the original eighteenth-century houses.

glassmakers, considers this to have been the first glasshouse in Ireland for the manufacture of flint glass. We also learn that seven people were burned to death during an accident in the glasshouse, in 1696, when part of it collapsed. 'Good flint drinking glasses' were advertised in *Dublin Intelligence*, a newspaper of 1707, for sale at the Round Glass House in St Mary's Lane. *Lloyd's Newsletter* advertised some years later: 'At the Round Glass House at St Mary's Lane, Dublin (the fire now being in), is made and sold the newest fashion drinking glasses, and all other sorts of flint glasses as good as any made in England, at very reasonable rates.' Captain Roache's wares included the newest patterns of drinking glasses, decanters, large globe lamps for halls, bells and shades, sweetmeat glasses, flint wine glasses, decanters and water glasses.

By the middle of the eighteenth century there were several other glassmakers and sellers in Dublin, including a famous Mrs Johnson who, at the Sign of the Robin Hood in Dame Street, admitted the public to watch her spinning thousands of yards of glass. Another firm of noted glassmakers were the brothers Thomas and John Pugh, who established a glasshouse at 13 Lower Liffey Street in 1854. Interestingly enough, their premises were later occupied by the Dublin Glass and Paint Company.

In 1850 at least sixteen of the thirty houses on North Anne Street were described as tenements, illustrating the social and architectural decline which was already setting in.

An interesting map of 1802 shows that part of the site between Mary's Lane and Cuckoo Lane, now occupied by the warehouse of Fyffe's fruit wholesalers, was then the sugar manufactory of Bartholomew Maziere.

This comprised a sugar house, warehouses and stoves, as well as a cistern and pumps, a dwelling house and offices.

In the 1850s part of the site was also occupied by a malt-store belonging to Henry Jameson. Twenty-five years later, Jameson had enlarged his maltstore and had erected the fine stone warehouse occupying the sites of 7–21 Beresford Street, a large building designed by his partner James Pim, which has now been converted into apartments.

Two houses, used for many years as offices by Jameson and Pim, survived at the corner of North Anne Street up until the 1990s. During the nineteenth century the ground-floor ceiling in the corner house was removed to create a large, square hall for public meetings and recreation. The adjoining house, which dated from the 1760s, had all the usual Georgian features, including a beautiful stone doorcase, an internal fanlight, a handsome staircase with wooden balusters and well-proportioned rooms. Despite attempts by the Dublin Civic Trust to acquire these buildings and restore them, they were allowed to deteriorate and were eventually demolished. Though it was unsuccessful in its efforts to preserve these buildings, the Dublin Civic Trust adopted a drawing of the North Anne Street doorcase as its logo.

All of the old brewery buildings, including a fine warehouse on North Anne Street itself, were eventually cleared by Fyffes, leaving only the large nineteenth-century stone warehouse on Beresford Street. New buildings, one of which incorporates an office block, have been erected on this site within the last year, creating an interesting but entirely new streetscape.

The district surrounding the Green Street Courthouse, including Green Street itself and Halston Street, was full of derelict sites in 1990 and was at that time identified by the Dublin Civic Trust as an area suitable for residential renewal. In 1991 plans were announced to restore the old Debtors' Prison, and since then it has become almost impossible to keep up with the number of changes and improvements, in the form of new apartment blocks and other buildings, which have taken place here.

There are several interesting and historic buildings in this area, including Halston Street Church, otherwise known as St Michan's Catholic Church and its Presbytery, the Green Street Courthouse, the Debtors' Prison, the warehouses on Beresford Street and George's Hill Convent. Though most of the original houses which gave the area its character have now gone, these key buildings remain as landmarks in the district.

Other modest buildings also remain, such as the offices of Carton's, the poultry and egg merchants, whose fine red-bricked premises stand on the corner of Halston Street and Cuckoo Lane. Entrances for the offices and goods entrance of these premises were constructed in cut granite. The old schoolhouse in Cuckoo Lane is another good building, with an imposing stucco façade and railings fronting onto the street. It was, until recently, in use as Leonard's fruit and vegetable store.

A small but attractive warehouse at Halston Street, facing the Debtors' Prison, was demolished in 1996, despite protests from the Heritage Council. It was unfortunate that it should have been Dublin Corporation who demolished the warehouse; the same body, a few years earlier, had made an excellent job of restoring the stone setts in nearby Cuckoo Lane, and were clearly dedicated to the rejuvenation of the district. It had been pointed out in the 1990 Dublin Civic Trust report that the area had the potential to become a sort of northside Temple Bar, if the historic building stock were conserved and the derelict sites infilled. Another remarkable improvement in this area has been the redevelopment of the depressing, concrete-surfaced playground into the pleasantly landscaped St Michan's Park. There is a monument to the 1798 Rebellion in the centre of the park.

As we have already mentioned, at the time of John Rocque this entire area, 'the Green', was an open space, but the 1790s saw the site used for the development of three important buildings of a judicial nature – the Debtors' Prison, the Green Street Courthouse and Newgate Jail, which has since vanished.

The impressive Green Street Courthouse, with its sombre façades facing both Green Street and Halston Street, was opened in 1797. Both façades have engaged white Portland-stone columns. The interior was remodelled in 1842, and many of the fittings from this period, such as the panelled benches and galleries, survive intact. In 1803 Robert Emmet was tried here. Later it housed the Recorder's Court and the Lord Mayor's Court. The Green Street Courthouse now serves as the Special Criminal Court and until relatively recently was subject to very tight security.

The Debtors' Prison, erected in 1794, is an interesting, U-shaped structure, rising to three storeys over a basement. Such prisons were common in the eighteenth century, and were used to accommodate individuals who ran up debts, often through gambling. As prisons went, it was not particularly uncomfortable – many of the rooms were large and well lit, with decent-sized Georgian windows. There were ten cells or rooms on each floor, and three in the basement, amounting to thirty-three cells altogether. The larger rooms fronted onto Green Street and two stone staircases provided access to the different floors. The hallways were vaulted to render the building fireproof. The prison was at one time used as a Garda barracks and later as accommodation for Garda widows.

Above: The cut-granite Victorian entrance to Carton's offices on Halston Street.

Below: The stone setts of Cuckoo Lane have been carefully maintained by Dublin Corporation.

For many years the Debtors' Prison stood with 'a sentence of demolition' hanging over it, as it occupied the line of a proposed new road linking Parnell Street to North King Street. The building was saved when the controversial road plans were amended, and the prison became a listed structure some years later. A trust formed in 1991 by members of Students Against the Destruction of Dublin set about restoring the building for community housing. The group acquired a long lease from the building's owners – the Office of Public Works. The roofs have been repaired and broken windows mended, but the project has stalled due to funding problems. Office use is now proposed for the building. Many of the ex-students who initially became involved with this project have since become engaged with heritage or environmental work elsewhere in the city.

The original Newgate Jail was situated between High Street and Thomas Street and was originally part of the medieval New Gate in the city wall. This jail was replaced in 1781 by the opening of a new building in Green Street, which was three storeys high and had four conspicuous corner towers. This formidable jail, with its thickly barred windows, was equipped with a grisly piece of machinery, displayed above the arched main entrance. It took the form of a balcony with a specially constructed collapsible floor, a gibbet with pulleys attached and, above all of this, a pair of executioners' axes. The flimsy bodies of many executed prisoners must have made a pathetic sight against the sombre magnificence of this building.

Following its closure as a prison in 1860, the walls of Newgate Jail were demolished down to first-floor level and it was turned into a temporary fruit market. When the prison was finally demolished in 1899 to create St Michan's Park, the bases of two of the corner towers were left, and may still be seen today at the corners of the park. The prison's ninety-seven cells were accommodated around two courtyards, and there was also a chapel and an infirmary.

Just across the street from the former Newgate Jail site stands St Michan's Catholic Church. The principal façade of the church, which was completed in 1817, faced onto North Anne Street and was built in a subdued but attractive Gothic style, very similar to the façade of the Church of SS Michael and John on Blind Quay. This original front, with its finely chiselled granite masonry, Gothic doors and windows and public clock, is now seldom used as an entrance. Churchgoers instead use the alternative entrance on Halston Street, where a new and elaborate façade was erected in 1891. As Peter Costello commented in his book, *Dublin Churches:* 'The contrast between these two faces

Above: Prior to 1990 the Debtors' Prison was scheduled to be swept away for road-widening.

Below: Newgate Jail opened in 1781 and was cleared in 1899 to make way for the present St Michan's park.

[of the church] tells the whole story of the Catholic Church in Dublin during the nineteenth century, a movement of obscure plainness to a dominant extravagance.' The interior of the church remains largely unaltered from the time of its original construction in the early nineteenth century. It has a fine balcony and a stucco-ornamented ceiling adorned with sculpted heads, which bear a close resemblance to those of its contemporary, the Chapel Royal in Dublin Castle. There are also a number of very attractive early nineteenth-century stained-glass windows.

Most of the new developments in the Green Street area enhance the appearance of the district. For example, the premises at the corner of Green Street and Little Britain Street have an interesting curved elevation, the roofs and brickwork of the new buildings in Halston Street respect the existing streetscape, while the more radical design of Cuckoo Lane introduces new colours and textures into the street.

A group of impressive, limestone-fronted warehouses remains on Anglesea Row. These three- and four-storey buildings are of Victorian date. The ashlar stonework is of outstanding quality and an original projecting crane may still be seen, high up over one of the warehouse doors. For many years a

Above left: The nameplate on the North Anne Street frontage of St Michan's Catholic Church.

Above: The new streetscape of Cuckoo Lane.

Left: This cut-stone warehouse, typical of those that housed nineteenth-century industry in the city, is on Anglesea Row.

large stone mill wheel stood at the corner of Anglesea Row and Little Britain Street, where it was a feature of interest. Unfortunately, the stone was stolen in 1996 and never recovered!

Capel Street

Capel Street is probably the most intact old commercial street remaining in the north city. Thanks to the efforts of the Wide Streets Commissioners in the middle of the eighteenth century, the vista down Capel Street is completed by the view of City Hall on the south side of the river. For most of the eighteenth century, Capel Street was the main access route to the old city centre around Dublin Castle. All traffic coming from the north city and beyond was funnelled down Capel Street and over Essex Bridge, which must often have been jammed with carts and carriages making their way across the Liffey. It was perhaps the continuity of the commercial life of the street throughout the nineteenth and twentieth centuries, coupled with the fact that it was not itself subject to any recent road-widening proposals, which prevented it from being destroyed. Neither was it sufficiently attractive or successful to warrant the attention of property speculators in the late twentieth century. The street managed to walk the tightrope, perhaps by accident, of maintaining just enough business to survive while remaining something of a commercial backwater. In this respect, it is not unlike many streets in provincial Irish towns, which also survived the often crude hand of change of the twentieth century.

Above: The Capel Street area was first developed in the 1670s and was named after the then Lord Lieutenant, Arthur Capel, Earl of Essex.

Below: An engraving of the late seventeenth-century mint, which once stood in Capel Street.

Following the construction of the first Essex Bridge in 1676, houses were built on the new street and it was named after the then Lord Lieutenant, Arthur Capel, Earl of Essex. Proceeding north from the river, Capel Street follows a straight line, first crossing Strand Street, so called because of its original proximity to the shore or strand of the Liffey, then passing St Mary's Abbey and Abbey Street, St Mary's Lane and Mary Street, Little Britain Street and Great Britain Street, ending in a curious twist whereby it finally meets Bolton Street and North King Street.

There are many old houses surviving along the full length of the street, though few of them retain their original internal features, such as the panelled rooms and early staircases. A very old house, with a bold classical cornice and prominent roof, which was known as the King James Mint, once occupied the site of number 27, but vanished long ago. There was a second detached house on Capel Street, which is shown on Rocque's map of 1756 as a large mansion with a substantial garden backing

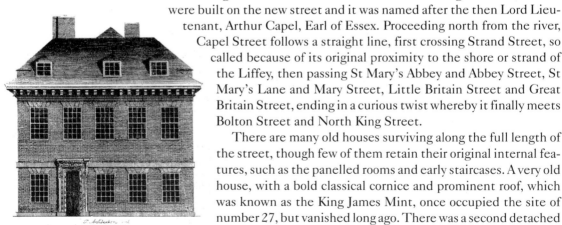

King James II^d Mint House, N° 27, Capel St.
Where the late Thomas Sheridan was born.

onto the old green of St Mary's Abbey and Little Green Street. The house was built in the 1720s for Thomas Connolly, the builder of Castletown House in County Kildare and Speaker in the Irish House of Parliament. It occupied the site of the present-day 103–108 Capel Street, but unfortunately there is no known picture of it.

A unique survivor from old Dublin is the small triangle of properties that once faced Connolly's house and is bordered by Capel Street, Ryder's Row and Parnell Street. If this tiny fragment of historic Dublin is to remain intact, it is imperative that no further demolitions or gutting of buildings be permitted.

Number 66, the oldest surviving building in this group, is a small house of the 'Dutch Billy' type, probably built about 1730. It features a fairly plain cut-stone doorcase, and is panelled throughout with bolection-type mouldings and timber cornices. The hall, stairs and rooms of the ground floor were, until recently, in use as a tailor's place of business. According to Ian Lumley, who is an authority on such buildings, it is one of the most intact small panelled houses remaining in the city.

Across the street a house of slightly later vintage, 95 Capel Street, was almost demolished in 1993. The façade and front rooms of the building were dismantled, even though an engineer's conservation report showed that it could be made structurally sound. Work went ahead in complete defiance of the city councillors, in the absence of an enlightened decision from Dublin Corporation. The building was declared a national monument, and the remaining panelled staircase and rooms were protected pending its reconstruction and full restoration.

This controversy showed that it was not only desirable but possible to preserve such an historic Dublin house. The Office of Public Works, now Dúchas, made history by making this house the first ever post-1700 building to be designated a National Monument. With its beautiful raised and fielded panelling, the house had for years been used by a repairer of prams and the rooms were a graveyard for these four-wheeled vehicles. This house and its early nineteenth-century neighbours, numbers 97 and 98, were for many years scheduled for demolition to facilitate the creation of the Inner Tangent road, which would have cut through Capel Street at this point to link Parnell Street and North King Street. The pair of houses, which were acquired by Dublin Corporation for that purpose, have only recently been restored, but with the loss of their original plasterwork. However, the ceiling of the drawing room of number 98 is still ornamented with delicate plasterwork dating to the early nineteenth century.

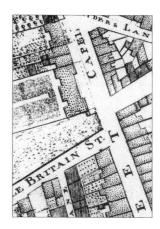

Above: Rocque's map shows part of the eighteenth-century Capel Street.

Below: Number 66, probably the oldest surviving house in Capel Street, dates from the early eighteenth century and has important internal features.

Above: Panelled staircases, such as those at number 95 Capel Street (right) and at number 51 Mary Street (above), were once a common feature of Dublin houses.

Below: Malton's engraving (1797) of Essex Bridge shows the busy street life outside the Georgian shops at the end of Capel Street.

Nearby, a block of apartments has been built on a long-vacant site. The adjoining house, 88 Capel Street, was completely stripped of all its original cornices, joinery and floors in 1999, leaving only the front wall. The ungainly modern façade of number 87 belies the fact that it is possibly one of the oldest surviving houses in Capel Street – it may have been built in about 1700. Early features include a staircase with barley-sugar-type banisters and simple panelled doors, which were common at this time. Staircases of similar style, which suggest an early date for the construction of the houses, were discovered at numbers 48 and 57 Capel Street. Unfortunately, the original panelling was stripped out of the latter house in 1992, but the staircase itself, with its barley-sugar banisters and fluted Doric newel posts, still survives. Number 59, another early eighteenth-century house, lost its original interiors in 1993, but number 37 still retains an attractive eighteenth-century ceiling, with plasterwork in the style of Michael Stapleton on the first floor.

Malton's engraving of Essex Bridge, made in 1795, shows the bottom of Capel Street with people standing outside the eighteenth-century shops. Apart from the modern shopfront and the fact that the original brick façade was plastered, the corner premises on the east side of the street remains unaltered. This building held an agency for the old State Lottery, which was popular in the late eighteenth century. The Georgian house and shopfront that stood on the opposite corner were replaced by the fine granite and red-brick Bank of Ireland premises, with its curved corner, in the early twentieth century.

As we can see from Malton's print, Capel Street was a thriving commercial thoroughfare with a great variety of shops. In a street directory of 1806, for instance, we find two jewellers and watchmakers, a feather manufacturer, four druggists and apothecaries, four haberdashers, a glover, a pianoforte-maker, several hosiers and milliners, four shoe-makers, a paper stainer, two linen drapers, three gunmakers, an engraver, a lottery office, a seed merchant, a confectioner, two printers and booksellers, a tin plate worker, a tobacco-nist, two cabinetmakers, two perfumers, a stay-maker, a goldsmith and a starch and hair powder manufacturer. Now, 200 years later, Capel Street still offers a rich cross-section of shops and services, including a large number of furniture stores, several hardware and paint shops, an art gallery, a model shop, several so-called adult shops, a number of cafés, a music shop, tailors, a monumental sculptor, electrical and telephone shops and travel agents, and lately a small supermarket.

Following the completion of the Civic Offices at Wood Quay, the Architects' Department of Dublin Corporation moved out of the old Baxendale building at the corner of Strand Street and Capel Street, and this building has now been converted into a bar and café. John Lemass, the father of Taoiseach Seán Lemass, was born at 2 Capel Street, where his family were hatters. Patrick Boland of Boland Bakeries, described as a biscuit manufacturer, occupied numbers 133–135 Capel Street in the late nineteenth century. His premises adjoined the old Presbyterian meeting house, which stood on the site of St Mary's Abbey.

Of the several ironmongers in the street, Joshua Edmundson & Company was one of the leading firms. In 1880 they specialised in gas fittings, grates, stoves, fenders and fire irons. They also sold gas ranges, gas chandeliers and a wide variety of household goods. Edmundson's had their own iron foundry in the city. An old bill from William Mooney, brass founder, lamp maker and gas fitter at 38 Capel Street, shows that in 1842 the

Above: The trade card of William Mooney, one of the many nineteenth-century gas and lamp fitters in the area.

Left: Joshua Edmundson was one of the leading dealers in domestic appliances and ironworkers in the city.

Above: The ornate Victorian
stucco façade of Slattery's
public house on Capel Street.

Below: Brereton's, the
pawnbroker, forms part of the
unspoilt streetscape of
Capel Street.

installation of gas fittings and brasswork was not cheap. The fitting of gas light in a ware room or showroom at that time came to almost £30. George Butler, another Capel Street iron-monger, also sold a wide range of products, but his illustrated billhead shows that he specialised in stoves and fireplaces. Henry Smith's establishment was to be found at the Sign of the Golden Key, at 154–155 Capel Street, where he sold builders', cabinet- and coach-furnishers' ironmongery, copper boat-nails, rivets and washers and coffin furniture. Smith advertised him-self as a nut and bolt manufacturer, and also sold harness-room fittings, brushes, mops, rainwater pipes and gutters.

Tait's seed warehouse at 119–120 Capel Street was estab-lished in 1780. Another seed merchants, which closed in the 1970s, was M Rowan & Company, founded in Capel Street in the late nineteenth century.

In the early 1960s, following the 1963 Planning Act, Mr Paul Rowan, the then director of Rowan seeds, and several other businessmen in the area challenged the Corporation's designa-tion of Capel Street as 'an obsolete area'. Mr Rowan expressed strong concerns about the Corporation's use of this term and their adoption of the Lichfield Plan, to redevelop the entire north inner city, which he said would 'end up with monolithic ownership, instead of multiple ownership' of businesses. He was concerned that the area would find itself with 'only one landlord and several developers and if you disinte-grate the philosophy of multiple ownership you will disintegrate the society itself as nobody will own anything'. Mr Rowan's concern for the ownership of businesses by non-nationals may not have happened over-night, but his predictions, for good and ill, have in large part come to pass.

Of the few pubs in Capel Street, Slattery's, at the corner of Little Mary Street, is one of the most striking in appearance. Though a considerable amount of the elaborate stuccowork has been removed, the pilasters, along with the arched first-floor windows and the large pendants combine to create an unusual effect. Grainger's Pub, which has now been renamed GF Handel's, occupies the corner of Little Strand Street. It is an interesting Victorian building of about 1870. About a year ago the Boar's Head, which for years stood as a single-storey pub on the corner of St Mary's Abbey and Capel Street, was rebuilt as a three-storey building and has greatly improved the streetscape.

McNeill's Music Shop, probably the longest existing business in continuous ownership in Capel Street, has been in operation since about 1830. As such, it is probably one of the oldest functioning shops in Dublin. Its mod-estly detailed shopfront, which dates from that time, has been carefully maintained, along with the interior, which has an old counter and built-in glazed presses. In 1850 it was advertised as McNeill's Military Musical Instrument

Makers. The building, at number 140 Capel Street, was carefully restored several years ago under the direction of conservation engineer Christopher Southgate.

Numbers 78–84 Capel Street are an important block of houses laid out by the Wide Streets Commissioners in about 1823. The houses, which are thin and tall and were originally designed with shopfronts and Wyatt windows above, constitute a unique surviving group of buildings. Some of the original shopfronts, with their modest joinery and slender columns, remain intact, and one has recently been restored. These buildings stand at the top of Capel Street, where it meets Bolton Street.

Brereton's, the pawnbroker, occupies one of the best-kept properties in Capel Street. Their shop at number 108 is carefully painted in black and gold and displays its original pawnbroker sign. The old-time lettering, which reads 'money office', is still featured on the wall above the shopfront. Oman's antique showrooms at numbers 114–116 feature an arcaded ground floor, probably erected in the 1860s. The handsome façade, with its brick and stucco ornament, at one time housed the Torch Theatre. In 1935 it was the headquarters of the United Trades Council and Labour League.

Meeting House Lane, a short cul-de-sac running north off St Mary's Abbey, derives its name from the existence of an old Presbyterian meeting house, a square-shaped building that is evident on Rocque's map. The first Ordnance Survey map shows a Scots church on the same site, with entrances from both Meeting House Lane and Capel Street. The church had a gallery on three sides, with boys' and girls' schools adjoining. It would appear that the site of the Scots church was incorporated into Boland's Bakery sometime after 1860. Nearby stood the timberyard and veneer loft of Messrs Holbrook, which backed onto Meeting House Lane. These premises and Warren's printing office are shown on a map of about 1800 in the Longfield Collection in the National Library.

The charity schools of the meeting house in St Mary's Abbey catered for about thirty children in 1835. It is not certain whether any of the meeting house survives, although some of the external walls may form part of the present gym, which occupies an old hall on this site. At the end of Meeting House Lane, behind the gym, is a large building, now used as a car park, where two substantial arcades, erected in 1882, support a heavily constructed steel floor above.

Above: McNeill's have been selling music and musical instruments in Capel Street since 1830.

Below: The trade card of Clifford's, who supplied oil candles and spermaceti tapers for lamps and lighting.

Sir Humphrey Jervis

An interesting collection of petitions, letters and other documents concerning the affairs of Sir Humphrey Jervis shed some light on his role as a developer north of the Liffey. The papers, which were donated to Trinity College by the Hutchison family, descendants of Jervis, record the changes to the old St Mary's Abbey, and document the laying out of streets there in the late seventeenth century. 'The dissolved Abbey of ye Blessed Virgin Mary near the city of Dublin' was held by Robert Piphoe during the sixteenth century. Piphoe died in 1610 and is buried in the vaults of St

Michan's Church. It appears that he acquired the estate for 'military services and soccage'. Some years after Piphoe's death, his residence was described as 'the former abbot's lodging at St Mary's Abbey', and included a common orchard, a columbarium, a stable, a ten-acre ash park and the Anckesters Park, which measured six acres. At this time there was also a townhouse, a water-mill and a horse-mill, along with various other dwellings and gardens.

Above: Number 30 Jervis Street, drawn by H Leask in 1907 just before its demolition, shows a large, early eighteenth-century house with a curious double gable.

In 1619 we come across the first mention of Sir Garret Moore, Baron of Mellifont and later Earl of Drogheda. His family, as we have already seen, was to play an important role in the development of the eighteenth-century city north of the River Liffey. In 1619 there is mention of a mortgage from Piphoe's estate to Sir Garret Moore, and there are various references to Lord Drogheda's house near St Mary's Abbey. In 1671 we find John Power, otherwise Lord Power, as lessee or tenant of 'the Burnt House', described as 'a great mansion house forming part of the St Mary's Abbey estate'. Two years later the St Mary's Abbey estate was described as including the Abbot's lodge, a dormitory, the porter's lodge, a cloister, half of Lord Drogheda's residence, the Burnt House, the Ash Park, the Calfe Park, the Pigeon Park, Brock's garden, Millar's garden, Reeve's garden and a coach house in Boot Lane.

In the following year, 1674, the Earl of Tyrone proposed to purchase Piphoe's Park for £3,000, but a year later he assigned his interest in all of St Mary's Abbey to Sir Richard Reynell and Sir Humphrey Jervis. It would appear that in the 1670s, Sir Humphrey Jervis (sometimes spelled Jarvise) was living in 'the great mansion house of St Mary's Abbey', the house formerly occupied by the Earl of Drogheda. The lease to Jervis was again confirmed in 1680 by Arthur, Viscount Loftus of Ely.

This mansion house was then described as having 'cellars, a drawing room, a bed chamber and other apartments'. The nearby Burnt House was situated close to Pill Lane and contained four large cellars. It had two large gardens and a bleaching yard. Close by in Boot Lane there were four cottages, a brew house and an inn known as the Red Lyon.

In 1676 the Lord Lieutenant, who was then the Earl of Essex, authorised the building of a new bridge, to be called Essex Bridge. The bridge was to span the river from 'the lands near the Custom House to St Mary's Abbey'. Five overseers were appointed, including Sir Humphrey Jervis, to carry out the project. By agreement with Sir Richard Reynell, Jervis would acquire the 'old walls, stones and rubbish' of St Mary's Abbey to assist in the construction of the bridge. Fortunately, the Chapter House of St Mary's survived, as it was in use as an underground storehouse.

For some reason, Jervis found himself alone in agreeing to build the new bridge, and this public-spirited enterprise was to lose him a substantial

Left: Grattan Bridge stands on the site of the first Essex Bridge, which was built by Sir Humphrey Jervis in 1677.

Below: St Mary's Church, with its adjoining graveyard, occupied a prime site in the development of the Jervis Estate.

amount of money and earn him a spell in prison! The following year, 1677, he entered into an arrangement with John Greene, a carpenter and builder, and William Robinson, the surveyor, and Jervis advanced money for the construction of the bridge. Naturally, there was a strong element of self-interest in Jervis's desire to build the bridge – he now held much of the land of St Mary's Abbey, which was being laid out in new streets.

The Corporation of Dublin had for some time disputed the right of St Mary's Abbey to the foreshore of the River Liffey, including the Strand – important land that would eventually become the Liffey quays and their hinterland. Accordingly, in 1674 the Corporation granted a lease to Anthony and Jonathan Amory of the Strand, which included that area now occupied by Ormond Quay and Bachelor's Walk. In the same year, Humphrey Jervis acquired the Amory interest in the lands stretching from the Pill, an area slightly to the west of Essex Bridge, to Gilbert Mabbot's new water-mill, which was situated opposite Dirty Lane, otherwise known as Hog Lane, now Fownes Street. Jervis's lease of 1674 included all of the land 'submerged at fulled high tide by the Annliffy for 299 years'.

Jervis's new Essex Bridge had a drawbridge or lifting section at one end, to allow ships with masts and larger boats to sail upstream to the area in front of Wood Quay. There were various complaints from the gabbardmen, or boatmen, about the operation of this drawbridge. As a result, it was decided in 1685 that arches should replace the drawbridge. Things were going well for Sir Humphrey Jervis, and in 1681 the new Lord Lieutenant of Ireland, the Duke of Ormonde, made him Mayor of Dublin for a second year. We also learn that Jervis 'will narrow the Liffey with lime and stone', indicating that at that time he was beginning to construct what would become known as Ormond Quay. However, the foundation of Ormond Quay may have been laid some six years earlier, as Richard Mills certified that a wall some 786 perches (2 miles!) long had been built on the strand.

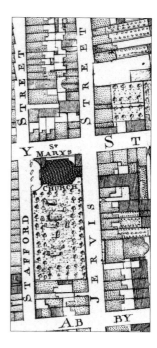

The Pill was originally leased to Lord Santry in 1662. In 1681 Jervis acquired an interest in the lands of Sir Richard Fleming, which had been laid out in streets and included the former land of the Pill. Shortly afterwards, he conveyed part of his interest in this property to William Ellis, who went on to develop Ellis Quay.

Between 1682 and 1684, Jervis laid out Ormond Quay and 'a quay at Bachelor's Walk'. In that year he also undertook to repair Bloody Bridge (now Queen Street Bridge) and to replace an old wooden structure with a stone bridge at a cost of £700.

By 1684 Jervis was in financial difficulties. He had entered into a dispute with the City of Dublin over the two 'bridgehouses' that he was supposed to have handed over to the city. In various petitions, Jervis claimed that he had not been reimbursed for monies laid out by him on the reconstruction of Ormond Bridge and Essex Bridge.

In 1685, following his refusal to hand over the two houses, Jervis was committed to prison, where it seems he spent some ten months. It transpired that the principal reason for the jailing of Sir Humphrey Jervis was the alleged slur or reflection on the government that was implied in his petition. However, the parties later agreed that there had been no such 'reflection'. In the meantime, Jervis claimed that he was owed £2,674/10s/10d, and suggested that he might be given forfeited land in settlement of the State's debt to him. The State eventually conceded that he was owed a sum of money, and decided to raise duty on the importation of coal in order to pay him off. Jervis put forward another proposal to cover his debts – he suggested that the city should raise a tax on 'hacking coaches and cars'.

In 1681 Jervis entered into an agreement to take a portion of three lots of land in Capel Street with Dr Christopher Dominick and Mr Tongue. A year later there is mention of leases being granted to Sir John Cole (after whom Cole's Lane is named) for lots east of Capel Street and south of Abbey Street.

The new streets of the Jervis Estate were first planned in 1685. Some of the earliest houses in Jervis Street had gabled fronts and cruciform roofs covered in tiny slates, indicating a late seventeenth-century or early eighteenth-century date. Jervis Street was a mixture of modest Georgian houses and those of a grander scale, such as number 30 and number 52 which had fine cut-stone doorcases. That of number 30 had rusticated stonework with a stone pediment supported on brackets. One of these houses was illustrated in the *Georgian Society Records* before its demolition in the early 1900s.

In 1691 an inquiry was held to investigate the property of Sir William Ellis at Oxmantown and Arran Quay, and shortly afterwards it was announced that he had been outlawed.

Above top: A carved and gilded fragment from the once-splendid reredos of St Mary's Church.

Above: Part of the classical carved-timber reredos, removed from St Mary's Church in about 1988.

In 1703 Jervis leased land at the east side of his garden in St Mary's Abbey to John Eccles, Alderman. The land, 'belonging to his present dwelling in St Mary's Abbey', was bounded to the east by tenements in Capel Street, and to the west by the middle walk or passage through Jervis's garden to 'the great gate'. Presumably this great gate was the original entrance to St Mary's Abbey, which was still standing in 1703. On the north, Eccles's property was adjoined by the tenements in Mary Street and by Anthony Henderson's sugar house.

The Presbyterian meeting house, built in the lane of St Mary's Abbey, was erected on part of the land leased to Eccles in 1703. When Sir Humphrey Jervis died in 1707, a public notice was issued to advertise the letting of his property and the sale of all goods by cant, or public auction. The auction included 'beds and bedding of all sorts, pewter, brass and copper, glasses, tables, chairs, chariot, sheas, horses, hay'.

Brooking's map of 1728 shows how the development of the city centre north of the River Liffey proceeded apace, even allowing for some artistic license on the part of the map maker. Ormond Quay and Bachelor's Walk, Abbey Street, Henry Street and Mary's Street are shown as complete, while to the east, Drogheda Street and Marlborough Street were in their infancy.

Stafford Street is now a forgotten area, running along the west side of the railed-in park that was once the graveyard of St Mary's Church. The design for this church is attributed to the noted architect Thomas Burgh. Named after the Cistercian Abbey of St Mary, it was built in the early 1700s to cater for the new population that was beginning to inhabit nearby Capel Street, Mary Street and Abbey Street. It is rectangular in shape with a short projecting chancel, and has a barrel-vaulted ceiling. A substantial timber gallery is continued around three sides and tall, fluted pilasters support the ceiling. The organ, built in about 1700 by the famous organ-maker Renatus Harris, is believed to be the oldest organ in Ireland but is now in a state of ruin. The richly carved wooden case of the organ is one of the most important features of the church.

By the 1980s St Mary's, like so many other city-centre Church of Ireland churches, had almost no parishioners and was forced to close. The church remained in use until 1986, when, for a short time, the Greek Orthodox Church used it for their services. The Representative Church Body, responsible for such Church property, decided to sell it in 1987. In a blatantly commercial move, the church was advertised as a mere site, and

Above top: Jervis Street now accommodates new apartments, shops, a shopping centre and the new Morrison Hotel.

Above: The Jervis Street Shopping Centre, which opened in 1996, covers the old Jervis Street Hospital site.

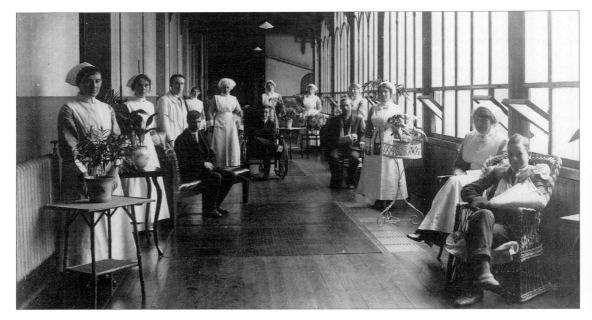

Above: Nursing staff and patients in the glazed verandah at the back of the Jervis Street Hospital.

the crypt was unceremoniously emptied of all its coffins and artefacts. The crumpled remains of fine lead coffins, many of them dating from the early eighteenth century and belonging to such noted people as the dukes of Ormonde, were flung on the back of a cart and taken away for scrap. This was the historic church, where the playwright Richard Brinsley Sheridan was baptised, along with Wolfe Tone and Seán O'Casey. It was also the wedding venue of Benjamin Guinness and Ann Lee, and it was associated with John Wesley's first visit to Dublin in 1747.

The church was initially acquired for commercial use, first as a shop selling paints and wallpaper and later as a bookshop. In the meantime, following the unfortunate removal of all the original box pews and the loss of the entire carved reredos, it was used for various exhibitions by a voluntary arts group. The church has recently changed hands again and the present proposal to turn it into a public house has resulted in raising the level of the floor by some three feet.

The Jervis Street Hospital, originally known as the Charitable Infirmary, began in a small way, occupying the site of no more than two houses in the middle of Jervis Street. The hospital was founded as early as 1718 and originally operated in Cork Street, later moving to Inns Quay and finally, in the late eighteenth century, to 14 Jervis Street, into the former townhouse of the Earl of Charlemont. The house was rebuilt in 1803 and remained in use until 1886 when the massive, red-brick-fronted Jervis Street Hospital was finally completed. Today only the façade of this once very large structure now survives; the original front hall with its arcade and grand staircase was swept away in the 1980s, along with the rest of the hospital. The hospital was noted for its lofty wards and elaborate cast-iron veranda, where patients could sit out and enjoy the morning sun or the fresh air.

Unfortunately, several eighteenth-century houses adjoining the hospital on Jervis Street were also demolished in the 1980s.

The Jervis Street Hospital, occupying a site of over two and a half acres, was sold in 1988. The Jervis Street Shopping Centre, with its grand arched entrance and copper dome, its double height ground floor and glass-domed centrepiece, was built in its place. The façades of two Victorian premises were also incorporated into the new shopping centre. One of them carries the initials 'TB' in terracotta and was no doubt a branch of Todd Burns. The centre was opened in 1996, and is bounded by Mary Street, Jervis Street and Abbey Street. A massive car park with space for 750 cars was also incorporated into the development. It is topped by a red-brick tower with the name Jervis emblazoned on it. What would Sir Humphrey Jervis, who lived three hundred years ago, have thought?

There are not many streets that have been so comprehensively cleared of their houses as Jervis Street and Stafford Street, which ran parallel to each other on either side of St Mary's Church. A photograph taken by the Dangerous Buildings' Section of Dublin Corporation shows an intact stretch of Jervis Street, with the former Simpson's Hospital (later Williams and Woods) closing the vista on Great Britain Street (now Parnell Street).

While the original concern of the Dangerous Buildings' Section of the corporation was the safety of citizens and the prevention of injury from falling masonry from neglected buildings, it would appear that they often undertook their work with unnecessary zeal. Undoubtedly there were many dangerous buildings in the city and some which had seen no maintenance for decades did collapse, sometimes tragically with the loss of life. However, photographic records of buildings subsequently demolished showed that slight movement in the front wall of a building or loose parapet stones were enough to condemn a building or possibly a whole street. From the 1960s onwards, a policy of demolish rather than repair seemed to operate, and as a result large chunks of the city, both north and south of the river, were literally erased, eradicating all sense of place. The demolitions were fuelled by grandiose road-widening schemes, which required many acres of land sometimes occupied by such old houses.

People will still say that conservationists are wrong in their desire to preserve everything that is old and that we must demolish to make way for buildings of our own time. However, it must be said that in Ireland there has never been the slightest danger of preserving everything that is old. In fact, we are only now, very belatedly, beginning to preserve *anything* that is old. Had we begun the process of historic building preservation earlier, we could have

Below: Jervis Street Hospital, showing the chapel (right) and the park, which was originally the graveyard of St Mary's Church.

been more discerning and ensured that the best of our streetscape survived and that dangerous buildings and architectural rubbish were indeed replaced. I have never yet met anybody concerned with historic building preservation who is against the erection of new buildings *per se* – their concerns relate more to what may be lost, and the location and appearance of any new replacement building itself.

Of the many city houses that once occupied the block bounded by Mary Street, Jervis Street and Abbey Street almost no trace now remains. The main entrance to the shopping centre was once occupied by the large, eighteenth-century Langford House, but most of the buildings in this block were already cleared away by the nineteenth-century expansion of Jervis Street Hospital.

Above: The late nineteenth-century billhead of Todd Burns & Co., showing the large corner premises now occupied by Penney's in Mary Street.

While Henry Street managed to maintain its position as a major shopping district in the north city, the western area including Mary Street and Capel Street had remained somewhat in the doldrums during the 1980s. The decision to build a major shopping centre in this area was seen by many as an act of faith in the north city centre and, though it has imported more English chain stores into Dublin, it cannot be denied that it has given the whole area a lift. The centre is connected, via Marks and Spencer's, to Liffey Street and another entrance is provided at the Jervis Street and Abbey Street junction to cater for pedestrians coming from the south city across the new Millennium Bridge – and in the future for those travelling on the Luas rail system, which is planned to come down Abbey Street.

Unfortunately, a fine pub which stood on the corner of Mary's Street and Jervis Street was also demolished in recent times. Last known as Keating's, it had been in use as a public house since at least 1850.

The streetscape of Mary Street is dominated by the great green copper dome which was erected for Todd Burns, now Penney's. The large, red-brick building is enlivened by ornamental panels and urns in yellow terracotta. The date 1902 appears on a copper weather vane above the cupula that stands on top of the great Baroque dome.

Mary Street, Liffey Street and Henry Street are today crowded with shops and boutiques selling clothes of every description. Mary Street is comprised of a great mix of buildings and commercial activity, and apart from clothes, shops selling household goods, hardware and furniture seem to predominate. There is great competition among the many shops and it is an area where the shrewd shopper can get great value. Unfortunately, there are very few if any of the old nineteenth-century shopfronts surviving in this district. Where it was first pedestrianised the street was paved with reddish-coloured bricks, which soon became drab and grubby. The entirety of Henry Street and Mary Street have recently been repaved in granite. In the evening, when the shops are closed up and the street is almost empty, the long vista to the east is closed by the elegant Italianate tower of Connolly Station.

Henrietta Street

Henrietta Street, which is one of eighteenth-century Dublin's most remarkable streets, lies a short distance from the top of Capel Street. When the street was described as 'Dublin's Street of Palaces', it was a fair description of this short cul-de-sac, which contains some of the earliest, largest and grandest houses built in the city. It was Luke Gardiner who, in the 1720s, laid out this enclave of palatial houses, which was connected to Bolton Street, but in the early eighteenth century lay some considerable distance from the heart of the city.

Most of the present houseowners in the street, some of whom are resident there, acquired the properties during the 1970s and have endeavoured since that time to repair and restore them.

One of the most notorious slum landlords of the late nineteenth century, Alderman Michael Meade, a successful building contractor and a member of Dublin Corporation, was responsible for stripping out many original features, such as carved woodwork and mantelpieces, and then dividing up the interiors to be let as tenements. Two of these houses belong to the Underwood family, who in the 1960s and 1970s acquired large numbers of eighteenth-century houses throughout the city.

Number 15 is owned by Dublin Corporation and leased to Na Píobairí Uilleann, the Piper's Club. It has been substantially renovated, but over half of the house had already been demolished in the 1950s when it was deemed to be in a dangerous condition. Number 13, the home of Michael and Aileen Casey, has frequently been photographed in colour magazines and used in films on account of its remarkable interiors. The majestic proportions of the interior, along with its boldly modelled plaster cornices and a sense of crumbling antiquity, give the house a unique quality – one which the Casey family have been careful to preserve. The original features of the building are being slowly stitched back, including a painstakingly accurate replica of the original staircase, which had been completely removed.

Ian Lumley, the owner of number 12, has carried out major structural repairs to the front and back walls of his house, which was once the Earl of Shannon's townhouse. The rooms of number 12, which are also of gigantic proportions, were considerably altered in the later eighteenth century when the present incredibly tall windows were inserted at first-floor level.

Above: The Casey family, outside number 13 Henrietta Street.

Below: The stone doorcase of number 9 Henrietta Street has a crisp, sculptural quality.

Above: A nineteenth-century engraving, showing the Kings Inns at the top of the Henrietta Street cul-de-sac.

Below: A furnished room in number 14 Henrietta Street. The scale and proportion of the rooms in the houses of Henrietta Street are among the largest in Dublin.

Uinseann MacEoin, who has campaigned to protect Dublin's historic buildings since the 1950s, acquired numbers 5, 6 and 7 as rent-controlled tenements. The mews or stables of these houses are used, appropriately enough, for the horses that draw the tourist carriages in St Stephen's Green and by the workshops of Advance Joinery, who have done much to assist in the restoration of old buildings by producing accurate replica windows, doors and other architectural features.

In some cases, major repairs to roofs and walls of these houses are still required. Some of the houses in Henrietta Street have received small grants from the Irish Georgian Society and Dublin Corporation, but the scale of the work that would be required to achieve their full restoration would call for a very large financial commitment.

The Bradogue River can be heard rushing beneath the manholes near the stable lane at the bottom the street.

The convent building of the French Sisters of Charity, occupying numbers 8–10, is now partly used as a crèche and training centre. Number 10 was Luke Gardiner's own house, but its original entrance disappeared when it was joined with numbers 8 and 9. Number 9 is the most outstanding house in architectural terms, and is probably the best preserved house in the street. The remaining nine houses are in various states of repair, most of them having been severely abused since they were turned into tenements in the late nineteenth century.

The Kings Inns, along with its library and the office of the registrar, occupies further buildings at the head of Henrietta Street. The Inns was built in 1804 to the designs of James Gandon, while the library was erected on the site of an early eighteenth-century house, the residence of a former archbishop of Dublin. It has often been observed that the location of the Kings Inns is somewhat strange, with the park on one side and the cul-de-sac of Henrietta Street on the other. The interior, with its ceremonial dining hall, is very noble and still retains its original furniture.

CHAPTER SIXTEEN

Abbey Street
and the North Quays

bbey Street, which runs parallel to the north bank of the River Liffey, extends eastwards from the site of the original St Mary's Abbey all the way to the present Custom House. It is divided into three sections: Upper Abbey Street, which begins at Capel Street and was known in the eighteenth century as Little Abbey Street; Middle Abbey Street, which continues east as far as O'Connell Street and was called Great Abbey Street in the eighteenth century; and Lower Abbey Street, which runs from O'Connell Street as far as Beresford Place at the back of the Custom House.

Most of Abbey Street and all of the present O'Connell Street had originally belonged to the Earl of Drogheda, who, in 1729, sold out his interest to the Right Honourable Brabazon Lord Duncannon and Luke Gardiner for the sum of £16,000. In 1730 Luke Gardiner bought Duncannon out for £21,230, and thus came into possession of most of the land and property of Abbey Street.

The earliest leases for houses to be built on Abbey Street seem to date from the 1720s. The records of the Wide Streets Commissioners state that Adam Fleming, a carpenter, built 69 Abbey Street. The site was at that time described as being 'on the south side of the strand leading from Dublin to Clontarf'. Sure enough, early maps show that Abbey Street did indeed eventually lead out along the Liffey by the strand to Clontarf – Strand Street took its name from its proximity to the shore or strand of the River Liffey. Records show that another early house was built in 1728 by another carpenter, named Samuel Allison.

Ever since the eighteenth century, all of Abbey Street was a hive of commercial activity. In 1806 we find paper manufacturers, delf (or

Above top: A carved Georgian doorcase at number 55 Middle Abbey Street.

Above: Rocque's map (1756) shows the convergence of Abbey Street, the Lotts and Bachelor's Walk before the creation of Sackville Street and Carlisle Bridge.

'delph') sellers, booksellers, printers and stationers, haberdashers, corn chandlers, coopers, apothecaries, brush-makers, gunmakers, several cabinetmakers and upholsterers, a whip-maker, a tallow chandler, engravers, brass manufacturers and iron merchants. There were also silk dyers, bakers and cutlers.

The creation of Sackville (now O'Connell) Street in the early eighteenth century dramatically changed the streetscape. It necessitated the purchase and demolition of at least eight Abbey Street houses; records show that James Sullivan, a wine cooper at number 72, and John Jones, a baker at number 71, sought compensation from the Wide Streets Commissioners.

Francis Booker, the noted maker of mirrors, acquired the lease of a house in Abbey Street as early as 1728. It would appear that the house, which Booker had sublet to a confectioner named Teresa Lindimire, was eventually demolished to make way for the newly widened Sackville Street. Unfortunately, none of these very early houses survive on Abbey Street today, although a few of mid-eighteenth-century date may still be seen in Middle and Upper Abbey Street.

Middle Abbey Street was always the more important part of this thoroughfare and had a greater number of good houses, many of which were sacrificed during the making of Sackville Street and the realignment of Abbey Street by the Wide Streets Commissioners.

Also lost in the creation of the new Sackville Street was an old watch-house, which stood just to the east of the present O'Connell Street. This had to be demolished to make way for the realignment of Abbey Street. The watch-house stood at a point of convergence of Abbey Street and another small street known as 'the Lotts', part of which still survives behind Bachelor's Walk. Watch-houses were the property of the various parishes in which they lay. Their operation, which amounted to a kind of twenty-four-hour policing of the city, was also the responsibility of the parish. The Abbey Street watch-house belonged to the churchwardens of the parish of St Thomas. In their claim for compensation they stated that the watch-house had been erected in about 1758 at a cost of £70 or £80. It is a great pity that none of the many original watch-houses in Dublin have survived.

On the north side of Abbey Street the Wide Streets Commissioners were obliged to buy five

Below: These two remaining eighteenth-century houses in Middle Abbey Street are among the very few remnants of the original Abbey Street.

Below bottom: Michael Butler's antique furniture warehouse flourished from the 1800s onwards at number 127 Upper Abbey Street.

Left: Butler's furniture-making and repairing workshop in Abbey Street.

Below: A late eighteenth-century map prepared for the Wide Streets Commissioners, showing the two circular furnaces of a large glassworks in Lower Abbey Street, backing onto the grounds of Tyrone House.

large houses, which they demolished. A large glasshouse, situated close to the Liffey quays, was also acquired by the Wide Streets Commissioners for the new Sackville Street. In 1784 a valuation for the three glasshouses on the site came to £16,140, and other buildings which were necessary for carrying on the flint glass manufactory were valued at £7,127. These glasshouses belonged to the Bottle House Company and the Window Glass Company of Abbey Street. These glasshouses, and others situated off Marlborough Street and near the North Wall, were presumably located near the strand so that they could obtain the fine sand required for glass-making. Another famous works, known as Chebsey's Glass House, was situated not far off at Ballybough, and had the distinction of making one of the largest glass chandeliers to survive in Dublin today – the great chandelier that still hangs in the House of Lords in College Green.

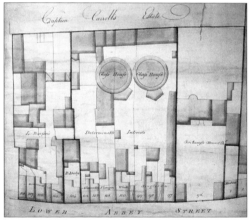

After the building of the new Custom House and Carlisle Bridge in the 1790s, Abbey Street, as it ran eastwards veered toward the river, was straightened and whole blocks of new buildings were erected. Lower Abbey Street and Eden Quay were laid out in a regular and uniform manner with plots of equal size for house building.

Rocque's map of 1756 shows that Abbey Street did not originally continue all the way to the river; it was blocked by the existence of the iron yards and 'the Iron Key' (or quay). To the east of the Iron Key were a number of timberyards, which are also shown on Rocque's map, and these fronted directly onto the Liffey.

Union Lane, a small lane beside the iron yards, gave access from Abbey Street to a set of small steps from which a ferry plied across the river,

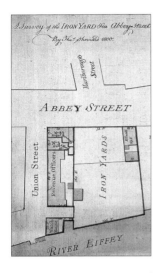

Above: A Wide Streets
Commissioners' map from
1800, showing the proximity
of Abbey Street to the River
Liffey before its realignment
(note the Ferry steps beside
the watch-house).
Below: This fine stone building,
the entrance and foyer of the
Abbey Theatre, was originally
designed a Meath Street
Savings Bank branch. It now
awaits reconstruction.

arriving at a point almost opposite Hawkins Street. The Revenue Offices
were located between the lane and the iron yards and were adjacent to the
watch-house on the river. This entire area, including another old
watch-house on the river front, was swept away when Eden Quay was created, shortly after 1800.

The new Eden Quay and the straightened-out Abbey Street were both
planned in the late 1790s, following the completion of the Custom House,
and were designed to enhance both the access to and the appearance of
that important new building.

Lower and Middle Abbey Street

If Abbey Street is today known for anything it is for the Abbey Theatre,
which stands at the corner of Abbey Street and Marlborough Street and
was originally entered through an old cut-stone building that once housed
the Mechanics Institute. Opened in 1904, the theatre hosted some of the
most celebrated plays in the English-speaking world. Ireland's fame in
terms of its playwrights, actors and performances largely emanated from
this building. An arched entrance led to a grand staircase, which in turn
gave access to the gallery of the intimate theatre.

In a fire on 17 July 1951, the theatre's auditorium and stage were
destroyed, leaving only the entrance hall and booking offices. The old
paintings which hang in the present Abbey Theatre were rescued from the
fire, and the vestibule and entrance hall remained in use as a booking office
for the Queen's Theatre (used by the Abbey Players) until 1961 when their
demolition was finally ordered. The cut-stone building, which incorporated the vestibule, was about to be sent to the dump when Daithí Hanley,
the then Dublin City Architect, stepped in and had the salvaged stones
removed to his garden in Dalkey. Even the old canopy above the theatre
entrance survives here, along with the original
railings and all the old billboards. That was nearly
forty years ago; today this historic building still
lies carefully stacked under the trees in his
garden overlooking Killiney Bay. These stones,
which make up the façade of the original Abbey
Theatre, speak of great names – Yeats, Lady
Gregory, Moore, O'Casey and Synge. They await
the moment when they will be re-erected in an
appropriate site somewhere in the centre of
Dublin. The most obvious way to give the various
salvaged elements from the theatre a new role in
the cultural life of the city would be to re-erect
them as part of a National Theatre Museum, perhaps close to the Abbey Theatre itself.

There was, and still is, much dissatisfaction
with the modern Abbey Theatre, which was built
in the 1960s. Even today there is talk of the

government sponsoring the complete rebuilding of a new Abbey Theatre, but as yet no plans have been made.

When the new Abbey Street Lower was formed, an 1828 map of the Wide Streets Commissioners shows Mulvany's Glass House, a shop situated at the new junction with Marlborough Street.

Several significant new public buildings appeared on Lower Abbey Street in the early nineteenth century, including the new Royal Hibernian Academy, which stood next door to the site of the present Wynn's Hotel, a new Savings Bank and, on the north side of the street, no less than three chapels. These were the Union Chapel, the Methodist Chapel and the Baptist Chapel. The large brick-fronted Metropolitan Hall, which became the headquarters of the YMCA in Dublin, was also erected on the north side of the street in about 1830. Apart from the Savings Bank, all of these buildings were demolished in the 1980s by Irish Life. The demolition included most of the buildings at the corner of Marlborough Street and Abbey Street, which had been built at the instigation of the Wide Streets Commissioners. Still surviving is the corner premises of TP Cummins and Sons, suppliers of paints and plumbing. The Savings Bank on the north side of Lower Abbey Street is a modest building erected in 1839 to the designs of Isaac Farrell. It is a neat classical-style building and is still in use by the Trustee Savings Bank.

The large, red-brick-fronted Dublin Metropolitan Hall was erected during the 1830s on the north side of Lower Abbey Street as a music hall,

Above top: The attractive Savings Bank in Lower Abbey Street dates from 1839, and is still in use.

Above: A billhead (1837) from Charles Mulvany's glassworks.

Below: Lower Abbey Street in 1981, prior to the removal of all buildings except Cummins on the corner with Marlborough Street.

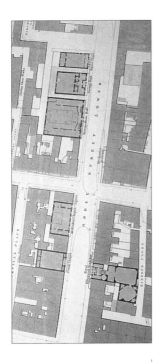

Above: An Ordnance Survey map (1866) of Lower Abbey Street, showing the Royal Hibernian Academy (bottom right) and the various non-conformist chapels, Metropolitan Hall and the Savings Bank (on the left side of the street).

Below: An architectural drawing (c.1823), showing the elevations of the new Royal Hibernian Academy and adjoining houses.

and was one of the largest buildings on Lower Abbey Street at that time. The music hall was sold in 1877, and following its demolition a new structure, known as the Metropolitan Christian Union Buildings, was erected in its place. The purpose of the new building, which was sponsored by various Protestant denominations, including Methodist, Presbyterian and Quaker, was to promote 'Evangelistic work of an undenominational character' and to provide facilities for the 'spiritual, intellectual and physical wants of the young men in the city of Dublin'. The new building was, in effect, the headquarters for the Young Men's Christian Association (YMCA), but had other objectives as well, including 'religious work amongst the sailors in the Port of Dublin'. In the early nineteenth century, various charitable religious bodies occupied the building, and 'penny dinners' were served in the basement. The main hall with its large gallery was an impressive space, but this functional, although rather dull, red-brick building was eventually demolished in 1982.

The original Methodist Chapel, with its six arched windows facing Abbey Street, was rebuilt in 1901 to form the building now occupied by the Dublin Central Mission, another solid but somewhat uninspired structure with a nineteenth-century, red-brick façade. When the early nineteenth-century church was rebuilt, the old galleries were converted into a smaller chapel. While the façade disguises the fact that a church lies behind, its modest appearance reflects the work of the Dublin Central Mission, which helps people on the streets of the city.

Further eastwards, a building belonging to the Salvation Army stands out alone against the backdrop of Irish Life's office blocks. Across the street once stood the offices of Dunlop House, a large, four-storey building with arched windows, which was later to become the headquarters of Voluntary Health Insurance. Beside it stands the small Scots Church, built in 1867 and still in use today. This Presbyterian church incorporated the congregation of the Ormond Quay Presbyterian Church, which closed in 1938.

The Royal Hibernian Academy (RHA), founded in 1823, erected a fine stone-fronted headquarters the following year. It was designed by the architect Francis Johnson, the Academy's first president, who very generously bore the cost of its construction. The Academy building incorporated offices to the front and three exhibition galleries to the rear. The three purpose-built galleries were lit from above and the paintings

were hung one above the other right up the walls. An octagonal room was used as a sculpture gallery. On either side of the recessed entrance with its Doric columns were the carved heads of three great Renaissance artists: Palladio, representing architecture; Michelangelo, as sculpture; and Raphael, as painting.

The Academy's headquarters were completely destroyed by fire in the bombardment of Dublin during the Easter Rising of 1916. The entire annual exhibition of paintings and sculpture was lost; an approximate estimate of the catalogued values of the exhibits exceeded £10,000. The treasurer of the Academy, a Mr JM Kavanagh, escaped from the burning building with the chain of office and the charter under his arm. Following the fire, the upper portion of the façade of the Royal Hibernian Academy was dismantled. It was re-erected in 1929 and may now be seen above the offices of CIÉ Travel on Abbey Street.

The original Wynn's Commercial and Family Hotel was a nineteenth-century establishment, which occupied 35–37 Lower Abbey Street, adjoining the RHA. The hotel was located at a convenient distance from the packets or ships for Liverpool and Holyhead and catered particularly for commercial travellers. Wynn's Hotel, like so many other buildings in the area, was burnt out in 1916.

On the eastern side of the Academy, at 84 Lower Abbey Street, there once stood an elegant Georgian house, which had been for many years the offices of the famous magazine, *The Irish Builder.*

Middle Abbey Street developed a reputation for ironmongers, brass and iron founders, and among the most noted businesses were those of Thomas Henshaw & Company and W Curtis & Sons, brass founders. Henshaw's were located at 81 Middle Abbey Street and had an ironworks on the River Dodder at Clonskeagh. They specialised in the manufacture of tools, including spades, shovels and all manner of garden and farm implements.

The wholesale brass foundry at 99 Middle Abbey Street originated in the 1820s and fifty years later was employing over 150 men in manufacturing taps and cocks for breweries, valves, engine fittings, bikes for the fire

Above: The interior of the Royal Hibernian Academy (RHA), with two of the exhibition galleries that were destroyed in 1916.

Below: Middle Abbey Street after the bombardment, showing the site of the present Easons and Independent Newspapers. Abbey Street was a popular address for the offices of newspapers and publishers since the nineteenth century, which included *The Nation* and Alexander Thom & Co.

Above: WH Smith's, the bookseller and newsagent at 85 and 86 Middle Abbey Street, were taken over by Charles Eason during the 1880s.

Below: Abbey Street was noted for its many wine merchants. The eighteenth-century premises of Turbett's (now restored) are now used as the offices of the radio station Today FM.

brigade, copper and brass wire and, in the 1880s, various materials required for fitting houses with electric bells.

The noted builders' providers Brooks Thomas & Company also originated in Middle Abbey Street where, in the 1850s, we find Maurice Brooks at numbers 90 and 91, selling plate glass, sheet glass and crown window glass, along with paper hangings, ironmongery, white lead and paints. Brooks later moved to Lower Abbey Street and Sackville Place, where they established a sawmill and continued to enlarge their range of building products.

Middle Abbey Street was once famous for the Adelphi Cinema, first opened to the public in 1939. The Adelphi replaced a dance hall, restaurant and billiard room which had been opened in 1928, under the name of the Plaza, but it burned down after some ten years in existence.

Since the early nineteenth century, Liffey Street Upper and Lower was noted for its second-hand dealers. Out of some seventy registered dealers in the two streets, in the 1850s, there were over forty furniture brokers and a few basket-makers, cabinetmakers and bottle dealers. Today Liffey Street connects the quays with Mary Street and Henry Street but in the time of John Rocque, Upper Liffey Street continued north towards Parnell Street, passing a widows' almshouse and parish school. This section of Liffey Street was later renamed Denmark Street, but the thoroughfare completely vanished with the building of the ILAC Centre in the 1970s.

In the 1980s all that was left of Lower Liffey Street were the tattered remains of a few ancient antique shops, such as Cohen's. The transformation of the street over the last ten years from a collection of old, abandoned shopfronts and derelict sites into a thriving and busy shopping street is one of the most remarkable examples of Dublin's recent resurgence.

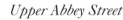

Upper Abbey Street

There is now little of interest in Upper Abbey Street except for a few surviving Georgian houses, as much of it has now become a service area or back-lands to the Jervis Street Shopping Centre, while other parts are currently being redeveloped.

The premises of Turbett's, the wine merchants, at 123–125 Upper Abbey Street are the last remaining mid-eighteenth-century Georgian houses on the street. Robert Turbett & Sons acquired the premises in 1895, taking over from a previous wine merchant of French-Huguenot origin who went by the name of Bartholomew M

Tabuteau. In 1850 we find Mr Tabuteau at 124 Upper Abbey Street, a wine merchant with a residence at 11 Fitzwilliam Place. Even in the 1980s, Turbett's offices had a Dickensian quality and were fitted out with mahogany counters and old-style cabinets. The wine cellars, stores and bottling department were originally located to the rear of the building and large cellars ran out beneath one of the houses. Following a short period of use during the 1980s by Sotheby's, the fine art auctioneers, it was proposed to demolish the houses as part of the planned Jervis Street Shopping Centre complex. Through the intervention of the Dublin Civic Trust the owners were persuaded to restore the houses instead and this was done to a very high standard, providing elegant offices now occupied by Radio Ireland (Today FM).

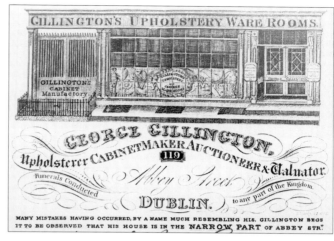

Since the late eighteenth century, the area of Upper Abbey Street, Stafford Street and Mary Street was particularly popular with cabinetmakers and upholsters. A noted maker of furniture was George Gillington, whose trade card illustrates his beautiful Georgian-style premises at 119 Abbey Street. The strong tradition of carvers, gilders, cabinetmakers and upholsterers working in Upper Abbey Street lived on until the twentieth century. In 1850 there were four carvers and gilders in this street – D Hulbert, Thomas Marshall, William Telford and Valentine Hoban. There were also many upholsters, woodturners, cabinetmakers and one chair-maker by the name of P Hicks, whom we shall discuss later. In nearby Stafford Street, Patrick Beakey carried on the business of cabinetmaker, upholsterer and auctioneer in no less than six adjoining houses. His neighbour, Williams & Company, who had inherited the business of Mack, Williams & Gibton, occupied two buildings at 42–43 Stafford Street. William Scott and Thomas Mason, who were also cabinetmakers and upholsterers, carried on their business in 47–49 Stafford Street.

Above: In the nineteenth century Upper Abbey Street was the focus of the furniture industry in Dublin.

Below: The impressive stucco-fronted Victorian premises of Patrick Beakey, on the corner of Stafford Street and Mary Street, is now used as offices.

The noted firm of William Hicks, cabinet and chair-maker, was located in Farrell's Court, a former stable lane on the north side of Upper Abbey Street, later built over by the Jervis Street Hospital. Hicks developed a reputation for high-quality pieces of furniture during the second half of the nineteenth century, and their replicas of original Georgian pieces are now much sought after.

Another important business in nineteenth-century Dublin was the construction of coaches, and in the 1880s we find Thomas Doyle's Abbey

Above: An early eighteenth-century trade label from a safe, sold by this Bachelor's Walk firm.

Below: The impressive façades of numbers 5, 6 and 7 Bachelor's Walk.

Carriage Works located at 30 Upper Abbey Street. Doyle's showrooms illustrated a wide variety of vehicles, including family carriages, phaetons, wagonettes, covered cars, outside jaunting cars and cabs.

Bachelor's Walk

Bachelor's Walk lines the northern side of the River Liffey, adjacent to O'Connell Bridge, on the most prominent part of the quays. It has a long and interesting history, beginning in 1675 when the City of Dublin leased the riverbank or strand to Jonathan Amory. Amory made leases to various builders, including Sir Humphrey Jervis, and in 1764 we find references to a Jervis Quay, presumably part of Ormond Quay. Jonathan Amory's seventeenth-century lease from the Corporation included all of the land, which was in the possession of Lord Santry and is now part of Ormond Quay, between the wall of the Pill (a small inlet) and the water-mill 'lately built by Gilbert Mabbot'. Mabbot Street, which is shown on Rocque's map of 1756, can today be found off Talbot Street.

Construction of the houses on Bachelor's Walk began in the early 1700s. They were built overlooking the quayside where ships could be moored. They were four storeys over basement and many had handsome cut-stone doorcases. However, various developments over the centuries have deprived Bachelor's Walk of its early residences. Numbers 36–41 Bachelor's Walk disappeared when the Wide Streets Commissioners undertook the creation of Sackville Mall, today's O'Connell Street. In 1782 the Wide Streets Commissioners valued an old house at 39 Bachelor's Walk at £574, while two new houses built by a Mr Thwaite were considered to be worth £2,250.

The first thoughts of creating a new bridge on the site of O'Connell Bridge were alive in the 1770s. From a lease granted to the sculptor Simon Vierpyl in 1779, we learn that he was required to pay '£73 a year and £5 per annum advanced rent, in case of new bridge eastwards of Essex Bridge'. The sculptor occupied a house at 41 Bachelor's Walk and had a stone-cutting yard in the adjoining property. We also learn from the minutes of the Wide Streets Commissioners that Simon Vierpyl repaired the quay wall in about 1779 at a cost of £41. It would appear that he bought his house in 1768 and had a 'shew shop' there, which must have served as a showroom or gallery for his sculptures. His neighbour, who took over his yard at 40 Bachelor's Walk and was also displaced by the Wide Streets Commissioners, was the strangely named Dr Achmet Borumbadab, who had established 'the great cold baths' here in 1772. He must also have operated hot water baths as we discover that Robert West, who 'says he is a plaisterer', carried out the plastering for the baths, which contained twenty-one tunnels of arched brickwork and twenty-one grates.

Bachelor's Walk suffered persistent urban blight and dereliction in the 1970s and 1980s. In the late 1970s a block of five buildings was cleared at the corner of Liffey Street. Following this demolition, the site, which had once included the corner premises of McGrath, tea, coffee and sugar merchants, lay vacant for many years. Despite the continued efforts of An Taisce to highlight the fate of the buildings on the Liffey quays, and in particular those on Bachelor's Walk, many were demolished at this time. During the 1980s a company named Arlington Securities managed to acquire the entire Bachelor's Walk frontage, except for three separate properties.

At the time, particular attention had been drawn to the houses at 5, 6 and 7 Bachelor's Walk, which were one of the few remaining groups of early eighteenth-century merchant

houses on the quays that were left standing with their interiors intact. In the late eighteenth century we find two merchants, Ebenezer Colvill and William Geale, as residents of 6 and 7 Bachelor's Walk respectively. The Colvills were noted merchants who were to remain in Bachelor's Walk well into the nineteenth century. The hall of number 6 was divided from the stairs by fluted Ionic pilasters. In the late twentieth century structural problems had arisen in the back wall, but the rest of the building was in good condition. A large factory, which covered the former gardens and yard, was used as a printing works by the firm of John T Drought. In spite of voluminous correspondence with Dublin Corporation and frequent press coverage, the demolition of numbers 5 and 6, with their attractive panelled interiors and original carved staircases, was permitted in 1989.

Above: The remarkable entrance hall and staircase of number 7 Bachelor's Walk, before the theft of the staircase and subsequent reconstruction of the hall.

Below: The spacious panelled hall of number 6 Bachelor's Walk, demolished in 1989.

Number 7, the only house of this group to survive the 1980s, was eventually restored in the mid-1990s, but not before almost all of the original staircase and panelling had been stolen and proposals for its complete demolition had been promoted by various unprincipled developers. This disgraceful and wanton neglect, as recently as ten years ago, of what was probably the last and finest merchant house on the quays was merely indicative of an overwhelming lack of interest in the city's heritage and a blatant refusal to respect listed-building status under the Planning Acts.

It is to the credit of all concerned that 7 Bachelor's Walk was meticulously restored.

Above: The streetline of
Bachelor's Walk was
reconstructed in the 1990s.

Below: Brown's – one of the
many cabinetmakers and
auctioneers who once
occupied premises on
Bachelor's Walk.

Every detail of the house was carefully measured and accurately repro-
duced where necessary. The façade was returned to its original brick finish.
The restoration of number 7 was carried out by Zoe Developments, the
company who were responsible for erecting the apartments on the Liffey
Street/Bachelor's Walk block. The restoration was supervised by David
Kelly Architects, while the panelling and carving was executed by Breffni
Joinery. Photographs of the interior of the house with its beautiful carving
and elegant proportions speak for themselves.

Other quayside houses of eighteenth-century date, including various
auction rooms and house-furnishing establishments, had been demolished
by 1989. It was cases such as Bachelor's Walk that were eventually, and very
belatedly, to result in the government's introduction of new legislation to
protect the nation's architectural heritage, which has only just come into
force in the last year.

But it should be said that in the 1980s some imaginative proposals were
put forward for the development of the quays. As early as 1983, a group of
young architects organised by Valerie Mulvin and Niall McCullough proposed a series of interesting individual new buildings, which might infill
the gaps where buildings had disappeared on Bachelor's Walk. The
designs were contemporary but would have harmonised with the
older houses.

The rebuilding of Bachelor's Walk in the mid-1990s incorporated
three eighteenth-century houses and what was once a small CIÉ bus
station. There has been some criticism of the so-called Georgian-
style façades, with which the quay was fronted, when the new apartments were built, but it should be remembered that some horrific

designs for office blocks and shopping centres had previously been proposed, which would have produced monolithic buildings of glass and concrete slabs. The question may be asked: are these neo-Georgian façades any more or less whimsical or appropriate than a pastiche of a Mies van der Rohe building might be?

A lane which runs parallel to and behind Bachelor's Walk, known as the North Lotts, originally accommodated the stables and warehouses of both Upper Abbey Street and Bachelor's Walk. In the 1850s there were at least eight wine vaults and stores in the North Lotts, mostly serving businesses in Abbey Street. In the mid-nineteenth century, a large, bonded warehouse was constructed there. This three-gabled brick structure was built by one of the many wine and spirit merchants in Abbey Street.

Above: The shopfront of Sheeran's, the auctioneers, is still in situ on Bachelor's Walk.

Below: Bennett & Son was one of Dublin's leading auctioneers, and had their salerooms at numbers 5 and 6 Ormond Quay.

In the 1870s the lane accommodated: Butler & Scott's wine vault; the ale stores of William Cairns of Drogheda; Irvine King's wine merchants; Carson's bottle stores; Thomas Brennan's wine stores; Sir John Arnott's ale stores; Henry Crawford Sharman's wine merchants; Rambout & Sons stores; Barry and Norton & Company's stores; Gaynor's cork stores; the Foreign Wine Shippers' Association stores; Glass & Company's ale stores; the printing works of George Drought; Turbett's wine stores; and James Colvill's flour stores.

McGrath's bonded tea warehouse also stood on Lower Liffey Street, and the narrow but ornamental premises of this tea and coffee merchant faced onto Bachelor's Walk. The bonded warehouse was a handsome cut-stone building with red-brick window dressings. In more recent times, Liffey Street was noted for its antique dealers and hucksters. Number 31 Liffey Street was the premises of Israel Cohen's antique shop, whose dingy-looking exterior was deceptive and belied the great treasures held within. Only two storeys remained of this building in 1974.

Ormond Quay

Ormond Quay now presents one of the most intact ranges of eighteenth-century buildings along the River Liffey. There is considerable variety in the scale and type of houses, reflecting the various rebuildings and alterations at different times. The fact that there are houses fronting on to the quays at all is generally credited to James Butler, the first Duke of Ormonde, who in the late seventeenth century persuaded Sir Humphrey Jervis to lay out plots for buildings which would face the river across an intervening quayside or thoroughfare.

Various late eighteenth-century prints show that the quays, especially those no longer in use by ships – such as Inns Quay in front of the Four Courts and all of Ormond Quay – had stone parapets to protect citizens from falling into the river. The present quayside parapet, which runs continuously from Heuston Station to Butt Bridge, would appear to have been

Right: The Liffey in tranquil mood, during the construction of the Millennium Bridge at Ormond Quay. Some original houses and Morrison's Hotel can be seen on the left.

Below: A seventeenth-century oak staircase with its broad handrail and 'ramp' construction. It was salvaged from number 30 Lower Ormond Quay.

erected in the middle of the nineteenth century by the Dublin Port and Docks Board. This fine stone wall with its curved top is only broken at the Four Courts where the parapet was replaced with a classical balustrade, which provides an elegant addition to Gandon's great masterpiece.

The area was famous for many years for its auctioneers, antique shops and book dealers. For instance, Bennett & Son Auctioneers had specially constructed salerooms, one of which is now the Bridge Art Gallery, to the rear of 6 Upper Ormond Quay, while Tormey's and Lawlor Briscoe's operated on Lower Ormond Quay. The well-known Butler's antique shop occupied 28 Lower Ormond Quay for much of the twentieth century. The tradition is still kept alive there by the weekly auctions held by Town & Country.

The stealthy destruction of the quays occurred on a piecemeal basis throughout the 1970s and 1980s. Demolition on the quays in the 1980s brought about the discovery of many remarkable interiors. For instance, behind the late-Georgian façade of 30 Ormond Quay Lower, a former solicitor's premises, lay an intact seventeenth-century staircase, with its original oak, barley-sugar balusters, wide handrail and panelling. This house, which was demolished in 1984, would almost certainly have dated from the time of the first building developments on Sir Humphrey Jervis's new estates. Fortunately, the staircase was salvaged.

A similar staircase was discovered in an adjoining house, 29 Lower Ormond Quay, which was bought by Patrick and Maura Shaffrey in 1990 and subsequently restored. In an act of faith, the Shaffreys later erected the first new apartments on Ormond Quay on the adjoining vacant sites. Other individuals, such as the Kenyon family, who operate an antiques business here, have also restored an eighteenth-century house on Ormond Quay. Their house and its neighbour have particularly fine cut-stone doorcases, with intricate carving on the undersides of the pediments. Number 6 Ormond Quay, restored by Michael Smith, was discovered to contain a staircase dating from 1686. The house was built by Sir William Doyne, secretary to the Privy Council.

The presence of trees along the Liffey would appear to be a twentieth-century addition, and one which is far more aesthetically pleasing than the ugly flagpoles which presently line the river. The flagpoles, which date from the late twentieth century, are representative of a time when it was thought that they would proclaim some symbol of the city's culture, while all of the buildings of the quays would be destroyed for the purposes of road widening.

Left: An ornamental urinal or *pissoir,* one of several erected along the quays in 1932 for the Eucharistic Congress. It was sold to a student for £10 in the early 1970s!

Below: The noble Four Courts building took ten years to construct and was completed by 1796. It replaced the old Law Courts, which stood beside Christ Church Cathedral.

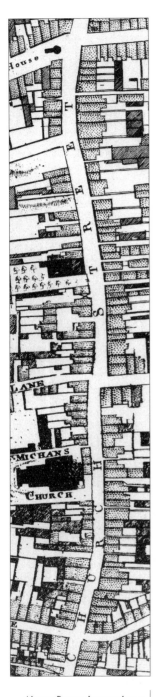

The Smithfield Area

Church Street

*C*hurch Street, which is now a very busy traffic route leading to the north Dublin suburbs of Phibsboro, Glasnevin and beyond, could be described as the oldest street north of the River Liffey. Speed's map of Dublin of 1610 shows that the bridge at the foot of Church Street was the only crossing on the River Liffey at that time. His map indicates a substantial group of buildings, called the Inns, standing on the grounds now occupied by the Four Courts. Further north is the ancient Church of St Michan, originally founded in the late eleventh century but largely rebuilt in the eighteenth century. A medieval tower is shown lying to the west of the church, and beyond that the open land of Ostman, or Oxmantowne.

Until quite recently, Church Street was a place of many industries, including iron foundries and engineering workshops. However, the last half of the twentieth century saw the gradual decline of all of these businesses and, more recently, the redevelopment of their old sites as office accommodation and apartment blocks. Hammond Lane iron foundry, Maguire & Patterson's match manufactory and Millar's the iron founders were among the last to go.

A collection of maps belonging to the Wide Streets Commissioners, and dating from the early 1800s, provides an interesting insight into the uses of the houses in Church Street. A group of some seven houses are shown adjoining St Michan's Church on the northern side, with extensive yards, sheds and stables to the rear. Another map shows the premises described as 'the late Tandy's Tavern' on the east side of Church Street, through which an arch gave access to a passage, where there lay a yard with extensive cow houses, stables and kitchen along with a catgut manufactory.

Tradesmen to be found in Church Street included Edward Kelly, a distiller; Patrick Darling, a cooper; James Elliot, a slater and slate merchant; and Field & Company, starch and bluestone manufacturers. There was also

Above: Rocque's map shows the narrow, residential nature of Church Street and the dominant position of St Michan's Church.

a selection of smaller businesses, including a cork cutter, a tallow chandler, a whip-maker, a grocer, an apothecary, a brush-maker, a tobacconist's and a rope-maker.

The nearby Pill Lane was also an important commercial district with similar trades. Here we find a button manufacturer, a hemp and sail cloth merchant, a tobacco and snuff manufacturer, a linen draper, a hosier, pin-makers and a rope-maker trading under the name of Eliza Gibson. Samuel Gatchell, an iron merchant, occupied premises at 87 Pill Lane. Fifty years later, Samuel Gatchell & Sons had moved into fine premises at 8–9 Mountrath Street, just adjoining the Four Courts. Here they manufactured beams, scales and weights, along with agricultural and ornamental gates. Gatchell's were one of the leading ironmongers in Dublin.

Above: Samuel Gatchell the ironmonger, whose fine premises in Mountrath Street are shown in this billhead of the 1850s.

Below: Church Street was once a narrow thoroughfare, which was lined with old houses from North King Street to the Liffey.

The Eagle Foundry, which stood opposite St Michan's Church, was operated throughout the nineteenth century by the Sheridan family. James Sheridan, a millwright and engineer, ran an iron, brass and bell foundry. In the late nineteenth century his son, Thomas Sheridan, proudly announced in an advertisement that they had made bells for many churches in Ireland and abroad. Bells had been supplied to places as far afield as Calcutta and Granada. At home, large signal bells were produced for the Dublin Ballast Board, for lighthouses, for the Pro-Cathedral in Marlborough Street and for St Audoen's in High Street. Earlier in the century, James Sheridan's advertisement 'beggs to inform Millers, millwrights, engineers, distillers, brewers, builders, and manufacturers in general, that he can supply, on the shortest notice, mill and other machinery suited to their use'. The Eagle Foundry also supplied cast-iron columns, kilns, boilers, weighing machines, ploughshares, anvils, pig troughs, kitchen ranges, cottage windows, pumps, gates, wheelbarrows and bedsteads. James Sheridan's foundry occupied premises at 162–164 Church Street.

Perhaps because of its age and busy commercial life, Church Street never had pretensions to being a grand residential district. It was instead the focus of St Michan's Parish, with the ancient church at its heart. St Michan's is well known for the mummified remains of bodies, which may be seen in their coffins in the vaults beneath the church. It is said that the salt in the limestone of the vault absorbs all

Above: Three of the famous mummified bodies in the crypt of St Michan's Church.

Below: A pre-1881 photograph, showing the narrow and congested Church Street with the Capuchin chapel on the left.

Below bottom: The interior of the 1796 Capuchin chapel.

moisture in the air and prevents the complete decay of the bodies. The Sheares brothers, who were implicated in the 1798 rebellion along with Oliver Bond, are among those buried in the vaults of St Michan's Church.

With the assistance of funding from the Department of the Environment, the church has recently undergone major renovations. Like most Protestant churches of this period, St Michan's has a gallery on three sides. The carving on the front of the gallery beneath the organ, representing musical instruments, is of outstanding quality. An original early eighteenth-century staircase leading from the tower to the gallery remains unaltered.

Rocque's map shows St Michan's Church with its long graveyard running back to Bow Lane. Church Street was then a largely residential district comprising of many small houses. Rocque also indicates a small, rectangular church further up the street. This was the Chapel of the Capuchin Fathers who settled here in the early eighteenth century. This chapel was rebuilt in 1796 as a simple rectangular structure, with two Gothic windows facing onto Church Street. In the great burst of Catholic church building in the 1860s, the chapel was replaced by a new and splendid Gothic-style church. The new church was designed by JJ McCarthy and was completed in 1881. The Gothic-style east front faces across Church Street to Father Matthew Square, a pleasant residential district. The interior, with its tall Gothic apse behind the altar, is impressive.

In the context of today's Church Street, it is difficult to imagine what it would have looked like in the 1860s, with its three- and four-storey Georgian houses facing across a narrow and busy street. The Capuchin order, whose monastery had been constructed to the rear of the church, erected a temperance hall on the corner of Church Street and the newly created Nicholas Avenue in 1890.

The Father Matthew Hall, as it became known, was intensively used by the local community, especially for events of a musical or dramatic nature. The hall was built by Joseph Kelly & Sons, the builders' providers of Thomas Street, and cost about £3,000. It was designed by Walter G Doolin, and was greatly embellished in 1909 when an elaborate proscenium arch, stage and gallery were added. The arch was ornamented with the most extraordinary Celtic revival plasterwork – the entire wall surrounding the stage was decorated with plaster panels of Celtic interlace, inspired by early Irish art such as might be found in the Book of Kells. The panels incorporate animals and shields bearing the emblems of the four provinces of Ireland. In the centre, over the proscenium arch, is a bust of Father Matthew, the great humanitarian who did so much to encourage temperance and fight alcoholism in Ireland. Two matching panels on either side of the stage have large reliefs figuring a round tower, an Irish wolfhound and a harp, set against a rising sun. The *pièce de résistance* is a pair of life-size figures, representing drama and music, which sit on pedestals in Irish Romanesque arches on either side of the stage. The entire ensemble is painted in white and gold and set off by a Wedgwood blue background. The plasterwork was carried out by the firm of John Ryan of Upper Abbey Street, to the designs of Mr A Scott of O'Connell Street, who almost certainly designed similar proscenium arch decorations in the Queen's Theatre in Pearse Street.

Left: One of the life-sized figures, representing Music, from the remarkable proscenium arch in the Father Matthew Hall.

Below: Sheridan's iron and brass foundry in Church Street produced metalwork of every kind, including church bells. The tower of St Michan's Church may be seen in the picture of their works.

A separate hall was allocated to girls and women and here a band, a debating society and an athletics club were formed. The fate of this building remains in some doubt, as it has lain empty for some time and the Capuchin order has decided to sell it. The fact that this unique interior was not recorded as a protected structure highlights the shortfall that exists in the the recording and listing of such structures in Dublin. However, once they became aware of the importance of the Father Matthew Hall, Dublin Corporation made provisions for its protection.

In the overall context of the renewal of this part of Dublin, designated the HARP (Historic Area Rejuvenation Project), the retention of such key buildings must be of prime consideration. It is especially significant given the lack of buildings with a cultural or community use in the area. The fate of important public buildings has been further threatened by the closure of St Paul's Church on Arran Quay, which now lies vacant.

Smithfield

Within the last year, the provision of a glazed observatory at the top of the old chimney of Jameson's Distillery in Smithfield has created the opportunity to get a bird's eye view of the square and the surrounding area. This inventive idea, along with the dramatic new steel mast with their braziers and sails, which illuminate the square at night, has certainly put Smithfield

Right: The monthly Smithfield horse fair now takes place against the backdrop of Smithfield's dramatic steel masts.

Below: An early nineteenth-century weight master's docket from Smithfield, an official record of the weight of a cart's load.

Below bottom: The emblem of Carton's of Smithfield.

back on the map. However, it is unfortunate that all of the old houses that once ranged around the sides of Smithfield have been allowed to go, including some which dated from the seventeenth century. The challenge now facing Smithfield is how to recreate the space of the old market that used to exist here by the erection of new buildings on the west side.

Smithfield is a long, rectangular space, first laid out in the 1660s in the hope of attracting fashionable residences, only some of which were ever built. It was hoped that Oxmantown Green, of which Smithfield was a part in the seventeenth century, would attract the same sort of fashionable residences as had St Stephen's Green, in the south of the city. The Duke of Ormonde, who acquired a site here but did not build a house, commented in 1666 that the construction of new houses at Smithfield was impeding the exercising of his majesty's horses and troops, who had used it freely when it had been waste ground.

In a historical report for Dublin Corporation in 1995, Gráinne Doran brought together much information about Smithfield. The city cattle market had been moved from the south city to Oxmantown Green in 1541. The area, which developed a reputation for the sale of hay, straw, pigs, sheep and cattle, was also 'the scene of extensive fairs'. By 1664 parts of Queen Street and a new market area were already laid out and built on and the cattle market was well established. At about this time a petition was made to the City of Dublin, calling for Oxmantown Green to 'be wholie kept for the use of the citizens and others to walke and take the open air, by reason cittie is at this present growing very populate'. The year 1665 is the date given by Gilbert for when the City made provision for a marketplace in Oxmantown Green. The name Smithfield was then adopted, probably after the London cattle market of the same name.

At this time, the land at Oxmantown Green had been divided into about ninety-six plots, and building leases were then granted. Number 39 Smithfield, which contained a seventeenth-century staircase, remained standing until the 1990s. The authenticity of this staircase is reflected in the heavy joinery and the barley-sugar balusters. Among the early tenants of Smithfield was George Putland, whose descendants were later to build fine houses in Mount Street and in Bray, County Wicklow.

By 1666 it had been decided that trees should be planted in the vicinity of Oxmantown Green, and that a stone wall should be erected to stop cattle straying into the nearby bowling green. From Gilbert's *Calendar of Ancient Records of Dublin*, we learn that Sir Daniel Bellingham acquired plots on Oxmantown Green in 1662, at a place called Lough Bouy – an area that in recent times became the headquarters of the Irish Distillers' Group. In 1667 there were many complaints about traders' stalls cluttering up the streets and blocking shops. The City ruled that no stalls, other than those selling victuals, would be allowed in Smithfield, except on market days.

In 1675 the city decreed that all the streets and lanes in Oxmantown were to be cleaned, and scavengers were appointed to do the job. In 1712 the considerable sum of £200 a year was paid to a scavenger to 'clean all streets, lanes and other publick pavements on the north side of the Liffey'. The cost of cleaning the streets in the Oxmantown area in the late seventeenth century was raised by a tax on breweries, which were then quite plentiful. Such breweries that had carts 'whose wheels are bound with iron' were also obliged to pay ten shillings per annum, plus a barrel of table beer each, towards the support of the King's Hospital.

The King's Hospital, officially known as 'the Hospital and Free School of King Charles II, Dublin', was founded in 1669 to clothe and educate the poor and needy children of the city. The first school was situated in Queen Street. It was heavily supported by the City of Dublin, to the extent that the Corporation assigned almost all of the ground rents from both St Stephen's Green and Oxmantown Green to the hospital. Even now, 300 years later, the King's Hospital School is the beneficiary of certain ground rents in the areas of St Stephen's Green and Oxmantown. In her comprehensive book *A History of the King's Hospital* (1975), Lesley Whiteside makes the following succinct summary:

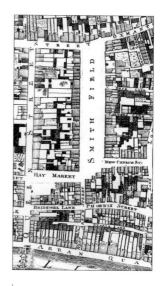

Above: The long, rectangular square of Smithfield and the adjoining Haymarket were lined with houses in the mid-eighteenth century.

Below: The ambitious front elevation of the King's Hospital, as planned by Thomas Ivory, from an engraving by Pool and Cash.

The history of the King's Hospital follows closely that of the Anglican community in Ireland: establishment in the heady days of the Restoration, peril under James II, closure during the Williamite War, reopening after the triumphs of the Boyne and Aughrim, a prominent position in the heyday of the Protestant ascendancy, disillusionment and decline in the days of Catholic Emancipation and growing Irish nationalism, reluctant integration into the State educational system, leading finally to a great broadening in the twentieth century and a ready identification with most aspects of modern Irish society.

Below: The now-vanished terraced Georgian houses of Blackhall Street were erected on Oxmantown Green in about 1789.

Below bottom: Speed's map (1610) shows the importance of St Michan's Church, with Oxmantown Green to the west.

In architectural terms the King's Hospital is chiefly remembered for having left behind its beautiful building in Blackhall Place, now occupied by the Incorporated Law Society of Ireland. An architectural competition was held to choose the design of the building, and it was won by Thomas Ivory; the original plans are today in the British Library. Ivory initially intended that there should be an elaborate spire and a substantial cloister of stone arches at the rear, but some of these features had to be eliminated due to a shortage of funds. An impressive list of craftsmen was assembled

to work on the new school, including stone cutters Simon Vierpyl and John Morgan, carpenters John Chambers and Joshua Parker, a bricklayer named Semple, woodcarver Richard Cranfield and plasterer Charles Thorpe. The foundation stone was laid in 1773 by the then Lord Lieutenant, Lord Harcourt.

Blackhall Place, where the new building was situated, was named after Sir Thomas Blackhall, who had been made Lord Mayor of Dublin in 1769. As a governor of the school he played an important role in overseeing the building work. It is interesting to note that in the late eight-

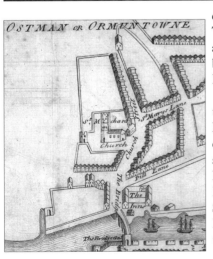

eenth century one of the governors of the school was James Napper Tandy, the United Irishman, and that some years later a bitter adversary of those Irish patriots, Major Henry Sirr, would also become a governor of the school. Blackhall Street, on axis with the King's Hospital, was laid out in lots for building in the early 1780s.

Rocque's map also illustrate sthe relationship of Smithfield and the Haymarket to Oxmantown Green. The original Blue Coat Boys' Hospital is shown in its first location on Queen Street, quite close to Smithfield, with a bowling green and artillery ground just slightly to the west of it. To the west of Oxmantown Green lies the Royal Barracks (now Collins's Barracks), with Palatine Square, Little Square, the Royal Square and the Horse Square. North King Street connects the top of Oxmantown Green with Smithfield. Here, the original St Paul's Church is shown, with its graveyard in the northern corner of the Green.

Apart from St Michan's, there was no other church in the Oxmantown Green area, until 1697 when ground was set aside in North King Street for the building of St Paul's. The church was replaced in 1821 by a rather plain structure in the Gothic style. The proceedings of the church are recorded in its minute books, which survive intact back to the year 1698. In the early eighteenth century places were reserved for the 'Blue Boys of King Charles's Hospital' in St Paul's, although they had their own chapel in the school. By the early twentieth century the congregation, mainly comprised of Protestant tradesmen, was already in decline and St Paul's finally closed its doors to worshippers in 1987. However, a year later the Protestant archbishop of Dublin, the most Reverend Donald Caird, and the then Minister for Labour, Bertie Ahern, who were both present at the deconsecration of the church, officially re-opened its doors as an enterprise centre to serve the north city centre and help alleviate some of the employment problems of the area. Three floor levels were constructed within the church to create twenty-five small business units.

In 1738 Sir Thomas Taylor, the Earl of Bective, constructed a large mansion on the west side of Smithfield. With its great cut-stone and brick façade, designed by Richard Castle, this must have dominated the marketplace. It stood out among the smaller, three-storied houses of the square. The Earl of Bective had large farming interests, and it has been suggested that he built his mansion here so that he could supervise the sale of his animals. His descendants eventually moved to Rutland (now Parnell) Square in 1790, leaving Smithfield to its salesmasters and other industries.

From 1816 Robert L'Estrange operated a foundry and iron-works at the mansion at number 33 Smithfield, until the 1850s, when the house was probably converted into sheds. By 1858 L'Estrange's business had been taken over by William Graham, who manufactured farm machinery, including rollers, crushers, winnowing machines, harrows, ploughs and threshing machines. An advertisement of 1858, showing Graham's new premises, suggests that the former house of the Earl of Bective had already been demolished. In the early 1900s the site was occupied by E&D Carton, who were auctioneers but also dealt in corn, hay, straw and potatoes. The Cartons also manufactured cattle feed and pig meal and were suppliers of seed potatoes and grains of all kinds. A small fragment of the rusticated cut stonework of the ground floor of the mansion remains embedded in a wall on this site.

Up until the middle of the eighteenth century, it had been the role of the water bailiffs, who were employed by the city of Dublin, to collect customs or dues on 'horses, black cattle, sheep, lambs, calves and swine', and also collected dues for the City on certain imports, such as wine and coal.

Above top: One of the last eighteenth-century houses overlooking Smithfield has been carefully restored.

Above: A rare seventeenth-century staircase survived in a house in Smithfield until the 1980s.

The water bailiffs generally operated on the river. Augustine Thwaite, who had a house on Essex Quay overlooking the Liffey, was mentioned as a water bailiff in 1742. However, in that year the City of Dublin decided that a collector would be appointed to collect the dues in Smithfield, in a system of subcontracting not unlike today's car clamping! One John Usher undertook the job on a commission basis, but ran into difficulty when he tried to extract fees from Smithfield's salesmasters!

At the northern end of Smithfield there was once a passageway, going by the colourful name of Thundercut Alley, that linked Smithfield to Queen Street. The alley, which is shown on Rocque's map of 1756, was bounded by a large iron foundry in the nineteenth century. This part of Smithfield is still used today by various wholesale fruit and vegetable sellers.

Ordnance Survey maps of the 1840s indicate that there were five or six weigh houses in Smithfield and the adjoining Haymarket. We learn from the Corporation's records that the Farming Society presented two weighing machines to Smithfield in 1815. The Corporation decided to build two small offices to accommodate these machines. Under the 1849 Act for the Improvement of the Corporation, the Lord Mayor and his agents had the right to inspect, weigh and seize any goods exposed for sale that might not be up to scratch. The Corporation also had the power to issue fines.

All carts entering the market were required to be weighed, registered and numbered. In 1870 the regulations governing the Smithfield market, which were posted on boards in the vicinity, dictated that hay and straw were to be sold only on Tuesdays and Saturdays. Tickets were issued by the weighmasters recording the number of each cart, the tare (the weight before the load was added), the gross weight and the net weight, which was the difference between the two. Traditionally, farmers were obliged to pay a ha'penny for weighing, and they were not happy when new charges were introduced in the late nineteenth century.

Rocque's map showed Smithfield to be a rectangular space, largely lined with houses. Many of these were still standing a century later, though many premises and backyards had by then been converted for industrial use.

By the nineteenth century Smithfield was regarded as the main cattle market in Ireland. In the 1880s the Corporation proposed to move the pig market to the North Circular Road, but this met with opposition from local residents, as well as from farmers and dealers, who liked Smithfield because of the many yards and lairs around it.

Above: An unusual photograph, taken by George Jameson from the top of the distillery in the 1890s, shows hay for sale in Smithfield and the Haymarket.

Many people in the market's area, which stretched from St Mary's Abbey to Smithfield, lived by what has been termed 'chance employment' in the nineteenth century. Men did casual work in the markets during the morning, while women acted as dealers and street traders during the day.

The Smithfield Female Penitentiary once stood on the east side of Smithfield, on the site of the present Corporation houses. It was opened in 1805 by the then Lord Lieutenant, the Earl of Hardwick. A plain Georgian façade disguised the heavily barred cells that were ranged around an extensive quadrangle to the rear. Each cell had an iron door with a heavily barred semicircular opening above it, devoid of any glazing and open to the elements. For much of the nineteenth century it served as a convict depot, until it was taken over by the Royal Irish Constabulary in the 1870s. In the

Above: Two photographs of the Smithfield Female Penitentiary, showing the galleried courtyard and cells above the façade (right).

Below: There were a number of farm implement suppliers in the Smithfield area.

Opposite top: An early twentieth-century artist's impression of Jameson's Bow Street distillery.

Opposite middle: A magnificent steam engine in the former distillery, 1984.

Opposite bottom: A photograph of one of the main distillery yards, 1984, showing the vandalised wreckage.

twentieth century the building was converted into a makeshift stable for horses and the whole complex was swept away in the 1970s.

In the 1850s there were eighteen salesmasters in Smithfield, dealing in corn, wool and cattle. Numbers 8 and 9, on the west side of Smithfield, were occupied by Christopher Dodd, whose name is still partly visible. Rooney & Headon, Kavanagh & Bull, Burke Valentine & Co., Hickey & Hanbury, AE Graydon, Stephen Thomas Matthews, Richard Coffy, James Newman, Duffy & Mangon, WJ Murphy and Whelan & O'Brien were just some of the other sales masters of Smithfield. Many of these families made great fortunes and owned large houses in the countryside surrounding Dublin.

In 1850 the Nag's Head Hotel and tavern and livery stables occupied 3–4 Smithfield and was run by Christopher Boshell. Hostelries once abounded in this district but farmers could also spend their cash in the many farm implement manufactories, which, as we have already seen, surrounded the Smithfield area. The agricultural implement factory of Courtney & Stephens was located in Blackhall Place, and sold a great variety of mowing machines and ploughs. In 1867 the firm had a steam threshing machine available for hire. The firm of Paul & Vincent, another farm implement manufacturers and iron founders, was also based here, at numbers 5–7 Blackhall Place.

Even in the 1890s there were reports of the various old houses in North King Street, Blackhall Place and around Smithfield becoming derelict.

Some areas were cleared and artisans' dwellings were built, such as in Bridewell Lane (now Arran Quay Terrace). The 1890s saw the repaving of Smithfield with stone setts, and the installation of porters who were equipped with uniforms, caps and badges. The pig market was moved to nearby Phoenix Street and the horse market was re-established. (The Corporation permitted trading in hay and straw until 1972.) A commission was established in 1885 to examine housing conditions, and some of the first Corporation flats to be built in the city were erected in Benburb Street, close to here.

By the middle of the nineteenth century, Jameson's distillery occupied the larger part of the east side of Smithfield, including the entire block of buildings running back to Bow Street. The distillery is said to have originated in 1789 and was responsible for the production of one of the most famous Irish whiskeys in the world. The Bow Street Distillery created a significant amount of employment in the general area, although much of it was seasonal.

Jameson's closed in Smithfield in 1970 and several companies were amalgamated to form the Irish Distillers' Group. Jameson's whiskey distilling operations were relocated to Middleton, County Cork. Between 1975 and the late 1980s the old distillery was set on fire several times. Three old houses occupying the northern portion of the site, two of which were of eighteenth-century origin, were demolished following years of neglect and vandalism. The interior of the distillery lay open to curious passers-by, scrap dealers and vandals. The scene was like an industrial ghost town, with its narrow passageways running between enormous derelict warehouses, containing the remains of huge machines. Though many of the more important steam engines were removed and preserved, I personally witnessed the smashing of a fly wheel on a beautifully made, green-painted steam engine so that it could be carted away for scrap.

Following a malicious fire in 1988, one warehouse was reduced to a mess of tangled metal and charred wooden beams. Small offices, mechanics' stores, rusting clocks and shattered drinking fonts were to be found throughout the distillery. Weeds and buddleia were growing from the roofs and walls. In the late 1970s stone setts were being removed from Smithfield and but for the vigilance of Gerry O'Callahan, a student of architecture in Bolton Street College, many of the stones would have disappeared. On being questioned, the Corporation replied that the cobbles or setts were being saved for the new Arts Block in Trinity College!

Above: The successful conversion to appartments of the dramatic cut-stone Bow Street distillery frontage.

Right: The headquarters of Irish Distillers occupies the Lough Bouy area of Oxmantown Green.

The OPW acquired the old distillery site with the intention of constructing a new courts' complex there. In 1991 the OPW sold the Smithfield distillery site to Duffy's car dismantlers for £1.5 million. Duffy's first site, sitting opposite to the distillery, was sold in 1998 for £8 million, a figure that reflects the growing interest in redeveloping this part of Dublin. An interesting stone stable and cobbled yard survive amid the debris of Duffy's site. It should probably be preserved as a reminder of all the centuries past when horses served Dublin citizens so well.

The distillery was acquired by Mr Terry Devey in 1995, and the subsequent development plan incorporated apartments, an underground car park, a museum, where some of the old kilns and vats may be seen, and a variety of commercial uses. The scheme was devised by architects Danuta and Andreij Wejchert. Openings were carefully made in the giant brick wall that faces onto Smithfield, and a brick-faced screen was continued in front of the old chimney to the furthest corner of the development to preserve the appearance of continuity at this old industrial landmark. Apart from the large chimney, none of the industrial buildings or machinery were listed for protection, and part of the magnificent limestone wall fronting onto Bow Street had been demolished following a spate of malicious fires.

It is remarkable that this property, which had been left so unprotected in every sense of the word, has now been successfully rejuvenated, with many of the original features incorporated into the new development. In conjunction with Irish Distillers, Heritage Properties have opened a small

museum where it is possible to take a guided tour of part of the old distillery. This replaces the former museum and visitors' centre at the Whiskey Corner on Bow Street.

The new Irish Distillers' headquarters at the southern end of Smithfield occupies a sizeable site, converted from an old spirits store that had been constructed in the 1890s. This fine limestone building, which backs onto Bow Street, was opened as their new offices in 1980. Although this development represented an early vote of confidence in the Smithfield area, further projects were slow to emerge. However, the Linders Motor Group built an office block, and a juvenile courthouse was eventually constructed at the corner of Smithfield and New Church Street. The courts, with their limestone and red-brick façades, designed by John Tuomey, fit in well with the neighbouring buildings of the former distillery. Perhaps appropriately, there is a gravity about this building, which Frank McDonald described in 1988 as 'the first truly "post modern" building in the centre of Dublin'.

There were once several other small distilleries in the Smithfield area. One belonging to a Mr Hayes is shown on a map of 1833 in the Dublin City Archives. Another distillery, which was situated in Hammond Lane, is shown to have had a large circular 'warm tub' and another 'still head'. Another map in the same collection, dated 1757, shows a still house located between Church Street and Bow Street. This map shows two dwellings, facing Bow Street and Church Street respectively, which are bounded on either side by 'the horse shoe holding' and 'the ball yard holding'. All of these are described as being 'in the parish of St Michan's, and the Liberties of the city of Dublin'. The ground was held on lease from Dublin Corporation and ran from Pudding Lane to Church Street. The bottom of Bow Street or Bow Lane was known as Pudding Lane in the eighteenth century, and it ran from Arran Quay to Hammond Lane. Hammond Lane was then spelled Hammon, thought to be a corruption of Hangman's Lane. The Hammond Lane ironworks was another important business in this district, and it thrives today on its Ringsend site. There were four separate ironworks in Hammond Lane in the 1870s.

The existence of the market and related businesses were in some respects responsible for the lack of investment in the area. This downward trend towards abandonment and dereliction, coupled

Above: A coal-hole cover from the Hammond Lane foundry.

Below: Smithfield's predominantly manufacturing and agriculture-related industries prevented it from becoming a fashionable residential area.

with the demolition of nearly all of its old buildings, had reduced Smith-field to nothing by the late 1970s, and in 1979 the Corporation officially closed the market. Many fortunes had been made in the Smithfield market in its heyday, for instance, James Ganly & Sons, the forebears of Ganly Wal-ters auctioneers, who advertised themselves as 'Smithfield Salesmen' also had offices on Usher's Quay and in Longford town.

The Smithfield horse fair is still held on the first Sunday of every month and has now been re-established in a more controlled manner, with the assistance of the Gardaí and the Dublin Society for the Prevention of Cruelty to Animals. It is a colourful and interesting event, which maintains Smithfield's links with its centuries-old heritage.

In spite of the partial demolition of the great limestone wall of the Bow Street distillery, Bow Street has man-aged to maintain a sense of its history. Apart from the distillery building, this is due to the surface of stone setts that pave this slightly curving, sloping street. Part of an old stone doorcase survives in the wall at 46 Bow Street. This was the original front door of Lord Bowes's townhouse. Another significant building on Bow Street is the former Irish Distillers' headquarters, a late Victorian three-storey, red-brick premises which boasts a large sandstone porch. This substantial building, facing the impressive five-storey ware-houses of the distillery, was sold in 1993.

Pedestrians can now walk from Smithfield through the new Smithfield Village development to emerge onto Bow Street. From here it is short walk to the fruit markets and on to Capel Street.

Most of Arran Quay was laid out by William Ellis, who acquired this parcel of land along the shore of the River Liffey in 1682. Ellis and his descendants reclaimed the land and erected quays, which were required by the Corporation to be thirty-six-feet wide in front of the houses.

Little now survives of the early eighteenth-century Arran Quay. Several significant blocks of houses were demolished there in the 1980s. The first to go was a group of five houses belonging to the Linders Motor Group, and these were followed soon afterwards by another five houses standing to the east of St Paul's Church, and owned by the Dunloe Group. In the National Museum of Ireland there is a cast-iron fireback inscribed 'IP 1737'. The fireback, which has ornamentation depicting a vase holding flowers sur-rounded by a floral scroll, is said to have come from a house on Arran Quay.

Above: These Arran Quay houses, which were demolished in the 1980s, were typical of the Georgian buildings which once lined the Liffey.

Below: A cast-iron fireback, dated 1737, from a house in Arran Quay.

CHAPTER EIGHTEEN

O'Connell Street

*I*n 1981 the *Evening Press* ran a full page photographic feature entitled 'Main Street, Ireland'. It was a shocking collage of pictures of boarded-up premises, derelict sites, cut-price emporia with tacky shop-fronts and slot machine joints. The only surviving Georgian house in the street, which adjoined the Royal Dublin Hotel, was semi-derelict. Dublin's 'Main Street' has had a noble and a troubled history, and is hopefully about to enter a new 'gracious' period once again. It is hard to imagine that O'Connell Street, called Sackville Street until 1880 and before that, in the eighteenth century, known as Drogheda Street, was once lined with Georgian houses like those of Merrion Square. Rocque's map of 1756 shows the many Georgian houses which filled Upper Sackville Street. Many of these houses had bow-shaped windows to the rear, overlooking long back gardens. A row of mews buildings or stables stood at the end of the back gardens, fronting onto lanes, such as the old Brickfield Lane, that could be accessed from Great Britain (now Parnell) Street or Moore Street.

Left: A continental air sometimes pervades today's O'Connell Street, with its leafy central mall.

Above: The Georgian shopfront of Butler's Medical Hall.

Below: The signature of Luke Gardiner from a Drogheda Street deed of 1749.

A well-known engraving of Sackville Street and Gardiner's Mall shows this great thoroughfare without the GPO and with the central mall lined with small stone obelisks. This mall was treeless and was reserved for pedestrians only, while a row of stone bollards marked the edge of the footpath in front of the houses. All of the eighteenth-century houses of Sackville Street and Gardiner's Mall originally had railings in front, protecting the basement area of each building. The engraving states that the street was begun in the year 1749 by Luke Gardiner and that it is over 1,000 feet long. Most of the people depicted in the print are pedestrians, but some are travelling by sedan chair.

Luke Gardiner, an astute speculator and a wealthy banker, had in 1714 acquired virtually all of the land north of the Liffey, which had been the property of St Mary's Abbey, but had been confiscated during the Reformation. Luke Gardiner was married to Anne, the daughter of the honourable Alexander Stewart, and in this way the Gardiners inherited the titles of Viscount Mountjoy and Viscount Blessington. During the eighteenth century, as we shall see, he and his descendants gradually developed much of what is now the Georgian north city. Sites were leased out to builders, carpenters and bricklayers, and others were developed by the titled families who would eventually occupy the houses. It was Gardiner who laid out the Mall in the centre of the present O'Connell Street in 1750.

The *Georgian Society Records* suggests that the game of Mall was played in this open space, and that it was later ornamented with gravelled walks and trees. One of the finest houses in the street, Drogheda House, was built by a wealthy banker named Richard Dawson, ancestor of the Earl of Dartry. This was the largest house in Drogheda Street, being a full six windows wide and four stories high and having a fine cut-stone doorcase. Dawson sold it in 1771.

The plasterwork decoration of the interiors of Drogheda House was very beautiful, and it is a great tragedy that the building was completely destroyed in 1916. The staircase, ceiling and walls were lavishly decorated

Right: Sackville Street in an early nineteenth-century engraving, showing the Georgian streetscape with shipping at Eden Quay.

Opposite top: A lease specially printed for Luke Gardiner, dated 1749.

Opposite middle: Sackville Street and mall as completed in the eighteenth century.

Opposite bottom: Elevation for Sackville Street as proposed by the Wide Streets Commissioners, which included shops at street level.

in rococo-style plasterwork panels. The ceilings of the principal reception rooms on the ground and first floors were also sumptuously ornamented in the same style. The house was furnished with fine marble mantelpieces and featured a Venetian window at

the back. After Lord Drogheda's death in 1822 the mansion was divided in two, becoming numbers 9 and 10 Sackville Street. In the late nineteenth century these buildings became the offices of the Hibernian Bible Society and the Dublin United Tramways Company respectively.

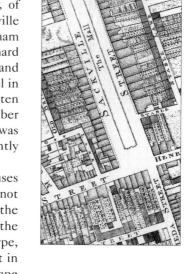

The finest houses of Gardiner's Mall, which stood in the middle of Sackville Street, were ranged along the east side and many were owned by the gentry of counties Meath and Louth, who used them as their townhouses. For instance, number 17 was owned by Blayney Townley, of Townley Hall, County Louth. This house later became the Granville Hotel. Number 18 was owned by Henry Bellingham of Castlebellingham in the same county and was designed by the prolific architect Richard Castle in about 1750. This house also had fine plasterwork ceilings and panels painted with classical subjects. It became the Waterford Hotel in the nineteenth century. Number 15 was owned by John Graham of Platen Hall, County Meath, while his neighbour, Mr Hancock who owned number 16, came from Waterston House in County Westmeath. Number 16 was also thought to have been designed by Richard Castle and subsequently became the premises of Mackey's Seeds Ltd.

In 1767, at the top of the street near the Rotunda Hospital, fine houses were built by George Darley, a stone cutter and builder, but these did not have the scale and grandeur of those previously mentioned. Similarly the houses built by the Wide Streets Commissioners at the lower end of the street, between Abbey Street and the river, were of a more modest type, but formed handsome Georgian terraces, with ground-floor shops set in arcaded doors and windows. The houses of this new Georgian streetscape were of a different scale and significance to the large mansions of the 1750s further up the street.

Nathaniel Clements built two houses on the west side of Sackville Street, on the site now occupied by the Royal Dublin Hotel. In 1811 Clements' son sold one of the houses to Joseph Wedgwood of Staffordshire, England, the son of the famous pottery manufacturer, for over £4,000. As far as we know, Wedgwood never actually lived in Ireland, and the house must have been purchased as an investment. The Hammam Hotel, at 12 Upper O'Connell Street, was once the residence of the Coopers of Markree Castle in Sligo.

An interesting collection of documents relating to Sackville Street was found by

Above and below: Two Sackville Street watch- and clock-makers of the early nineteenth century. Law's (above) and Chancellor's (below) both occupied buildings designed by the Wide Streets Commissioners.

Opposite top: A busy traffic scene, c.1855, showing the original narrow passage of Carlisle (O'Connell) Bridge.

Opposite bottom: Nelson's Pillar after the explosion in 1966.

this author in a derelict solicitor's office in Nassau Street during the 1980s. The earliest deeds are leases of sites made by Luke Gardiner in 1749. One of them, which unusually for the time was printed, was for a site that was later incorporated into the Gresham Hotel. The plot was taken by Gustavus Hancock of County Westmeath who built 'a large brick house thereon', which had a frontage onto Drogheda Mall of thirty-one feet. In 1761 this house was purchased by Nathaniel Clements for what was then a large sum, nearly £1,800. The various deeds indicate that Luke Gardiner had already built houses on the mall before 1749. Gardiner died in 1755, leaving vast debts of just under £10,000 to his son, Charles Gardiner. Theobald Wolfe, of the City of Dublin, obtained a judgement in the Court of Chancery, then located beside Christ Church Cathedral, against Charles Gardiner, for the sum of £9,923/8s/7d sterling. Various Gardiner properties were then sold by public cant or auction.

A bundle of deeds concerning number 1 Sackville Street shows how the plans of the Wide Streets Commissioners were realised. In 1792, having cleared the site of old buildings, the Commissioners leased 'a lot of ground, number 1 on the east side of Sackville Street and Bachelor's Walk, Dublin' to William Pemberton, a bricklayer. Under the terms of his lease, Pemberton was obliged to build the new house according to the plan, elevation and level directed by the commissioners. Four years later the new house with its vaults, standing on the corner of Sackville Street and Eden Quay, was sold to William Law, a goldsmith, for £600 with an annual rent of £100 payable to William Pemberton. Law was one of the most prominent goldsmiths and jewellers in the city and his son, Matthew Law, continued the business well into the nineteenth century.

Later in the nineteenth century these premises were taken over by the firm of Hopkins and Hopkins, who were also jewellers, silversmiths and watchmakers. In about 1900 they produced attractive headed notepaper with a small engraving of their premises and the O'Connell monument.

When it was first developed, this fine residential street, like the adjoining Rutland Square (now Parnell Square) and nearby Henrietta Street, was connected to the important commercial and administrative centre of Dublin around Dame Street and Dublin Castle only by means of Essex Bridge. The fashionable northside districts were isolated from the rest of the city, and remained so until 1795, when Carlisle (now O'Connell) Bridge was completed. The building of this bridge, along with the present Custom House, in the 1790s was all part of a grand plan for Dublin, by which the Georgian north city was linked, via Sackville Street and Westmoreland Street, to the Parliament House in College Green. Dame Street, newly widened since 1780, linked the old city around City Hall to the eastwards-spreading city and port.

The joining of Drogheda Street to the new Carlisle Bridge involved the demolition of many houses in Abbey Street and Bachelor's Walk. Most of these houses had been erected in about 1730, and one or two examples of this period remain.

The newly completed Carlisle Bridge and Sackville Street were acclaimed in the late 1790s as the city's grandest thoroughfare, and raised Dublin to the status of one of the great cities of Europe. Considered to be the first boulevard ever built in England or Ireland, it was chosen in the early 1800s as the location for an important new building – the General Post Office. The GPO may not seem to be a place of much importance in today's world, but in 1814 it was the centre of communication, with responsibility for mail, coach roads and the post. It had possibly the equivalent combined prestige and power of today's An Post, RTÉ and all the telephone companies put together! Accordingly, it was thought fitting to house the GPO in a building of great style and magnificence and the architect Francis Johnson was commissioned to design it, with its imposing classical portico.

Sackville Street was also chosen as the location for a monument to Lord Horatio Nelson who, in the eyes of the merchants of Dublin, had restored the world's shipping routes to normality by defeating Napoleon, and thus merited a grand monument in the city. The grandeur of the portico of the GPO was

greatly enhanced by the presence nearby of Nelson's Pillar and by the surrounding Georgian houses that once filled the street. Nelson's Pillar was erected at the junction of Henry Street and Sackville Street in 1808 to the designs of William Wilkins, a London architect, and the statue of Nelson was carved by Thomas Kirk. The pillar cost about £6,857 to build, and over half of the cost was subscribed by the merchants of Dublin.

Above and below: Sackville Street (above) on the occasion of a royal visit to Dublin in the early 1900s, and (below) after the bombardment of 1916. The Dublin Bread Company building may be seen in both pictures before and after the Rising.

The image of the GPO and Nelson's Pillar became something of a symbol of Dublin in the middle of the nineteenth century. Engravings of this subject frequently featured on the covers of sheet music, on trade cards and as souvenirs. Regardless of what one thought of Nelson, the pillar was one of Dublin's best-loved monuments and a favourite meeting place. Its destruction in 1966 was not just a great loss to the heritage of this city, but it deprived O'Connell Street of an architectural focal point, a classical column of great beauty that could be ascended by the public. It was the

only high vantage point in the city to which the public had access, and the views were sensational. I was fortunate to have been brought up the pillar for the first and last time just three weeks before it was blown up. For children, the long climb up the narrow spiral staircase was exciting, to emerge onto a windy platform below the statue of Nelson and see Dublin spread out below. After the explosion, the head of Nelson was stolen from a Corporation yard and ended up in an antique dealer's shop in London, but it was later returned and is now in the Dublin Civic Museum.

Sackville Street attracted wealthy residents in the eighteenth century, many of whom were landed families and also members of parliament. Following the Act of Union in 1800, most of these residents moved back to the country and their houses were sold or let. Three such houses, one of which had belonged to Nathaniel Clements, were acquired by Thomas Gresham in the 1820s, and there he established a hotel. With the steam age came greater mobility and easier travel, and by the end of the Victorian era Sackville Street had become a street full of hotels – including the Metropole, the Hammam, the Imperial and the Waverley to name but a few.

Throughout the Victorian period, Sackville Street was recognised as Dublin's 'Main Street', filled with prestigious and well-known firms such as Findlater's, Gilbey's and Clery's. The central mall later attracted an interesting mix of public statuary erected to commemorate great men such as Charles Stuart Parnell, Father Matthew and Daniel O'Connell.

A Whammond guidebook, published in 1875, commented:

Visitors will be readily disposed to admit that it is a noble looking street. It is allowed to be one of the finest in Europe. It is occupied on both sides with some of the best shops, several hotels, clubhouses, insurance and other public offices. Within the past few months were planted numerous trees which, it will be observed are taking root and flourishing ... The O'Connell monument is intended to occupy the site at the end of Sackville Street facing Carlisle Bridge.

Below: Clery's late nineteenth-century billhead, showing their extensive shop, with electric trams in Sackville Street.

Below bottom: Clery's clock, on the stone-fronted reconstructed 1920s building.

The foundation stone for the O'Connell monument was laid in 1864, but the elaborate memorial with its many separate sculptures was not completed until 1882. The sculptures are the work of John Henry Foley and are remarkable for their size and sense of power.

In 1896 O'Connell Street underwent yet another change with the arrival of electric trams. Tracks had already existed for horse-drawn omnibuses or trams, but the new electric-powered trams required overhead wires supported by poles.

In 1916 O'Connell Street was the focus of the Easter Rising, and in the ensuing battle between the rebels and the British troops much of the street was destroyed. Afterwards, there was considerable discussion as to how the street should be rebuilt. A consensus was eventually reached – that a single harmonious design should prevail, that stone should be used and that a broadly classical style should be adopted, while giving each development a certain flexibility. There are several impressive 1920s buildings to be seen in O'Connell Street today, including the rebuilt Gresham Hotel, the Carlton and Savoy cinemas, the façade of Clery's and the Allied Irish Banks building at the corner of O'Connell Street and Abbey

Street. Many of the corner buildings, like the bank, were ornamented with stone-built turrets or cupolas. The common feature of all of the 1920s buildings in O'Connell Street was a grand first and second floor, often emphasised by stone columns, and a continuous cornice at attic level.

In 1924 the new Irish government passed a special act, entitled 'Dublin Reconstruction, Emergency Provisions'. This act enabled Dublin Corporation to acquire land compulsorily for the purpose of improving the street and gave them powers to do away with narrow or inconvenient sites. The city architect was empowered to impose design criteria on the new buildings in the interest of the 'preservation of amenities'. The Corporation could also remove any unsuitable premises on the new street frontage. Licenses for public houses or hotels were deemed to be invalid until the rebuilding or restoration of the various premises was complete.

In the middle of the twentieth century, O'Connell Street was seen as the ideal location for major semi-state companies such as Aer Lingus and CIÉ, both of which located their principal tourist offices in the street.

During the 1980s the attendance at city-centre cinemas fell sharply and several of them closed down, including the Carlton on O'Connell Street. This cinema, with its handsome stone façade, columns and Egyptian-style capitals, closed during the 1980s and only the gound floor remains in use, now occupied by several shops. There had been a cinema on this site since the 1920s.

It is unfortunate that in the last fifty years, O'Connell Street has not succeeded in becoming a prestigious commercial shopping area, as would befit the status of the street. Some would say that the fate of O'Connell Street was sealed when the various burger joints arrived in the 1970s with their vulgar, plastic fronts and their cheap, processed food. They remain in the street today, producing vast quantities of throw-away cartons and mountains of black refuse bags.

As we have already seen, there were many criticisms of the neglect of O'Connell Street and its deteriorating condition, and in about 1986 a Metropolitan Streets Commission was established to take matters in hand. The mission of this group was to upgrade the capital's principal street – to improve the quality of shopfronts and signs, get the derelict sites built on, improve pedestrian facilities and possibly consider a new monument to replace Nelson's Pillar. However, the government that appointed this body lost an election and the incoming government quickly abolished the commission, which had scarcely had time to set about its business.

There are, of course, many businesses on O'Connell Street that reflect the dignity of the street and have gone to great lengths to maintain high-quality shopfronts: Eason's, Clery's and the Gresham Hotel lead the field. A new restaurant, Café Kylemore, was opened in 1987 on the corner of North Earl Street and O'Connell Street, in the former Burton's Tailors premises. The new timber shopfront did much to improve the appearance of this part of O'Connell Street, which has been blighted with plastic signs for many years.

Above and above top: A billhead and trade card from two O'Connell Street businesses – one of the more unusual businesses (top), and Thwaites mineral waters.

Opposite top: A view from the top of Nelson's Pillar, showing a military parade against the background of the tram tracks.

Opposite middle: North Earl Street, nowadays a busy, pedestrianised shopping street.

Opposite bottom: An early nineteenth-century card from the Gresham Hotel boasts that it was 'one of the largest and best appointed hotels in Ireland'.

The erection of a fountain in 1988, to commemorate Dublin's millennium and representing the river goddess Annalivia, did not succeed in creating a new focal point in the street or in winning any great public respect.

There have been several attempts to recover the dignity of the street over the last twenty-five years, and substantial sums have been spent on widening and repaving the central mall, which has improved the general aspect of O'Connell Street greatly. One thing is certain: only the highest quality buildings should be permitted in the street. This was the guiding principle of the committee that oversaw the rebuilding of O'Connell Street in the 1920s, and those structures, with their cut-stone façades, have the mark of quality. They may not be highly original in their design, but they are appropriate to the status of the street. Dublin Corporation has made a commitment to enhance the overall quality and public perception of O'Connell Street and its neighbouring districts. This difficult task will address the issues of the presentation of premises, of paving, of the uses of buildings and the linking of various districts together. The Corporation hopes that the proposed 120-metre spike, the millennium monument, which will take the place of Nelson's Pillar, will become a new symbol of the street. Out of over 200 entries to the competition for the new monument, the spike was by far the simplest and most sculptural design. The fact that it is a symbol of nothing in particular is perhaps an appropriate monument to our single-minded, economy-driven age.

The story of Thomas Gresham, founder of the Gresham Hotel, is intriguing. It is said that as a child he was discovered abandoned on the steps of the Royal Exchange in London, and was named after the founder of the Exchange, Sir Thomas Gresham. He came to Dublin and worked as a butler in the house of a wealthy family in Rutland Square. In 1817 he managed to buy numbers 21 and 22 Sackville Street, where he opened his first hotel. Business flourished and by the 1830s we find him as the owner of a hotel in Kingstown (now Dun Laoghaire) and the builder of Gresham Terrace, now the site of the Dun Laoghaire Shopping Centre. Gresham's nineteenth-century hotel in Sackville Street was a handsome building, the façade of which was ornamented with stucco architraves and a balustraded parapet.

THE GRESHAM HOTEL
SACKVILLE STREET, DUBLIN.
ONE OF THE LARGEST & BEST APPOINTED HOTELS IN IRELAND, ELECTRIC LIGHT, SANITARY CERTIFICATE.
THERE IS A SEPARATE READING & WRITING ROOM FOR COMMERCIAL GENTLEMEN ALSO A SPECIAL TARIFF.

The hotel was nine windows wide, comprising three four-storey houses. This building survived the 1916 Rising, but perished in 1922, during the Civil War. The new hotel building that replaced it was wider and a storey higher, and its relatively plain stone façade was only enlivened by an arcaded ground floor. In the middle of the twentieth century the Gresham Hotel flourished under the management of Toddy O'Sullivan and often accomodated many famous and important guests such as Prince Rainier and Princess Grace of Monaco, and various film stars, such as Audrey Hepburn.

Clery's department store was built on the site of the Imperial Hotel, another very grand and imposing building, which was destroyed during the 1916 Rising. The hotel dated back to 1837 and was acquired by Clery and Company in 1902. Since 1884, Clery's had operated a department store on the ground floor beneath the hotel. The present grand elevation of Clery's with its majestic columns was completed in 1922. For many years Clery's has had the reputation of attracting country shoppers, and in 1941 the firm was purchased by the Kerry draper Denis Guiney.

Across the street, the site of the present Penney's shop has seen at least four, and possibly five, different manifestations over the last 200 years: In 1973, to construct the shop, British Home Stores unfortunately demolished the very impressive stone-fronted structure of the Metropole restaurant and cinema, built in 1922 to replace the old Metropole Hotel, which had been destroyed in 1916. Like other hotels in the street, the Metropole dated back to the 1830s. However, the building of this Victorian hotel had itself brought about the demolition of the Georgian houses erected by the Wide Streets Commissioners in the late eighteenth century and those, in turn, had necessitated the removal of even earlier eighteenth-century houses! The present building occupied by Penney's, on the prominent corner adjoining the GPO, is a particularly bland modern structure.

Eason's bookshop, a fine, stone-fronted premises, whose clock has become a modern landmark in O'Connell Street, was also rebuilt in the 1920s following the destruction of the original shop in 1916. Charles Eason, the founder of the firm, came to Dublin from England in 1856. Eason had been an employee of WH Smith's railway bookshops in England, and on his arrival in Ireland he quickly monopolised the bookstall business at Irish railway stations. While Eason's were once famous for their Circulating Library, they are better known today for their sale of newspapers and magazines. Eason's is today probably the largest Irish-owned bookshop chain in the

Above top: The elegant nineteenth-century Gresham Hotel was composed of three Georgian houses.

Above: The Hammam Hotel, 11–13 Sackville Street, also occupied three large eighteenth-century houses and boasted 'Turkish baths'.

Opposite top: Eason's 'subscription library, newspaper and advertising' office opened at number 40 Sackville Street in the 1880s.

Opposite middle and bottom: Findlater's large store at 29–31 Upper Sackville Street sold a wide variety of branded products.

country and stocks one of the widest selections of books and magazines in Ireland.

The Hibernian Bible Society building and the Hammam Hotel were also among the Georgian houses destroyed on the east side of O'Connell Street during 1916. The Hammam Hotel was unique for its Turkish baths, which were opened in 1870 by the famous Dr Barton of Blarney, County Cork. Further up the street the premises of Mackey's, the seed and implement merchants, at 23 Upper Sackville Street were also destroyed. Mackey's had been established as early as 1777, and was one of the principal suppliers of farm and garden implements and seeds and plants of all kinds. The firm still operates a nursery at Sandycove in County Dublin.

The headquarters of Alex Findlater and company, wine and spirit merchants and grocers, was situated at numbers 29–32 Upper Sackville Street. They occupied a group of buildings which had been refronted in the Victorian style. Findlater's first appeared at Burgh Quay in 1828 and had opened a grocery in Sackville Street by 1835. A century later they took in the buildings on the corner of Cathal Brugha Street, which in 1882 had been renamed Findlater Place. Findlater's was completely demolished in the 1970s and replaced with an office block.

Another well-known business situated in Upper O'Connell Street was that of Gill and Son, publishers and booksellers. Gill's, established in 1855, became well known as a publishing house for the Catholic hierarchy and as publishers of educational books. Their large premises, with its galleried interior, stood in Upper O'Connell Street until twenty years ago.

The firm of Lawrence and Son, photographers, jewellers and toy importers, was equally famous, and their premises was situated at 5 and 7 Upper Sackville Street. Initially, William Lawrence made his name as a portrait photographer and as a supplier of toys. The shop also sold sports equipment and souvenirs made from Irish bog oak and Connemara marble. But the name of Lawrence is best known today for their remarkable collection of photographs, many of which were taken by Frederick H Meyers in the late nineteenth century, and bought by Lawrence. Lawrence took thousands of photographs all over Ireland between 1870 and 1920, and these are now housed in the Photographic Archive in Temple Bar. The quality of the Lawrence photographs is outstanding and the pictures are justly famous for their crisp images of Ireland's streets and landscapes.

Thwaites, the mineral water manufacturers, were also located in Upper Sackville Street and their original shopfront was uncovered ten years ago during renovations to a building there. Augustine Thwaites had been prominent in business during the eighteenth century in Dublin, and records from the 1790s identify him even then as a manufacturer of soda water. A&R Thwaites and Company soda-water syphons are still

quite commonly found, but the firm also manufactured ginger ale, tonic water, lemonade and champagne cider. By the end of the nineteenth century, Thwaites was one of the leading stockists of mineral waters in Ireland.

Among the significant losses in the vicinity of O'Connell Street was the Capitol Cinema, located in Prince's Street. This wonderful theatre, founded in 1919 by FW Chambers and George P Fleming, had an auditorium not unlike that of the Olympia Theatre, furnished with three tiers of gilded and plaster-decorated boxes and a double gallery. The narrow front with its arcaded terracotta entrance was very distinctive and its demolition represented a major loss to Dublin's heritage. The theatre, which could seat 1,400, was demolished in 1974. The demolition was a long drawn-out and sad affair – as the theatre had been built in reinforced concrete, it took a long time to knock down. At one stage in the proceedings, the great proscenium arch, with its gold, pleated curtain, stood before a pile of mangled steel and concrete rubble. Though many of the interior fittings had been sold, the oak panelling and marble staircase were smashed up.

The nearby Prince's Bar was a well-known Dublin pub. The original Prince's Bar, with its handsome façade and shopfront of Ionic columns, was built for the Tierney family, but was burned down in 1916. The pub was rebuilt in 1922 and much of the interior panelling is said to have come from a wrecked ship in Belfast Harbour. Along with the Capitol, it was demolished in 1974, but some of the fittings were re-used in the Henry Grattan pub in Lower Baggot Street and the Sutton House Hotel.

An impressive building which survived the 1916 Rising but was demolished in the 1970s was the O'Connell Street premises of W&A Gilbey. The French-style, stucco-fronted façade was erected in 1865 to front the Georgian interiors of two earlier houses that stood here. Frederick O'Dwyer, in his book *Lost Dublin*, tells us that this façade was designed by William

Above: A medal commemorating the fiftieth anniversary of the founding of Eason & Son Ltd.

Right: Many prominent businesses had branches in Sackville Street, such as Tyler's Shoes and the Dartry Dye Works.

George Murray, and that the elaborate porch featured the busts of Lord Palmerston and William Gladstone, who had been responsible for reducing the tax on wine! The Georgian houses that stood behind this façade had once been the premises of Sneyd, French and Barton, wine merchants, who had extensive wine cellars there. Gilbey's erected their own wine stores to the rear of the building, above the old cellars. O'Dwyer notes that the busts of the prime ministers were salvaged and presented to the National Gallery and that the magnificent plasterwork ceiling of the adjoining house, 49 Upper Sackville Street, was dismantled and re-erected in a house in Enniskerry, County Dublin. The florid rococo ceiling had a centrepiece of cherubs surrounded by swags of fruit and flowers and a profusion of free-hand foliage that covered every inch of the ceiling.

Number 42 Upper O'Connell Street is the only Georgian house of the 1750s to survive in the street. Built for Robert Robertson, a state physician, the house has important plasterwork ceilings. It was built in 1752 and is believed to have been designed by Richard Castle, the architect of the nearby Rotunda Hospital. Although owned by the adjoining Royal Dublin Hotel, the house remained in a derelict condition for many years. Incredibly, even though it was listed for protection by Dublin Corporation, plans for its demolition went before An Bord Pleanála in 1983. The architect for the developer declared that the house was 'never a particularly distinguished example of Georgian architecture', while a conservation architect and historian maintained that the demolition of a building of such historical importance would be unthinkable in any other country. Fortunately, the house was in fact saved, and has been incorporated into the hotel, though the upper floors remain unused.

The General Post Office

The General Post Office is by far the most important building remaining in O'Connell Street today. As we have already seen, the General Post Office moved from the medieval city of Dublin to Temple Bar, on to College Green, and then in 1818 to its new and final resting place in Sackville Street. The foundation stone was laid by Earl Whitworth in 1814 and the building was completed at a cost of £50,000. It was designed by Francis Johnson in the Greek-revival style, and its magnificent Ionic portico became the focus of the street. Early engravings of the General Post Office show that it originally had railings in front of the ground-floor windows and a row of oil lamps suspended from scroll-shaped lamp standards. The royal coat of arms was incorporated into the pediment and there was a public clock underneath the portico. Five arched openings, closed off at night by means of gates, gave access to the interior of the post office.

The GPO was the principal departure point for coaches leaving the city for destinations all over the country and was the depot for English mail, which left via Howth or Kingstown harbour for Holyhead. There was originally a sizeable courtyard to the back of the GPO, which, in the nineteenth

Above top: Number 42 Upper O'Connell Street is the only remaining house from Luke Gardiner's mid-eighteenth-century development.

Above: The stone doorcase of number 42.

century, must have been crowded with coaches and horses arriving and departing with their passengers and mail.

The GPO, as the headquarters of the rebel leaders, was, of course, completely gutted by fire during the Rising of 1916. Restoration work was not completed until 1929, and during this long period the stonework of the post office lay exposed to damage by water and frost. Because of this, some of the granite, which makes up the greater part of the post office façade, had begun to disintegrate. In 1991 repairs were carried out by the Office of Public Works, using granite from the same County Wicklow quarries that had provided the original stone. Repairs were also made to the beautifully carved Portland-stone portico and parapet. The three statues, representing *Hibernia*, *Mercury* and *Fidelity*, had by the 1990s become quite eroded and replicas were carved to replace them.

Above: The imposing portico of the GPO has dominated O'Connell Street since 1818. Note the Imperial Hotel to the left of the GPO.

Opposite top: Fruit and vegetables have been sold in Moore Street since the late nineteenth century.

Opposite bottom: Horseman's Row was part of a network of street markets off Parnell Street. All of them were closed in the 1970s.

Since 1929, the GPO arcade has linked Henry Street with the short cul-de-sac known as Prince's Street. The opportunity to create a covered shopping arcade arose in the late 1920s, during the time of the rebuilding of the GPO, as the coach and stable yard were no longer required. The arcade was refurbished in 1989 and is now an extension of the successful boutique and clothing businesses that occupy much of Henry Street.

Moore Street

The Moore family had arrived in Ireland in the sixteenth century and acquired the Abbey of Mellifont in County Louth, where, in the seventeenth century, their descendants received the title of Earl of Drogheda. In 1619 another confiscated abbey, St Mary's, was granted to Garret Moore, along with all its lands north of Dublin. The Moores adapted part of St Mary's Abbey as their city residence, but it was not until the early eighteenth century that the family capitalised on their land holdings north of the River Liffey by laying out the estate for building purposes. The family name is commemorated in Henry Street, Moore Street, Earl Street and Drogheda Street.

We are very fortunate that the late Seamus Scully, Dubliner and historian, has left us his vivid account of life in Moore Street, in an article in the *Dublin Historical Record*. As a boy, Seamus lived for several years at 31

Moore Street, above his family's butcher shop. He described the view from his window:

> Horse-drawn vehicles pranced and clattered on the skiddy cobble-stones to the abusive shouts of confused drivers trying to avoid the surging mass of shoppers who swelled out from the crowded path onto the slimy rubbish of the roadway. Along Britain Street [Parnell Street] clanked the cumbersome swaying tram-cars, their jerking trolleys spluttering col-oured sparks from the overhead shiny steel wires, and their iron wheels thudding and grinding over the shrieking iron rails.

Among the many butchers' shops in the street, Seamus recalls a poultry shop just across the road from his own house, where chickens and scarlet-skinned rabbits were sold from the cracked marble tabletops. Seamus describes the activity in their own shop, where things had changed very little since the eighteenth century:

Underneath the parlour was our shop and I could faintly hear Father's voice and his assistants bargaining with the women over the price of pigs' cheeks, backbones and ribs which were being sold from the pickle barrels. From the ceiling, dangling overhead, were the flitches of bacon and the dried ling fish, all haphazardly guarded by the whistling messenger boy in his knickerbocker trousers.

In another shop he describes the gruesome scene:

Under the tables lay the sheeps' and cows' heads dripping with blood – and with their stark eyes – which a few days previously had been driven up the street by the shouting drovers, followed by the yelling youngsters beating the animals with sticks, to the slaughter-houses behind the shops in the surrounding lanes.

The picture painted here describes a way of life that had survived in the city almost since medieval times. In today's world of packaged and sanitised food production, we are getting further and further away from that aspect of city life. Scully also described the dismal situation of many of the street traders:

Little did my childish mind, in the midst of pampered comfort, as I watched the mothers load their unsold goods onto the perambulators, realise, as they cautiously pushed them along, followed by their shivering children, the scanty meal that awaited in their bleak Dominick Street homes – once the stately residences of the wealthy, with their lofty rooms, decorated ceilings and delicate Bossi fireplaces, now the dismal draughty tenements, the tombs of Dublin's poor.

His memory of many of the tumbledown houses in the Riddles Row and Moore Street market area was that they were in a deplorable state, with dreadful sanitary conditions. He recalls in later life being embarrassed and ashamed to hear Big Jim Larkin refer to the 'slums surrounding Moore Street' as being the worst in Dublin.

Above top: Taaffe's, a poultry shop, was a noted business in Cole's Lane, now vanished under the ILAC centre.

Above: Riddles Row, paved with stone flags, was one of several alleys which were once part of a large outdoor market standing between Moore Street, Parnell Street and Little Denmark Street.

In the middle of the eighteenth century Moore Street was lined with small Georgian houses. During the nineteenth century the Street gained a reputation for its victuallers, poultry shops and butchers, and by the turn of the century a dense network of small shops and stalls had evolved in the district between Moore Street and Little Denmark Street. It was then the largest market in the city. Though the market catered for the daily needs of the less well-off in the north city centre, it was not very organised. An early nineteenth-century commentator remarked:

It is much to be regretted that such markets, so convenient in every other respect, and so well supplied with cheap and excellent meat, should not be better laid out or kept in neater order. The approaches are narrow and inconvenient and the avenues confined and dirty. To increase the objections there are no public slaughterhouses, and the animals are killed behind the stalls or in the very place where the meat is sold, and the accumulation of odours and offal in the market is sometimes highly offensive.

By the 1890s the activity of the more permanent market stalls began to spill over into Moore Street, where fruit and vegetables continue to be sold. Many of the street traders inherited the business from their parents. In 1974 students from the UCD School of Architecture carried out their own survey of stall holders in Moore Street. They found that eighty percent of the business concerned fruit, vegetables, and flowers, while thirteen percent was involved with clothes and shoes. Many of the permanent shops were occupied by butchers. Even today, the great majority of shops on Moore Street are in the butchering business. In the old Anglesea market there was a greater emphasis on the sale of second-hand clothing, shoes and furniture. This activity remained until the early 1970s.

The planned development of the ILAC Shopping Centre, in the early 1970s, brought about the demolition, in 1968, of virtually all of one side of Moore Street. In one stroke, a whole area of markets was swept away, including the Rotunda Market, Taaffe's Market, the Norfolk Market, Anglesea Market and the Moore Street Market. The Corporation architect reported that the demolished buildings were largely 'good-class shops' with no structural problems. Even more unfortunate was the grim frontage presented by the new shopping centre itself.

The planned clearance of the old markets area, much of which was undoubtedly very run-down, dated back to the 1930s. In 1957 the Corporation employed an American consultant, Professor Abraham, to give his views on the redevelopment of the whole area. He concluded that it was 'full of shacks, one-storey buildings and a few decrepit two- and three-storey buildings. Contributing to the general drabness are some old slaughterhouses.' He described Cole's Lane as 'a narrow alley composed of one- and two-storey buildings set among a few vacant lots and shacks. On some weekdays some small-scale peddling is done in one of the alleys and there are the push-carts on Moore Street with its busy retail shops giving an atmosphere of activity amid squalor.'

Professor Abraham suggested that part of the site might make a good location for department stores with the addition of a parking area. The large site between Little Denmark Street and Moore Street was cleared in the years leading up to 1972. With the clearance and disappearance of Denmark Street in the 1970s went Denmark House, a perfectly sound early twentieth-century building, which was demolished in 1976. Denmark House, with its neat corner tower, was occupied by a tailoring concern and as a building was in perfect condition.

Above: The ILAC Shopping Centre, which opened in 1981.

Below: The early nineteenth-century billhead of a cheese and provision warehouse in Cole's Lane.

Below: The now-vanished Cole's Lane, which joined Henry Street and Parnell Street, was a fashionable shopping street in the eighteenth century.

Shortly afterwards, a lease was granted to Irish Life, who proposed to develop the site and build a multi-storey car park there. For this, Irish Life paid a premium of £3 million to Dublin Corporation and an annual ground rent of £70,000. Some of the street traders were provided with lock-up facilities in the new centre, while the traders in clothes and shoes were offered basic retail facilities on Parnell Street. In spite of all these changes, Moore Street has survived and is still famous as one of Dublin's most colourful and busy streets.

Above: Denmark House was demolished to make way for the ILAC Shopping Centre.

Henry Street

The pedestrianisation in 1973 and the eventual repaving of Henry Street underlined its position as an important shopping street. Rocque's map shows that Henry Street was already fully developed by 1756. Like Mary Street, Henry Street did not remain residential for very long. In his history of Arnott's, Ronald Nesbitt states that: 'Narrow streets make good shopping streets and Henry Street was destined to become a centre of shopping in Dublin.' John Arnott, who was of Scottish origin, started in the drapery business in Cork in the late 1840s. There he became involved in business with George Cannock, who opened a shop in Henry Street, in 1843, under the name of Cannock White & Company.

The business originated in Number 14 Henry Street and by 1850 included two adjoining houses and was listed as 'a general drapery and haberdashery' in the street directories of the time. The firm was renamed Arnott & Co. in 1865 and their premises were gradually expanded. In the late nineteenth century, Arnott's, along with Todd, Burns & Company of Mary Street and Pim's of South Great George's Street, were leading wholesalers in the drapery trade in Dublin. Early photographs of the store show that its three floors were supported by cast-iron columns and that galleries overlooked the central space.

Arnott's diversified into many areas of business, including the sale of furniture. In 1894 the shop and its entire stock was destroyed by a fire which broke out in the carpet department. Such was the public interest in the fire that a large detachment of about 500 soldiers were requested to come from the barracks at Dublin Castle not only to assist the firemen but to keep the crowds back for their own safety. A contemporary newspaper report described the scene:

Above: Arnott's impressive department store was rebuilt in the late 1890s.

Opposite: Henry Street, seen here at Christmas time, is one of Ireland's busiest shopping streets.

Walls and partitions mingled with flooring and ceilings in their headlong collapses, and sank into the depths of flames with an immense crash, causing blinding upheavals of smoke, sparks and flame. The

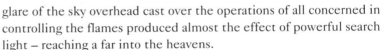

Above: The 1900s' equivalent of today's 'pound shop' was the 6½d World's Fair Stores in Henry Street. Note the statue and the proliferation of shopfronts with carved brackets.

Below: Bewley & Sons' wine, tea and grocery establishment in Henry Street. There were extensive wine vaults under this large building.

glare of the sky overhead cast over the operations of all concerned in controlling the flames produced almost the effect of powerful search light – reaching a far into the heavens.

A fine new premises complete with an elaborate tower were designed by the architect George Beater and built in the late 1890s. The imposing façade, which is thirteen windows wide and four storeys high, was originally crowned by a central tower that contained large water tanks for the building. But this, unfortunately, was removed in 1949. While many other buildings nearby were destroyed in the disturbances of 1916, Arnott's was lucky to survive with only minor damage.

Another Henry Street business with an imposing premises in the late nineteenth century was Bewley & Sons whose wine, tea and grocery establishment was located at numbers 18–20 Henry Street. These Bewleys were very distantly related to the family which went on to found the cafés on the south side of the city. In their vaults at Henry Street, Bewley's maintained a large stock of all varieties of wine, whiskeys, teas and a wide variety of hams, cheese, butter and bacon. Their large store, with its eight-bay frontage and arched windows facing onto Henry Street, maintained a great variety of dried and preserved fruits, jams, jellies, pickles, sauces, preserved meats, soups, soap, starch and many other household items.

Henry Shaw's *Dublin Pictorial Guide and Directory* of 1850 illustrates the façades of some of the premises in Henry Street and includes four early houses whose upper floors terminate in Dutch-style gables. The presence of single windows at the top floor of another four or five houses suggest that they may have been of similar early eighteenth-century date. Shaw also illustrates the fairly plain premises of Cannock White & Co., later to become Arnott's.

CHAPTER NINETEEN

The Rotunda Hospital
and Parnell Square

*T*he history and development of Parnell Square and the Rotunda Hospital are inextricably linked, for the building of the houses that surround the square followed the erection of the hospital and its pleasure gardens. Bartholomew Mosse, whose lying-in hospital we have already discussed in connection with Great George's Street South, took a lease of lands off Great Britain Street, now Parnell Street, in 1748. At that time, the land stretching away to the north and east of Dublin was open countryside. As the old building was no longer adequate, Mosse planned to erect a large, purpose-built hospital on this new site. To fund this ambitious project, he began by laying out a pleasure garden and opening a coffee room, equipped with an orchestra, to entertain the gentry and wealthy citizens who he hoped would support his plan.

Left: This early nineteenth-century engraving of the Rotunda Hospital shows that this fine group of buildings have changed little.

Below: Rocque's map (1756) shows only one side of Parnell Square completed, at Cavendish Row, overlooking the formal gardens of the Rotunda Hospital.

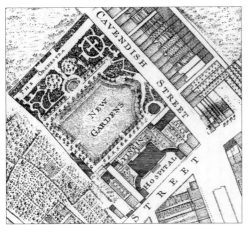

Below: The elaborate plasterwork which ornaments the Venetian window in the chapel of the Rotunda Hospital.

The pleasure gardens were originally laid out in a formal manner and were surrounded by a low wall, inside of which were two rows of elm trees. Mosse planned to build a pavilion on the east side and ornament the gardens with many statues, some of which were commissioned from the sculptor Van Nost. Van Nost supplied a variety of classical statuary, including copies of *Venus de Medici, Mercury, Apollo* and a sitting *Venus*. He also supplied marble busts of Lord Sudley, Lord Shannon and Bartholomew Mosse, at a cost of almost £80. The residents of Parnell Square were entitled to make use of the gardens, and could acquire a key on payment of the sum of 11s/4½d per annum.

The foundation stone of the new hospital building, which was designed by the eminent architect Richard Castle, was laid in 1751. CP Curran, in his most informative book *Dublin Decorative Plasterwork* (1967), notes that Castle does not appear to have charged the hospital for his work in designing the building. Mosse and Castle were friends, and it appears that Mosse was adept at getting his friends to support a worthy cause. Mosse placed an engraved copper plate underneath the foundation stone, giving details of the occasion, and various gold and silver coins were thrown in. For several years the building work proceeded, with funding coming from Mosse's limited personal resources, including revenue from the pleasure gardens and from the holding of several lotteries. But, in 1755, a charter was obtained for the hospital and a grant of £6,000 towards the expenses of its erection. In the same year the House of Lords in Dublin voted to give Mosse £2,000 in recognition of his great work and personal expenses.

The hospital opened in 1759. The hospital, which had all the appearance of a large, eighteenth-century country house, was entered through a spacious hallway. Vaulted corridors, which run on axis through the building, provided access to the various wards on each floor. The kitchen and other service areas were accommodated in the vaulted basement. The entire construction of the building, with its stone staircases and brick-vaulted corridors, was designed to minimise the risk of fire. An elegant tower and cupola sit, somewhat uncomfortably, on top of the building and once provided it with fresh air, by means of metal ventilators in the floors.

The chief architectural splendour of the Rotunda Hospital is its remarkable chapel. At an inaugural sermon preached in the new hospital chapel, a clergyman extolled the virtue of charity and praised subscribers as 'acting the part of good citizens'. He continued as follows:

The increase of inhabitants is most to be desired amongst the lowest ranks. The direct influence of this charity will be to increase hands for tillage; to supply hands for carrying on

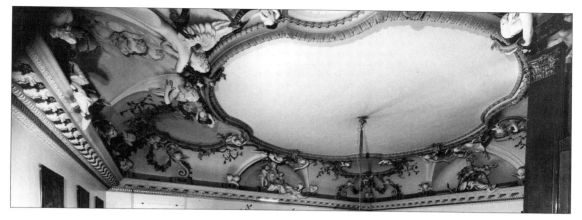

manufacture and for doing the laborious part and drudgery of mechanics; for maintaining the safety and glory of our nation in warlike forces...

He concluded that it was right to: 'relieve these poor objects, but why in a palace? ... Such a building should be large and strong and lasting, neat and warm for health.'

The chapel is reached by ascending the main staircase to the first-floor landing. It is square in plan, surrounded by an elegant gallery and ornamented with magnificent plasterwork. The carved woodwork of the fluted Corinthian columns, which support the gallery and its delicate wrought ironwork, are of the highest quality. The woodcarving was carried out by John Kelly, and the plasterwork is the creation of Bartholomew Cramillion, a European stuccodore invited especially by Mosse to create one of the most beautiful chapels in Dublin. Cramillion, who is thought to have been from southeast Belgium, and of French extraction, was paid 300 guineas for his work. Mosse originally planned that the space in the centre of the chapel ceiling would host a painting of the nativity, to be executed by Cipriani, an important Italian artist. Sadly, Mosse died in 1759 before this work could be carried out. The symbols captured in Cramillion's plasterwork are appropriate to a maternity hospital, featuring an abundance of cherubs, allegorical figures and various biblical texts. Above the altar we see a representation of the Lamb of God, along with a representation of *Charity*, symbolised by a mother with her children. On the right wall, *Hope* is represented as a

female figure supporting an anchor, while on the left wall *Faith* is symbolised holding a bible and a plumb line, to symbolise righteousnes, while underfoot she crushes a fox, the spoiler of the vine. A pair of angels floats above the organ, one of which points to the ten commandments. The pews were made from the finest mahogany, imported from the Caribbean.

Above: An unusual close-up view of the ceiling of the Rotunda Hospital chapel, showing the remarkable three-dimensional quality of the plasterwork. The centre panel was intended to carry a painting of the Nativity.

Below: This vignette shows the main façade of the completed Rotunda Hospital.

Some time after Mosse's death, the governors of the Lying-in Hospital undertook the building of a great circular room which would hold 2,000 people and would be called the Rotunda. This Rotunda was built in 1764 and gave the hospital its name. Malton's view of the hospital, originally painted in the 1790s, gives a very good idea of the circular Rotunda and the adjoining assembly rooms. The assembly rooms were officially inaugurated in 1787 and today incorporate the pillar room, or ballroom, with the Gate Theatre overhead. The pillar room was restored in 1987, 200 years after its first opening. On 12 March 1787, the *Dublin Journal* had described it thus:

New Garden.

AT a Meeting of the GOVERNORS and GUARDI-ANS of the *Lying-in Hospital*, on *Monday*, the 25th Day of *March*, 1765, it was Refolved, that any Perfon or Perfons who fhall mifbehave, by raifing any Riot or Difturbance in the Garden, fhall be profecuted at the Expence of the Corporation; and that any Perfon who fhall difcover and profecute fuch Offender or Offenders, fhall, upon Conviction, be intitled to a Reward of Twenty Guineas.

Dublin: Printed by S. POWELL and SON, in *Dame-ftreet*.

Above: A public notice of 1765, concerning behaviour in the Rotunda Gardens, issued by the governors of the Lying-in Hospital.

The ballroom was everything that could be expected. Over one of the chimneypieces was a brilliant girandole, composed of the insignia of the different ornaments of the Knights of St Patrick. This had a splendid and beautiful effect, and the temporary pillars were ornamented with artificial flowers, and festoons of evergreen which hung the whole room and gave it an appearance of simple elegance.

The basic layout of Mosse's original eighteenth-century garden is still discernible today where the nurses' home backs onto a terrace. The most northern part of the Rotunda Gardens was acquired in 1966, in order to lay out the Garden of Remembrance.

The Rotunda gardens are today much taken up with car parking, and what was once lawns is now covered with tarmac. However, the presence of various trees on the hospital grounds allows one to imagine the former pleasure gardens as they might have been in the eighteenth century. Some of the six- or seven-foot-high obelisks that once graced these grounds may still be seen; they are some of the few relics of the ancient pleasure gardens.

Necessity has dictated that the large red-brick nurses' home, along with an unfortunate collection of various low buildings – consulting rooms and offices – be built on the gardens. These many buildings within the original gardens detract significantly from the sense of Parnell Square as an actual square. In an ideal world, an underground car park could be constructed here, which would serve the hospital by day and the neighbouring Gate Theatre by night. This would allow for the reconstruction of the formal gardens above, which would be of great benefit to both patients and staff alike. If I could be permitted a further fantasy, it would be to demolish the ugly nineteenth-century four-storey wing and extension to the west of the original hospital, and rehouse the paediatric unit and other wards in a new, perhaps circular, building, which would echo the original Rotunda.

Although the Rotunda Hospital was originally built to cater specifically for the poor – the well-off tended to have their births at home – it eventually became a hospital for everyone. It was founded in the heyday of the Protestant ascendancy, but it catered for women of all religions and developed a reputation for a humanitarian approach to childbirth. The hospital chapel, which had been established as Church of Ireland, is now in use by all denominations. The Rotunda Hospital is one of the few public buildings in Dublin that is still being used for the purpose for which it was initially designed. The hospital now employs some 500 people and 5,000 deliveries are made every year. When the Rotunda Hospital celebrated its 250th Anniversary in 1995, the historic building received light cleaning, which greatly improved its overall appearance.

The Houses of Parnell Square

The houses of Parnell Square were erected contemporaneously with the building of the Rotunda Hospital, in the middle years of the eighteenth century. The houses tended to be large, with frontages varying in width from thirty feet up to more than fifty feet. The architect John Ensor, who oversaw the building of the hospital, is known to have built at least two houses on the square in partnership with the builder and architect Henry Darley. Parnell Square was completed by 1789.

The east side of Parnell Square was the first to be built, with the first leases being made in 1753 on land belonging to Luke Gardiner. The original six houses, known as Cavendish Row, were eventually extended to create a terrace of sixteen houses, which would be known as Cavendish Street. These houses exhibit a variety of fine cut-stone doorcases. Two types predominate: one is a simple doorcase with a fanlight, surrounded by a frame of rusticated stonework and finished with a pediment supported by scrolls; the other, more elaborate, variation is the tripartite doorcase, which incorporates side lights or flanking windows and four columns. Examples of the first type may be seen at numbers 1, 5 and 6 Parnell

Above: The northeast corner of Parnell Square in the 1890s from a photograph by George Jameson.

Left: Parnell Square East (formerly Cavendish Street), was the first range of houses to be built.

Square, while numbers 14 and 15, both of which were demolished in the 1980s, had the more elaborate type of doorcase. The side lights of number 14, once occupied by Conradh na Gaeilge, featured elaborate lead tracery. Number 10, which is an exceptionally large, five-bay house, exhibits another type of classical doorcase, this time supported by Doric columns. A

Above top: An elaborate 1750s wooden overdoor from number 9 Cavendish Row, carved by J Kelly.

Above middle: A typical mid-eighteenth-century staircase from Parnell Square West, with hand-turned and carved balusters and brackets.

Above: Carved stair bracket, number 15 Parnell Square.

similar example may be seen at number 11, which at one time housed the offices and council chambers of Dublin County Council, whose crest may still be seen over the door. Many fine examples of the elaborate tripartite type of doorcase may be seen on the west side of Parnell Square, for instance, at numbers 40 and 41.

In keeping with other Georgian houses of this style and date, many of the principal reception rooms in Parnell Square were elaborately decorated, with elegant plasterwork ceilings. For instance, both the ground and first floors of 4 Parnell Square were decorated with elaborate rococo compositions, featuring delicate swirls and garlands and incorporating bunches of roses. The ceilings, with their rich repertoire of garlands, strapwork and faces, are attributed to Robert West and were carried out between 1754 and 1758. West is also thought to have created the ceiling at 9 Cavendish Row.

In 1758 leases were taken for various plots on what would become Granby Row, or the west side of Parnell Square. In his study of the houses of Parnell Square, published in the bulletin of the Irish Georgian Society in 1995, Anthony Duggan suggests that most of the houses on the west side were built by about 1766. The first to be built here were numbers 32–34, facing Palace Row at the top of the square. Numbers 33 and 34 appear to have been built as a pair, as were numbers 40 to 41 on the east side, whose magnificent tripartite doorcases were divided by a short but elaborate wrought-iron railing, now unfortunately vanished.

Number 33, at one time occupied by the National Association of Transport Employees, has an exceptionally ornate interior. The staircase has balusters in the form of fluted Ionic columns. The walls are decorated with panels of lavish rococo plasterwork. The ceiling of the ground-floor front parlour is ornamented in a most unusual style, using *papier mâché* instead of plasterwork and featuring cockatoos and other birds. The *papier mâché* does not allow for the same level of refinement as plasterwork, and the ceiling, though beautiful, is a little clumsy.

The rear of 34 Parnell Square, occupied by INTO, the Irish National Teachers' Union, has an unusual feature – an arcaded yard at basement level. This yard gave access to a variety of vaulted cellars, the arched entrances to which are ornamented with classical heads. These heads, which are copied from antique models, serve as keystones to the arches and are signed by the maker, Coade. Number 34 also possesses an unusually attractive staircase which, like that at number 33, forms part of the entrance hall. A second staircase, which provided access for servants, was tucked into the middle of the house, directly behind the main staircase.

This elaborate layout signified a grander and more costly house, and having two staircases was no doubt a point of prestige for the noble owner.

The houses of Palace Row, on the north side of the square, were built between 1758 and 1766, with the exception of numbers 17 and 18, which were added several years later.

In 1786 an act 'for better lighting, paving and cleansing of the streets of Dublin' was passed and the subsequent taxes raised went towards the maintenance and development of the Rotunda

Lying-in Hospital. Under the act, the owners of sedan chairs had to pay £1/15/6d per annum. Lists of people who owned sedan chairs and were holders of licences were published for various years during the 1780s. All chairs had to carry numberplates, and a fine could be imposed for not keeping the plate legible. Of the annual tax levied on every sedan chair 'in the city of Dublin or within one mile thereof', the police were entitled to receive ten shillings.

At its simplest, a sedan chair was a covered box containing a seat or chair in which the owner was carried about the city to do his business. Two men carried the chair, which was supported by a pair of poles and was often leather-covered and highly ornamented. When not in use, sedan chairs were left sitting in the spacious hallways of Georgian townhouses. Following the act, a notice was issued to the public that all private sedan chairs (except those chairs that were still in the possession of makers), were 'liable to information and fine' unless registered. In 1787 there were 257 private sedan chairs in Dublin, and their owners were contributing towards the upkeep of the Rotunda Hospital. Such modes of transport had been taxed previously – as we learn from an earlier act of 1772, which contained the following provision: 'to keep or use any private chair or sedan without such licence as aforesaid, under penalty of £20 for every such offence'.

The 1786 act also decreed that railings were to be erected in place of the walls around Rotunda Gardens, in accordance with the wishes of the residents of Granby Row, Palace Row and Cavendish Row. It was also at this time that the name Rutland Square was first adopted. The act determined that the width of the streets should be the same on all three sides of the square and that, for instance, the occupants of numbers 26–48 must pay 1s/9d per foot of frontage for lighting and lamps. The governors of the hospital were given power to remove any irregular lamps, lamp posts, brackets or any other projecting features. These were to be replaced in a regular manner, to be of uniform height and spacing, and the inhabitants would be obliged to pay for such

Above: An attractive feature of Parnell Square West and East is the way in which the houses are stepped, each one slightly higher than the next.

Below: This sedan chair, which was sold in Dublin in 1999, is typical of those used in the eighteenth-century city.

Right: Number 15 Parnell Square, once occupied by display artists, was one of three houses demolished in the early 1980s to make way for an office block.

Below: The refined ceiling, with flowing foliage, from the drawing room of number 15 Parnell Square.

Opposite top: A now-vanished doorway on Gardiner's Row, with its original eighteenth-century oil lamp brackets.

Opposite middle: An unusual feature, a carpenter's name stamped into the back of a timber moulding, from the hall of number 14.

Opposite bottom: An old nameplate recalls the Gardiner family's role in the development of this area.

alterations. Stone tablets carved with the name Rutland Square were to be erected on the various terraces around the square.

Iron lamp standards with glass globes were erected, at a cost of £1/14s/– to each resident, and were put up at intervals of thirty feet along the length and breadth of the square. Anyone caught defacing these lamps or their stone bases could be subject to a fine of £5 and a prison sentence of up to three months! Eight armed watchmen were appointed and were paid £12 per annum. These regulations show that a sophisticated system of street lighting had been implemented in certain parts of Dublin, and that the policing of anti-social behaviour in the city was more efficient at that time than it is today!

The houses of Parnell Square are characterised by their fine brickwork, excellent cut-stone door-cases and heavy, hand-forged railings. The sloping site of the square, and the resulting stepping down of the houses on the east and west sides, creates a pleasant variety in what otherwise could be a monotonous Georgian streetscape. Almost all of the fifty original Georgian houses that stood around Parnell Square had some internal decorative plasterwork and fine joinery in their staircases and doors.

In the mid-nineteenth century, the west side of Parnell Square was almost exclusively occupied by solicitors. For instance, number 39 was used as offices by Robert Warren, solicitor, who resided at Killiney Castle. Number 36 was occupied by several members of the Cornwall family, including Gustavus Cornwall, secretary to the General Post Office, John Cornwall, a land agent, and William Cornwall, a solicitor.

Remarkably, Parnell Square is still relatively intact, despite the depredations of the 1980s when numbers 13–15 were demolished on the east side, and another three houses were torn down on the west side. The destruction of 15 Parnell Square in the early 1980s was a disgraceful act of vandalism, as it contained, in its first-floor drawing room, one of the most beautiful ceilings in the square, a delicate rococo composition with light and airy swirls of foliage, fruit and flowers of great beauty. This ceiling was in fact salvaged before the building, latterly occupied by FOS display artists, was replaced by a crude office block with a neo-Georgian frontage.

The neighbouring house, number 14, had been wrecked by 1980, its roof stripped and its ceilings collapsing from the flow of water dripping through unchecked. The floorboards and fittings had all been stolen. The first-floor drawing room of this house was quite unusual. It had had large niches and a coved ceiling, which incorporated four semicircular paintings by Jacob Ennis. These paintings, copied from those in the Palazzo Pitti in Florence, represented such classical figures as *Mercury* and *Vulcan*, and were fitted into the panels of the ceiling. During the demolition work, a pair of stucco-decorated Ionic pilasters were salvaged from the inside of the front door and they were discovered to contain the signature of I Mack, the carpenter. The firm of Mack, William & Gibton were well-known cabinetmakers in the early nineteenth century, but Mack's forebears were obviously joiners who were proud of their work in these mid-eighteenth-century Dublin houses.

Number 16, which stood on the corner of Gardiner Row, was demolished as recently as 1998 by veteran developer John Byrne, and is currently under reconstruction. This house once had a separate entrance on Gardiner Row, which was ornamented by two distinctive wrought-iron lamp brackets.

Across the street stands the Abbey Presbyterian Church, which was built in 1864 on the site of 17 Parnell Square, a house originally owned by the Earl of Bective. This Gothic intrusion sits lightly into the Georgian square, with its elegant Gothic façade and slender tower built mainly of limestone and Portland stone. The delicate stonework over the entrance and on the traceried windows, and the use of white Portland stone, prevent any heaviness from predominating.

The interior of the Abbey Presbyterian Church has an open aspect, with cast-iron piers supporting its dark-stained timber roof. Large Gothic windows on the eastern wall light the church. The focus of the church is the pulpit, behind which is a large organ. There is a substantial gallery to the south end. The aisles of the church are covered by polished cast-iron gratings, which disguise Victorian heating ducts. Carved stone corbels, featuring birds and naturalistic foliage, support the roof. The church is often known as Findlater's Church, in deference to the well-known Dublin grocery family who largely paid for its erection.

Numbers 18 and 19 Parnell Square today house the Dublin Writers' Museum and the Irish Writers' Centre respectively, which were officially opened in 1991. It is thought that the first owner of number 18 was Lord Farnham of Cavan and that in 1832 it passed to a Mr Andrew Vance, who was a merchant in Lower Bridge Street. In 1891 George Jameson, a member of the wealthy family that owned the John Jameson Distillery in Bow Street, acquired number 18 and made major alterations to the rooms. These included combining the major reception rooms on the ground and first floors of the house and redecorating the staircase with Italianate arabesques or murals. Jameson also commissioned the stained-glass windows of the main staircase, which represent Music, Literature, Art and Science, and incorporated his own monogram and the date: 1894.

The house was acquired from the Jamesons in 1914 by the City of Dublin Vocational School, at one time known as the Parnell Square Technical Institute. Until about 1980 it served as the College of Marketing and Design, then the house was left empty for several years. The unusual, boldly carved balusters of the main staircase were stolen in 1990, along with the elaborate overdoors and other fittings, and it was remarkably lucky that the staircase was later recovered from a Dublin antique shop. The plasterwork of the principal ceilings is in delicate Adam style, and the main drawing room at the back of the house incorporates four circular paintings of classical subjects. From the upper floors of the house there is a

Above: The interior of the Abbey Presbyterian Church on Parnell Square.

Below: Malton's well-known print of 1795 shows the houses of Parnell Square North, including Charlemont House and a small classical shelter for the men who carried sedan chairs.

magnificent view of the city, framed by the Dublin Mountains in the background. A continuous balcony was erected across the front of the house to take advantage of these fine views. It was Jameson, when joining the two first-floor rooms, who added the columns and the nineteenth-century lincrusta wallpaper below the cornice, creating a very bold, though perhaps slightly fussy, effect. He also commissioned the paintings of the seasons on the backs of the main doors, but only those representing the months of autumn are original. The others are so well executed, however, that it is almost impossible to distinguish which are original and which are modern.

In 1985 An Taisce alerted Dublin Corporation and Dublin Tourism to the fact that 18 and 19 Parnell Square were rapidly falling into decay and that, apart from the fact that they were listed buildings, their interiors were of outstanding importance. Ian Lumley (then of An Taisce) suggested that number 18 could be opened as a furnished eighteenth-century house, as at that time no such reconstruction existed in Dublin. Despite a series of break-ins and robberies, which resulted in the theft of various important mantelpieces and other architectural fittings, including the staircase of number 18, Matt McNulty of Dublin Tourism took the initiative to restore the house as the Dublin Writers' Museum. Bord Fáilte, the National Lottery and the European Regional Development Fund (ERDF) provided funding, and a major refurbishment got under way, including the building of a new restaurant and bookshop to the rear and the restoration of the house to its former magnificence.

The Writers' Centre now occupies number 19 Parnell Square, a house of slightly earlier date than number 18. The house is entered through a delicately proportioned stone doorcase with Ionic columns and a pediment, while the hall inside has one of the most perfect black-and-white flagged hallways to be seen anywhere, from which double doors and a beautiful internal fanlight lead to the staircase. The first-floor drawing room has one of the prettiest plasterwork ceilings on the square, featuring violins, French horns and lyres interspersed with portrait heads in laurel wreaths. Images of parrots, both sitting and flying, are also represented, along with a trophy showing a bow and quiver and a harp. The Writers' Centre is used for meetings, readings and concerts, and also accommodates an important collection of paintings that are on permanent loan from the art collector Frank Buckley.

Several proposals have been put forward to develop the former ballroom at numbers 20 and 21 for cultural purposes, and perhaps to extend the Hugh Lane Municipal Gallery of Modern Art, better known as the Municipal Gallery. The building, with its wide front, six arched windows and long unifying balcony, lies between the Writers' Centre and the

Above top: A fragment of wallpaper, probably of the 1890s, from the library of number 18 Parnell Square.

Above: A corner of the drawing-room ceiling in number 18 Parnell Square shows the skilful composition and modelling of the plasterwork.

Municipal Gallery. Again, the first-floor ceiling is ornamented in magnificent rococo plasterwork. A most unusual feature of the house is a marble mantelpiece, whose (vandalised) centre panel depicts *Hibernia*, accompanied by a wolfhound, a harp, a shield with a shamrock and a round tower.

Charlemont House, now the Municipal Gallery, stands out among the brick-built terraced houses of Parnell Square, as it is a detached house faced entirely in stone. This central position at the top of the square created a dramatic location for Lord Charlemont's townhouse, which he and his descendants owned until the middle of the nineteenth century. Although the house was significantly altered in the twentieth century through its conversion into the Municipal Gallery, the main building retains many of its original features and even the hall, which is the most altered space in the building, has an air of Georgian graciousness about it. Old photographs illustrate the now-vanished Venus Library, with its circular lantern, and the interesting Rockingham Library, which was apse shaped, had an elaborate plasterwork ceiling and was lit by oval windows.

Lord Charlemont was an avid collector, and he purchased many antiquities, including paintings, sculpture, books and medals, all of which he displayed in Charlemont House. Indeed, documents have come to light showing the original designs by his friend, Sir William Chambers, for a medal case, which was constructed around a fireplace in a unified and highly decorative design. The medal case was sold by auction in 1984 at Christie's in Suffolk, England. The ceiling of the room that housed the medal collection is currently being restored by Dublin Corporation, who manage the gallery.

By the 1870s Charlemont House had become the General Register and Census Office, where births and deaths were recorded. Old photographs of the Library Wing, taken in 1864 and now in the collection of the Royal Irish Academy, show it to have been elaborately ornamented, with carved overdoors, pilasters, niches and built-in bookcases. A few examples from the collection of seventy-eight busts, made in terracotta by Simon Vierpyl in Rome, still survive. These classical busts were made for the Reverend Edward Murphy, who was Lord Charlemont's agent, and they were arranged around the principal library in Charlemont House.

The initial plans of 1917 for the Municipal Gallery involved minor alterations to the house. It was not until 1930 that the new gallery was built, replacing the old library block and passageway to the rear of the house. The staircase, with its dramatic apsidal wall pierced by three circular windows, leads to a series of eighteenth-century rooms, which remain relatively unaltered. These rooms contain several delicately carved white-marble mantelpieces, along with a rare example of a mantelpiece, inlaid with coloured paste in the style of Bossi.

Above: The elegant and pleasing proportions of Charlemont House, as depicted by Pool and Cash.

Below: A late eighteenth-century engraving of Lord Charlemont on horseback.

A group of six houses, numbers 23–28 Parnell Square, which stand to the west of the Municipal Gallery, are now occupied by Coláiste Mhuire, and although they are all fine houses they contain no elaborate ceilings. The end house, number 28, whose entrance faces onto Granby Row, has an unusual side elevation, with a curved bow that accommodates the main staircase and an octagonal projection that incorporates the entrance hall.

Apart from one noticeable gap where the lane of Granby Place joins Parnell Square, the west side is relatively intact, although some of the houses are still in poor condition. At the top of Granby Row a number of houses were sold by SIPTU in the mid-1990s, and these have been converted into apartments. Two houses in the middle of the west side of the square have been opened as a hotel. The functions of the premises remaining on this side of Parnell Square continue to be institutional, with a variety of occupants, including solicitors, trade unions and Sinn Féin. Some of the houses here have narrower frontages and interiors, which, though very fine, are less ornate than some that have already been mentioned. Many of the houses have balconies at first-floor level, which enabled occupants of the drawing rooms to enjoy views of the Rotunda Gardens and the activity on the surrounding streets. It is curious that Parnell Square is still to some extent a neglected part of Dublin, despite the fact that it contains some of the finest houses in the city.

Above: Number 12 Dorset Street, the family home of playwright Richard Brinsley Sheridan, has been reduced to ruin, but could still be restored.

Below: The environs of Parnell Square in 1831.

The Environs of Parnell Square

Writing in the *Irish Times* in 1982, Frank McDonald described the area surrounding Parnell Square as follows:

> Dorset Street's cancerous condition is mirrored in the surrounding area. Ravaged Eccles Street, awaiting redevelopment by the Mater Hospital ... Parnell Street laid waste by the Corporation and Irish Life ... Dominick Street, destroyed by a combination of housing schemes and road-widening plans ... and North Great George's Street, which may yet be saved from decades of criminal neglect.

It is heartening that Parnell Street has at long last made a significant recovery, and that many new buildings, though none of any great architectural merit in their own right, now accommodate a mixture of apartments, shops and cinemas.

North Great George's Street, which we shall discuss shortly, could be considered a model of the successful conservation of an entire street. While opposition to the demolition of houses at the bottom of this street failed, apartments screened by replica Georgian façades were eventually erected in their place. Purists may throw up their hands in horror and shout about pastiche, but this is one place where the solution of stylistic replicas may have been justified. Although the standard of such replication is rarely adequate, and architects and builders seldom get the detail exactly right, nonetheless there are instances when such an approach is appropriate.

Another case that could be mentioned in this context is Mountjoy Square, which in the early 1980s languished with almost two entire sides ravaged and derelict. Twenty years later, the square is once again intact, at least in terms of streetscape. Of course, the magnificent houses should never have been demolished in the first place, but there are cases for insisting on replacement structures where authentic details are correctly reproduced.

The role of the Gardiner family in the development of the northeastern section of the city has been well documented, and we have already seen how Luke Gardiner was responsible for the original layout of what would eventually become today's O'Connell Street. By the time of his death in 1755, Gardiner had played the lead role in the development of Henrietta Street, Dorset Street and other areas stretching across to Henry Street and O'Connell Street. His second son, also named Luke, continued to develop the estate up until the time of his death in 1798. Gardiner's Row was erected by 1769, Eccles Street in 1772, Temple Street in 1773, North Great George's Street in 1776 and Gardiner Place and Mountjoy Square in 1790. Rutland (now Parnell) Square had been completed by 1791 and Gardiner Street by 1792, while Fitzgibbon Street, North Frederick Street, Blessington Street, Great Charles Street and Belvedere Place had all been completed by the early nineteenth century.

Parnell Street

Parnell Street, originally called Great Britain Street, connects the top of Capel Street to the top of O'Connell Street and continues in a northeasterly direction through Summerhill. The street never had any buildings of great architectural distinction, but consisted mainly of small shops with three- and four-storey houses above. The shops and houses of Parnell Street, many of which were refronted in Victorian times, were swept away in the 1970s and 1980s to make way for the present wide thoroughfare, which was intended to be part of the Inner Tangent relief road.

Above: The premises of Robert Gibton, druggist, at 124 Great Britain Street (now Parnell Street).

Below: The former Simpson's Hospital was once the dominant feature of Parnell Street.

The most impressive building on this street was Simpson's Hospital, a large, stone-built structure erected in 1787 as an asylum 'for blind and gouty men in reduced circumstances'. The hospital was founded by George Simpson, a merchant whose business was located in Jervis Street. The building consisted of four storeys over a basement and was seven windows wide, with a façade of fine granite ashlar and a grand Doric doorcase. The boardroom was ornamented with a remarkable mantlepiece, depicting a sensuously carved female figure. The mantelpiece cost £140 at the time the hospital was built.

The hospital moved to Wickham House in Dundrum in 1925, and the Parnell Street building was acquired by Williams & Woods Ltd, manufacturers of jams, jellies and marmalade. The company, which had originated in Dame Street in 1856, now used the old hospital building as their headquarters and erected factory buildings on the gardens at the rear. *The Industries of Dublin*, a commercial directory of the 1880s, noted that since the abolition of duty on sugar, the price of confectionery had come down and demand was greatly increased. In the late nineteenth century, Williams & Woods were manufacturing a wide variety of sweets, including candies, drops, toffees, liquorice and gum. Their factory extended along the side of Kings Inns Street and, in 1885, the firm took over an old leadworks in Loftus Lane. Here they

continued the manufacture of sheet lead for roofs, vartry water pipes and a variety of plumbers' requisites – a strange combination!

This massive site was sold by Williams & Woods in 1978, and the factory was demolished. The demolition of this building was a great loss not only to Parnell Street but also to Jervis Street, where it had closed the view at the north end. Part of the site was eventually acquired by Bolton Street College of Technology, while the Parnell Street frontage was rebuilt in the 1990s as a cinema complex. Within the last ten years, Parnell Street has begun to assume the appearance of a street once again, as long-vacant lots are redeveloped as apartments. Various pubs, including the well-known Commodore and the Parnell Mooney, were also scheduled for demolition. The Parnell Mooney, which had been established at number 78 in 1885 by JG Mooney, a wine and spirit merchant, was somehow spared.

Above: Although reduced to tenements, this 1949 photograph shows that Dominick Street was once among the finest Georgian streets in the city.

Dominick Street

It would appear that the first construction work to take place on Dominick Street was carried out by Sir Christopher Dominick himself in the early 1720s. At that time we find a house being built by Lady Alice Hine, which was described as 'bounded on the north by the house of Sir Christopher Dominick'. The rest of the street was not developed until thirty years later.

Rocque's map of 1756 shows Dominick Street laid out, but with only three or four houses built. In 1785 the residents of Dominick Street included two peers, six Irish MPs, one judge, six barristers and several sheriffs, attorneys and doctors. One hundred years later the street was mainly occupied by lawyers and merchants, and several houses had been converted into schools, hotels and one boarding house.

In the early years of the nineteenth century, there were still a number of titled families and several merchants listed as residents in Dominick Street, but by the 1870s the street was largely given over to the offices of various professionals, such as solicitors and surgeons. By the 1850s, for instance, number 1 Lower Dominick Street was occupied by the offices of William Dargan, the railroad contractor, while twenty years later we find Sandham Symes, architect, and Robert Symes, barrister, at number 58. Number 13 remained in the possession of the Dukes of Leinster, who had acquired it through marriage in the eighteenth century.

The townhouse of the Earl of Howth was located at number 41, and it was eventually sold to the Carmelite Fathers in 1854 as a school. The Holy Faith Girls' School and Convent, which occupied 39–42 Dominick Street, was sold in 1981 following the closure of the school. Like the Dominican Convent School in Eccles Street and the Sacred Heart Convent School in Leeson Street, this school was relocated to a suburban area of Dublin. The houses were well looked after by the religious order and most of their original features, in terms of woodwork and plaster cornices, were maintained. Number 41 is the most spacious of the four houses, having a large open-well staircase. An unusually elaborate carved doorcase may be seen at number 40, beside which is a grand cut-stone carriage entrance to the yards at the rear.

Number 20 Lower Dominick Street is the largest house remaining in the street, and also the most important in terms of its interior decoration. It was built in 1755 by Robert West on land leased from Usher St George, who was a son-in-law of Sir Christopher Dominick. Robert West, considered to be one of the finest stuccodores in eighteenth-century Ireland, was also a master builder and erected several other houses in Dominick Street. In this house, West produced his most flamboyant and exuberant plasterwork, in the form of gigantic birds, flowers and foliage. West's boldly modelled and theatrical plasterwork is seen at its best on the staircase, where the ceiling is a controlled extravaganza of flowing acanthus leaves, scrolls, busts, birds and musical instruments.

The ceiling of the drawing room, which was converted into a chapel during the occupation of the Dominicans who ran an orphanage at number 20 from 1927, is also of remarkable quality. With generous financial assistance from the Department of the Environment, the Heritage Council and the Irish Georgian Society, these ceilings have recently been cleaned and stripped of 250 years of paint, to reveal all of West's craftsmanship in its original state. Timber windows of correct Georgian proportion have also been reinstated in the façade to replace the inappropriate aluminium glazing which was installed twenty years ago.

Number 20 Dominick Street became the school for the Parish of St Mary's in the 1850s. Seamus Scully, who grew up in this part of Dublin and wrote about its streets in the *Dublin Historical Record*, remembered 'the scared children [from the orphanage] with shaven heads, clad only in unshapely uniforms and noisy hobnailed boots'.

Above: Number 40 Dominick Street, once part of the Holy Faith convent, retains its unusual carved-stone doorcase.

Below: A charming detail, from the centre of the first-floor drawing room, of the partially cleaned plasterwork of number 20 Dominick Street. This photograph was taken in 1998.

 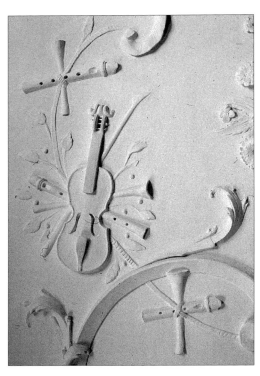

Above left: This detail, from the drawing-room ceiling of number 20 Dominick Street, shows a basket of flowers by the remarkably confident hand of Robert West.

Above right: Musical instruments from the ceiling of the first-floor drawing room at number 20 Dominick Street.

Dominick Street was also the territory described in some of Seán O'Casey's writings. In particular he refers to attending a miserable and sadistic school run by the 'scowl-faced, pink, baldy, whorey old-headed teacher, Slogan!' Seamus Scully also records that there was once a plaque on the wall of number 38, recording that it was once the home of Sir Rowan Hamilton, a mathematical genius of his time. Laetitia and Eva Hamilton were daughters of the great scientist and both later became noted painters of the Irish landscape.

Two houses, numbers 13 and 14, once housed the Leinster Estate Office. The houses, whose gardens ran back to Granby Lane, became Fitzgerald property when Emily Olivia St George, the granddaughter of Sir Christopher Dominick, married the second Duke of Leinster in 1775. Seamus Scully quotes from the childhood memories of the daughter of a caretaker in these two houses in Dominick Street:

> Number 13 was the residence, with lovely period furniture and a number of valuable pictures – original paintings by Old Masters – in the drawing and dining rooms. The hall, floored with black and white large tiling, held a cosy, covered 'booth' for the hall porter. Number 13's mews was covered with an ornamental pear tree; number 14's with Virginia creeper ... a gravel path ran down the garden and there were lawns on each side, with two raised circular groups of ornamental shrubs. The Fitzgerald family, aunts, uncles, etc., of the duke all stayed at number 13 when visiting or passing through Dublin. They

were Lords Frederick, Walter, George, and the Ladies Alice, Mabel, Nesta. They were charming people – kind, interested in their employees and their families.

Number 11 was occupied in the eighteenth century by Sir Hercules Langrishe who, with Henry Grattan, Lord Charlemont and Napper Tandy, formed the Irish Volunteers. However, it later transpired that Sir Hercules had accepted a bribe of £15,000 so that he might abstain in the vote against the Act of Union!

The opening of Broadstone Station in 1847, not far from the top of Upper Dominick Street, saw the introduction of various hotels and boarding houses into the street. The Midland Hotel, for instance, accommodated guests and travellers arriving on the Great Midland Railway from Mullingar and beyond.

Soon afterwards, in 1852, the foundation stone was laid for the Church of St Saviour in Dominick Street, and the fine building in the Gothic revival style was dedicated in 1861. The church was designed by JJ McCarthy. St Saviour's, which is attached to the Dominican priory, is one of the finest Gothic revival churches in Dublin, although its elegant Gothic interior was marred, in recent times, by the removal of a beautiful stone and marble altar and reredos.

Below: St Saviour's Church, Dominick Street, is one of the best examples of the Gothic revival in Dublin.

By the early twentieth century over half of the houses in Dominick Street had been converted into tenements and much of the street had sunk into the worst of slum conditions, where large families were reared in one room, often undernourished and prone to every kind of disease. The creation of these notorious slums seems to have originated around the 1880s, when so-called slum landlords bought the large Georgian houses cheaply and sublet them, often with fifty to eighty people occupying one of the large houses.

Most of Dominick Street was cleared away in the late 1950s and replaced by Corporation flats, at the time providing much-needed modern accommodation for the residents of the area. Only five houses on the east side, adjoining the magnificent Catholic church, and six on the west side remain standing. The building of a new block of apartments at the top of the street, adjoining numbers 38–43, has to some extent repaired the damage to the streetscape on the west side.

CHAPTER TWENTY

Mountjoy Square and Surrounding Streets

Mountjoy Square

*T*he creation of Mountjoy Square was the work of Luke Gardiner, grandson of the earlier Luke Gardiner who had developed O'Connell Street. William Stewart, Lord Mountjoy, was a relation of the Gardiners by marriage, and on his death in 1769, Charles Gardiner, son of the first Luke Gardiner, took on the title of Lord Mountjoy. Charles's son, the second Luke Gardiner – and designer of the square – also inherited the title, but died at the Battle of New Ross in Wexford in 1798, when he was hit by a cannonball as he led the Dublin Militia against the rebels. He was buried in the crypt of St Thomas's Church in Marlborough Street.

Luke Gardiner's original plan for Mountjoy Square, which he began to build in 1790, was that each of the four sides would have a unified composition, with a central feature incorporating pilasters and a pediment. This grand piece of town planning and architectural design did not materialise however, and the square evolved in a similar fashion to Merrion Square, its southside contemporary, with individual plots being developed by a variety of owners and builders. For instance, the Darley family of stone cutters and builders, who we have already come across, took several sites and built houses. Some of the first residents of the square, in 1793, included William Pemberton, the noted Dublin builder, and Michael Stapleton, the famous stuccodore who decorated so many of Dublin's Georgian houses. GN Wright, writing in 1825, comments: 'The air in this neighbourhood is considered extremely pure, being at the extremity of Dublin, and on the most elevated grounds.' He also observed that the park 'is enclosed by an iron railing, and is laid out with much taste in serpentine walks, and planted with shrubs and evergreens'.

A history of Mountjoy Square and its environs, entitled *Gardiner's Dublin*

Above: A variety of designs were used for late-Georgian boot-scrapers such as this.

(1991), noted that the completed square consisted of sixty-nine houses. The Whitelaw Census of 1798 found that on the north side, 100 people occupied ten houses, while sixty-seven occupied nine on the west side, and 190 occupied sixteen on the south side. These figures show that even in the late Georgian period a typical Georgian house was home to ten or twelve people, which presumably included an extended family and their domestic staff. Throughout the nineteenth century the inhabitants of Mountjoy Square were mainly professional people and included a variety of merchants, civil servants and solicitors.

During the twentieth century the houses were increasingly divided up into tenements, particularly on the south and west sides, and it was here that most of the demolition was later to take place. By the early 1970s only three of the original Georgian houses survived on the south side and seven on the west side. However, the north and east sides remained intact. Dublin Corporation owned six houses on the north side, which it kept in reasonably good repair.

Uinseann MacEoin criticised the Corporation's policy in a comprehensive article on the square, written in the 1970s: 'A minor fault on a building suffices to have it warranted "dangerous" by the Corporation who inspect these buildings.' MacEoin, one of the earliest campaigners for the protection of Dublin's historic streets and buildings, fought many battles over the demolition of Georgian Dublin, especially in the north city, where few people seemed to care. He acquired a number of houses on Mountjoy Square and in Henrietta Street, some of which have been fully restored, and which now incorporate a mixture of commercial and residential uses.

During the 1960s property developer Matt Gallagher had gradually bought up houses on Mountjoy Square, which he intended to demolish. He eventually agreed to sell his holding of twenty houses to the Irish Georgian Society for £68,000. Unfortunately, the deal did not materialise, and most of the houses were subsequently demolished.

Above: Decorative details, such as this cast-iron urn, were commonplace on late eighteenth-century railings.

Below: The south and west sides of Mountjoy Square were converted to tenement use, and by 1980 many of the houses had been demolished.

Above: A typical design for a late eighteenth-century entrance door.

Below: Sights such as this, blocked-up windows and doors and a smashed fanlight, were commonplace on Mountjoy Square in the 1970s and 1980s.

In the 1960s the Irish Georgian Society offered substantial sums of money to the owners of neglected Georgian properties in order to acquire the houses and sell them on to sympathetic people who would restore them. One such house, number 50, was acquired and restored by Mariga Guinness, the first wife of Desmond Guinness, but even it was eventually demolished. It seemed that there was a certain perverse determination to raze as many of these houses as possible, even though in 1968 they were listed for preservation. However, there was some support for the restoration and reuse of these buildings. For instance, Mr Michael Gill of MH Gill & Son, publishers, commented that the Georgian houses were 'absolutely suitable' for the publishing business, partly because they had the advantage of being away from the busiest parts of the city centre.

An article published in the *Evening Press* in 1975, entitled 'The Jekyll and Hyde Square', showed pictures of the disgraceful condition of Mountjoy Square. A similar article was published in the *Evening Herald* in 1982, asking what the 10,000 or so people who had stayed at An Óige's hostel at 61 Mountjoy Square, on the east side of the square, could have thought of the derelict sites and the half-demolished terraces with blocked-up doors and windows and ragged gable walls. The An Óige hostel building itself is a good example of the kind of refinement which is to be found in the interiors of the houses on Mountjoy Square, for it has beautifully decorated ceilings and fine mantelpieces.

Several people narrowly escaped injury or death when part of the front wall of 64 Mountjoy Square collapsed into the street in June 1983. The

house, which had been in tenement use, had been vacant for several years and the roof and joists had been stripped out.

But some of these abandoned houses were restored, such as number 47, which was carefully renovated and became the home of John and Ann Molloy and their family. For many years the Molloys' home, and its neighbour, number 46, stood in virtual isolation, with nothing but derelict sites surrounding them. On the west side, number 54 was restored by Karen Flanagan in the early 1980s.

Numbers 25 and 26 were carefully restored by Edward Dillon, wine importer. These are among the finest houses on the east side of the square and are thought to have been built by Frederick Darley. As is the case with most other Mountjoy Square houses, the interior decoration is delicate in style, displaying refined plasterwork in the style of Robert Adam. One contains elegant staircase

balustrades of wrought iron, and the discreet use of gesso ornamentation in the entrance hall. Frederick Darley, who lived at 88 Lower Abbey Street, came from a family of distinguished stonemasons. Two of his brothers practised the same trade, while a third was a bricklayer living at Essex Quay. Frederick Darley Snr had been Sheriff of Dublin City in 1798 and was elected an Alderman in 1800. Other members of the Darley family were involved in brewing and wine importation. A subsequent generation in the nineteenth century became well-known solicitors.

In the late 1980s Zoe Developments, one of the leading apartment builders in the city, undertook a development that would lead to the reconstruction of part of Mountjoy Square. Another major redevelopment was the construction of an office building by the PMPA, which included the creation of replica Georgian façades for numbers 40–45.

The building interests of the Gardiner Estate had also extended to the creation of Upper and Lower Gardiner Street and Beresford Place, behind the Custom House. Further terraces of fine houses were also erected on the south side of Summerhill, on Rutland Street Upper and on Gloucester Street Upper and Lower (subsequently renamed Seán McDermott Street). With the exception of the lower part of Gardiner Street, virtually all of the houses on these streets were razed to the ground in the early 1980s. In most cases this was because they had deteriorated into some of the worst slum housing in the capital city.

Two of the last buildings to disappear from Seán McDermott Street were a pair of partly stone-fronted Georgian houses, one of which once

Above: This photograph, looking towards Mountjoy Square, shows Belvedere Place, which is little changed today.

Next page, top: The rear of houses at Summerhill before their demolition c.1980. Once the bow-shaped drawing rooms of an elegant Georgian terrace – later, Dublin's shameful slums.

Next page, bottom: A pair of stone-fronted houses on Seán McDermott Street were cleared in 1984.

Page 437, top: A long-vanished, unusual entrance with wrought-iron grille in Gloucester Street, now Seán McDermott Street.

Page 437, bottom: A panoramic view of Eccles Street, showing its junction with Dorset Street.

accommodated Murray's bar. The arcaded ground floors of these houses were finished in rusticated cut-stone, while the upper floors had carved stone window surrounds. Had these houses stood on Merrion Square, there would have been no question of pulling them down. Following the demolition of the remaining houses on Seán McDermott Street –

including the old Gloucester Diamond, a formal composition of eighteenth-century houses – Dublin Corporation set about constructing 240 new townhouses in the early 1980s. Some of the residents, however, liked the old houses of the Diamond and would have preferred if they had been modernised rather than replaced.

Following these wholesale clearances, few people expected to see new buildings, never mind apartments, being re-established here. However, in 1992 one of Dublin's leading apartment builders,

Cosgrave Brothers, erected a major development of apartments on Gardiner Street, creating a new streetscape once again. While there has been some criticism of the apartments' neo-Georgian façades, most people were simply amazed that this had once again become a residential district, with new two-bedroom apartments selling for modest prices by today's standards.

Eccles Street

Eccles Street was named after an early eighteenth-century lord mayor of Dublin, Sir John Eccles, who once owned much property in this area. It was Eccles who is said to have built the first St George's Church in 1714 in Hill Street, of which only the tower now remains.

It was during the early 1770s that Luke Gardiner Jnr commenced the development of Eccles Street, a residential thoroughfare that would ultimately connect Dorset Street with the North Circular Road. Almost eighty terraced Georgian houses were built on Eccles Street, and they were mainly occupied by the affluent professional classes. The rear elevation of quite a number of the Eccles Street houses were bowed, creating interestingly shaped rooms lit by three windows.

The houses followed the usual Georgian format, though the earlier examples, many of which were demolished to make way for the Mater Hospital in the 1980s, had simple Gibbsian doorcases. These stone doorcases, which were popular in the mid-eighteenth century, consisted of a classical architrave punctuated with blocks of stone and carried around a small arched fanlight. Number 7 Eccles Street, the imaginary home of James Joyce's character Leopold Bloom, had one of these doorcases. The door was fortunately salvaged at the time of demolition and found its way into the Bailey pub on Duke Street. When the Bailey was taken over by Marks and Spencer's, this landmark, with its wonderful old cracked paint, was donated to the James Joyce Cultural Centre in North Great George's Street, where it can be seen today.

The noted architect Francis Johnson lived in a house, designed by himself, at 64 Eccles Street. Four relief plaques depicting classical subjects are incorporated into the façade of Johnson's house, and the interior boasts some unusual features, such as an octagonal room that receives natural light from a lantern above. This room must have housed part of Johnson's art collection, which was apparently open to the public on a limited basis. The collection consisted of a large number of paintings, including one of

Left: This fine ceiling from the Dominican convent in Eccles Street was destroyed in 1984.

Below: A decorative relief plaque from the façade of Francis Johnson's house in Eccles House.

the Piazza San Marco (St Mark's Square) in Venice, attributed to Canaletto. There were also Swiss and Italianate scenes and a series of paintings of saints, all attributed to great masters such as Dürer, Murillo, Cuyp, Caravaggio, Rubens and Poussin.

Number 59 has a fine interior with delicate plasterwork in its barrel-vaulted hallway, and in alcoves and over doors.

By the middle of the nineteenth century the houses on Eccles Street were largely devoted to office use and, like many other nearby streets, were monopolised by solicitors and barristers along with a few physicians, merchants and engineers.

The demolition of one entire side of Eccles Street in 1984, to make way for the Mater Private Hospital and its car park, was yet another sad chapter in the story of the destruction of Dublin. The hospital had purchased the buildings of the Dominican Convent back in 1978. The Dominican College was founded in Eccles Street in 1882 and had closed almost exactly 100 years later and moved to the Dublin suburbs. The college had first started at 23 Eccles Street, and later expanded to include nine houses on the north side of the street. The houses, though modest compared with Parnell Square or Dominick Street, contained much fine plasterwork. For instance, the ceiling of the first-floor drawing room in number 19 was decorated in Adam style, while the original dining room on the ground floor of number 18 had an alcove and cornices adorned with garlands and swags of plasterwork. An elegant Art Deco theatre, designed by the architect Butler in the 1920s, was one of the finest of such halls in the city. The line of the houses was interrupted only by the convent chapel, with its apse-like projection.

Many past pupils have fond memories of the old Dominican College, with its elegant stuccowork of draped urns and swirling clusters of leaves. They recall the ever-present smell of wax polish and old wood. Many of the nuns and parents were reluctant to leave Eccles Street and see the school buildings destroyed, and when the nuns finally left the old convent on 1 September 1984, the buildings were in perfect condition. The roofs were well maintained and there was no dampness, no rot and no rising damp. Unfortunately, the red brick façades of many of these houses had at one time been rendered with unattractive hard, grey cement, but even so, they were part of an impressive streetscape.

There was widespread outrage at the destruction of the beautiful convent chapel, with its arcaded nave supported by Ionic columns. There is something particularly brutal about watching, as I did, the demolition of an entire streetscape by a crane operating a wrecker's ball. The houses were reduced to a pulverised mountain of rubble, broken masonry and smashed-up timber.

Prior to the demolition, various important features, including mahogany doors, carved architraves, cast-iron balconies and staircases, had been salvaged. During the removal of the gesso-decorated, wooden staircase brackets from the house which once accommodated Scoil Bhríde, an inscription in pencil was found: 'sent by this bearer, three dozen – for the Lord Mayor; signed Arthur Mooney'. This indicates that these pretty brackets, which were so typical of the later Georgian period, were made in a Dublin workshop by a craftsman of that name.

A new St George's Church, designed by Francis Johnson, was begun in 1802 and took seven years to complete. Considered to be one of the finest classical churches in Dublin, and designed to accommodate 2,000 people, it opened in 1814. The church, which occupies a central position in Hardwicke Place, was strategically placed to close the vista of a number of streets, including Eccles Street, Hardwicke Street and Temple Street. Unfortunately, the original setting of the church was disfigured by the demolition of the original terraces that had lined the approaches and formed a crescent in front of it.

Mrs Louise Kavanagh, a former parishioner, recalled that in the early 1900s the large church was packed on Sundays. By the 1980s the numbers had dwindled down to twenty or thirty at most, and it was becoming clear that the closure of the church was inevitable. St George's was closed in the late 1980s and subsequently sold. The spire of the church has remained partially scaffolded for many years because very costly repairs to the stonework – estimated in 1990 at £1 million – have been postponed. Damage to much of the decorative stonework of the frieze capitals and other mouldings is thought to have resulted from rusting iron cramps, which were used to secure the stonework of the spire.

Above: In 1984 one entire side of Eccles Street was demolished.

Below: A decorative coal-hole cover from Eccles Street.

Left: The houses of the still-intact south side of Eccles Street frame the view of St George's Church.

A small number of coffins, thought to contain the remains of the Earl and Countess of Blessington and members of the Gardiner family, were removed from the crypt of St George's in the early 1990s. The Gardiner remains had been moved here from St Thomas's Church in Marlborough Street.

The Mater Hospital on Eccles Street is an impressive building, erected between 1855 and 1861, and has a long granite façade with a classical entrance. The development of the hospital's holdings elsewhere on Eccles Street was controversial during the 1980s. In 1988 the Students Against the Destruction of Dublin occupied three Georgian houses owned by the Mater Hospital on the opposite side of the street, which the hospital was planning to demolish. The councillors of Dublin Corporation strongly condemned the hospital for its neglect of the listed buildings and for its plans to demolish them. Even the hospital's medical council issued a statement saying, 'Regrettably, the Mater Hospital is now associated in the press with acts of architectural vandalism so that fund-raising efforts, particularly, on behalf of the Mater Foundation, will meet with a cynical response.' Unfortunately, even in the face of much protest, the Mater Hospital proceeded to demolish the three houses.

The Bertrand School in Eccles Street, which was established in 1801 by Peter Bertrand for female orphans, was joined with the Rutland High School in 1946 to become the Bertrand and Rutland High School. The houses of the Bertrand and Rutland High School were acquired by the Mater Hospital and, though listed for preservation, were also demolished in 1982.

The Mater Hospital was opened at the corner of Eccles Street and Dorset Street in about 1985. On the south side of Eccles Street, most of the houses are still intact, though attempts were made by the Mater Hospital in the late 1980s to demolish various properties here as well. The rest of the hospital's site on Eccles Street has lain idle as an ugly parking lot for almost twenty years.

North Great George's Street

North Great George's Street's gentle gradient, rising from Parnell Street
to Belvedere House, creates a fine vista. The story of North Great George's Street during the last twenty years is one of the more notable
successes of conservation and rejuvenation in Dublin. In the early 1980s
the prospects for this street were quite bleak, although a number of individuals, such as Harold Clarke, Tom Kiernan and David Norris, had
already rescued some of the houses from destruction and carried out
remarkable restoration work.

At the head of the street stands Belvedere College with its magnificent
interior, while the Loreto convent and school occupied another four fine
Georgian houses. The four houses, which date from 1775, were acquired in
1836 when Loreto College started in North Great George's Street. There

was considerable opposition to the closure of the school, which some
saw as a short-sighted move. Following the school's closure, the
property was put on the market in 1987. The school then moved to a
new eleven-acre site at River Valley in Swords. The largest house has
since been successfully converted into a hostel, and is used by young
people visiting Dublin, who have the pleasure of staying in these elegant and historic surroundings.

By 1980 much of the southern end of the street had been reduced
to ruin and Dublin Corporation was proposing to demolish the
remaining four houses and replace them with a new housing scheme.
Opposition was mounted by the North Great George's Street Preservation Society, which had been founded in 1980 and insisted that
the original houses could be saved. Though there had been considerable support from the City Council for the conservation of the
houses if funding could be found, they were in fact demolished and a
new development with replica Georgian façades of similar proportions was erected.

Number 35 North Great George's Street adjoined this site. Having been reduced to a deplorable condition, by 1980 it was a mouldering wreck. Stripped of its floorboards and other internal features, it faced demolition. But there can have been few restorations as dramatic as that of this house. Much of the original character of the house has survived, including a magnificent fanlight and doorcase and a good deal of the original plasterwork. The reconstruction of the two first-floor ceilings, based on photographs taken in the early 1900s for the *Georgian Society Records*, is an outstanding piece of work. Many visitors are quite unaware that the elaborate ceilings, decorated with dancing figures, are not original. In 1980 Dublin Corporation agreed to make the house available to the James Joyce Foundation for the purpose of using it as the James Joyce Cultural Centre. The Joyce connection is the fact that in the early 1900s a professor Denis J Maginni, who ran a dancing academy in this house, is mentioned in *Ulysses*. The magnificent building was officially opened in 1991, and attracts a large number of visitors throughout the year.

Above: Restoration work in progress at number 35 North Great George's Street. This room is now the Maginni Room in the James Joyce Cultural Centre.

Below: The restored elegance of a bow-ended dining room in number 38 North Great George's Street.

A few doors away, at number 38, is another beautifully restored townhouse. It was built in 1785 by stuccodore Charles Thorpe, whose exquisite plasterwork may be seen in the hall and principal reception rooms. The plasterwork has recently been restored by its owner, Desirée Shortt, who has lived there since 1975, and, in the drawing room, it has been returned to its original delicate colour scheme. Between 1870 and 1914 the house was occupied by Professor John Pentland Mahaffy, the tutor of Oscar Wilde, who later became provost of Trinity College.

Remarkable transformations have also been achieved by other dedicated owners, including the beautiful ceilings of number 11, owned by

Above: The centrepiece of an unusual plasterwork ceiling at number 50, showing a collection of Masonic instruments.

Below: An old photograph of Belvedere House, North Great George's Street, illustrates the original oil lampholders, almost all of which have now vanished from the railings.

John Aboud and John Hanley. The architect John O'Connell restored number 14, while Nabil Saidi rescued number 50. In this house, the removal of old wallpaper in the former dining room on the ground floor revealed the most beautiful, undamaged classical figures, represented with musical instruments in roundels. The elaborate drawing-room ceiling incorporates a fascinating collection of Masonic instruments, including an architect's dividers, a ruler and a plumb line. Like most of the houses on the street, number 11 was slowly restored from its tenement condition and gradually brought back to its full splendour. Layers of paint have been painstakingly removed from the ceilings, partition walls have been removed and the rooms have been painted in delicate colours. In most cases the owners have created small but magical gardens, and in the case of number 11 a small rectangular pond surrounded by flagstones forms a tranquil centrepiece.

Perhaps one of the most unfortunate losses in North Great George's Street was a series of frescoes that had existed at number 41, a house built in 1786 by Henry Darley. It is thought that the Italianate scenes may have been painted by Gaspare Gabrielli.

Number 19 was built in the 1780s as the residence of the King family, who were substantial landowners in County Roscommon. Harold Clarke, who bought the house in 1967 as a semi-derelict wreck, was a pioneer, one of the first private individuals to attempt the restoration of such a large Georgian townhouse in the centre of Dublin. Clarke's house had been designated a dangerous building by Dublin Corporation when he bought it.

Belvedere House, which stands in a prime position on Great Denmark Street, at the head of North Great George's Street, was built in 1786 by George Rochford, the second Earl of Belvedere. He spent the massive sum of £24,000 on constructing and decorating the house. The Earl of Belvedere, who developed a reputation for lavish entertainment, is thought to have been one of thirteen Irish lords who protested against the Act of Union. Later, however, it was discovered that Lord Belvedere had received £15,000 to persuade him to vote in favour of the act!

The walls and ceilings of the staircase of Belvedere House are among the most richly decorated of any house in the city. Even the underside of the staircase is ornamented with plasterwork, while the pilasters around the staircase window bear emblems of the Roman army, military trophies and the Roman motto, SPQR. The discovery of sixty original drawings in the 1950s showed that the decorative plasterwork in Belvedere had been carried out by Michael Stapleton. The ceilings of the three principal upstairs reception rooms, now the sitting room, library and dining room, are fine examples of his work. The ceiling of the Diana Room, now the library, incorporates many references to hunting, including a hunting horn, a stag and a fox. The ceiling of the neighbouring dining room carries representations of musical instruments and must once have served as a music room.

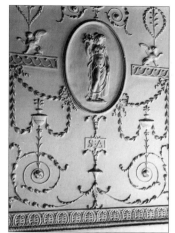

Marlborough Street

As we have already seen, Marlborough Street had been laid out and partially built on by 1728, when Brooking produced his map of Dublin. The few mid-eighteenth-century terraced houses that survive on Marlborough Street may be seen adjoining the north side of the Pro-Cathedral.

The most ambitious eighteenth-century house to be erected here was Tyrone House, built in 1740 for Sir Marcus Beresford, later the Earl of Tyrone. This house was designed by Richard Castle, and although the exterior now looks somewhat institutional, it contains an elegant and spacious staircase and beautiful plasterwork, which may have been carried out by the La Francini brothers. Rocque's map shows the completed house set back from Marlborough Street, with no other development from north to east. A large bowling green stood between Tyrone House and what would eventually become Abbey Street.

An engraving of Tyrone House by Pool and Cash in their book *Views of the City of Dublin* (1780) shows the house as it was originally built. It had a fine classical doorcase, a Venetian window at first-floor level and an oculus above. These features were removed and much altered when, in 1835, Tyrone House was taken over by the Government to house the Department of Education. Shortly afterwards a replica of Tyrone House was built to the north and the Central Model School, which George Bernard Shaw once attended, was constructed in between. In 1998 a fire completely gutted the 1835 replica building that matched Tyrone House, but, to the credit of the Office of Public Works, it was quickly restored to its original condition.

The *Georgian Society Records* give details of the interiors of 86 and 87 Marlborough Street. These once formed a single house, probably the residence of Barry Yelverton, later Viscount Avonmore. It contained a magnificent coved ceiling in the rococo style.

Towards the end of the 1750s, the fine, Palladian-style St Thomas's Church was erected on the west side of Marlborough Street, facing down the newly planned Gloucester Street (now Seán McDermott Street). The church was built to serve a new parish that was created in 1749. When it was built, the church looked out over fields towards the estuary of the River Liffey. The church was closely modelled on the façade of Palladio's Venetian church, the Redentore. It was destroyed in 1922 and replaced by

Above top: Outstanding decorative plasterwork from the staircase at Belvedere House.

Above: One of the unusual ironwork uprights from the staircase at Belvedere House.

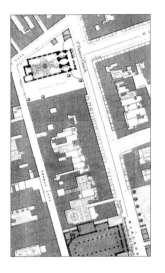

a modern church in the Byzantine style, standing in the middle of Cathal Brugha Street. The demolition of the church presented the opportunity to continue Gloucester Street through to O'Connell Street.

Whyte & Sons, glassworks, had been in business at 3–4 Marlborough Street since the eighteenth century. Their Marlborough Street premises occupied the corner site now covered by the present Abbey Theatre. A billhead of the 1880s illustrates the glassworks, showing a large, conical tower and four furnaces beneath. Glass blowers are shown working in a high, open-sided shed at the bottom of the tower. This provided some relief from the intense heat of the furnaces and the molten glass. In the late nineteenth century Whyte & Sons specialised in engraved glass, some of which was decorated to the very highest standards. Although Whyte's main premises and manufactory were located in Marlborough Street, from the 1880s onwards they also had fine corner premises in the South City Markets at South Great George's Street.

In 1815, some time before Catholic Emancipation, work began on the building of the Pro-Cathedral on the corner site at Marlborough Street and Elephant Lane. The laying of the foundation stone was 'an ecumenical event' in the sense that it was attended by the Dean of St Patrick's Cathedral, the banker John David La Touche, the brewer Arthur Guinness and Daniel O'Connell. The neo-classical cathedral is not particularly large, but it was erected in anticipation of a greater and finer Catholic cathedral being built in the future. Its portico, inspired by Ancient Greek temples,

Above top: Tyrone House – now the headquarters of the Department of Education – was built in 1740.

Above: This nineteenth-century Ordnance Survey map shows the positions of St Thomas's Church and the Pro-Cathedral on Marlborough Street.

Right: Whyte's billhead of 1883 show an eighteenth-century glasshouse in Marlborough Street with the furnaces and shelters for glassworkers.

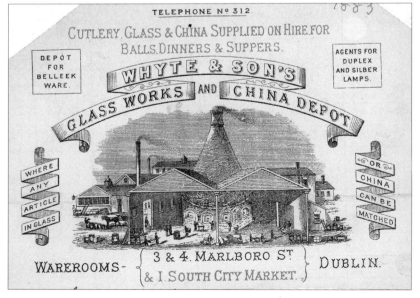

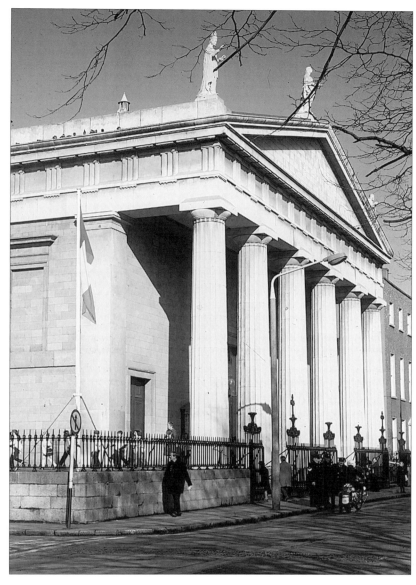

Left: The Greek-revival portico of the Pro-Cathedral was completed by 1825.

creates a bold statement on Marlborough Street. Following the early Christian tradition, the interior is laid out with its focus on the apse, and the nave is lit by great Diocletian windows, whose arches support a dome. The high altar was carved by the noted Dublin-based sculptor Peter Turnerelli. The cathedral was dedicated in 1825.

CHAPTER TWENTY-ONE

Dublin Port

Dublin's port, for centuries the hub of both the city's and the nation's overseas trade, is a subject of great historic interest. Here we will glance briefly at it.

Today's port is far removed from the shipping scene of eighteenth-century Dublin, when trade was concentrated around Essex Bridge, near Capel Street in the centre of Dublin city. Not alone has the Port of Dublin moved relentlessly eastwards over the last 200 years, but the ships themselves have become so massive in scale that it is hard to think of them as the descendants of the picturesque sailing ships that once crowded the Liffey quays. As we have already seen, the principal shipping activity of the eighteenth century and earlier took place in front of the Custom House, which was located in the city centre in what is now the Temple Bar area of Dublin.

But by the early 1800s maritime commerce was firmly established downstream, with the building of the new Custom House, followed by the Custom House Docks, St George's Dock and the North Wall Quay. This northside development complemented the existing southside quays, which had been built by Sir John Rogerson and stretched from the city to Ringsend, and the huge new basin at the Grand Canal Docks near Ringsend.

Below: Rocque's map (1756) shows the activity in the eighteenth-century port, with a multitude of small sailing ships and timberyards on the quays.

One of the earliest maps in the possession of the Dublin Port and Docks Board was drawn up in 1704 and shows the River Liffey as an irregular channel, very shallow in places and with few quay walls. Prior to the opening of the present Custom House in 1791, most shipping had to make its way upstream as far as Essex Bridge. This was no easy task and the channel had to be regularly deepened and made safer for shipping. In fact, Dublin had the reputation of being one of the most dangerous ports in Europe. In response to this, in 1708, a body known as the Ballast Office Committee was established by an Act of Parliament.

One of the first premises of the Ballast Office, in the eighteenth century, were located at the bottom of Temple Lane, beside a boat slip that was used by ferries and small boats. Later, on a map dated 1811, we find the Ballast Office in a building on City Quay, with a substantial yard to the rear containing sheds, account offices and a sawpit. By the late eighteenth century the office had developed beyond its simple utilitarian functions and had become an important administrative body, which required an imposing building for its headquarters. An appropriate site was chosen in the late 1790s. It was to be situated at the corner of a newly formed public thoroughfare, Westmoreland Street, where it joined Aston Quay. Designs were prepared for the new building in 1800 by Henry A Baker, under the direction of the Wide Street Commissioners. The building was to match the rest

Above: Logs at Sir John Rogerson's Quay in the nineteenth century. Large quantities of timber continue to be imported through Dublin today.

Below: Jonathan Fisher's aquatint (1792) of the South Wall and lighthouse.

of the new houses on Westmoreland Street, being five storeys high and having a stone-built ground floor and pillared doorcase. It was altered in 1860 and lasted until 1979, when it was demolished and replaced by a replica.

From early in the eighteenth century it was decided that a breakwater, in the form of a wall running eastwards from Ringsend, should be constructed, which would contain the course of the river and assist in the scouring action by which the river channel would deepen itself. This was created by means of a double row of huge tree trunks that were rammed into the sand. Some of these great timbers, fixed together in the form of a box, were called kishes. They were sunk onto the sandbar or riverbed and filled with gravel, stones and sand as ballast. The very first piles laid were put in place at Ringsend around 1720. By 1728 piles had been driven into the muddy sandbanks of the South Bull, extending right out into Dublin Bay, but they were not as yet connected to Ringsend. A map of Dublin Bay by Gibson, dated 1756, shows that a wall had been built part of the way out to Poolbeg and was now connected to a substantial double row of piles that ran out to the present Poolbeg. John Rocque's map, which was made in the same year, shows the same wall, and the river packed with ships of varying sizes and types. Nearest to Ringsend he depicts the 'pacquet moorings', where the mail pacquet or passenger boat moored while waiting to discharge its passengers. An old lightship was anchored at Poolbeg and a light was displayed from its mast. Further seaward was the Quarantine Sloop, a ship presumably moored in the Liffey to accommodate persons infected by disease who needed to be quarantined.

During the 1760s the lightship was replaced by the present Poolbeg lighthouse. The original lighthouse, as designed by Smyth, was encircled by a balcony or gallery about two-thirds of the way up. This has long since vanished, but must originally have allowed for an excellent view of all the shipping in the bay. The South Wall was not finally completed until about 1786 and ran from close to the site of the present ESB power station out to the Poolbeg lighthouse.

By 1800 a second and equally important breakwater had been constructed. The Great North Wall, as it is called, runs from Clontarf in an easterly direction. It assists in narrowing the mouth of the Liffey, thus helping to prevent a sandbank, the Bar, at the mouth of the river, from silting up. The Great North Wall brought about the eventual creation of Bull Island, as we know it today, through the build-up of silt.

In 1791 a small harbour or basin was constructed at the Pidgeon House and this became known as the Pidgeon House Harbour. Two years later a plan was mooted to build a hotel beside the harbour and work was completed in 1795. The Pidgeon House Hotel, now in office use, is a fine granite structure, three storeys in height, which offered excellent accommodation. The hotel originally stood, in a rather bizarre manner, on the sands of Dublin Bay, and had an unrivalled view across the sandy shore to the mountains beyond.

The Custom House

The 'new' Custom House was opened for business in 1791. It was built at a considerable distance downstream from the original Custom House at

Below: Unloading a small coaster opposite the Custom House in the late nineteenth century.

Essex Quay. This noble building, one of Ireland's finest pieces of architecture, underwent a major restoration during the five years leading up to 1991. The Custom House is remarkable for many reasons, not least for the length of its magnificent cut-stone façade, which fronts onto the River Liffey. It is also unique as a public building in that it is possible to walk right around it and that each of its four façades is finished to a very high level. The new Custom House, promoted by politician and property owner John Beresford, was built as a symbol of Ireland's prosperity and as a crowning monument to the new neo-classical city. As we have seen, this Dublin was symbolised by many new developments, such as Mountjoy Square and Gardiner Street.

Above top: Eighteenth-century ships from the pediment of the Custom House, some of the unseen sculptures of Edward Smyth.
Above: The signature of James Gandon, from an early nineteenth-century document.

The building as we know it today is different in some respects from its original appearance, mainly because the dome was rebuilt in grey Irish limestone after a fire in 1921, rather than in the white Portland stone used in the rest of the building. Also, all of the original chimney stacks have been removed, somewhat altering the roofline of the building.

Much damaged stonework was also replaced and several of the impressive sculptural features were restored, including the enormous statue of *Commerce* which topped the dome of the building. The massive sculptures were carefully lifted down onto the ground and restored in stonemasons' workshops on the site. The quality of stonework achieved in the building of the Custom House is outstanding, and the decorative details are of particular note. The fourteen carved keystones, which represent the rivers of Ireland, are justly famous. The various faces depicted in these keystones represent the Liffey as a serene female face, the Boyne as a noble king and the Shannon as a powerful old man, while the Nore looks like a rather miserable old man! These keystones, which measure over two-and-a-half feet in height, are carved from single blocks of Portland stone. The carving is deeply undercut and the faces are very striking.

Many books about Dublin extol the architectural qualities of the Custom House, but few explain why such a very large building was required for the business of collecting excise and duties. Most of the building was taken up with offices, where all the work of extracting dues and tolls was carried out, and records were kept. The many offices housed numerous clerks who recorded all of the trade that came through the port of Dublin. The Custom House also housed many related Government departments, such as the Fisheries Board or the Receiver of Wrecks. The only large rooms included a boardroom and the Commissioner's Court. GN Wright describes the only office worthy of the visitors' attention as being

Left: An aerial view of the Custom House and Custom House docks area prior to its development as the Irish Financial Services Centre (IFSC).

Below: The old sugar refinery in the Grand Canal Docks, now the Business Enterprise Centre run by the Industrial Development Authority (IDA).

the Long Room, which was over seventy feet long and decorated with a range of composite columns, between which were counters where forfeited goods were sold.

The Docks

The earliest and most impressive large-scale docks to be built in Dublin were those at the Grand Canal, generally known as the Grand Canal Docks. The docks consist of two large rectangular basins joined together by a lifting bridge. Opened in 1796, the new docks were equipped with three graving or dry docks, and the triple entrance locks, each of varying size, were beautifully constructed from granite. The docks cover an area of thirty-five acres and the water is on average sixteen feet deep by the quayside. Unfortunately, silting outside the lock gates made access difficult and the docks were to prove unsuccessful as a financial venture. They were eventually purchased by the Port and Docks Board. The total cost of construction came to nearly £113,000. In his *History of the Ports of Ireland* (1858), Anthony Marmion estimated that 300 square-rigged sailing vessels could be accommodated in the Grand Canal Docks.

Across the river, beside the Custom House, St George's Docks were constructed some twenty-five years later, and were formally opened by George IV in

1821. These docks cover an area of eight acres, and also have a depth of about sixteen feet of water and were provided with bonded warehouses for the storage of wines, spirits and tobacco. The docks, also known as Custom House Docks, consist of two large, connected basins that were once linked to the Liffey by means of a lock. One of the most interesting features of the docks is the former Harbour Master's house, a small, early nineteenth-century brick residence with a tower and slated roof.

Special warehouses were also built that could contain up to 80,000 hogsheads of sugar and tobacco and 20,000 chests of tea. There was also cellar space for up to 12,000 pipes (large casks containing over 100 gallons) of wine. Throughout the nineteenth century the quantities of tea, coffee, sugar, tobacco and wine that were imported into Ireland continued to increase steadily. Dublin also imported timber and coal in large quantities. Exports included bacon, butter, wheat, barley, oats, flour, hams, eggs, beef, port, candles, feathers, hides, lard, leather, whiskey, porter, linen cloth, printed cottons, wool, oxen, pigs and sheep.

Although there are records of coal being imported into Dublin since medieval times, its consumption rose dramatically during the nineteenth century. Not alone was coal the most efficient means of heating – a medium-sized house might easily have eight or ten fireplaces – but it was also the fuel most widely used for industry. Hospitals, offices, barracks, hotels and many factories such as bakeries all relied on coal, and in the Victorian period the railways consumed great quantities of it. One of the best-known firms in the coal trade were Messrs J McCormack & Company. McCormack's had been prominent in the business since the 1840s and had their offices at 7 D'Olier Street. Like their competition – Robinson's, Robert Tedcastle, Michael Murphy & Company and Thomas Heiton – they had their own fleet of sailing vessels, which in the 1870s was replaced with a fleet of steam ships.

Many cut-stone bollards, which were used for tying up shipping, and many of the original stone setts survive in the docks area. The most impressive bonded warehouse was known as Stack C and was built to the designs of engineer John Rennie. This, unfortunately, was demolished during the 1980s, although it had been listed for

Above: One of the many stores owned by Merchant Warehousing Ltd, from their early twentieth-century billhead.

Below: A steam crane unloading coal at Thomas Heiton's depot in the early twentieth century.

ONE OF OUR
STEAM CRANES WORKING.

preservation. The warehouse had contained a remarkable series of vaults or cellars and the exterior was articulated with fine cut-stone coigns and stone details.

Another impressive warehouse, known as Stack A, still stands and restoration work is now in progress, although its future function has not been decided. Like Stack C, this warehouse also has an extensive vaulted basement area. Various cultural uses have been proposed for this building, including at one time a museum of modern art, which was instead located in Kilmainham.

The original Custom House Dock eventually fell into disuse and was filled in in 1927. It is situated partly under Memorial Road, close to the Custom House, and partly under the new Irish Financial Services Centre (IFSC). Begun in the late 1980s, the IFSC is undoubtedly a most impressive development, even in terms of its scale. It stretches from the Custom House back behind Connolly Station as far as Sheriff Street. The development has triggered a whole wave of building – mainly offices and apartment blocks, but also a hotel. The extent to which the docks have changed within the last fifteen years is almost unbelievable, considering its previously run-down, derelict state. The North Wall now boasts new hotels, the Point Depot, which is a major venue for concerts, and various retail outlets, such as the Tile Style building.

The Custom House Docks Development Authority was established in 1986 and its brief was to create a dramatic new development out of the redundant dockland area. The Authority set out with a clear vision of building timescales, conservation principles, planning and townscape guidelines, coupled with very favourable tax exemptions and incentives. Apart from the loss of Stack C, the development has proved extremely successful in preserving the main features of the dock area while creating a remarkable new cityscape with water as its focal point.

The old Dublin Port with its quays and cranes was a testimony to the great trading traditions of Dublin city. That port

WALLER & Cº DUBLIN.

ON BOARD THE CITY OF DUBLIN STEAM PACKET Cº.S R.M.S. ULSTER.

Above: For over a century, the City of Dublin Steam Packet Company operated a fleet of fast passenger ships across the Irish Sea.

Below: Stack C, a fine bonded warehouse that stood on the site of the present IFSC offices, now demolished.

Above: The building of apartments in the redundant port area continues apace.

has gone, and the cranes have almost completely vanished from the quays. All is changed. Everything in the new port is now highly mechanised. Gone are the dockers; gone are the horses and the drays and most of the goods trains. Many goods remain completely out of sight in their containers, and sometimes the only visible products are bulky commodities like coal, timber or cars. Today trailers, trucks and containers represent the new form of transportation which is part of the ever-increasing volume of traffic on the city's streets.

On the river, some things, however, never change. The pilot boats still rush up and down the Liffey to guide vessels in and out of Dublin Bay, while container ships glide downstream on the ebb tide. There is still the smell of tar and gas near Poolbeg power station and the few remaining idle cranes are reflected in the still waters of the docks.

As we have seen, much of the heritage was indeed lost, but a good deal of the city's historic fabric remains which is beginning to be recognised as worthwhile. In the decades leading up to the 1990s the colour of Dublin was grey and the buildings of the city reflected a drab tone. It was as if the years of black soot on the buildings of the city seemed to symbolise neglect. Over the last ten years the cleaning and refurbishment of many landmarks, and the addition of some new ones, has brightened the spirit of the capital. Examples of renewal abound – from the two principal railway stations, Heuston and Connolly, which have recently been revamped, to the ongoing work at the Fruit and Vegetable Market and the Iveagh

Market. The former Harcourt Street train station has been stylishly converted into a pub, and the sparkling Gate Theatre has a new entrance and canopy, discreet but modern. Most of Dublin's major monuments have by now been renovated and are well maintained and the profusion of new hotels, restaurants and bars in the city tell their own tale. Who would have thought that in the year 2000 people would be sitting outside on Liffey Street drinking cappucino? Alongside the ever-expanding tourist industry, it is pleasing to see high-quality facilities being provided for the citizens of Dublin, such as the new Markievicz swimming pool and the excellent Larkin and Whitefriar community centres.

Most recently, the restoration of City Hall provides a powerful symbol of Dublin's new confidence in its past. This and other restoration projects, such as the crypt of Christ Church Cathedral and St Catherine's Church, display the highest level of workmanship in conservation, and show a commitment to both beautify and utilise the city's heritage.

Some trends, like the disappearance of manufacturing centres, the dominant role of 'the office' and our addiction to the motor car, are typical problems of the late twentieth century. Other achievements, such as the pedestrianisation of certain streets, the addition of new bridges on the Liffey, the successful story of Temple Bar and the ongoing renewal of Smithfield, will be recorded in future histories as significant events.

Acknowledgements

*A*t the outset I would like to thank David Freeman, James O'Halloran and Brian Coyle and Stuart Cole of James Adam and Sons, for their generous financial assistance in the production of this book. It is an honour to be supported in this way by such a long-established and highly esteemed Dublin firm.

A great many people have contributed to the research and production of this book, and I am very grateful to them all. They have assisted in many different ways: some by providing information or loaning historical material, others by allowing me to visit their buildings or browse through their precious collections of photographs, trade cards or postcards. There are almost 1,000 illustrations in this book, and such a rich profusion of images was only possible due to the generosity of many individuals and organisations.

I am particularly indebted, once again, to Mr Daniel Gillman for allowing many items from his Trade Card collection to be reproduced, and at the age of ninety-one for his unwavering interest in Dublin's past. Mary Clark and all of the staff at the Dublin City Archives must be specially thanked for their co operation and great helpfulness in finding maps and other records, and in allowing them to be reproduced. I would also like to thank Tom O'Connor, Philip O'Brien Gleeson and Tommy Grennan of the Dublin Civic Museum for their assistance. To Seamus Kearns, President of the Old Dublin Society, and the Society itself, I am very grateful for access to their postcard and photographic collections. I am also indebted to the staff of the National Library of Ireland, and to its energetic director, Brendan O'Donoghue, and Matthew Cains for facilitating the use of maps from the Longfield collection, and for allowing the reproduction of various prints from the Lawrence collection.

I wish to thank the National Gallery of Ireland, the National Museum of Ireland, Dublin Corporation's Press Section and the Office of Public Works for the use of various pictures.

It would have been almost impossible to assemble the pictures for a book of this sort without the resources and assistance of the Irish Architectural Archive, and I would especially like to pay tribute to its director, David Griffin, along with Colum O'Riordan, Simon Lincoln, Anne Henderson, Aisling Dunne and Ann-Martha Rowan.

I am very grateful to Paddy Healy for sharing with me his large collection of photographs of Dublin streets, many of them now vanished, and for providing other important pictures of houses in the Liberties. I am equally indebted to Ian Lumley for the use of many of his beautiful photographs of city buildings, for his useful comments on the text itself and for his research on Capel Street and South William Street.

I would like to thank Dr Edward McParland and Ruth Sheehy of the Art History Department of Trinity College for their generosity in regard to access to theses and photographs, and particularly to Dr McParland for directing me towards the Jervis papers in the College archives. I would like to acknowledge the research carried out for theses by Siobhán Barry, on Merrion Square; Rachel MacRory, on Fumbally Lane; Lesley Kavanagh, on Dublin churches; and Susan Sharkey, on the Tholsel. I would also like to thank Mary Bryan of the Irish Georgian Society for her excellent study of Fitzwilliam Square, and Antony Duggan for his analysis of houses on Parnell Square.

I am very grateful to Alderman John Gallagher of the Liberties Association for making the Thomas Street Survey, carried out by Mairin Doddy and her team in the 1980s, available to me. I would like to thank Temple Bar Properties, in particular Eve-Anne Cullinan, for their archaeological reports, and Claire Walsh for her report on the archaeology of Thomas Court. I am also grateful to Linzi Simpson, Claire Dolan and Dara O'Rourke, the City Archaeologist.

I would like to pay tribute to the late Maura Shaffrey for her dedication to conservation matters, and for her research into the work of the Wide Streets Commissioners. I would also like to thank the Dublin Civic Trust, Geraldine Walsh and her team, and in particular Julie Craig and Emmeline Henderson for their architectural studies of South William Street and the Father Matthew Hall.

I am indebted to David Byers, Tommy O'Shaughnessy and Denis McCarthy for access to all parts of Dublin Castle, even with dogs (!) and for the use of various photographs. I would like to thank the following newspapers, some of which loaned photographs: *The Irish Times*, the *Sunday Business Post*, the *Irish Independent* and the former *Irish Press*. I would also like to thank Teresa O'Donnell of Guinness, and Peter Walsh for the use of photographs, and for his contribution to the story of old Dublin houses. I am also grateful to the families of the late Larry O'Connor, and of the late Malachy Hynes, some of whose excellent photographs have been included in the book.

I wish to thank Dr Maurice Craig, Alex Findlater, Inge Clissman, Seamus Daly, Hamilton Osborne and King and Fonsie Mealy of Mealy's auctioneers for the use of particular illustrations, along with Desirée Shortt, Andrew Bonar-Law, James and Teresa Gorry, Michael and Helen Purser, Kevin Mulligan, the Gardaí at Kevin Street, Daithí Hanley, Mark Boland, Colin Scudds, Marcella Senior, Bewley's Oriental Cafés, the Irish Distillers' Group, Pat Casey, the late Nuala Burke, the Geography Department of Trinity College, Dublin, Andrew Smith for his beautiful photographs of plasterwork at 20 Dominick Street, Nabil Siadi, Mary Boydell, John Lenehan and Garda Brendan Duffy of Kevin Street.

I would also like to thank John Fitzgerald, the City Manager, and his office for their support, the Gilbert Library in Pearse Street, the Royal Irish Academy, the Royal Society of Antiquaries of Ireland, Bord Fáilte, the Irish Landmark Trust and Dublin Port and Docks Board. Thanks also to Mervyn Percival and Christ Church Cathedral, the staff at St Patrick's Cathedral and Canon David Pierpoint of St Werburgh's Church.

I must here record the names of Deirdre Kelly, Matt Byrne and Rico Ross, three stalwart defenders of the city, who are sadly no longer with us. I would like to acknowledge the pioneering work done by John Lenehan in salvaging important Dublin interiors and features.

I wish to pay particular tribute to all at The O'Brien Press who were involved in producing this very large and detailed book. I would like to thank Michael O'Brien for facilitating the production of the book, and Ivan O'Brien, who had the unenviable task of scanning and organising the vast number of illustrations. Also Eoin O'Brien, Íde ní Laoghaire, Rachel Pierce, Marian Broderick and Susan Houlden for their unending patience in editing the book, and Lynn Pierce for the cover and layout. Also thanks to Gráinne Farren who undertook the index.

I would like especially to thank Lindis Page, Vanessa Sweeney and Kelly-Ann Sweeney for their great assistance in the early stages of preparing the text.

I wish to particularly thank Robert Vance for his many beautiful and specially taken photographs, and also Sarah Durcan, Hugh Doran and David Davison for the use of other fine photographs.

Finally, I must pay tribute to Phil and my sons Adam and Jerome, who have survived all of the anti-social rigours of book-writing and book-making yet again!

Picture Credits

Illustrations from author's collection: pages 2, 6, 7 (bottom), 8 (top), 9 (bottom), 13 (bottom), 14, 19 (bottom), 20 (top), 23 (both), 24, 27, 30, 34 (both), 35 (both), 36 (both), 37 (top), 38, 39, 42 (top), 45, 46, 47 (top and bottom right), 48, 49 (bottom), 50, 51 (bottom), 53, 54, 57 (bottom), 59 (bottom), 63 (bottom), 64 (top), 65 (middle), 66, 69, 70 (top), 71, 73 (top), 74 (both), 75 (both), 78, 79 (top and bottom), 80 (top), 81 (both), 86, 88 (bottom), 89 (both), 90 (both), 92 (bottom), 93 (bottom), 95 (both), 96 (middle and bottom), 97 (both), 99 (bottom), 101 (bottom), 102, 105, 106, 109 (both), 110 (top), 111 (top), 112 (bottom), 113 (bottom), 114 (top), 115 (both), 116, 118, 121 (bottom), 122 (both), 123 (bottom), 124, 125, 127 (bottom), 135 (left), 137, 140 (both), 144 (top), 145 (bottom), 146 (top), 147 (top), 148 (bottom), 150 (top), 153 (top and middle), 154 (bottom), 155 (top and middle), 156 (top), 157 (both), 158 (bottom left), 159 (bottom), 162 (bottom), 164 (both), 165 (both), 166 (middle), 171 (bottom), 176 (bottom), 177 (top), 178 (both), 179 (both), 180 (top), 181 (both), 183 (top), 189, 191 (both), 193 (both), 194 (both), 195 (top), 200 (top), 201 (bottom), 202 (top), 203 (bottom), 204, 205 (top and middle), 206 (both), 209 (bottom), 213 (bottom), 215 (all), 216 (top), 217 (bottom), 218 (both), 219 (bottom), 220 (bottom), 221 (top), 226 (both), 228 (top), 229 (both), 230, 231, 232, 233, 240, 245 (all), 251 (top), 256 (bottom), 257 (both), 259, 262, 263, 265 (top), 267 (bottom), 268 (top), 271 (both), 272, 274 (top and bottom), 275, 276 (all), 277 (top), 278 (both), 279 (top), 280 (both), 281, 282 (top), 283 (both), 284 (all), 285 (bottom), 286 (both), 287 (both), 291, 292 (both), 293 (bottom), 294 (bottom), 295 (bottom), 296, 297, 298 (bottom), 299 (both), 300 (both), 301 (top), 303, 306, 308 (bottom), 309 (both), 312, 313 (top), 315, 318 (bottom), 320 (bottom), 324, 325, 329 (bottom), 330 (top), 331 (top), 332, 333 (both), 335 (top), 336, 337 (right), 340 (both), 341 (top), 342 (bottom), 343, 345 (both), 347 (top left and right), 350 (top right and bottom), 351 (both), 352 (top), 353 (both), 356 (both), 357 (top), 360, 361 (top), 362 (both), 367 (all), 369 (bottom), 370 (both), 371 (both), 372 (both), 373 (both), 374 (both), 375 (both), 376 (both), 377 (top), 379 (both), 380 (bottom), 381 (both), 382 (middle and bottom), 385 (top), 388 (bottom), 389 (all), 390 (bottom), 391 (top), 392 (top), 394 (all), 395 (top), 396 (both), 398 (top), 399 (top), 400 (top), 401 (bottom), 402 (bottom), 403 (all), 404 (top), 405 (both), 406, 408 (top), 409 (top and middle), 410 (top), 413, 414 (bottom), 418 (middle and bottom), 422 (bottom), 423 (both), 426 (bottom), 431, 432, 439 (bottom), 440 (both), 442 (bottom), 443 (both), 446 (middle and bottom), 449 (bottom), 451, 452 (both), 453 (bottom), 454 (top), 455 (top).

New photographs by Robert Vance: pages 7 (top), 8 (bottom), 9 (top), 10 (bottom), 11, 12, 13 (top), 18 (top), 20 (bottom), 25 (top), 28 (bottom), 33, 40, 56, 58 (left), 60 (top), 62 (bottom), 65 (both), 68, 72 (top), 76 (bottom), 77, 79 (middle), 83, 98 (bottom), 99 (middle), 100 (both), 101 (top), 108 (all), 110 (bottom), 117, 123 (top), 129 (both), 130, 131 (top), 143 (both), 163 (top), 167 (bottom), 173, 175 (top), 180 (bottom), 185, 195 (bottom), 196, 227 (both), 235 (top), 236 (bottom), 237, 241 (bottom), 248 (bottom), 251 (bottom), 267 (middle), 269 (top and middle), 270, 279 (middle and bottom), 302, 335 (bottom), 357 (bottom), 368 (top), 382 (top), 393, 399 (bottom), 401 (middle), 456.

The Daniel Gillman Trade Card collection: pages 29, 51 (top), 57 (top), 76 (top), 82 (both), 84, 85 (both), 87, 103 (top left and right), 107, 111 (bottom), 148 (top), 160 (both), 161 (bottom), 166 (top and bottom), 171 (top), 175 (bottom), 182, 201 (top), 202 (bottom), 225 (top), 264 (bottom), 266 (bottom), 273, 290 (bottom), 293 (top), 294 (top), 301 (bottom), 304, 322, 387, 397 (top), 400 (bottom), 410 (bottom), 417 (top), 427 (top), 435, 442 (top).

Ian Lumley: pages 21, 31, 43, 64 (bottom), 121 (top), 144 (bottom), 153 (bottom), 242 (top), 244 (top), 344 (top), 346 (top), 348 (top), 349 (bottom), 350 (top left), 364 (top), 390 (top), 417 (bottom), 433 (both), 434 (bottom), 441, 455 (bottom). Seamus Daly: page 1.

The Irish Architectural Archive: pages 9 (middle), 19 (top), 42 (bottom right), 44 (top), 52, 58 (right), 59 (top), 60 (bottom), 67, 72 (bottom), 88 (top), 91, 93 (top), 104, 126 (bottom), 128 (both), 131 (bottom), 134 (bottom), 136, 152 (bottom), 154 (top), 156 (bottom), 163 (bottom), 167 (top), 168, 170 (bottom), 174 (top), 183 (bottom), 184, 186, 192, 198 (both), 199, 200 (bottom), 212 (both), 214 (bottom), 216 (bottom), 219 (top), 220 (top), 221 (middle), 242 (bottom), 250, 260, 305, 307, 308 (top), 310 (both), 311 (both), 314 (top), 316 (both), 317 (both), 318 (top), 319, 323, 326, 327 (bottom and top right), 328 (bottom), 329 (top), 330 (bottom), 334 (both), 337 (left), 358, 364 (bottom), 365 (top), 385 (bottom), 386 (both), 388 (top left and right), 391 (bottom), 420 (both), 421 (middle), 422 (top), 429 (top), 436 (both), 437 (both), 438 (top), 439 (top), 445 (both), 453 (top); Irish Architectural Archive, David Davison: pages 61 (both); Irish Architectural Archive, Foras Forbaithe collection: page 380 (top).

Dublin City Archives: pages 22 (both), 25 (bottom), 42 (bottom left), 44 (bottom), 49 (top), 63 (top), 73 (bottom), 113 (top), 132 (top), 134 (top), 135 (right), 138 (bottom), 142 (bottom), 174 (bottom), 242 (middle), 252, 267 (top), 269 (bottom), 290 (top), 365 (bottom), 366 (top), 395 (bottom).

Sunday Business Post: pages 12 (bottom), 228 (bottom), 289, 298 (top), 411; Andrew Smith: pages 15 (both), 429 (bottom), 430 (both), 457; Bord Fáilte: pages 17, 366 (bottom); John Speed's map: pages 18 (bottom), 70 (bottom), 145 (top), 158 (top), 172, 209 (top), 264 (top), 338, 384 (bottom); John Rocque's map: pages 19 (middle), 26 (bottom), 41 (top), 94 (top), 120 (top), 151 (bottom), 217 (top), 222, 243 (top), 274 (middle), 288, 331 (bottom), 342 (top), 349 (top), 355 (bottom), 363 (bottom), 378, 383 (top), 395 (middle), 414 (top), 448; the Guinness Museum: pages 28 (top), 258 (top and middle); Mark Boland: page 37 (bottom left and right); the National Gallery of Ireland: pages 41 (bottom), 151 (top); Irish Landmark Trust: page 47 (bottom left); Paddy Healy: pages 62 (top), 132 (bottom), 133 (bottom), 139 (bottom), 141, 142 (top), 149, 152 (top), 203 (top), 207 (left), 221 (bottom), 224 (bottom), 244 (bottom), 247, 258 (bottom), 344 (bottom), 384 (top), 409 (bottom), 419 (top), 438 (bottom); Office of Public Works, Dublin Castle: pages 92 (top), 94 (bottom), 103 (bottom), 155 (bottom), 210 (both), 214 (top), 314 (bottom), 327 (top left); Royal Irish Academy: page 369 (top); Royal Society of Antiquaries of Ireland: pages 96 (top), 133 (top), 261 (top), 407 (bottom), 421 (top), 444 (bottom); the Gorry Gallery: page 98 (top); Glenn Thompson: page 99 (top); Dublin Corporation: pages 112 (top), 341 (bottom); Dublin Penny Journal: pages 119; *Georgian Society Records*: pages 120 (bottom), 354, 363 (top); the *Independent*: page 127 (top); St Werburgh's Church: page 138 (top); Malachy Hynes: pages 26 (top), 139 (top), 187, 224 (top), 401 (top); Dublin Civic Museum: page 146 (bottom); Old Dublin Society: pages 150 (bottom), 158 (bottom right), 159 (top), 176 (top), 177 (bottom), 188, 190, 205 (bottom), 207 (right), 208 (top), 238, 239, 243 (bottom), 248 (top and middle), 253, 254 (bottom), 255 (top and bottom), 256 (top), 261 (bottom), 266 (middle), 285 (top), 380 (middle), 397 (bottom), 404 (bottom), 408 (bottom), 421 (bottom), 425 (top), 426 (top), 427 (bottom); Sarah Durcan: pages 147 (bottom); Bewley's Oriental Cafés: pages 161 (top), 295 (top), 412 (bottom); O'Brien Press collection: pages 162 (top), 266 (top), 346 (bottom), 348 (bottom), 415 (both), 416; Pool and Cash engravings: pages 169, 383 (bottom); Hugh Doran: page 170 (top); Leonard R Strangways: pages 208 (bottom), 241 (top); Larry O'Connor collection (ex Mason photographers): pages 211, 213 (top), 223, 246; Larry O'Connor: page 225 (bottom); Christ Church Cathedral: pages 236 (top and middle); National Library of Ireland: pages 234, 254 (top), 265 (bottom), 268 (bottom), 368 (bottom), 434 (top); the Lawrence Collection, in the National Library of Ireland: pages 16 (top), 277 (bottom), 282 (bottom), 355 (top), 377 (bottom), 402 (top); the National Archives (Pembroke Estate): page 313 (bottom); the Electricity Supply Board: page 320 (top and middle); Rex Roberts: page 321; Trinity College, Dublin, Department of Fine Arts: pages 328 (top), 339 (both), 361 (bottom), 418 (top), 424, 425 (bottom), 446 (top), 447; Nessa Roche: page 347 (bottom); Michael O'Brien: page 352 (bottom); National Museum: pages 392 (bottom), 407 (top); Radió Teilifís Éireann: page 398 (bottom); Seamus Kearns: pages 359, 412 (top), 449 (top), 454 (bottom); Hamilton Osborne King: page 419 (bottom); Nabil Saidi: page 444 (top); Port and Docks Board: pages 450; Maurice Craig: page 428.

A great number of pictures were culled from the author's own collection of photographs, billheads, trade cards and other ephemera, some of which may include pictures taken by others. The author has tried to establish the origin of all images used, and apologises if any name has been omitted.

Select Bibliography

Anon. *The Industries of Dublin. c.*1888.

Ballagh, R. *Dublin*. Dublin: Ward River Press, 1981.

Bennett, Douglas. *Dictionary of Dublin*.

Campbell Ross, I. *Public Virtue, Private Love*. Dublin: The O'Brien Press, 1986.

Clarke, HB (ed.). *Medieval Dublin: The Making of a Metropolis*. Dublin: Irish Academic Press, 1990.

Costello, Peter. *Dublin Churches*. 1989.

Cowell, John. *Dublin's Famous People and Where they Lived*. Dublin: The O'Brien Press, 1980.

Craig, Maurice. *Dublin, 1660-1860*. London: Cresset Press, 1952.

Craig, Maurice. *James Malton's Dublin Views*. 1981.

Crawford, John. *Within the Walls: the story of St Audoen's Church, Cornmarket, Dublin*. Dublin: 1986.

Cullen, LM. *Princes and Pirates*. 1983.

Curran, CP. *Dublin Decorative Plasterwork*. 1967.

Curtis, Joe. *Times, Chimes and Charms of Dublin*. 1992.

Daly, Mary. *Dublin, The Deposed Capital*. 1985.

De Courcy, JW. *The Liffey in Dublin*. 1996.

Dickson, D (ed.). *The Gorgeous Mask – Dublin 1700-1850*. 1987.

Dublin Civic Trust. *South William Street*. 1999.

Duffy, Sean (ed.). *Medieval Dublin I*. 2000.

Farmar, Tony. *Holles Street, 1894-1994*.

Farmar, Tony. *The Legendary Lofty, Clattery Café – Bewleys*. 1988.

FER. *Historical Reminiscences of Dublin Castle*. 1900.

Ferguson, Kenneth. *Fox, history of a family tobacco shop, 1881-1981*. 1981.

Gilbert, Sir JT *A History of the City of Dublin*. 3 vols, Vol. 1, 1854, Vols 2 and 3, 1859.

Gilbert, Sir JT (ed.) and Gilbert, Lady. *Calendar of Ancient Records of Dublin*. 19 vols, 1889–1944.

Gillespie, E (ed.). *The Liberties of Dublin*. Dublin: The O'Brien Press, 1973.

Gilligan, KA. *A History of the Port of Dublin*. 1988.

Guinness, D. *Georgian Dublin*. London: Batsford, 1979.

Guinness Dublin, A History and Guide. 1931.

Haliday, C. *The Scandinavian Kingdom of Ireland*. Dublin: Alex Thom, 1881.

Harvey, John. *Dublin: a study in environment*. London: Batsford, 1949.

Haverty, Anne. *Elegant Times – Switzer and Brown Thomas*. 1995.

Horner, Arnold and Simms, Anngret, essays by. *Dublin – From Pre-history to Present*. 1992.

Kearns, Kevin. *Dublin Tenement Life – An Oral History*. 1994.

Kelly, D. *Hands Off Dublin*. Dublin: The O'Brien Press, 1976.

Kennedy, Roísín. *Dublin Castle Art*. 1999.

Lindsay, Deirdre. *Dublin's Oldest Charity*. 1990.

Loeber, R. *A Biographical Dictionary of Architects in Ireland*. 1981.

Lyons, JB. *Brief lives of Irish Doctors, 1600-1965*. 1978.

Martin, Liam C and Logan, Patrick. *Medical Dublin*. 1984.

McCready, CT. *Dublin Street Names*. Dublin: Hodges Figgis, 1892.

McCullough, Niall. *Dublin, An Urban History*. 1989.

McDonald, F. *The Destruction of Dublin*. Dublin: Gill and Macmillan, 1985.

McDonald F. *The Construction of Dublin*. 2000.

McDonnell, Joseph. *Irish Eighteenth-Century Stuccowork and its European Sources*. 1991.

Maxwell, C. *Dublin under the Georges*. London: George Harrap, 1946.

Meenan, J and Clarke, D. *The Royal Dublin Society, 1731-1981*. 1981.

Meredith, Jane. *The Custom House, Dublin*. 1997.

Mitchell, D. *A Peculiar Place*. 1989.

Mitchell, Flora. *Vanishing Dublin*. 1966.

Nesbitt, R. *At Arnotts of Dublin – 1843-1993*. 1993.

O'Donnell, EE. *The Annals of Dublin Fair City*. Dublin: Wolfhound Press, 1987.

O'Dwyer, Frederick. *Lost Dublin*. Dublin: Gill and Macmillan, 1981.

Scully, Seamus. *The Dublin Rover*. 1991.

Shaw, H. *The Dublin Pictorial Guide & Directory 1850*. Dublin: 1850.

Stalley, Roger. *The Cistercian Monasteries of Ireland*. 1987.

Sweeney, Claire L. *The Rivers of Dublin*. 1991.

Warburton, J, Whitelaw, J and Walsh, R. *History of the City of Dublin*. 2 vols. London: 1818

Webb, JJ. *The Guilds of Dublin*. Dublin: 1929.

Williams, Jeremy. *Architecture in Ireland, 1937-1921*. 1994.

Whiteside, Lesley. *A History of the King's Hospital*. 1975.

Periodicals and Journals

Corporation of Dublin (A Diary). 1950.

Dublin Builder, The. 1857-1966.

Dublin Historical Record, The – journal of the Old Dublin Society. Various.

Dublin Penny Journal, The. 1835.

Georgian Society Records. 5 vols. Dublin: Dublin University Press, 1909-13.

Irish Architectural and Decorative Studies I and II.

Irish Arts Review Yearbook, The. Various.

Quarterly Bulletin of the Irish Georgian Society, The. Various.

Thom's Directory. Various.

Wilson's Directory. Various.

Wright, GN. *An Historical Guide to Ancient and Modern Dublin*. 1821.

Young, A. *A Tour of Ireland*. 1779.

Pamphlets

Dixon, FE. *The Dublin Tailors and their Hall*. 1969.

Hayes, Conyngham and Robinson, 1897-1997.

Milne, Kenneth. *A History of the Royal Bank of Ireland*. 1964.

O'Neill, Michael. *Marks of Unheeded Dilapidation*. St Patrick's Cathedral 800 series. 1991.

Quakers in Eustace Street, The. 1985.

Royal Irish Academy, The – A Brief Description, 1971.

Stalley, Roger. *Christ Church, Dublin: The late Romanesque building campaign*. 1973.

Ulster Bank, 1861-1991.

Weir and Sons, 1869-1994.

Index

H